Real in all the ways that matter:

Weaving learning across the curriculum with Mantle of the Expert

Real in all the ways that matter:

Weaving learning across the curriculum with Mantle of the Expert

Viv Aitken

NZCER PRESS

NZCER PRESS
New Zealand Council for Educational Research
PO Box 3237
Wellington
New Zealand

www.nzcer.org.nz

© Viv Aitken, 2021

ISBN: 978-1-99-004008-5

No part of the publication (other than the worksheets and other student resources) may be copied, stored, or communicated in any form by any means (paper or digital), including recording or storing in an electronic retrieval system without the written permission of the publisher.
Education institutions that hold a current licence with Copyright Licensing New Zealand may copy from this book in strict accordance with the terms of the CLNZ Licence.

A catalogue record for this book is available from the National Library of New Zealand.

Designed by Smartwork Creative Ltd

Dedication

For my daughters Caoimhe and Siobhān.
LYATT ...

Contents

Whakataukī	xi
Mihi | Greeting	xii
Acknowledgements	xiii
1. Introduction	**1**
Aims of the book	9
An appeal to the reader	11
Glossary and definitions	12
Drama terminology	12
2. Some history and context	**15**
Dorothy Heathcote and the development of Mantle of the Expert	15
Mantle of the Expert in New Zealand	20
How Mantle of the Expert relates to other Dramatic Inquiry approaches	23
The elevator pitch	26
Defining features	29
Ten core elements	29
Three teaching modalities	32
Metaxis: Learning in real and imagined worlds	33
Theoretical underpinnings	38
Learning and development	39
Role, frame, and children's play	40
Cognitive, affective, and psychomotor domains	42
Enactive, iconic, and symbolic learning	44
Power and agency	45
Positioning	46
Social practices and signature pedagogies	50
3. Three Aotearoa New Zealand examples	**52**
Junior primary—Toy Museum	53
Introduction	53
The big idea/key learning objectives	54
Key planning decisions	54
Implementation—the hook	56
Deepening the learning	60
The commission	63
Tensions	64
Links to curriculum	72
Afterword	72

Senior primary—Shark Tank	74
Introduction	74
The big idea/key learning objectives	75
Key planning decisions	75
Implementation—the hook	76
Deepening the learning	78
Tensions	81
Outcomes	88
Links to curriculum	90
Afterword	90
Objects of Significance	92
Introduction	92
The big idea | Key learning objectives	93
Key planning decisions	93
Implementation	99
The hook	100
Deepening the learning	102
Tension	104
Outcomes	105
Links to curriculum	106
Afterword	107
More examples	107
4. Planning and teaching in Mantle of the Expert	**113**
Introducing the weaving metaphor	114
Gathering materials	119
Whenu | Core elements	120
Ngā aho tapu | The sacred thread	121
Aho | Interweavings	121
Mahi whatu | Working the weave	122
Ua | Hems and edges	123
Models and patterns	123
The four stages of planning and teaching	124
Stage 1: Laying out the whenu—pre-planning and research	125
Summary of preplanning process	145
Stage 2: Choosing the overall shape—mapping	146
Stage 3: Interweaving the aho—microplanning and teaching	154
Stage 4: Refining and defining—recording and assessment	209
5. Tools to enhance teaching in Mantle of the Expert	**214**
Choosing an opening—three modalities	215
Setting up the imagined world—elements of drama	220
Building commitment—continuum of engagement	222

Selecting drama strategies and conventions—
    enactive, iconic, symbolic   224
Sequencing drama strategies and conventions—
    narrative, poetic, reflective   225
Working with signs and symbols—divisions of culture   226
Teaching in role—registers and positions   230
Working with the aesthetic—six dimensions of dramatic imagination   234
Supporting affective and cognitive learning—
    enactive/iconic/symbolic triad   236
Point of view and protection—frame distance   238
Balancing student agency and teacher leadership—
    the teacher compass   243
Varying delivery and elevating language—three teaching voices   247
Uncovering meaning—five levels of meaning-making   251
Encouraging critical distance—describe first, then interpret   253
Making critical connections—brotherhoods and otherhoods   254
Marking moments of significance—dropping to the universals   257
Co-constructing—principles of improvisation   259

6. Advice and cautionary tales   263
Getting started   263
    Giving it a go and learning through trial and error   263
    Warming up with preparatory activities   265
    Easing in through drama for learning and process drama   267
    Making use of existing planning   268
    Adapting for early years and junior classrooms   269
    Teaching in collaborative settings   271
    Using Mantle of the Expert as a subject specialist   273
    Taking account of specific learning needs   276
    Sustaining professional learning   279
Planning   280
    Taking time to plan   280
    Considering culture   280
    Trusting the process to take you to curriculum   284
    Weighing up when to use the commission model   286
    Finding alternatives to real-world names   289
    Keeping things ethical   291
    Avoiding light-hearted names   292
    Focusing learning with a narrow commission   293
    Conducting research into content and the professional
        world of the team   295
    Including other perspectives   296
    Working with the mythological   297

    Teaching   300
        Moving beyond the surface features   300
        Avoiding deceit   301
        Signalling the imagined world   304
        Using de-rolling rituals   305
        Maintaining the grace element   307
        Overcoming uncertainties about teaching in role   308
        Dealing with resistance to role   311
        Avoiding the temptation to pre-teach   313
        Using manipulations in time   314
        Keeping the sense of a team   315
        Working with fictional others   316
        Ensuring curriculum is taught in depth   317
        Including participants who come and go   319

7. Looking to the future   322
    Mantle of the Expert: A teaching approach for our times   322
    Where's the evidence?   332
    Priorities for 21st-century education in Aotearoa New Zealand   334
    Where to next?   342
    Further information and support   343

Appendix
    Four handouts to help with pre-planning   344

References   350

Index   363

Tables
    Table 1: Core elements of Mantle of the Expert   30
    Table 2: Summary of learning domains   43
    Table 3: Examples of Mantle of the Expert experiences   109
    Table 4: Suggestions for working with the elements of role, time and space, and action   221
    Table 5: Eight possible positions and registers when teaching in role   232
    Table 6: Adapting planning from overseas   283
    Table 7: Effective vs ineffective new pedagogies   330

Whakatauākī

E kore e taea e te whenu kotahi

Te raranga i te whāriki

Kia mōhio tātou ki a tātou

Mā te mahi tahi o ngā whenu

Mā te mahi tahi o ngā kairaranga

Ka oti tēnei whāriki

I te otinga

Me titiro ki ngā pai ka puta mai

Ā tana wā, me titiro ki ngā raranga i makere

Nā te mea, he kōrero anō kei reira

The tapestry of understanding cannot be woven by one strand alone

Only by the working together of strands

And the working together of weavers

Will such a tapestry be completed

With its completion let us look at the good that comes from it

And in time we should also look at those stitches that were dropped

Because they also have a message

Kūkapa Tirikatene (1934–2018)

Mihi | Greeting

I whānau au ki Ingarangi

Ko Chosen Hill te maunga

Ko River Severn te awa

Ko Cotswolds te rohe

Ināianei kei Te Papaoiaia taku kāinga, a

Ko Kirikiriroa taku tūrangawaewae

Ko Rosemary Rowe / Aitken taōku whaea

Ko Tom Aitken tōku matua

Ko Michael Donkin tōku hoa tāne

Ko Caoimhe McKeogh rāua ko Siobhān Maglalang āku tamariki

Ko Viv Aitken tōku ingoa

Tihei mauri ora

My greeting acknowledges a joint attachment to England, the country of my birth and to Aotearoa New Zealand where I've lived for almost 30 years, with ancestry ties going back five generations on my father's side. I grew up in the limestone hills of the Cotswolds, with a strong connection to the granite cliffs of Cornwall, where my mother's family has lived for hundreds of years, and where my first daughter was born. Hamilton holds a special place in my heart—it's where my second daughter came along and where many friendships and memories were made. These days, though, home is a small block of regenerating bush I tend with my husband in the foothills of the Tararua ranges near Palmerston North.

Acknowledgements

First, the story behind this book's title. A few years ago I was teaching a Mantle of the Expert experience to a class of 9-year olds. One of the children asked whether what we were doing was "real" or "made up" and I replied, "we're creating a story together using imagination". The child seemed satisfied with this clarification. Just then another boy in the class spoke up: "It's real" he said quietly and emphatically, "in all the ways that matter." His words capture the depth and complexity of Mantle of the Expert so perfectly I could think of no better title for this book.

Next, a few formal acknowledgements. Sections of this book have previously been published in other forms. The table of 10 core elements in Chapter 1 previously appeared in *Connecting Curriculum, Linking Learning* (Fraser et al., 2013). Initial ideas and images associated with the weaving metaphor were first explored in a conference presentation at the *Heathcote Reconsidered* conference in Greenwich, London in 2013, with a subsequent paper published in *Drama* (Aitken, 2014). Many of the handouts and charts reproduced and referred to in this book are from the UK website www.mantleoftheexpert.com. All have been used with permission.

Some of the Mantle of the Expert examples I have described were based on or influenced by other people's planning. The *Objects of Significance* example in Chapter 3 was inspired by a process drama by Trevor Sharp (Sharp, n.d.), while in the table of examples in Chapter 3, *Little Wild Thing* was an adaptation of a process drama by Shireen Garrett (Garrett, 2001), the Rata plan was inspired by planning by Tanya Batt (2001) as well as *Fairy Tale Problem Solvers* by Tim Taylor (Taylor n.d.). The *Animal Carers* example was based on something I saw Luke Abbott model in a school in the UK in 2012 and *Diamond Demolition* was my attempt at a New Zealand version of Julia Walshaw's plan of the same name (Bealings School, n.d.).

The process of reconceptualising Mantle of the Expert in a culturally sustaining way is only just beginning but I'm already grateful to Rawiri Hindle for his generous insights and for being so willing to walk alongside our Dramatic Inquiry community on this journey. I'd also like to thank Makaira Waugh for helpful guidance on the whakatauākī and mihi used to open this book.

In relation to the weaving metaphors that run through the planning chapters, I'd like to acknowledge Tasman (Tahimana) Maude, a teacher from Northland who first referred to Mantle of the Expert as "Te Korowai o te tohunga" and encouraged me to explore this new way of conceptualising the approach. Special thanks to Robin Hill who kindly talked through terminology with me and whose helpful guide *Weaving Your First Korowai* (Hill, 2013) provided an opportunity for a hands-on experience at making a mini kākahu. Thanks to Veranoa Hetet whose website, blogs, and articles have provided valuable insight and terminology, particularly in clarifying the difference between kākahu and korowai (Hetet, 2016, 2018). I must also thank Pare Kana for years of gentle mentoring into cultural practices during our years together at Waikato University, including the privilege of seeing her own beautiful kākahu in creation. Thanks to Patricia Tepania, kaitiaki on the Te Wānanga o Aotearoa tikanga course I took in 2019, who provided further information and resources. I'm grateful to all those who have supported me to take my first steps in understanding this rich metaphor and I welcome feedback to help me continue my learning journey.

As mentioned in the text, the metaphor of korowai weaving has been employed in other contexts including *Tu Rangatira*, a Ministry of Education (2010) resource for Māori-medium educational leaders, *He Korowai Oranga*, a Ministry of Health resource (2002) and *Tā Tātou Mahere Korowai*, a production of Te Rau Matatini (2010), designed to offer guidance to advisory groups in mental health services. I found these documents inspiring and acknowledge echoes of their imagery in my writing.

The narratives of classroom practice in Chapter 3 are such an important part of this book, so my heartfelt thanks to Melissa, Andy, and the other classroom teachers for kindly welcoming me into their spaces and letting me publish about our shared adventures all these years later. Thank you to the student teachers who participated so bravely in these examples. Thanks to Gay for your years of vision, friendship, and amazing support and to Peter, Stuart, Marie, and other senior leaders for generously making space in your schools and giving permission for these accounts and photographs to be shared. Special thanks to Whakarongo, Materoa, Kylie, Whitney, and the team for assisting with the writing and implementation of the *Objects of Significance* example. I'm so glad we could include even a little bit of our important work together. The best is yet to come!

Beyond the specific examples included in this book, there are so many colleagues within New Zealand and overseas whose ideas, practice, and support fed into its pages. The Introduction acknowledges some individuals and I would like to repeat my thanks here—along with my regret that it's impossible to name everyone I should. This book could never have been conceived without the hundreds of shared projects, explorations, reflections, and conversations I've enjoyed with dozens of mentors, teaching colleagues, research colleagues, and teaching students over the last two decades. Thank you all for the passion, commitment, and belief you have invested into your work in education. You have made it impossible not to at least try to write this book to capture some of the power of our work. This is true, also, of the many participants—children and adults—who have so willingly entered into imagined worlds with me and their teachers over the years. Though you are unlikely to ever read it, this book is really all about you.

While the imperative to write this book was never in doubt, actually finding time to write was a challenge and getting it to the point of publication was one of the hardest things I've ever done, so I want to give heartfelt thanks to some people without whom I would never have started or finished. Thanks to the inspirational Luke Abbott for supporting my first forays into Mantle of the Expert 10 years ago, for generous permission to use training materials, for opportunities to observe some masterful teaching, and for patiently explaining Heathcote's brotherhoods to me in a teashop in Cambridge. Thanks also to friend and mentor Brian Edmiston whose relentless quest to understand and theorise Heathcote's work has formed and informed so much of my own understanding. I'm indebted to you Brian for much of the terminology and thinking in these pages, particularly the stuff on teaching modalities and signature pedagogies. Without our collaborations and deep conversations this book would never have happened. Thanks similarly to Iona Towler-Evans whose skill in using Mantle of the Expert is second to none. Your stories about teaching transport me from the other side of the world right into your classroom and I learn so much every time. Very special thanks to the ever-supportive Tim Taylor without whom this book definitely would not have seen the light of day. Tim, you've been so generous with expertise and knowledge, particularly in relation to the tools in Chapter 5. You've inspired and indulged me with long reflective conversations, you've read and reread drafts, you've challenged and offered feedback, and you've encouraged me to keep going to the end. I can't thank you enough.

Thank you David Ellis from NZCER Press for encouraging me to write this book and for waiting patiently for the results. Thanks to my talented daughters: Keava for being my writing buddy and for skilful editing advice at just the right moments and Vonnie for help with images. And last, but not least, thank you to my husband Michael for carrying the "mantle" of love and support on the home front.

Chapter 1

Introduction

This book is the outcome of years of collaboration with inspirational people. As the whakataukī at the start of this book expresses, understanding can only come through learning with and alongside others, and through a process of trial, error, and reflection. That has been my journey while writing this book.

My first exposure to drama in education was as an undergraduate student in Wales in 1989. In a course on Theatre in Education, our lecturer David Rabey showed an overhead transparency with a list of "Paradigms regarding views of children" written by someone called Dorothy Heathcote (1926–2011). The list of metaphors included:

Child as flower—I will give you time and care
Child as friend—If I'm nice to you, will you ...
Child as clay—In time you'll turn into the students I want
Child as crucible—You and I must keep stirring our understanding around
Child as vessel—My knowledge will fill you up.

(Heathcote, cited in O'Neill 2015, p. 116)

I found the words intriguing. I'd never considered there might be different ways of looking at how children learn, and found myself reflecting on these as we created our Theatre in Education piece together. This experience was a turning point, sparking my interest in the educational potential of drama and theatre.

Another turning point came 12 years later. A lot of change had occurred in the meantime. I'd had 3 years in Dublin working as a stage manager, gained a Master's in Theatre Studies, emigrated to New Zealand with my husband and 3-month-old baby, spent 2 years teaching English and Performing Arts at high schools in Christchurch, moved to Hamilton, celebrated the birth of another daughter, and embarked on my PhD in Theatre Studies at the University of Waikato. Then, one day my supervisor loaned me a copy of *Three Looms Waiting*, a BBC documentary on Heathcote's early work (Smedley, 1971). He was less than complimentary about Heathcote's approach, but I was inspired and began devouring all I could about process drama, classroom drama, and Mantle of the Expert.

Around this time, I gained a position at the University of Waikato's Faculty of Education. My predecessor in that position, Lyn Shillingford, was a talented teacher with a huge understanding of Heathcote's work and I'm so grateful for the way she encouraged me to learn and build on her legacy at Waikato. I continue to use her notes and planning to this day and I still hear her voice encouraging me to "just trust the drama!"

This was the early 2000s. New Zealand had just introduced a new arts curriculum, with drama included as part of the Arts learning area for the first time. The document made a specific mention of process drama as "drama not intended for an audience" in which "participants build belief in roles and situations and explore them together, negotiating, interpreting, and reflecting on role and meaning" (Ministry of Education, 2000, p. 36). With the appointment of Arts advisers, I had the opportunity to attend workshops, speak to some really knowledgeable people, and continue to grow my understanding of Heathcote's approaches. I also joined Drama New Zealand, the subject society for drama teachers in New Zealand and many of the inspirational colleagues I got to know at this time have become lifelong friends and mentors, including Susan Battye, Terry Locke, Peter O'Connor, Michelle Hesketh, Hilari Anderson, Elizabeth Anderson, Angela Walker, Gaenor Stoate, Trevor Sharp, and Delia Baskerville.

I took every opportunity to practise teaching in the Heathcote tradition. My daughters were at primary school at this stage, so I arranged to take groups of university students into their classrooms and lead classroom drama experiences with the children. We spent time skulking around the university campus being spies, we helped out a lost monster, and we advised a farmer how to attend to a sick taniwha. I was very fortunate to have these opportunities to play, explore, and make mistakes and many of the cautionary tales shared later in this book emerged from this time of learning and experimentation. I'm so grateful to Coryn Knapper, Gay Gilbert, Jocelyn Williams, and other staff at Knighton and Hillcrest Normal Schools for these early opportunities.

I remember working in a class of Year 5s in which the children imagined they were running a factory producing "hyperleather"—an imaginary product made from recycled tyres but with all the qualities of animal skin. The children and I took on multiple roles, ranging from machinery parts, to business people planning out the different areas of production. I then introduced an ethical dilemma: we had insufficient product to meet a large order from an American pop star and the boss was asking us to substitute some real leather and not tell the client. Suddenly the children were intensely debating with a seriousness and conviction I hadn't known they were capable of. That was my first experience of the special quality of engagement that can arise with the responsible team, client, and commission so integral to Mantle of the Expert. Almost unconsciously, I'd introduced some of the key elements of the approach, including a key tension that challenged participants to stand up for what they believed in.

Soon afterwards I found and read Heathcote and Bolton's *Drama for Learning* (Heathcote & Bolton, 1994), the only resource available on Mantle of the Expert at that time. I was both excited and acutely aware of gaps in my understanding. I needed to see the approach in action. A trip to the UK in 2008 brought an opportunity to meet Luke Abbott and Tim Taylor and attend a training weekend. Watching these two stunning practitioners in action left me feeling I was part of something very important. On a subsequent trip back to the UK I met Dorothy Heathcote herself, and presented her with a kete as a gift from Drama New Zealand. I also visited Bealings School and saw the way teachers, including Julia Walshaw, were using Mantle of the Expert at every year level. I was struck by the children's engagement and the conviction the teachers brought to what they were doing. With naive enthusiasm, I became determined to offer opportunities for study in the approach at the University of Waikato.

The Master's paper in Mantle of the Expert began in 2009 with five students: Sue Bleaken, Priya Gain, Carrie Swanson, Dianna Elvin, and Gaenor Stoate. The first offering was both wonderful and intense with difficult assignments over several months of study. A shorter, more manageable version was developed and taught as a summer school every few years through to 2018, when I departed the university and the paper offering stopped. There is insufficient space here to list all the names of those who graduated from this course over the years, but many have become friends as well as fine practitioners leading Mantle of the Expert in their own schools. I have such fond memories of working with students on those courses, grappling with theory and practice and coming to grips with Mantle of the Expert in a New Zealand context. In many ways it was those experiences that first inspired this book.

Another important event occurred in 2009 when my very understanding boss, Dean of Education Roger Moltzen, allocated substantial funding for the first international conference in Mantle of the Expert: *Weaving our Stories*. A panel consisting of Sunny Amey, Carole Beu, Sally Markam, and Susan Battye presented on the history and development of Mantle of the Expert in New Zealand, and Dorothy Heathcote gave a memorable keynote address via live link. Luke Abbott, Tim Taylor, and Julia Walshaw all presented in person as did Allana Taylor, an experienced practitioner from the UK who had recently moved to New Zealand. The presenters repeated their workshops so that all attendees came away with shared experiences and resources (including some of the handouts and resources included in this book) and the conference closed with participants sharing their responses using drama conventions. *Weaving our Stories* honoured the existing work in Mantle of the Expert within Aotearoa New Zealand and internationally, and laid the foundations for new relationships and collaborations that have continued for over a decade.

Among those who attended the 2009 conference was a group of teachers who were part of a TLRI (Teaching and Learning Research Initiative) research project called Connecting Curriculum, Connecting Learning led by Deborah Fraser from the University of Waikato. I was on the research team along with Graham Price and Barbara Whyte. Working with these valued colleagues was a joy. Of the eight teachers who participated in this project, five—Michelle Parkes, Whakarongo Tauranga, Elicia Pirini, Penny Deane, and Lynette Townsend—made the decision to explore Mantle of the Expert as their chief pedagogy for the project. This gave us the opportunity to trial Mantle of the Expert in five classrooms across the Bay of Plenty and Waikato. Many of the teachers continue using Mantle of the Expert to this day and support other staff within their schools to do the same. This project's findings were disseminated in a book (Fraser et al., 2013) as well as a number of written articles and presentations. It was around this time the New Zealand Ministry of Education included Mantle of the Expert as an "effective pedagogy" on its TKI website (Ministry of Education, 2011a). Also emerging from the conference, a number of informal cluster groups were formed around New Zealand and I started convening a website to provide ongoing information and support for teachers. The story of this informal network, affectionately known as the "Mantle Underground", has been told in a book chapter (Aitken, V., 2017) and forms an important backdrop to this book.

Over the next few years I was fortunate to build relationships with people who helped strengthen my practice and understanding. The development of an undergraduate course in Mantle of the Expert opened up opportunities to work in partnership with local schools. Particularly special was the relationship with Hillcrest Normal School. Here, Deputy Principal Gay Gilbert invited me and a group of third-year teaching students to plan, implement, and deliver a programme of learning using Mantle of the Expert for one term each year. This was a fantastic training ground for me, the students, and the teachers. Two of the examples in this book are accounts of those collaborations. At the same time as working on my teaching practice I was able to deepen my theoretical understanding and investigate the field of drama education a little more. I stayed in touch with Luke and Tim and also got to know other international colleagues whose writing and research I admired. Brian Edmiston quickly became a friend and trusted mentor while I also enjoyed conversations and collaborations with Iona Towler-Evans, Pam Bowell, Brian Heap, Patrice Baldwin, Chris Hatton, Stig Errikson, Gerard Boland, Julie Dunn, John O'Toole, Helen Cahill, and Judith

Ackroyd through IDIERI (International Drama In Education Research Institute). So many drama education academics and practitioners from around the world have influenced my practice in lasting ways, as will be evident from how often their names are cited in this book.

I maintained regular correspondence with Dorothy Heathcote over several years until her death in 2011. Dorothy had a talent for ensuring anyone who communicated with her received individual attention and she always generously answered my questions and shared her thinking. On one of my trips to the UK, she said "You might want to do something with this", and handed me a photocopy of a handwritten transcript entitled *Mantle of the Expert: My Current Understanding*. It was an expanded version of the keynote she had given in 2009. I knew she had gifted me something really significant and I took it as encouragement to keep on with my efforts. I have indeed "done something" with the manuscript. The original is available online along with a commentary at www.mantleoftheexpert.co.nz and you'll see I make frequent references to this text throughout this book.

Over the next few years, with increasing numbers of students emerging from courses at the University of Waikato and more of my own and others' practice and research to build on, Mantle of the Expert became central to my practice and research. A particular privilege was the opportunity to supervise and mentor Master's and PhD students as they conducted research projects into drama for learning and Mantle of the Expert for their dissertations and theses (Abdul Samat, 2016; Bleaken, 2012; Stoate, 2013; Swanson, 2016). Working with these smart people as they drilled down into aspects of drama and Mantle of the Expert certainly influenced my own understanding. Then, in 2013, I had the pleasure of hosting Brian Edmiston as a visiting professor and co-teacher for several weeks. We taught a Master's paper together and spent many hours in rich discussions on theory and planning. I learned so much from these conversations and from observing Brian's teaching in action. Many of my ways of thinking about Mantle of the Expert and the terminology used in this book have emerged from these conversations.

A shift from Waikato to Hawke's Bay in 2015 was an opportunity for career advancement with the chance to co-ordinate an exciting teaching degree at the Eastern Institute of Technology. I really liked the programme and my new position, but it left me very little time to focus on drama in education. So, after 2 years, I decided to leave academia and see if I could make a job for myself offering professional development support in schools. In 2016, I became a Ministry-accredited facilitator, first with the Institute of Professional Learning at the University of Waikato and then Tātai Angitu E3 at Massey University. My dream job has slowly become a reality: now I spend my time travelling around the country supporting schools to learn about Mantle of the Expert and other forms of Dramatic Inquiry (Edmiston, 2010). Under the Ministry of Education's funding model, schools can access funding to support school-wide professional development including innovative pedagogy as part of local curriculum development. I love this work, which so far has included contracts with schools in Northland, Gisborne, Hamilton, Auckland, Christchurch, Tauranga, the King Country, and Wellington. Each collaboration has brought new discoveries and new questions that continue to shape my thinking.

It's impossible to do justice to the layers of new understandings and nuance that have emerged through working with teachers over the past few years: to attempt to do so would take as long as the book itself! However, I must mention some key turning points. In 2017, I had the privilege to work alongside Renee Downey, Principal Terry Brock, and a team of brave teachers at Otaika Valley School, on a TLIF (Teacher-led Innovation Fund) project exploring the use of Mantle of the Expert to support writing. The teachers also reflected on their evolving understandings of Dramatic Inquiry alongside their understandings of te āo Māori. As well as providing useful research data on the benefits for writing, this project sowed the seeds for the sections in this book on cultural responsiveness. In 2017–2018 I had a wonderful time with Michelle Hall and colleagues at Makaraka School exploring the concept of student agency. Our joint explorations were critical in consolidating my understanding of links between agency, play, and drama as expressed in Chapter 2. And 2018 saw a rekindling of the long-standing PLD relationship with friend and mentor Gay Gilbert and the staff at Hillcrest Normal School. The work with this team of highly reflective practitioners has really helped to clarify the Dramatic Inquiry framework shared in this book and provides a case study for how this can be embedded into local curriculum. Starting in 2019, I also had the pleasure of working with Whakarongo Tauranga and a team of 10 highly committed teachers at Knighton Normal School exploring how Dramatic Inquiry can support the teaching of New Zealand history. The learnings from this collaboration have been very profound. Some have made it into this book—including one of the case studies—others will need to wait for future volumes!

In addition to working in schools, there have been a number of other events and collaborations that contributed to this book in its final stages. In 2018, we were lucky enough to have Tim Taylor return to New Zealand to run a winter school for experienced practitioners. Tim's teaching was invaluable and most of my scribbled notes from the 2 days of workshops and our long chats in the car have ended up in this book somewhere. Tim's planned return in 2020 was interrupted by COVID-19 travel restrictions, but we still found a way to work together, by recording a podcast series in collaboration with our colleague Whakarongo Tauranga. Those rich conversations have definitely influenced the final redrafts of this volume, particularly the section on tools for enhancing pedagogy. I am also enjoying working alongside the visionary Lynne Cardy and her team at Auckland Theatre Company exploring the interface between Dramatic Inquiry and theatre making: it is early days for our collaboration in this exciting terrain and I look forward to exploring further. Last, but by no means least, as we go to press, I am thrilled to be working with a small group of colleagues from around New Zealand who have formed a charitable trust with the goal of supporting ongoing support and professional development for teachers and schools in Dramatic Inquiry, including Mantle of the Expert. It's so rewarding to be part of a passionate group with a shared commitment to the future of this pedagogy in New Zealand.

This book could not have happened without the input and support of many people. Truly, the tapestry of understanding that is offered here has been woven from many strands and by many weavers. I only hope what I have laid down in these pages goes some way to honouring this collective wisdom and experience.

Aims of the book

I opened this book with a whakataukī and a mihi because I want to write about Mantle of the Expert in a way that celebrates the unique context of Aotearoa New Zealand. This includes embracing our bicultural foundations; our specific environmental, social, political, and historical landscape; and our own distinct curriculum and assessment framework. I want to acknowledge and give voice to the many teachers around the country who, over many years, have explored Dramatic Inquiry and Mantle of the Expert within their own context, evolved it, and made it their own. Teachers here are expert at many things, one of which is making allowances for the dissonance we experience while working with teaching resources written by authors from the UK, the US, Australia, or other contexts. We become adept at adapting: tweaking the assumptions, world views, and language to make it work for our own situation. This is good for resilience, creative thinking, and the "number 8 wire" mentality that Kiwis are famous for, but it can also be quite hard work and somewhat othering. It's my hope that this book will be a different experience—one that uses language, references, and source material that feel local and appropriate to New Zealand teachers. If the book is also of interest to readers from other contexts by allowing a familiar approach to be illuminated in a new way, that's a bonus.

I realise that teachers using Mantle of the Expert come from every sector: early childhood, primary, intermediate, secondary, tertiary, community, and in contexts in which English, te reo Māori, and other languages may be spoken. I initially wanted to produce a resource that would speak equally to all these contexts but it proved impossible do this without overcrowding the text. So, this book focuses on teaching in primary school contexts, with some information and advice for those in other sectors. I'll refer only to *The New Zealand Curriculum* (Ministry of Education, 2007) and *Arts in the New Zealand Curriculum* (Ministry of Education, 2000) although I acknowledge some readers will be accustomed to using *Te Marautanga o Aotearoa* (Ministry of Education, 2008b) as their guiding curriculum, others will be working within the early childhood curriculum *Te Whāriki* (Ministry of Education, 2017), and many will be governed by special character considerations associated with their particular school. I hope colleagues can use their expertise to make connections with those frameworks and that—in time—other resources can be produced where these links are shared more explicitly.

Teachers are busy people, so while some might read the book from cover to cover, others are likely to skim or read certain sections and not others. Readers new to Mantle of the Expert will probably find the first three chapters most relevant, while those looking for support with planning will focus on Chapter 4. Chapter 5 looks at the nuances of teaching and will appeal more to those with experience in the classroom. Chapters 6 and 7 are broad enough to be of general interest. In terms of writing style, you'll find I will often address you/the reader directly—like this! At other times, where I refer to "the teacher" in the generic sense, I have opted for the gender neutral "they". When referring to those we teach, I'll usually use the word "participant" for generic descriptions and "child/ren" when talking about a particular group. I may occasionally also use the words "student" or "learner".

Mostly this book is illustrated with examples of teaching by a single teacher or a pair working with a group of around 30 participants in a single-cell classroom, though I realise that this is no longer the norm nor the anticipated future of teaching in New Zealand. I hope that readers who work in collaborative spaces and those who teach in online and blended settings can see the potential for Mantle of the Expert to be used in their environments. There is certainly exciting work being done in this area (Taylor, 2020) and in future I'm sure we will see books devoted to digital and online possibilities in Dramatic Inquiry. In the meantime, you'll find specific pointers for using Mantle of the Expert in Innovative Learning Environments (ILEs) and other collaborative learning settings later in this book.

There are some things this book does not aim to do. It's not an attempt to theorise Mantle of the Expert fully, or to offer a comprehensive review of research literature. While research provides a significant backdrop to the practical advice offered here, this is primarily a practitioner's handbook. This book is not a final word on Mantle of the Expert. I would argue that there is no such thing and nor should there be. One of the most fascinating things about the approach is its flexibility and adaptability. There are so many ways to understand Mantle of the Expert, so many ways to plan it, so many ways to continue to improve and theorise it. What is shared here is one perspective, one approach, one set of views. I encourage you to seek out others. Read widely, keep learning and practising, and ultimately you will make the approach your own.

An appeal to the reader

Having stressed the importance of forming your own understanding of Mantle of the Expert, I also want to urge you not to rush this process. I spend a lot of time speaking to people about Mantle of the Expert and demonstrating it in classrooms and, in my experience, one of the biggest obstacles is where someone forms a firm opinion right away. This might be a firm negative opinion such as thinking: "This is too complicated for me" or "Drama is not my thing"; or it might be overly positive: "I love it and I completely get it" or, "This is the whole answer to education and everyone should do it!" These are equally problematic as we need to remain both open and critical about any new pedagogy. Another temptation is to adopt a firm position based on existing practice. I often hear people say: "I'm already doing this" or "This is exactly like the X or Y approach". While it's great when people find something in Mantle of the Expert that clicks with their existing philosophy, this can become a barrier to further understanding.

The temptation to form strong opinions is part of our brain's natural response to new learning. As Jonathan Haidt explains, our desire to encapsulate and simplify is born of the brain's need for security in bias confirmation and pattern recognition (Haidt, 2013). I also think it's a positive part of the Kiwi mindset that we want to get to grips with new ideas quickly; make them our own and make them work, or drop them and move on. However, my appeal to you as you read this book is to try to maintain an open, curious, and questioning mind. As teachers, we talk a lot about developing "learning dispositions" and "growth mindsets" in our learners; celebrating a learning journey that includes moments of uncertainty and incomplete understanding, so see if you can adopt this approach to your own learning in Mantle of the Expert too. There's enough simplicity in the approach to be able to grasp aspects of it straight away, and enough complexity that you could find yourself using it every day for the next 20 years and still learn new things about it. It's not by chance that one of Heathcote's final written works was entitled *Mantle of the Expert: My current understanding* (Heathcote, 2009, my emphasis). I hope this book provides interesting reading for you wherever you are in forming your current understanding.

Glossary and definitions

This section provides explanations of education acronyms and definitions for key drama terminology used in this book. I have taken into account the language of *The New Zealand Curriculum* and the writing of esteemed colleagues in drama and Mantle of the Expert. However, there is healthy and ongoing debate within our field about the categories, definitions, and terms we use and so many definitions offered here will differ from those found elsewhere. Please note: I have not translated terms from te reo Māori that are used within the text, since it is one of the official languages of Aotearoa New Zealand. If translations are required, these can be accessed through reputable dictionaries.

Drama terminology

Compact: An informal agreement made between participants in a shared activity about how the situation will be organised. The compact covers how elements and techniques of drama will be organised, what social behaviours will be appropriate, and what will stand in for things from the imagined world. Details of a compact may be implicit or explicit. They are flexible and may be renegotiated as needed.

Convention: A generally agreed way of working (*see* Drama conventions, Role conventions, and Social conventions). Any conventional activity relies for its success on a mutually agreed compact between those engaged in it (*see* Compact).

Core elements: The fundamental components of something. In the planning model offered in this book, the core elements of Mantle of the Expert are described as whenu—the 10 things laid out in advance. These are then interwoven with aho—the signature pedagogies or teaching techniques that characterise the approach.

Dimensions of dramatic imagination: The sensory aspects of action within the imagined world—light and darkness, movement and stillness, sound and silence. These six dimensions can be manipulated by the teacher and participants to deepen the aesthetic aspects of the experience.

Drama conventions: A generally agreed way of working dramatically with a strategy for a particular purpose. Different conventions offer different ways to manipulate drama elements and techniques. For convenience, some of the tried and true ways of working are given labels, such as "freeze frame" or "speaking thoughts aloud", but, in fact, endless permutations are possible. Heathcote identified 33 conventions specifically related to the use of role (see Role conventions).

Drama elements: The fundamental components that all drama is made of. *The New Zealand Curriculum* identifies the elements of drama as role, time and space, action, tension, and focus.

Drama for learning: A term for any classroom activity where drama conventions and strategies are used to create an active learning experience. This can include one-off activities as well as those used within the sustained arc of a process drama or Mantle of the Expert. Drama for learning is described in this book as one of the teaching modalities within Mantle of the Expert.

Drama techniques: The different ways people can use their bodies to express themselves. In 2000, the *Arts in the New Zealand Curriculum* document (Ministry of Education, 2000) listed the drama techniques as voice, gesture, movement, and facial expression. This list was later amended to include use of space and body language, though I personally prefer the former version.

Dramatic Inquiry: An umbrella term used to describe a range of teaching approaches where participants are supported to explore questions and solve problems in imagined contexts. Includes dramatic play, drama for learning, process drama, Mantle of the Expert, commission model, and rolling role (see "How Mantle of the Expert relates to other Dramatic Inquiry approaches" in Chapter 2 for more detail).

Mantle of the Expert: An education approach developed by Heathcote that uses imaginary contexts to generate purposeful and engaging activities for learning. Within the fiction, the students are positioned and framed as a team of experts working for a client on a commission. The commission is designed by the teacher to generate tasks and activities that fulfil the requirements of the client as well as creating opportunities for students to study wide areas of the curriculum.

Process drama: An approach to classroom drama developed from the work of Heathcote and others, where participants, including the teacher, move in and out of an imagined world to engage with tensions, explore, create, and enact solutions. The experience is structured in episodes using drama conventions and the emphasis is on the process rather than any product in the sense of a final performance for an external audience.

Role conventions: Agreements between participants in a drama for how roles will be organised and depicted. Heathcote's list of role conventions indicates multiple ways in which a fictional other can be introduced to the class. The original list can be expanded with digital, online, and virtual possibilities.

Rolling role: A teaching approach invented by Heathcote in which different classes combine to carry out a collaborative inquiry based on an imagined community (see "How Mantle of the Expert relates to other Dramatic Inquiry approaches" in Chapter 2 for more detail).

Social conventions: Generally agreed ways of working between people about the organisation of space, appropriate behaviours, use of positioning, rules of talk, and other aspects of human behaviour in social situations, including classrooms. As with any conventions, they are sustained by compacts, or agreements.

Strategies: Ways of working that teachers employ with a particular purpose in mind. For example, using a doughnut circle to facilitate pair work and move between partners quickly. Drama strategies are ways of working in the real and the imagined world: for example, teaching in role, freezing a moment in time, or questioning a role to gather information (see "Selecting drama strategies and conventions" in Chapter 5 for more on the distinction between drama strategies and conventions).

Chapter 2
Some history and context

As Kūkapa Tirikatane's words reminded us at the opening of this book, the tapestry of understanding cannot be woven by one strand alone. To understand Mantle of the Expert it is important to know something of its origins. In this chapter we will look at the origins of the approach and its development here in New Zealand. We'll see how Mantle of the Expert relates to other classroom drama approaches and we'll grapple with the challenge of summing up the approach and teasing out its defining features. To close, we will take a brief look at some theories from education and sociology that can help us understand how Mantle of the Expert supports learning.

Dorothy Heathcote and the development of Mantle of the Expert

Mantle of the Expert was first developed in the 1980s by Dorothy Heathcote MBE (1926–2011), an accomplished classroom practitioner from the UK, who insisted on treating children and young people as capable and competent. Throughout her career, Heathcote sought out ways to bring children's play, drama, and theatre into the forefront of classroom learning:

> Man's [sic] gift with which we seem to be born, [is] of just putting ourselves instantly into someone else's shoes and having a sort of total

picture of how it must feel to be feeling like that person right now. Now, we haven't as yet done very much about harnessing this to the education of our children. But it's just about time, I feel, that we began to say to ourselves, 'can we use this in the classroom situation?'

(Heathcote, in Burgess, 1993)

There is insufficient space here to give Heathcote's full life story, but for those interested in finding out more, Gavin Bolton's biography (Bolton, 2003) and the documentary *Pieces of Dorothy* (Burgess, 1993) are well worth seeking out. Both explore Heathcote's personal and professional influences and give fascinating insights into how the Mantle of the Expert approach was developed. The BBC documentary *Three Looms Waiting* (Smedley, 1971) is also invaluable as an insight into her early work. While the film doesn't show Heathcote using full-blown Mantle of the Expert it remains a stunning record of her early methods.

Mantle of the Expert was one of four key approaches Heathcote identified as models within her practice. First was what she called "drama to explore people" (Heathcote, 2002). This approach, sometimes called "man in a mess" drama, involved participants encountering a figure in dramatic role and improvising a response. Another variant was what we now call "drama for learning" which involved using a drama strategy or convention to enhance learning in a curriculum area other than drama; for example, a teacher going into role to introduce a maths problem. In time, Heathcote's drama to explore people model became the basis for what we know as "process drama"—a more sustained approach in which teachers and participants create imagined worlds that they step in and out of together (O'Neill, 1995; O'Toole & Dunn, 2002; Bowell & Heap, 2013). Heathcote herself did not generally use the term "process drama" to describe this phase of her work, though in an interview towards the end of her life she seems to have acknowledged process drama and placed it alongside her other four models (Özen & Adıgüzel, 2017). Process drama builds on the socio-dramatic play of young children in that participants employ different drama conventions, play out ideas in role, and reflect on implications for their own lives. Like play and drama for learning, process drama has no final performance for an external audience. It is more like a long-form improvisation within a framework, which allows participants to sustain a narrative arc and to develop high levels of engagement and emotional affect. Any teacher who wants to understand Mantle of the Expert will benefit from becoming familiar with play, drama for learning, and process drama as a foundation.

Mantle of the Expert was the second model to emerge in Heathcote's practice. She explained that the approach "carries forward the elements of model one (drama for learning about people) except the point of view is taken into task situations where a fictional client is involved" (Heathcote, cited in O'Neill, 2015, p. 135). Mantle of the Expert retains many of the ingredients of process drama with the additional feature that participants are asked to imagine they are experts in a particular field, charged with carrying out an important job, or commission, for a fictional client. Through addressing this commission, and dealing with the tensions and problems that arise, participants encounter opportunities for cross-curricula learning. Mantle of the Expert combines drama, inquiry, and powerful positioning to give participants a real sense of responsibility, and for Heathcote it was this quality that set Mantle of the Expert apart from her other models (Özen & Adıgüzel, 2017). In her keynote address at the 2009 conference in Hamilton, Heathcote explained her reasons for giving Mantle of the Expert such an unusual name:

> Let us first examine the strange label. 'Mantle' is not a cloak by which a person is recognised. This is no garment to cover. I use it as a quality: of leadership, carrying standards of behaviour, morality, responsibility, ethics and the spiritual basis of all action. The mantle embodies the standards I [the wearer] ascribe to. It grows by usage, not garment stitching.
>
> (Heathcote, 2009, p. 1)

As for the word "Expert", Heathcote explained:

> 'Expert' is essential in the name because I value learning and curiosity to enquire. Schooling imposes such burdens of 'out there' information upon students, that ways must be found to inspire and reward curious enquiry and give children the first steps towards pleasure in exploring new fields, and shedding the insidious fear of error or making mistakes.
>
> (Heathcote, 2009, pp. 1–2)

For Heathcote, the metaphor of a mantle of expertise carried almost spiritual connotations, conveying the idea of a cloak of responsibility carried on the shoulders and passed on from one generation to another. This metaphor takes on particular resonance when we bring it into the context of Aoteaora New Zealand and relate it to kākahu including korowai. These literal mantles, lovingly created to be worn during significant ceremonial occasions, are more than garments. They are taonga that indeed symbolise "qualities of leadership … standards of behaviour, morality, responsibility, ethics and the spiritual basis of all action". While there's no suggestion Heathcote was conscious of kākahu when she chose the name for her teaching approach, extending her metaphor like this provides a powerful way for teachers in New Zealand to conceptualise Mantle of the Expert and this is something we will return to in the pages ahead.

Towards the end of her career, Heathcote went on to develop a third model which she called "rolling role" (Heathcote, 2002). Rolling role was originally designed for use in specialist settings such as a secondary school and was "Heathcote's attempt to reduce the isolation of subject teachers and to allow students to carry the same context with them from lesson to lesson while sharing skills and information" (O'Neill, 2015, p. 133). In simple terms, rolling role involves discrete groups of students and their teachers collaborating to create a fictional community such as a town, institution, or company. This is a much broader entity than the focused responsible team of a Mantle of the Expert and, critically, participants may not become the community so much as oversee it. The quality of engagement is more like projective play with dolls and puppets rather than embodied role play, though some enactment may be included. The fictional community, once established, becomes a shared context for inquiry, collaboration, and exchange. As in a soap opera, dramatic tensions—what Heathcote (2002) called "disturbance factors"—are introduced and these trigger further learning opportunities. Key to the rolling role approach is that the work is an exchange between different groups of participants, who each pick up certain aspects of the work, develop it, and share back for other groups to respond to and build on. There's not necessarily a specific client or a commission to fulfil, although sometimes the rolling role might have these qualities. In general, the inquiry is open ended and emergent and runs until the decision is made to stop. The products of inquiry are shared with everyone involved through live presentations, or in digital form. In this way, the approach employs the same practices as online communities and collaborative gaming. Heathcote considered that rolling role had particular potential for specialist teachers who need to teach within their own curriculum area but want to collaborate with colleagues and break out of a compartmentalised approach to curriculum. Rolling role has received much less attention than Mantle of the Expert, though recent scholarly work has argued a case for revitalising the approach for the digital age (Davis, 2016; Davis et al., 2014).

Heathcote's fourth and final model, the commission model, is much closer to Mantle of the Expert in that it involves engaging as a team with a client and a commission. However, in this approach, students work on a real-life commission rather than an imagined one and generally there is a real-world client too: "Commission model … carries the social element that is present in the other models right out into the community beyond the school" (O'Neill, 2015, p. 133). As in Mantle of the Expert, participants in the commission model may be positioned as a team of experts. However, they generally do the work "as themselves" rather than being framed with a fictional team identity in the imagined world. This might sound like a small variation and in some cases it can be. At other times it makes a huge difference, particularly in terms of how participants grapple with real-world responsibilities, time frames, and safety considerations.

The commission model has similarities with other recognised teaching approaches such as social inquiry (Ministry of Education, 2008a; Wood, 2013), project-based learning (Ministry of Education, n.d.-a), and design-based learning (Doppelt et al., 2008). What makes it different is the use of the dramatic, with tensions, drama conventions, and other strategies employed to enhance engagement and explore multiple perspectives. Heathcote saw the commission model as one that could revolutionise schooling. She envisaged schools as places where teachers and learners could engage with imagined commissions, as in Mantle of the Expert and respond to real-world commissions from the community with groupings and logistics designed to fit around the work at hand (Heathcote, 2002). To date, however, the commission model has not been widely explored. Some practitioners overseas, including Iona Towler-Evans, have used it with encouraging results (BBC News, 2017; Hopkins, 2017) and here in New Zealand a version of the commission model approach was trialled in a polytechnic course on interior design (Dunne, 2015).

Of Heathcote's four models, Mantle of the Expert has been by far the most widely explored, thanks to the commitment of Heathcote's former students and other practitioners, scholars, and researchers who have worked hard to sustain and grow it around the world. At the forefront of this effort are UK practitioners Luke Abbott and Tim Taylor who worked closely with Heathcote for many years and have continued to advocate for and support Mantle of the Expert since her death in 2011. Abbott and Taylor, both gifted teachers themselves, have embedded practice in the UK and beyond by offering a range of training options for teachers, building networks of training schools and recognised trainers, and developing an extensive website. One of the important principles of Heathcote's work that Abbott and Taylor have been careful to perpetuate is that all the teaching materials and planning tools are made available free to anyone who wishes to use them. This open source policy lends a special quality to the experience of using Mantle of the Expert: a sense one is part of a community with a direct link to Heathcote's legacy. These days, Mantle of the Expert is used in hundreds of schools around the world. It is probably the most accessible of Heathcote's four models for a school to implement (Sayers, 2011) and is the approach she is most remembered for.

Mantle of the Expert in New Zealand

Heathcote had strong links to New Zealand throughout her career and local teachers played a special place in the inception and development of Mantle of the Expert. Her first visit was in 1978. Then in 1984 and 1987, with the support of the British Council and Sunny Amey (then education officer for drama), Heathcote conducted two extensive tours of New Zealand in which she led workshops and classes up and down the country (Battye, 2010). Scores of teachers attended Heathcote's demonstrations and workshops and those who attended still talk about how transformative they were. It seems Heathcote felt the same way. Twenty years later, in a letter to Drama New Zealand, she recalled how much she had learned from her collaborations with New Zealand colleagues, particularly their "wrestling bravely" with a drama called *Those Who Sailed with Cook* (Heathcote, 2008; Shaw, 1986).

It was during her time in New Zealand that Heathcote's thinking about Mantle of the Expert started to consolidate. One can clearly spot elements of the approach in dramas developed during her time here. For example, *Sanctuary* (Department of Education, 1986) involved children setting up a home for runaway children with activities including dividing up the land for different crops. As for *Those Who Sailed with Cook*, Heathcote specifically states this was the drama that "initiated" her work in Mantle enterprises (Heathcote, 2009, p. 1).

Heathcote's visits had a significant influence on the development of drama in education in New Zealand (Battye, 2010; Greenwood, 2009). The subject society for drama educators, NZADIE (later Drama New Zealand) was formed in 1984 as a direct result of Heathcote's visits and she remained patron for the rest of her life. Today, the society continues to offer workshops and conferences fostering her methods, though it has also expanded to focus on supporting secondary specialists. During the 1980s and 1990s, several teachers travelled to the UK to study with Heathcote and then shared their learning back in New Zealand. In this period, teachers in New Zealand operated without any formal guidelines in drama but after Heathcote's visits a drama curriculum working group was established, with many of its members advocates of Heathcote's methods. In 2000, drama was recognised in the curriculum for the first time as part of the Arts learning area (Ministry of Education, 2000). The influence of Heathcote's practice can clearly be seen in the wording of this document, which makes specific reference to process drama and conceptualises drama in terms of elements, techniques, and conventions. The document specifically names Mantle of the Expert, though it is listed as a drama convention, which has led to misunderstanding about its full potential as a teaching approach.

The early 2000s were a lively time for drama in education in New Zealand, with advisers appointed around the country. Two process teaching resources, *Playing our Stories* (Ministry of Education, 2006) and *Telling our Stories* (Ministry of Education, 2004), were sent to every school in the country and these included excellent examples of process dramas, some with Mantle of the Expert characteristics. In 2007, when the New Zealand curriculum was revised, drama was firmly embedded once again as a discipline within the Arts (Ministry of Education, 2007). Drama's position within the curriculum since 2000 has meant, among other things, that all student teachers now receive some level of pre-service education in classroom drama.

Over the past two decades, New Zealand's political and educational climate has shifted as the country went through the era of National Standards, shrinking pre-service allocation, and the loss of advisory services in the Arts. In spite of this, interest in process drama and Mantle of the Expert has continued. In 2009, we held the first International Mantle of the Expert conference *Weaving our Stories* in Hamilton. This event was well attended and subsequent symposia have also been successful (Battye, 2016). Since the 2009 conference, informal cluster groups of teachers interested in the approach have continued to meet in various centres around the country (Aitken, V., 2017). Those who attended the conference, along with students from courses offered by the University of Waikato, have gone on to take leadership in their schools and carry out further research in the approach. At the time of writing, seven schools around New Zealand have a commitment to using Dramatic Inquiry, including Mantle of the Expert, across all levels of the school, and have begun embedding the approaches into their local curriculum. The Ministry of Education has included information about Mantle of the Expert on its teachers' resource website under the heading "effective pedagogies", which is a welcome clarification given the earlier characterisation of Mantle of the Expert as a convention (Ministry of Education, 2011a). The Education Review Office has also given positive feedback; including that in one Northland school, the use of Mantle of the Expert "is providing more opportunities for children to be leaders in their learning" and has "had a significant impact in increasing boys' engagement in learning" (Education Review Office, 2017).

A body of New Zealand-based research into Mantle of the Expert has also begun. The Mantle of the Expert Aotearoa website lists over 60 conference presentations, articles, and Master's and PhD theses produced in New Zealand since 2009. Between 2010 and 2012, Mantle of the Expert was a key focus for a TLRI project at the University of Waikato (Fraser et al., 2012a). This project found high levels of engagement and self-direction in classrooms where Mantle of the Expert was used, and benefits for children in grappling with difficult ethical issues (Fraser et al., 2012a). In 2017–18, a TLIF project led by teachers at Otaika Valley school in Northland, explored students' attitudes and achievement in writing in classrooms where Mantle of the Expert was used. Teachers found very positive results, particularly for those students who had experienced Mantle of the Expert over several years of schooling (Downey, 2017, 2018).

How Mantle of the Expert relates to other Dramatic Inquiry approaches

This book focuses specifically on Mantle of the Expert, but it is important to consider how the approach relates to and complements other classroom drama approaches. The Dramatic Inquiry framework shown below is one way to conceptualise this.

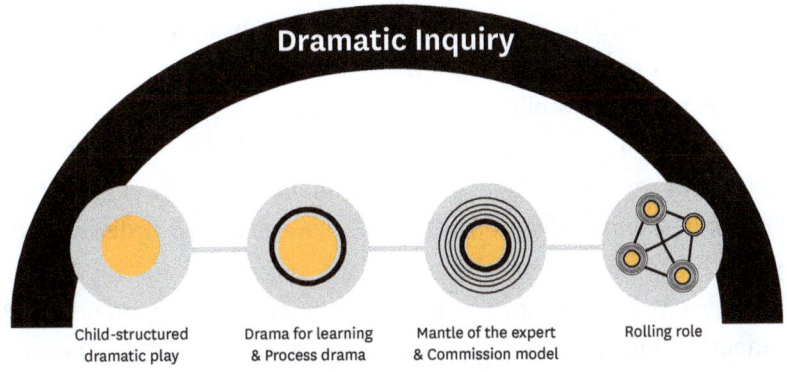

Figure 1: Dramatic Inquiry framework

This diagram has been developed with and for teachers in New Zealand schools, with input from a range of experts. The diagram proposes "Dramatic Inquiry" as an umbrella term or collective noun for the approaches nestled within. This term, first suggested by Brian Edmiston (2010) covers teaching and learning experiences that are *dramatic* in that teachers and participants collaborate to explore imagined worlds through role, tension, and other drama elements, and involve *inquiry* in that participants learn by asking questions, solving problems, taking ownership, and grappling with concerns that matter (Fraser, 2000). "Dramatic Inquiry" was not a term used by Heathcote herself: her four suggested approaches (drama for learning about people, Mantle of the Expert, commission model, and rolling role) were offered without any collective noun other than teaching models

(Heathcote, 2002). However, since all of Heathcote's approaches have an implicitly inquiry-based orientation, the name seems fitting. Over time, others have suggested other terminology; some preferring to use "drama for learning" as an overarching term and others conceptualising Mantle of the Expert as one component of process drama (Baldwin, 2010). Personally, I've found the term "Dramatic Inquiry" resonates well with New Zealand teachers, while the framework shown above provides a way of thinking about the interrelationship of different approaches. The framework can be helpful when deciding on the right approach for a group of participants and, just as importantly, it can help identify areas for professional development for teachers. Several primary schools around New Zealand now have this framework embedded in their local curriculum as the basis for a school-wide commitment to Dramatic Inquiry.

Beneath the umbrella of Dramatic Inquiry, the framework identifies the following sequence of approaches: child-structured dramatic play; drama for learning and process drama; Mantle of the Expert and the commission model; and rolling role. Rather than ordering them as Heathcote did in terms of when they were invented, the diagram sequences the approaches in order of the organisational and developmental complexity required for each approach. There are no fixed ages and stages within classroom drama, but in a sense the sequence reflects a child's developmental progressions. Each builds on the one before. We start with child-structured dramatic play on the left; this is represented by a gold circle which lies at the heart of all the approaches. As we move across the diagram to the right, the golden centre gains some layers around it, representing the conventions and other structures that teachers and participants place around play to generate drama for learning and process drama experiences. Further right again, and we see Mantle of the Expert and the commission model, which retain the golden centre of play and the structures of process drama and drama for learning while adding additional elements (the client, commission, and cross-curricula professional tasks). In the case of the commission model, some of these aspects will be situated in the real world but the features are the same. Moving on to the far right-hand side, we find rolling role, which involves groups of participants engaging in play, process drama, Mantle of the Expert,

Figure 2: Dramatic Inquiry approaches

Child-structured dramatic play	Drama for learning and Process drama		Mantle of the Expert and Commission model		Rolling role
Child-structured dramatic play is imaginative, embodied play where children imagine they are other people, or things in settings other than where they actually are. This includes socio-dramatic/ fantasy/ superhero play. Occurs at everyday life and in play-based educational contexts.	Drama for learning is where drama conventions and strategies such as teacher in role are used to enhance teaching and learning within a particular lesson or activity.	Process dramas are discrete lessons/ units/programmes where drama for learning is used to explore a pretext such as a book, story, or historical event. Participants move in and out of role using drama conventions and strategies to explore tensions and play out solutions.	Mantle of the Expert involves sustained programmes often lasting a term or longer, where learners are framed as experienced experts undertaking a commission for an imagined client. The commission forms the basis for a collective inquiry leading to authentic tasks across the curriculum. Drama conventions and strategies are used to explore tensions and play out solutions.	Commission model is an extension of Mantle of the Expert where the commission and usually the client are not imagined, but are in the real world. This involves social action and always has an outcome or product created for the client. The approach encourages engagement with the wider community beyond the classroom.	Rolling role involves sustained experiences in which groups of learners create a shared imagined world, organisation, or community. Groups work discretely but collaboratively, taking responsibility for an aspect of the shared community as it moves through a crisis or change process. Each group builds on the work of the others and feeds back information and ideas. Together they create a joint fund of information and a shared storyline.

or commission model experiences connected by their building of a shared imagined world. At each stage of the diagram, there are additional structural and organisational elements, though all involve inquiry within imagined worlds and in every case the golden centre of play remains at the heart.

In the online version of the framework, found on the Mantle of the Expert Aotearoa website, the diagram is followed by a table with more details on each approach: what teachers and participants do, developmental considerations, and resources needed. Only the first part of the table is reproduced here. The full version can be found at https://tiny.cc/nsclgz.

The elevator pitch

In 15 years of teaching, researching, and writing about Mantle of the Expert I have struggled to come up with an elevator pitch: that pithy statement you are supposed to have ready to deliver when you step into the lift and you have just a few seconds to explain something convincingly before you reach the next floor. In some ways, my favourite encapsulation is the one used in the title of this book: "It's real in all the ways that matter". As mentioned earlier, these words were spoken by a boy in a Year 5 class I taught some years ago, and were his attempt to explain to a peer how Mantle of the Expert works. To my mind, his words really sum up the essence of the approach. For a slightly fuller, yet still succinct definition (assuming we have internet access in our elevator) we could turn to the current Wikipedia entry, which succinctly describes Mantle of the Expert as:

> An education approach that uses imaginary contexts to generate purposeful and engaging activities for learning. Within the fiction the students are cast as a team of experts working for a client on a commission. The commission is designed by the teacher to generate tasks and activities that fulfill the requirements of the client as well as create opportunities for students to study wide areas of the curriculum.
>
> (Wikipedia, n.d.)

This gives a sense of the mechanics, but to really capture the flavour of the experience I still prefer the definition offered by the Year 5 participant. Beyond that, the elevator pitch probably depends on who has stepped into the metaphorical lift and asked for the information.

If I were talking to a professional colleague, such as a teacher or education researcher, I might tell them Mantle of the Expert is a form of inquiry learning that combines process drama with inquiry so there's room for lots of authenticity and engagement. I would tell them teaching in Mantle of the Expert is like improvising within a framework, and I would stress the use of conscious repositioning to shift the power between teachers and learners so that student agency is emphasised. I would also want to add that we don't have to compromise on deliberate acts of teaching and meaningful curriculum content; these are placed in a context so that deep learning can occur with key competencies and learning dispositions right at the fore. If the professional colleague were from New Zealand I would point out how, at its best, the learning that happens in Mantle of the Expert resonates with principles from te ao Māori including fostering ako, whanaungatanga, manaakitanga, kotahitanga, rangatiratanga, mōhiotanga, māramatanga, and tuakana-teina. If I knew the teacher was concerned with current educational literature and trends, I might describe how Mantle of the Expert promotes future-focused skills for 21st century and lifelong learning, including aligning with Fullan's six Cs: character, citizenship, communication, critical thinking, communication, and creativity/imagination (Fullan & Langworthy, 2014). I could talk about how this particular form of inquiry can encourage the development of a growth mindset (Dweck, 2006), or how it fosters deep learning through enhanced student agency, and how it requires collaborative and socio-emotional learning. Or I could describe how it can prompt higher-order, critical, and design thinking. I would definitely want to stress the central importance of empathy and how Mantle of the Expert aims to teach young people to take multiple perspectives and develop a critical mind; something humanity desperately needs as we face our uncertain future. Unfortunately, that's a lot to convey in the short time before the lift doors open!

If the fellow passenger were a parent or a learner I would present the case differently. To the parent, I would describe Mantle of the Expert as a way of bringing the real world into the classroom through imagination so that children can learn across the curriculum in an authentic way. I would make sure to tell them it would be likely to help their child get excited and engaged in school. If I were asked to explain it to a younger child, I would let them know that Mantle of the Expert is an adventure, a bit like when you play a game of pirates or superheroes. I would tell them that teachers join in the adventure as well, everyone solves problems, works together, and has fun. And everyone learns all sorts of things about the world along the way. For participants at primary or intermediate level, a pithy explanation might sound more like this: Mantle of the Expert is a way of learning that invites you to organise yourself in a grown-up sort of way. It gives you an opportunity to take charge and make some important decisions together. It's a chance to bring your best, most mature selves to the learning process and be the leaders of what happens. For a high school student or adult participant with clear expectations of outcomes and a concern about assessment, I might advocate for Mantle of the Expert as a way of working together that doesn't only focus on individual success but fosters deeper, more collaborative understanding. I would tell them that, while Mantle of the Expert might help them get better marks individually, the most rewarding thing is when everyone buys in and people start to care deeply and the learning often goes well beyond what's required to pass.

These various elevator pitches sound quite different but, between them, they convey some key ideas about Mantle of the Expert:

- It's a form of inquiry learning that includes drama for learning—so it's active, embodied, imaginative, and aesthetic.
- It's agentic in that it positions learners as responsible, competent co-constructors of meaning and allows them powers to influence, make decisions, and grapple with complex problems.
- It situates learning within authentic imagined worlds in ways that are safe and have real-world implications and meaning.
- It provides opportunities to develop all the key competencies and learning dispositions while facilitating deep learning across a range of curriculum areas.
- It fosters learning in ways that are appropriate to the cultural context of Aotearoa New Zealand, involving reciprocal teaching and learning, collaborative learning, building each other up, and the consideration of multiple perspectives and ways of knowing.
- It's engaging and seriously fun!

Any elevator pitch will fall short of the direct experience of Mantle of the Expert. After many years of attempting to talk about, write about, and introduce people to this approach, I have concluded that the best introduction is gained through experience as a participant or visitor to a classroom where Mantle of the Expert is in use. Chapter 3 of this book is devoted to stories of real Mantle of the Expert experiences and I would encourage anyone reading this book to supplement their learning by visiting a classroom to get direct experience.

Defining features

Here I will outline some of the defining features of Mantle of the Expert; its core elements, the three key teaching modalities used in delivery, and, last but not least, the way learning happens in a duality of real and imagined worlds.

Ten core elements

The figure below is reproduced from *Connecting Curriculum, Linking Learning* (Fraser et al., 2013) and sets out what I have previously identified as the 10 core elements of Mantle of the Expert. The word "elements" implies that the 10 things listed here are fundamental to Mantle of the Expert in the same way that hydrogen and oxygen are elements of water—they are the necessary components that make Mantle of the Expert what it is. Later in the book we will look at how the teacher selects these elements and weaves them together, but for now let's just identify what they are. More details on each element can be found in the original chapter (Aitken, 2013a).

This list of 10 elements is not definitive. As you will notice if you have read other books on Mantle of the Expert, there is no firm agreement among practitioners on what the core elements of Mantle of the Expert are. My list of 10 extends Heathcote's list of seven mandatory elements (Heathcote, n.d.-b). Taylor (2016) describes nine elements, divided into subcategories of foundational, core, and drama. Meanwhile, Brian Edmiston and I recently came up with a whole new set of possible terms (Edmiston, 2016; Aitken, 2016). This is an indication of the fact that Mantle of the Expert is not a fixed system with universal rules to follow but an approach based on certain key philosophies and principles. It's also an illustration of how Mantle of the

Expert is still evolving. We may, in time, move towards an internationally agreed set of definitions but, in the meantime, we can embrace the fact that there are multiple, slightly different perspectives out there. For this book, I've reproduced the same list of 10 core elements, as I know some readers are familiar with it and I want to make it easy to cross reference. Later in the book, you'll see these elements referred to as whenu or strands in a weaving, with the suggestion that the teacher needs to gather, tease out, and arrange these elements before the teaching process begins.

Table 1: Core elements of Mantle of the Expert

Core element	Definition	What it means for the learning
Fictional Context	The children and their teacher agree to operate together in a fictional context, using their imaginations to "agree to see" or "pretend" together.	A fictional context means: • learning tasks are both playful and serious • there is dual awareness of both fictional and real worlds *(metaxis)* • safety is ensured—there are no real-world consequences • learning is not bound by real-world limitations (time, power, finance, age).
"Company", "enterprise", "responsible team"	The children and their teacher take on a collective identity as members of a collaborative enterprise or company. Sometimes this may not be a fully realised "company" but some other "responsible team" with a common goal.	Taking on a collective identity means: • learning in collaboration • a shared sense of mission, values, and morals (e.g., through a mission statement) • a shared past history of excellence • opportunities for kinaesthetic response (e.g., setting up office space) • a real-world context.
Frame	The enterprise or company is "framed" as having a particular specialism or point of view on the issues being considered. Any further roles adopted during the drama are also "framed".	• Being framed as certain "kind" of company enhances collaboration and builds shared perspectives. • By framing roles, the teacher can increase or decrease the intensity of the experience and explore from a particular perspective (frame distance).
Commission	The enterprise or company is asked to undertake a particular important job.	The commission provides: • clearly expressed long-term learning goals—a shared purpose • an authentic bounded inquiry.

Core element	Definition	What it means for the learning
Client	The commission, or important job, is for a very important (fictional) client.	Involving a client means: • there is a clear purpose to the learning beyond "for the teacher" or "for its own sake" • a real-world context, that is relevant but safe • high status, high stakes, high standards • having a sense or audience, which gives a sense of obligation.
Curriculum framed as professional tasks	The tasks the children carry out in response to the commission are both appropriate curriculum tasks *and* professional tasks for the company	Framing the curriculum as professional tasks: • provides a real-world context • gives an immediate purpose for learning • involves an "incorporated" curriculum rather than discrete "subjects".
Powerful positioning	Children predominantly interact as "themselves" within the company, but they are positioned as *experts*: people who have been doing this a long time. The teacher positions children as knowledgeable and competent colleagues.	Powerful positioning: • provides a shared sense of past success, which increases group and individual self-efficacy • involves high-status positioning—learners as experts • results in shifts in language register • causes lasting shifts in the power relationships between teacher and student.
Drama for learning/ conventions	Along with their ongoing roles within the company, children and their teacher explore the perspectives of "others"—people with alternative points of view on the issues being explored. Various "conventions of dramatic action" are used by the teacher to evoke these other roles. Heathcote listed 33 conventions, and others can also be used (see http://www.manteoftheexpert.com).	Using drama for learning means: • multiple perspectives are explored • an embracing of complexity/ postmodernity • contesting binary/black-and-white thinking • exploring paradox and ambiguity • taking an approach that is not necessarily linear • not necessarily employing "naturalistic" drama.
Tensions	The teacher plans for certain obstacles or difficulties to arise during the completion of the commission. Often drama is used to reveal these tensions.	Introducing tensions means: • embracing the complexity and "messiness" of learning • engaging the children—maintaining their interest an intrigue • grappling and struggling, which teaches resilience.
Reflections	The teacher will allow times (both within role and out of role) for discussion *and* reflection on learning and the learning process in multiple worlds.	Reflection involves: • meta-learning • an awareness of multiple worlds (classroom, company, client, content), which makes meta-awareness more vivid.

Three teaching modalities

Mantle of the Expert draws on three key modalities of teaching: *inquiry learning, drama for learning,* and *powerful positioning.* I've called these modalities as an echo of the way the term is used by professionals such as counsellors, soldiers, or doctors, who use the word to describe methods or procedures they adopt, hone, and move between as they gain mastery in their field. Let's look at the modalities of Mantle of the Expert in turn. *Inquiry learning* is familiar to most teachers in New Zealand. It involves encouraging participants to formulate questions and carry out investigations in which they find things out for themselves. *Drama for learning* draws on the teaching strategies and conventions of process drama. It involves structuring experiences using role and other elements of drama so that participants can: build a shared narrative; explore multiple perspectives on an issue; build empathy; grapple with tensions; and tap into the aesthetic aspects of understanding. The final modality, *powerful positioning,* is about teachers ensuring they speak, move, act, and design experiences in ways that allow participants to co-construct and take leadership in the learning experience. The conscious repositioning of participants happens both inside the imagined world, where the participants are invited to see themselves as an expert team, and in the real world, where the teacher makes deliberate use of language, space, and other systems of power to ensure participants are treated as competent co-constructers of the learning experience.

Each of these teaching modalities involves its own skills and pedagogies, some of which will be teased out further in this book. Figure 3, adapted from Abbott (2007), provides a way of visualising how the modalities work together. While all three are used within Mantle of the Expert, the Venn diagram illustrates how sometimes the teaching and learning will foreground one over another, sometimes it will involve an overlap between two, and sometimes it will be a case of all three being experienced simultaneously.

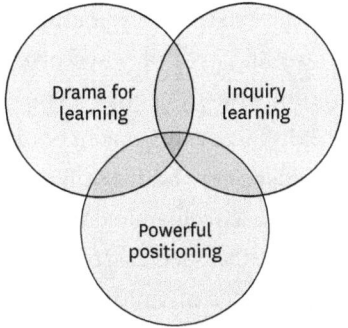

Figure 3: Three teaching modalities in Mantle of the Expert
(adapted from Abbott, see Fraser et al., 2013)

Abbott (2007) suggests that, for Mantle of the Expert to work at its best, the teacher needs to develop skills in all three modalities and he suggests that it's in the centre of the Venn diagram, where the three overlap, that the most effective teaching and learning takes place (2007, pp. 3, 23). Another way teachers can look at the diagram is as a guide for future growth: depending on your background, teacher education, and level of experience, you will probably bring existing strengths in one or more of the modalities and be able to identify at least one mode that could do with more development. Your personal Venn diagram might have three very different-sized circles. For teachers with a background in inquiry learning it is often the drama for learning aspects that are new territory, while those familiar with process drama may need to build skills in guiding student-led inquiry. As for powerful positioning, I've found this can challenge and stimulate some of the most experienced teachers. The diagram is helpful as a tool for planning, as a way of thinking about the pedagogies involved in Mantle of the Expert, and as a means to identify the ongoing professional development needs for yourself and others in your teaching team.

Metaxis: Learning in real and imagined worlds

A key premise of Mantle of the Expert, as in process drama and children's socio-dramatic play, is that the participants agree to operate in and between two worlds: the real world of the classroom and the imagined world that they set up together. I realise that by using a term like "real world" I'm opening a can of worms. For one thing, the real world completely depends on imagination. Every time we think, we draw on imagined memories of the past and projections into the future. And then of course there are all sorts of ways of thinking about reality, existence, perception, and the subjective experience of being in the world. The nature of reality in drama has been debated since the time of the ancient Greek philosophers and is still contested today; witness a recent drama education research article that referred to the "assemblage of reals" within the drama classroom (Gallagher & Jacobson, 2018). However, for the purposes of our discussion here, I'm simplifying things by assuming a shared ongoing experience that can be described as the real world and another shared experience identified as the imagined world. Mantle of the Expert occurs in both at once, as represented in Figure 4.

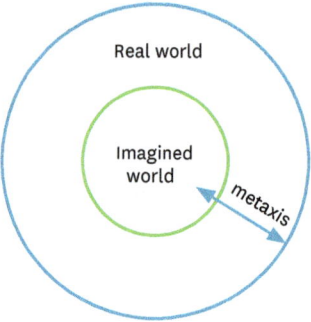

Figure 4: Duality of real and imagined worlds

Notice that, rather than placing the two circles alongside each other, or overlapping like a Venn diagram, the diagram shows the imagined world inside the real world. This is because participants enter an imagined world within their ongoing reality. The real world doesn't disappear, and participants remain aware of both worlds at the same time. If you have ever seen children playing imaginary games you will see this in practice as they easily shift between their real-life identities and their fictional roles: "Mummy, I'm a tank—and I want a biscuit!" In drama education literature, this capacity to operate in two worlds and maintain an awareness of both is termed "metaxis" (Bolton, 1985). The theory underpinning this duality is that, while there is a distinction between the two worlds, it is more like a porous membrane than a barrier. Learning can happen in either world—or both worlds at once—and can be carried over from one to the other. This deceptively simple idea is one of the most important principles of Mantle of the Expert, so let's spend a moment thinking about what that means and how it helps the learning.

The benefits for participants of operating in and between the real and imagined worlds can be said to include the following:

- The opportunity to experience being someone else or multiple other people.
- The chance to explore and play out new kinds of power and status and to reflect on how this felt.
- A safe place to explore—what Heathcote calls the "no penalty zone" for learning, where we can try out decisions and actions in role with minimal real-world consequences (Heathcote et al., 1991, p. 130).
- A sense of authenticity—learning in an imagined world can be meaningful, realistic, based in real-life situations, and carry a sense of consequence.
- An opportunity to engage in both worlds through the aesthetic and poetic. Teachers and participants employing dramatic and other elements such as tension, light and darkness, sound, movement, and music, as well as techniques of voice, body, and space to enhance the experience.
- A chance to explore within an imagined world with no limits, constraints, and boundaries other than those negotiated by the participants.
- Opportunities to play out and re-enact situations from the real world in order to understand and process them.
- Opportunities to rehearse or try out possible actions that might be employed in real-world situations, in multiple ways.
- Opportunities to explore and empathise with multiple perspectives on an issue.
- Opportunities to embody learning—not just imagining or discussing, hearing, or writing about something, but actually doing it with our bodies.

- Imagining that a situation is happening to us in now time. And yet being able to stop, rewind, step back, and replay time or jump forward into the future.
- Developing a watching eye or mindfulness about our actions and decisions. Not being swept up in imagination but maintaining a sense of distance and observing our own actions, behaviours, and responses, individually and collectively.
- Fostering meta-cognition—thinking about thinking—through opportunities to stop, think, reflect, and watch ourselves and the processes we use to gather information, make decisions, and develop ideas.
- Bringing the awareness of their learning into consciousness by making the structures under which learning is happening very explicit. As *The New Zealand Curriculum* reminds us, meta-learning—the ability to inquire into the ways one is thinking and learning—is an important skill and one that should be fostered by teachers (Ministry of Education, 2007).
- Learning that knowledge is provisional and framed by cultural and social perspectives—an awareness that comes through operating on the same content from different viewpoints.
- Fostering opportunities to explore, reflect on, and change the social and personal dynamics of the group in the real world—by rehearsing alternative structures in the imagined world.
- Demonstrating that systems of power are constructs. If we can make up and challenge systems of power in the fictional world, perhaps we can do this in the real world too.

This is complex stuff. One of the things I most appreciate about Mantle of the Expert is how it gives learners cutting-edge messages about the world. It's been described as "innovative" (O'Neill, 2015, p. 5), "ahead of its time" (Bolton, in Burgess, 1993), and, significantly for the context of this country, it's been found to have resonances with te ao Māori and culturally responsive pedagogy (Downey, 2017).

The opportunities opened up by offering learning experiences in the duality of the real and imagined worlds are enormous. In part, this is because imagined worlds have fewer limitations and greater space for exploration than the real world with all its constraints of time, space, power, and consequences. Even though the inner circle on the diagram are smaller than the outer one, in many ways it should be the other way round, since participants step from the limits and constraints of the real into the expanded potential of the imagined. It's important to remember this given the tendency, at least in the Western world view, to diminish the imagined as if it were somehow lesser than the real. We use language like "it's *just* pretend" as if imagination and invention were not significant human traits. Our capacities for thinking creatively, experiencing empathy, considering multiple perspectives, and acknowledging alternative points of view are at the heart of what makes us human. They are also the capacities we most need to draw on if we are to survive as a species. It's amazing, then, that we disparage them so readily in our common parlance; an attitude that may contribute to the devaluing of arts in our society including our schools (Barish, 1981; Robinson, 2006). So, while the diagram has the imagined world contained within the real world, this is not to suggest that it less significant, or smaller.

Where learning experiences work in the duality of imagined and real worlds in this way, this raises important implications and opportunities for the teaching too. The teacher needs to think about sustaining the two worlds by:

- explaining and celebrating the fact that learning is taking place in two worlds
- consciously avoiding and discouraging any disparaging language about imagination or drama
- signalling shifts between worlds—verbally and through simple props or signs
- ensuring internal coherence within the imagined world—avoiding inconsistencies or contradictory ideas
- helping participants establish the time and place and given circumstances within the imagined world
- modelling and inviting participation by being prepared to move between worlds themselves—including teaching in role
- using the client and the commission as agents to facilitate learning

- making use of a range of conventions and strategies to structure episodes in the imagined world and the real world
- drawing on aesthetic and sensory elements to enhance the experience of learning in both worlds
- manipulating the dramatic element of tension to arrest attention and make learning in both worlds enticing
- giving opportunities and time for solutions and resolutions to be explored in the imagined and the real worlds
- ensuring connections are made between the imagined and real worlds
- taking time to promote quality reflection on the events in the imagined world from back in the real world.

This is not a full list of considerations but gives a sense of the extra nuance involved in the apparently simple idea of introducing an imagined world to the classroom. Further discussion on how to support teaching and learning across real and imagined worlds can be found later in this book.

Theoretical underpinnings

There is a large body of existing scholarship on drama in education and process drama, much of which would be of interest for a teacher wishing to understand the Mantle of the Expert approach in depth. However, practitioner and scholarly literature specifically related to Mantle of the Expert is still harder to find. For practical guidance, Tim Taylor's *A Beginner's Guide to Mantle of the Expert* (2016) is the go-to text, along with Dorothy Heathcote and Gavin Bolton's *Drama for Learning* (1994). Gavin Bolton's excellent biography of Heathcote's life describes how the Mantle of the Expert approach developed and sets it within the context of Heathcote's other work (Bolton, 2003). Sandra Heston's thorough PhD study (Heston, 1993) outlines many of the features of the approach, while a PhD study by Ruth Sayers examines how Mantle of the Expert has been introduced and sustained in the UK (Sayers, 2012). It's only in relatively recent times, however, that researchers and academics around the world have started to produce the peer-reviewed research studies, articles, and books that will help us theorise Mantle of the Expert and other forms of Dramatic Inquiry in depth. If you visit the research tab on the Mantle of the Expert Aotearoa website (https//mantleoftheexpert.co.nz), you can see the work that is happening in this country.

Next we will look at some broad educational and sociological theories that can help us understand Mantle of the Expert and explain how it works. The theories discussed here provide the terminology and frameworks used within the rest of the book.

Learning and development

Mantle of the Expert aligns with social constructivist and sociocultural theories of education in that the approach is based on assumptions that learning is a social process, that people learn with and from others, and that all learning is situated in a cultural context (Smith, 2007). This is very different from theories of education that start from a more individualistic or behaviourist viewpoint. Applying the lens of social constructivism helps explain the strong emphasis on relationship building, collaborative activity, and group culture within Mantle of the Expert. However, this needs teasing out a little further, since social constructivist theories can be interpreted in at least two different ways.

According to the theories of Jean Piaget (1896–1980), learning occurs in stages that an individual learner moves through in an age-related progression. This suggests that the teacher's job is to suit the most appropriate tasks to the developmental stage of each learner. This "ages and stages" viewpoint, quite deeply ingrained in our ideas about learning and development, may not be the most helpful way to understand Mantle of the Expert. First of all, the assumption that learners necessarily get better at something with age is counter to a drama-based approach, since often it is younger children who are better at imagining. Secondly, Mantle of the Expert is not about aligning tasks to fit the age or stage that learners are perceived to be. On the contrary, the approach is about positioning learners as having levels of understanding and expertise way beyond their real-world age, to encourage them to grow into new understandings. Thirdly, Piaget's theory tends to regard children as individuals who each learn from their interactions with their environment, whereas in Mantle of the Expert, participants learn in social relations within cultural contexts (B. Edmiston, personal communication, 2020). For all these reasons, it can be more useful to theorise the learning in Mantle of the Expert through the ideas of another social constructivist, Lev Vygotsky (1896–1934). Vygotsky's theories suggest learning happens in a zone of proximal development in which a teacher and peers play a crucial role. Instead of seeing learning as dependent on development, Vygotsky suggests that development is a product of the process of learning, including playful exploration with others. This means the teacher's role is to look at what can be done to encourage the group beyond their existing abilities. Several drama scholars, including Edmiston and Davis, have used Vygotsky's ideas to illuminate Mantle of the Expert in really useful ways (Davis, 2016; Edmiston, 2014).

Role, frame, and children's play

To understand Mantle of the Expert, it helps to step back and have a look at the different kinds of role taking and dramatic activity humans get up to. According to role theory, developed by sociologists like Erving Goffman (1959), everyone in society takes on different roles all the time. For example, one person can adopt the roles of son, teacher, customer, road user, and cook within the space of an hour. This idea is useful for Mantle of the Expert teachers as it reminds us that role taking and role shifting are crucial to our social life and it dispels the idea that role taking is a special activity that only actors engage in. Goffman's writing also offers another, even more useful, theory: frame analysis (Goffman, 1986). Frame analysis suggests that the way we play our different roles in life is not fixed, but fluid, depending on context. For example, the role of son is played very differently when you are 9 and it is time for a bedtime story compared to when you're 59 and attending your father's funeral. Goffman suggests that we respond to social situations by adopting "frames" of behaviour that we think are most apt to the situation. We do this not only as an individual, but also collectively, within social groups. The frames we draw on are developed from cultural norms and we learn them, adopt them, adapt them, and possibly also discard them as we operate in different groups within our social lives. As well as helping us understand society, Goffman's sociological theories offer a useful way to illuminate Mantle of the Expert; you'll see the idea of "frames" and "framing" popping up frequently through Heathcote's writings and this book.

With all of the roles we play in everyday life, we are still being "ourselves". This is true for Mantle of the Expert, too. However, there's a particular kind of role taking—dramatic role—where we consciously imagine ourselves to be other people or things inhabiting other spaces and engaged in other actions than our own real-world selves. With dramatic role being so central to Mantle of the Expert, it's worth taking note of the different ways humans engage in it. It's also interesting to note that there is a developmental side to the taking of dramatic roles.

Dramatic play refers to the open-ended, semi-structured dramatic explorations enjoyed by young children. Dramatic play can involve playing out familiar roles from the real world, such as doctors and nurses or mums and dads. This is often called "socio-dramatic play" (though some commentators use that term to mean any dramatic play that happens within in a social group). Alternatively, it can be based more in fantasy, involving roles like superheroes, book characters, or sports stars. If you have watched children engaged in dramatic play you will know they are generally adept at taking on and moving between personas that allow them to explore different ideas and concepts, and learn about the world. This kind of play is process-based rather than being about a "product" or outcome. It requires only one player and no external audience.

Projective play (sometimes called "projected" play) refers to dramatic play where the participant does not take on the full role with their whole body, but instead uses objects to perform one or more roles indirectly. Examples might include: holding two dolls and "doing the voices" as they talk to each other; playing with trucks and blocks to build roads; using puppets and pieces of cloth to tell a story; or having an imaginary friend represented by their little finger. This kind of play is generally associated with young children as it allows them to play out ideas and concepts with greater distance and control over the events. They become "god-like" figures who can oversee, control, and "story" their imagined world from outside rather than being fully immersed in it.

Dramatic performance involves the very same basic elements as dramatic play and projective play—role, time, space, action, tension, and focus—but is generally more structured and rehearsed with less fluidity between the real world and the imagined world and more of an emphasis on a final product. The purpose of dramatic performance is similar, in some ways, to the purpose of dramatic and projective play—it's all about exploring ideas, roles, and concepts and learning about the world. The key difference is that it depends on an external audience to whom ideas are presented and therefore it involves at least two participants (Brook, 1995). This kind of dramatic exploration is generally associated with older participants and is the dominant form of drama experienced and appreciated by adults. It is familiar to children through TV, theatre, and movies.

These ideas about role taking, framing, and the different forms of dramatic role are very helpful in understanding how Mantle of the Expert works and in planning activities that are varied and age appropriate.

Cognitive, affective, and psychomotor domains

Many teachers will be familiar with Bloom's taxonomy, a hierarchical model for classifying learning, which has been adapted, amended, and used by teachers and students for half a century (Bloom et al., 1956). For the most part, though, educators have focused on only the part of the taxonomy related to the cognitive domain, or levels of thinking (Bloom et al., 1956):

1. Knowledge
2. Comprehension
3. Application
4. Analysis
5. Synthesis
6. Evaluation.

This list has been revisited and revised a number of times (see Krathwohl, 2002) and is still widely used by educators today. See, for example, Heick (2018) whose blog includes a diagram of the "hierarchical ordering of cognitive skills" presented as "a way to help teachers and students learn" (Heick, 2018). However Bloom and his team did not limit their theorising of learning to a study of thinking. In fact, they proposed a taxonomy covering three domains, as summarised in Table 2.

Table 2: Summary of learning domains (adapted from Bloom et al., 1956)

Bloom's domains	Where learning happens	How learning happens
The cognitive	The head	Thinking
The affective	The heart	Feeling
The psychomotor	The body	Doing

The theory that learning occurs across thinking, feeling, and doing is a useful one for the teacher using Mantle of the Expert and reminds us to consider all three in our teaching. Unfortunately, discussion of the cognitive domain has tended to dominate and the details of the affective and the psychomotor domains have received much less attention. Bloom and his colleagues did publish a taxonomy for the affective domain, consisting of five levels (Bloom et al., 1964):

1. Receiving
2. Responding
3. Valuing
4. Organising
5. Characterising.

However, they did not get as far as creating a taxonomy for the psychomotor domain. Other education commentators have suggested what should be on the list; for example, Simpson (1966), who offered the following seven categories for learning by doing:

1. Perception
2. Set (readiness to act)
3. Guided response
4. Mechanism
5. Complex overt response
6. Adaption
7. Origination.

The theories of Bloom and others are not without their issues. Any attempt to spell out levels of thinking, feeling, and doing is bound to oversimplify the complex and holistic nature of learning. For example, the taxonomies don't acknowledge the collaborative and social aspects of learning. Cognitive, affective, and psychomotor processes are presented as if they are individual phenomena occurring in each person's body, even though we know real learning is more social and collective than that. All the same, the language provided by the taxonomies can be useful in discussing Mantle of the Expert, as can the notion that learning happens across all three domains. Later in the book we'll draw on these ideas, particularly where we talk about sequencing teaching activities.

Enactive, iconic, and symbolic learning

Another theory that can be useful for illuminating Mantle of the Expert is Jerome Bruner's "three forms of representation", expressed in *Toward a Theory of Instruction* (Bruner, 1966). As the title of his book suggests, Bruner was attempting to theorise how teaching and learning work. His suggestion was that learners store, encode, and represent their knowledge and understandings about the world by moving from action-based, enactive learning through the body in the early years, to iconic learning through images, drawings, and pictures in the middle years, to the symbolic form of written language, beginning at about 6 years. These stages of development were seen as loosely related to age, but it's important to realise that Bruner did not suggest the teacher should limit instruction to one form of representation at a time, nor that once children were 6 they should stop learning through the body! This was not a stage-based theory. Rather, Bruner was suggesting teachers should encourage learners to engage actively through all three forms and that in primary school, secondary school, and beyond, all would benefit from learning through a combination of using the body, images, and symbols. Many practitioners and researchers have found Bruner's theory useful to explain Mantle of the Expert, or advocate for working in this way in their classrooms. Bruner's theory also provides a very practical planning tool, as we will see later in the book.

Power and agency

Most people who use Mantle of the Expert would agree that a core objective is to bring about shifts in how power operates between the teacher and the participants. However, that's a deceptively simple statement given all the different ways we can talk about and understand power, so it's important to clarify what theories of power are behind the thinking in this book. First of all, you will notice I avoid using the word "empowerment" though this is a term you hear a lot in teaching. The idea that teaching, or teachers, can "empower" participants goes back to the theories of emancipatory education associated with people like Paolo Freire (1921–1997). While Freire himself talked about empowerment as a dialogue and argued that it was a process rather than an endpoint (Freire, 1972), others have criticised his theories for encouraging us to think about power as something that some people hold and others don't. As one commentator puts it, "by conceptualising power as a commodity, identities are forced into a powerful–powerless dualism which does not always do justice to diverse experiences" (Pease, 2002, p. 135). Another criticism of Freire's ideas is that the way he describes power tends to characterise it as a negative thing used to oppress and suppress others. To get beyond these binaries, it can be useful to think about power using the metaphors found in the theories of Michel Foucault (1926–1984).

Foucault insists that power is not a commodity nor a process or dialogue, but more a "capillary" or network (1980, p. 201) that continually throbs and flows between places, systems, and people:

> What makes power hold good, what makes it accepted, is simply the fact that it doesn't only weigh on us as a force that says no, but that it traverses and produces things. It needs to be considered as a productive network which runs through the whole social body, much more than as a negative instance whose function is repression
>
> (Foucault, 1980, p. 199)

Foucault argues that power is *constitutive*—everything depends on it; *inevitable*—it's everywhere; it's *positive*; and it's *productive*—it makes things happen. He argued:

> We must cease once and for all to describe the effects of power in negative terms: it 'excludes', it 'represses', it 'censors', it 'abstracts', it 'masks', it 'conceals'. In fact, power produces; it produces reality; it produces domains of objects and rituals of truth.
>
> (Foucault, 1977, p. 194)

If we work from this kind of viewpoint, suddenly our job as teachers becomes not "handing over" power to participants but spotting, recognising, and critiquing the systems of power that are at play, including in our own practice and in the systems of education we are part of, so that we can create contexts where the flow of power is maximised for the benefit of participants. This might seem like a subtle difference in definitions, but the more you think about it, the more significant it becomes. I particularly like how Foucault's theories force us as teachers to shift attention to our own use of power and the systems of power we are part of.

Another idea that comes from Foucault's theories is the idea of "agency". This is something of a buzz word in education at present, though it's not always clear what people mean by it. My current preferred definition for "agency" is "the capacity and propensity to take action both individually and within a group, along with an awareness of the implications of that action for the self, for others, and for the environment" (definition developed in personal communication with staff of Makaraka School, 2018). By thinking of power in these terms, we begin to see that student agency depends on what Foucault calls the "habitus" or systems surrounding teachers and learners, as much as it does on the personal attributes or efforts made by any particular person. As a teacher in Mantle of the Expert, it is crucial to continually be alert to the visible, hidden, and invisible systems of power at play in the classroom and wider world, and be willing to question these.

Positioning

Another theory that can help teachers understand the complexities of Mantle of the Expert is positioning theory (Harré & Langenhove, 1999; Harré & Moghaddam, 2003). Positioning theory is a sociological theory that attempts to illuminate the ways people interact with other people and with non-human entities such as institutions, systems of rules, or countries. The theory resonates with the ideas of power just outlined and also builds on the ideas of role and frame discussed earlier. As we've seen, people take many roles in life, with lots of different ways of carrying out a role, depending on context (like the person who frames the role of "son" in one way when enjoying a story with his dad and in a very different way when attending his dad's funeral). Where frame analysis explains how roles are selected for context, positioning theory explains how people go about playing their roles from moment to moment: how they understand what Harré and Lagenhove call the "rules that shape the episodes of social life" (Harré & Lagenhove, 1999, p. 4).

According to positioning theory, every time someone engages in a social episode they are constantly figuring out, balancing, and shifting three things: position, storyline, and actions. These three aspects of positioning are illustrated as points on a triangle or "positioning triad" in Figure 5.

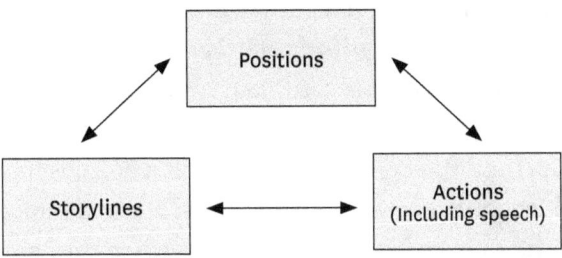

Figure 5: Positioning triad (adapted from Harré and Lagenhove, 1999)

The first word, *positions*, is to do with the power and responsibilities people have, or take up, in a certain situation. It's defined by Harré and Moghaddam as "the cluster of rights and duties to perform certain actions with a certain significance" (2003, p. 5). Imagine a school teacher moving through their familiar morning routines from road patrol duty, to staffroom banter, to participating in karakia and waiata with their class, taking the roll, and setting up for the first learning activity. Even before the first class begins, this person has moved between several positions of power and responsibility within their role as teacher. Indeed, they will have shifted position numerous times within each activity. For example, during roll call the teacher might shift within seconds from a friendly position where they are chatting with students to a more authoritarian position where they ask for quiet to take the roll, before flicking into a more helpless position where they ask the students for assistance because they can't log on to their laptop. It can help to think about social positions as akin to the physical "positions" our bodies take on in different situations—standing, sitting, stretching, or squatting. Just like physical positions, we adopt social positions temporarily, hold them for a particular purpose, and then drop them again when a new purpose arises.

The next word, *storyline*, is defined as the "loose cluster of narrative conventions" that unfold in the dynamics of a particular social episode (Harré & Moghaddam, 2003, p. 6). In simple terms, storylines are the things we tell ourselves about what's going on and therefore what position we should adopt. Consider the activities of the teacher described above. There might easily be a number of "storylines" running through the different things the teacher does as they start their day: culturally agreed narratives around what happens on road patrol duty, how to engage in social banter with professional colleagues, how tikanga is observed, and how to engage in classroom routines. The teacher doesn't need to learn everything each time as they've learned the conventions through prior observation, overt training, or negotiation with others. We are usually unconscious of storylines, and only become aware of them when they are new to us; for example, if we move to a new setting or when someone doesn't follow the storylines as we'd expect.

The final point on the triad, *actions*, refers to how we "perform" our understandings of positions and storylines to ourselves and each other. In the teacher's case, the actions taken might include things like putting on a high visibility vest for road patrol, laughing and joking with a colleague, carrying their mug of tea carefully, putting the empty cup into the dishwasher, and entering attendance data into a spreadsheet. It's through what we do and what we say—the "socially significant actions, movements or speech" that we either sustain positions and storylines or shift them to somewhere new (Harré & Moghaddam, 2003, p. 6).

I like how positioning theory illuminates aspects of Mantle of the Expert and helps explain how it works. It's particularly useful when thinking about powerful positioning, one of the three teaching modalities for Mantle of the Expert. If we look at what happens in a Mantle of the Expert classroom, we can see that operating in an imagined world and within a responsible team allows participants to change the storyline and positions. This, in turn, gives participants access to a whole new set of actions, including speech acts. Whether it's a group of new entrants invited by the tooth fairy to help solve a logistics problem, or a class of Master's students operating as a group of professional fact checkers asked to investigate the validity of research reports, participants in a Mantle of the Expert access new storylines and positions and they get to say and do things they wouldn't otherwise get to say and do in the classroom. Edmiston expresses this very well:

> One of the core reasons why as a teacher I use drama is because when we create an imagined world, we can imagine that we frame events differently so that our power and authority relationships are changed. A long-term aim of mine as a teacher is as much as possible to share power and authority with students. I want students to have more opportunities to use words and deeds to act appropriately but in ways that are often not sanctioned in classrooms. Additionally I hope that students' sense of their personal and shared authority will become more secure and more extended while at the same time more aware of others' authority. I want a culture to develop that is more egalitarian than most students expect walking into the room.
>
> (Edmiston, 2003, p. 225)

The repositioning of participants that occurs within Mantle of the Expert is, for many teachers, a core attraction, and part of a deliberate attempt to shift power structures, particularly when dealing with young people who may not have much power or authority outside the classroom.

One final thing to stress about the positioning triad is the idea that all three points on the triad are interdependent, with each influencing the other. Positioning theory says that any change in one point will automatically influence the others. So, a shift in storyline will affect both position and speech acts. Similarly, adopting a certain position will make some speech acts more or less appropriate and thereby alter the storyline. And so it goes on. For a teacher who is thinking about consciously repositioning learners, this is very useful. The positioning triad reminds us that at any time while we are teaching, or at any time in our lives, we can make a change to either storyline, positions, or actions and speech and this will change the whole experience. This way of thinking captures nicely the fluid, dialogic, and ever-changing "feel" of a Mantle of the Expert experience. Indeed, the whole practice of Mantle of the Expert can be understood as an exercise in positioning—which is why in this book "powerful positioning" is included in the Venn diagram of teaching modalities as well as appearing as a core element. Later, when we come to look at the teaching strategies used in Mantle of the Expert, we'll see that many of these—including Heathcote's role conventions—are suggestions for how to make shifts in position, storyline, or actions, or all three.

Social practices and signature pedagogies

There are two further theories that make a brief appearance in this book so should be mentioned here. The two theories are quite closely related and both come from sociology. "Social practice theory" is a way of studying people that focuses on understanding social actions and practices, not simply what they think, write, or say. To clarify, a practice is "a routinised type of behaviour which consists of several elements, interconnected to one another forms of bodily activities, forms of mental activities, 'things' and their use, a background knowledge in the form of understanding, know-how, states of emotion and motivational knowledge" (Reckwitz, 2002, p. 249). The study of social practices originated with examining the social and behavioural norms of those in professional roles, such as lawyers and doctors, and given that Mantle of the Expert involves participants taking on professional identities within the imagined world, it's a useful concept for us. The notion of teaching as a "practice" will run through this whole book, while social practices will be discussed in Chapter 4 as we consider how to plan to develop peer relationships among participants.

A second, and closely aligned, theory is that of "signature pedagogies"; a concept from the work of Lee Shulman, who suggests that different professional fields, such as nursing or law, can be said to have their own characteristic teaching techniques or approaches (Shulman, 2005). In other words, if you walk past a classroom, you can sometimes tell what is being taught by the *way* it's being taught. Of course, that's an oversimplification; especially in something like Mantle of the Expert where, depending on the context, you might expect to witness anything from practical science experiments to improvised dance routines. But the idea of signature pedagogies is still useful. For example, most primary school teachers would agree that participants framing their own questions and carrying out research could be seen as signature pedagogies for inquiry approaches, while those who work with the Orff approach to music education will be familiar with the signature processes of "imitation, exploration and improvisation" that are integral to the philosophy (Gain et al., 2018). In writing this book it's been really helpful to think about what might be nominated as the "signature pedagogies" of the Mantle of the Expert approach, and this idea will be discussed further when we look at planning and implementation in Chapter 4.

Chapter 3

Three New Zealand examples

Now we shift from the theoretical to the practical, to look at Mantle of the Expert in action. This chapter begins with case studies from three New Zealand classrooms, with participants ranging from junior to senior primary levels. As it happens, these examples all involved collaboration; the first two were planned and taught by a team, the third was planned collectively and taught by a single teacher. However, any of the three could just as easily have been planned and taught by a teacher working alone. The case studies are followed by a table of further examples of Mantle of the Expert experiences, to illustrate how the same core elements can be used to create vastly different experiences across the curriculum.

These narratives are *not* offered as exemplars of best practice; they are accounts of experiments where my fellow teachers and I were learning about Mantle of the Expert through trial and error. As our whakataukī reminds us, it takes the working together of many strands and many weavers to form a tapestry of understanding, and there is much to be learned from the dropped stitches. What's offered here are descriptions of real practice, where the flaws are just as interesting as the strengths. The case studies are organised as follows:

- *Introduction*—background context and information about the class.

- *The "big idea"*—key learning objectives underpinning the example.
- *Key planning decisions*—preparations and thinking that went on prior to the teaching.
- *Implementation*—an account of the classroom experience including the hook, deepening the learning, tensions, outcomes.
- *Links to curriculum*.
- *Afterword*—reflecting on the successes and limitations of this example.

The narratives draw on blogs and recordings used with permission (see Acknowledgements). While schools and individuals are identifiable in the original blogs, steps have been taken to preserve anonymity within this chapter: images have been digitally manipulated; children are referred to by pseudonyms; and only the first names of teachers and student teachers are used.

Junior primary—Toy Museum

Year: 3 **Taught by:** Viv, classroom teacher Melissa, and student teachers

Introduction

This Mantle of the Expert experience was taught in 2012 over 6 weeks in a Year 3 class at a decile 9 primary school in Hamilton. The classroom teacher, Melissa, was new to the approach although she had a bit of experience in process drama. We were joined by a group of student teachers who were there to learn about Dramatic Inquiry by assisting with the planning and teaching 1 day a week. This was all made possible with the support of the deputy principal, Gay, who set up the opportunity and supported us throughout by taking notes and video recordings for reflection. I acknowledge not everyone will have the luxury of working in this kind of way. Certainly, planning and teaching can be enhanced if collaborative effort and an extended timeframe are available, but these are not a prerequisite for success. This Mantle of the Expert experience could have been planned and implemented by a solo teacher or over a shorter timeframe.

The big idea/key learning objectives

Melissa mentioned she wanted to focus on creative writing, but she was open to any learning that might emerge from the process and there were no expectations from the syndicate or the school. This meant we were able to explore for ourselves Dorothy Heathcote's assertion that "the teacher can trust any Mantle to take them to curriculum" (Heathcote, 1983).

Key planning decisions

The preplanning process took several months. I held two meetings with Melissa and Gay, where we talked through possible directions. Using the planning process outlined later in this book, we began by thinking about the children in the class and their interests. Melissa filled a page with lots of information and noticed that one topic kept coming up—toys. So we selected this as our starting point. Next, using Heathcote's "list of possible enterprises" as recommended in the planning process, we generated a list of jobs of people who work with toys. Initially, we got excited about the idea of being toy designers, working on a new prototype transformer toy, or being specialists in a certain kind of toy—perhaps creating educational puppets? However, we knew from past experience it was good to think of multiple possibilities rather than settling on the first idea, so we kept thinking. Eventually, we decided our team would be curators running a toy museum: toys in a museum would have stories associated with them and this would fit nicely with the creative writing focus.

Having decided on our responsible team of curators, we considered our other core elements. For the client, we decided on a rich business person with an amazing toy collection who would commission a special exhibit to showcase their toys and their stories. I worked with the student teachers, listing the tasks that would arise from carrying out this commission. This included designing displays, restoring toys, and arranging insurance and transportation for the toy collection. Then it was time to think about tensions—the "what ifs" that could arise for a company embarking on this kind of work. As always in the brainstorming process, some ideas felt more productive than others but we could see how our ideas could lead to authentic curriculum tasks:

- What if there's a mystery toy of some sort and no one knows the story? *Researching what the toy might be. Using drama and creative writing to imagine and record the toy's story.*
- What if the exhibition venue has to change at the last minute? *Considering floor plans and layout, measuring the new space, and redesigning the exhibition layout. Phone calls, emails, and other communications.*
- What if the star item in the exhibition gets withdrawn by its owner? *Persuasive argument through oral language and writing. Problem solving and exploring solution as a group. Considering alternative exhibits. Arranging last-minute transport.*
- What if some of the exhibits get damaged? *Insurance claims process. Writing a letter of apology. Strategies for difficult conversations.*
- What if something goes wrong with restoring one of the exhibits? *Considering options for restoration. Telling the toy's new story. Discussions on different kinds of value.*
- What if all the promotional material gets destroyed? *Exploring options for low-cost promotion. Principles of poster design.*
- What if the toys come alive at night and get up to mischief? *Using drama to imagine the mayhem in the museum at night. Making a clean-up and safety plan. Giving advice to toys on appropriate behaviour.*

Working with Melissa and the students, I mapped out how the teaching and learning might pan out over the 6 weeks in the classroom. We allocated the first week or so to building the imagined world of the curators, the second week to introducing the commission and working on the exhibits, and the remaining 4 weeks to working through the various tensions towards a resolution and some kind of exhibit at the end. Many practitioners prefer to allow the Mantle of the Expert experience to develop in an emergent way but on this occasion I found it helpful to have an overview. This was partly for my own reassurance and partly because I was sharing the teaching. After plotting out the overall shape, we were ready to select a hook and plan our opening session.

Implementation—the hook

On the day before the student teachers would join us, I visited the class to introduce myself and do some activities exploring imagination. We played "Yes Let's"—an activity to practise making and accepting offers. I also asked the children about the signals used in their class for attention. Then I introduced a large piece of black paper cut to represent a "hole". I placed this on the floor and encouraged the children to imagine what might be down inside it. Someone suggested caverns, so we discussed how we might lower ourselves down into the hole and explore together. We spent quite a while figuring out how to attach ropes and make sure everyone could get down safely. Then, with teacher guidance, children set off to explore and soon reported back on what they had found, including some skeletons, jewel-encrusted stalactites, and a monster lurking nearby. Back up through the hole we went, back to the classroom. This open-ended play-based activity gave me an opportunity to notice which children were hesitant about working imaginatively. It also gave us all an opportunity to talk about how to work with each other within an imagined world.

The next day, the student teachers joined us for a session after morning tea. We needed a way to build relationships between the children and the student teachers. So we formed a circle and did an introductory activity where someone says something about themselves and steps forward, and others in the group step in too if what was said is true for them. I started with "I have two eyes", which got everyone stepping in to join me. The game went on for a while, with some children trying to pick things that made them unique. When one of the children made the statement "I have a toy", this provided an ideal segue into the activity that we had previously planned for our hook. I invited everyone to think about a special toy that they owned; to close their eyes and picture that toy in their imagination and to think about what made that toy so special. Next, I invited them to imagine

Figure 6: Children share their imaginary toys

that the special toy was in their hands, to hold it, feel the weight of it, open their eyes, and see it in their imagination. Then, in small groups, the children and student teachers described and demonstrated their toys. Some shared their toys around and imagined playing with different ones.

There was a nice energy in the room at this stage although I heard one of the children identified as having special needs—I'll call him Ben—say, "This is boring. I want to do something else." I made a point of thanking Ben for his patience. One of the things that can be tricky about the opening of a Mantle of the Expert experience is how much is conducted as a whole group. It's important to build the imagined world together, but this can be challenging for some children. One of the things I'm still working on is finding ways to include group and individual tasks without losing class unity.

We cleared a small space in the centre of the room and invited everyone to turn around and look at the space. I said, "We are going to imagine another toy now." I shifted to a "narrator" voice, and told the story of someone called David, once a young boy but grown up now, whose parents had bought him a wonderful gift—a large and amazing toy which we were now going to imagine standing in the space before us. The children were interested in the story of David. They didn't know it yet, but I was introducing their future client. Children offered lots of ideas for what David's toy might be like. The first boy mentioned lasers, so I asked him to stand up, move around the toy, and point out where the lasers were produced. I pressed for detail: "What colour are those cones the lasers shine from?" And then I folded the details into the story, using a narrator voice: "And just before he went to sleep at night, David loved to lie in his bed and watch as the lasers beamed out intricate patterns of light all over the walls of his room." Another child added six legs and a key that makes the toy scuttle like a spider, so I responded, "Where is the key, how does it turn?" and built this into the story too. There was an air of reverence as different children walked around the imagined toy to point out its features and listened to their ideas being layered into the story. I was pleased to hear Ben joining in with his own descriptions. Finally, we learned that the toy had another feature: when you rub one of the legs, it folds down to such a tiny size it can fit into a little boy's pocket.

Now the central idea of the dramatic world had been conjured up, it was time to ease the children towards the collective concern—in this case, taking responsibility for the toy. This shift can be a bit tricky, but it felt effortless on this occasion. I continued the story: "David always kept his amazing toy a secret. As an only child, the toy was his greatest treasure and he never told anyone about it. But now, as a grown man, he feels it's time for his toy to be shared with others. He's looking for a place that might look after his toy, care for it, and make it available for others to see." I had questions in my head such as "What places are there in the world that would care for treasures such as this?", but they weren't required. One of the children said "A museum!" straight away. Very quickly, children were using the "we" register and talking about "our" museum. It seemed to happen by itself. To slow things down and encourage thoughtfulness, I asked if anyone had concerns about David's toy being put in a museum. One of the children responded: "What about when he wants to pass it on to his child? Will he be able to get it back?" Another said, "We wouldn't want people to break or take it—we'll need good security." These questions were pondered over and recorded on the whiteboard.

From here, some children were keen for individual roles. One boy said, "I'll be in charge of security", and others started talking about particular jobs they wanted in the museum. I did not want to lose the collective "team" feel and wanted to maintain one blanket role for the class, to ensure we didn't compromise on depth of curriculum engagement. So while I did not pick up on the suggestion of allowing children to take specialist roles, I did say things like, "It's great to know we have specialists within the team—when we need security advice, we will come to you but I know we can depend on you when it comes to toy maintenance as well."

Next, I invited the participants to think about the things museum workers do and the equipment they use. The children each created a still image showing one piece of equipment in use. With the whole class frozen like statues, I moved through the group and asked people to unfreeze and tell me what they were doing: "I am holding a teddy in one hand and with the other picking off the bits of fluff." Others were cleaning: "I am using this mop to clean the entrance"; while others were conducting tours: "I am showing someone around the museum and this is my map." We also had quite a lot of security-based images: "I am handcuffing the thief—and talking on my walkie talkie to tell the other security guard I've caught him."

Next, we moved into a mapping exercise. I invited the children to describe the office spaces at the toy museum and we started a bird's eye plan on

Figure 7: Using different kinds of equipment around the museum

the whiteboard. Individuals added some details including a tea corner, an oval shaped meeting room, offices, and a storage room. Finally, children were invited to take a piece of paper and draw whatever was on their desk in their imagined office. There was a high level of engagement in this. Several children started shifting their desks away from other people to create their own office space. I saw lots of pictures of computers and one child whispered to me, "I have got the latest model—Toshiba." There were piles of maps, cleaning equipment, security screens, and also personal features such as photos of the family and bars of chocolate. It was quite difficult to persuade the children to pause in their drawing and gather to conclude the session.

Figure 8: A museum curator's desk

Over the next week, Melissa helped children to imagine the past successes of the company. Letters were delivered from satisfied clients and the company name was decided—History Mystery toys. The children designed a logo and drew up a timeline of the company's past, which included a dreadful fire that the children decided had gutted the offices a few years ago. They also continued to work on the map of the office and add details.

Figure 9: The logo for History Mystery toys

Melissa took the opportunity during the first week to teach the children about insurance; the museum curators received a letter from their insurance company saying it was time to renew policies on some of the valuable toys in the collection. The teaching was done in "shadow role" and in many ways it resembled a traditional lesson, with Melissa as the teacher transmitting new information and the children applying and practising their new understandings to estimate values and calculate what the premiums would be. But by framing it as part of the Mantle of the Expert experience, the financial literacy concepts could be taught within an authentic context that resonated for the children.

Deepening the learning

The student teachers and I revisited the class at the start of the second week. This session began with a company meeting. I adopted a formal register as I asked the company members what business we needed to attend to. Suggestions included: "We need to read the letters and check for recent messages." I framed the student teachers as part-time company members and asked the children to update them on what had happened during the week. Next on the agenda was a visit from the storeroom manager. The mention of the storeroom prompted some imaginative responses from Ben who reported, "I've been down there and it's really messy and untidy. Please can everyone put things away properly?" It was delightful to hear this level of commitment to the imagined world from someone who had been unwilling at first. I told children that I was going to take on the role of the storeroom manager and asked a quieter child to choose a name for this figure. She decided he was called Josh. I moved into role, signalled by a blue hat, and asked the children for advice in sorting some of the toys in the storage room. As Josh, I presented six slips of paper with names of different toys handwritten on them. Children were asked to use their expert opinion to order the labels with the most valuable toys at the top, and the least valuable at the bottom. This task was designed to build on from the learning about insurance and to deepen conversations about other kinds of value that toys might hold.

Figure 10: A visit from Josh the storeroom manager

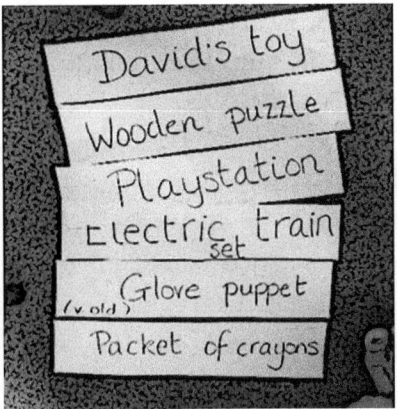

Figure 11: The labels

As they sorted the labels, children estimated the relative fiscal value of the toys and also made some thoughtful comments about different kinds of value. For example, one child said they had put David's special toy at the top of the list because it was "one of a kind" and couldn't be replaced. Children talked about the sentimental value of a toy that has been loved a lot. They also attributed value to toys that were "technological" and "educational". We built an extensive word bank on the board related to what gives toys value. At this stage, I thought we were finished but a comment from one of the children caught my attention. He noticed that every group had placed the "packet of crayons" label at the bottom of the list, suggesting it was the least valuable. He said, "That poor old packet of crayons is always left at the bottom!" I responded to his offer by saying, "That's true—if only we could hear what life is like for the crayons. Who could speak for the crayon and tell us what it's like to be at the bottom of all those lists?"

One of the girls stood up and said, "I'm a green crayon, but right now I feel blue." I asked the green crayon what her true value was and she replied, "I'm very good for drawing grass and leaves." Another child went into role as a crayon and added another value: "We are portable—you can heft us around. With a Playstation you have to stay plugged in, but crayons you can carry us out into the fields." Another student took things to a whole new emotional level with his monologue in role as the silver crayon: "They just take me outside and rub me on the concrete—they wear my tip right off. My friend the golden crayon died some time and I don't feel like colouring in the money anymore."

Figure 12: Ranking toys by estimated value

These children couldn't have known the book *The Day the Crayons Quit* (Jeffers, 2013) as it hadn't been published yet, but their responses were reminiscent of sophisticated ideas explored in that story and certainly helped reinforce the enduring understanding that value is about more than financial worth.

The final activity for this session was conceived as a lighthearted way to explore the imagined world further and promote writing. Company members were informed that

Figure 13: Activating the robot toy

some early robot toys had been discovered in storage. These only had a single function and were activated by voice command. Unfortunately, the labels had fallen off these toys and the team was asked to write a description of what each robot was and what it did. Children enjoyed "activating" the student teachers in role as robots and telling them what to do, before writing a few lines of descriptive text on the "label".

Over the following week, the children undertook a series of tasks springing from the premise of the disorganised storeroom. Whenever she wanted to evoke the role of Josh, Melissa simply used the same blue hat I'd worn. Children had no problem accepting a different person in that role. During the student teachers' next visit, they devised a toy hunt. The student teachers hid around the school in role as the toys and children searched for them. Through questioning, children were able to match the toy with the right information and add new details to "fact files" on each toy. Another day, it was announced that there had been water damage to the storeroom. Children wrote incident reports about the condition of each toy, filled in forms to claim on the insurance, and attended a meeting with David's lawyers to discuss how the museum might improve its storage conditions to avoid such an issue happening again. These activities provided rich opportunities for oral and written language to be used in authentic contexts.

The commission

About 3 weeks into the Mantle of the Expert adventure, the main commission was delivered to the class. It arrived in the form of a handwritten letter from David and a parcel, which Melissa left unwrapped at first, to add to the sense of intrigue. In his letter, David thanked the museum for caring for his expensive robot toy and sorting out the storage issues in the museum. He suggested he'd like to fund a special exhibition focusing on toys with different kind of value; those that had been on adventures or were very special and dearly loved. David proposed the displays could include such toys alongside their stories. He also suggested the exhibits could be interactive in some way. David offered to provide funding and promotion and attend the opening of the exhibition. And, finally, he offered his own most precious toy to be included as an exhibit—they would find it in the parcel. The children opened the parcel to reveal a very threadbare teddy.

And so the inquiry phase began. After collectively writing a response to David's letter, accepting the commission, children started to work more independently. They were each encouraged to decide what their exhibit would be about, and they chose whether to work individually or in groups. The long opening phase meant

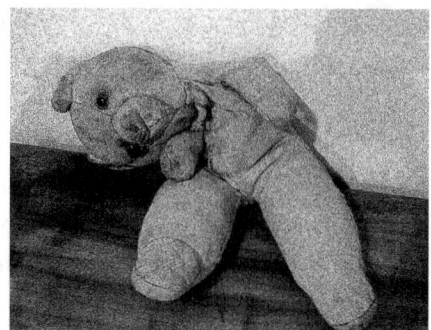

Figure 14: David's precious teddy

that children had a lot to draw on already. They could choose to make an exhibit around one of the toys in the storeroom, including the lost toys they had already written about; they could bring in a significant toy from home; or they might be inspired by a story. Melissa had made sure that the library corner in the classroom was populated with lots of stories about toys and during story time she shared some of these including *The Velveteen Rabbit* (Williams, 1922), *Winnie the Pooh* (Milne, 1926), and *The Trolley* (Grace, 1993).

Tensions

After a few sessions working on their individual exhibits, we introduced a key tension related to David's teddy. This idea was something we had thought up in the planning stage but kept up our sleeves until the moment felt right. Children were invited to a meeting of museum staff, with an agenda written on the board. Several brought pens and paper and made notes to record what was said. After catching up on where everyone was at with their exhibits, we turned to the next item on the agenda, which was a visit from Josh, the storeroom attendant. Once again, I took this role and signalled it with the blue hat. Josh had a large colour photo of David's old bear and black and white copies for everyone, which he handed out. Josh then advised that he'd had a call from the restoration group asking for advice about what work they should carry out on the bear to prepare it for the exhibition.

Originally, I had intended to group children by ability, with differentiated tasks for different levels: one group would write a list of words to describe the current condition of the bear, another would detail what restoration was required, and the third group would describe what the finished bear should look like. However, in the event the task was left open-ended with everyone simply invited to label what work they thought was needed on the bear. Where children needed help with spelling words, these were written on the board. I noticed children using a whole range of different strategies to approach this task. One child created a checklist on the back of the paper, another used a highlighter on the photo to show areas that needed work, and another just wrote the first couple of letters of each instruction "because I'm not great at writing—it goes crooked". The lack of structure allowed children to create their own ways to respond to the task.

At this point I wanted the children to put their pens and paper away so we could focus on discussion. So, we imagined the papers were sent off by fax (i.e., put in their desks). Some children did not know what a fax was so one of their peers gave a description of how a fax is "like a teleporter that zooms something to another place". Then I asked the children to agree that "several weeks have passed since our documents were faxed to the restoration team and now it's time to see their response". I told a story about how the restoration team had used a computer program to generate a new image of what David's bear might look like if it was completely restored. I asked the group to close their eyes and then I revealed a picture of the proposed restoration to them. Initially, the children were enthusiastic about what they saw but I was keen to complicate this response. On reflection, I could have done this through drama by inviting them to take the role of David and look at the picture through his eyes, or by overhearing a conversation in which David responded to the photograph. In the event, we got there through taking time for a deep discussion. And what happened next was the crux of the Mantle of the Expert journey.

Figure 15: The proposed reconstruction

First, the children were asked to think to themselves about whether we should restore the bear to look like the picture. Then they were asked to whisper their opinion to a neighbour. Then we moved into a physical continuum with children standing in a line according to whether they strongly agreed, were not sure, or strongly disagreed with the proposed restoration. Once children were grouped, I put a hand on someone's shoulder and asked them to state their opinion. This was another opportunity for quieter students to be heard. There was some fidgeting as children struggled to stand still and listen, but it was worthwhile to hear the complex and thoughtful points being made:

> "We don't want our customers to think we don't look after the toys—so we should make it clean and shiny."
>
> "I like new things."
>
> "David asked us to clean up and restore the bear—it's in the letter he sent, so we should go ahead."
>
> "I'm not sure if we should restore the bear—because I don't know what David would want us to do."
>
> "We definitely shouldn't because if he looked at that one, he wouldn't recognise it."
>
> "That's like a different bear—not the one that's full of memories."

As the discussion went on, some changed their place in the continuum, which suggests they were working out their own opinion and realising it was OK to take a different stance from a friend. The children were really respectful of others with a different point of view and, as the activity progressed, children's arguments got more sophisticated and unexpected, including:

> "I think we shouldn't do it because it's a lot of work to do all that."
>
> "Maybe if it does get restored it will remind him of what the bear looked like when it was new—which would be a GOOD thing."

Gay, who was observing the activity, commented on the depth of philosophical thinking and the level of buy-in to the imagined world. To deepen the discussion further, I asked those in the firm "yes" group to mix in with others who disagreed and have a "civilised conversation" about the issue. I was very impressed with how children managed this.

As I circulated between the groups I could hear lots of intense conversations and some people changing their minds.

The consensus seemed to be that we should consult David and get his view on the restoration. But before that I suggested we should consider the bear's perspective. I gathered the class around the photo of the old bear and raised the possibility of asking for his opinion. One child commented, "We can't talk to him—he's away at the restorers in Auckland." So we had to solve that first, by agreeing to imagine we were in Auckland too. A small chair was placed to the side of the group and I asked the group to gather in closer around it. By now the children were quite familiar with teachers going in to role so I just indicated that they would know the bear by his floppy neck. Before going into role I asked children how we could make the bear feel comfortable to answer our questions. One child was very clear that we shouldn't crowd him. Another child mentioned putting up hands. I asked children to think of questions that we might ask and suggestions came thick and fast.

I noticed a real shift in the mood of the room when I went into role. There was an air of hushed attention. I started with my eyes closed and one of the boisterous members of the class reminded the group not to shout out—which was lovely, given that he was often the one who did just that during class discussions. Questions came quickly. It was tricky to answer them without leading things too much—I wanted to encourage the children to gather data to help them take their own position—rather than delegate the responsibility to the bear. When I was asked, as the bear, if I would like to be restored I replied, "I think everyone who is old like me thinks about being young and beautiful again, but I'm not sure that's the same as actually wanting it to happen." At one point, the restoration process was compared to plastic surgery for humans. The option of a partial restoration was mentioned—perhaps just working to strengthen the neck? And the bear asked a question too: "Do you think I'm broken or less valuable because I look like this? Because I don't feel less valuable—I feel loved." After coming out of role, we discussed the options: full restoration, partial restoration, or leaving the teddy unrestored. I proposed that each person should write to David and spell out the various pros and cons, finishing with their professional opinion about the best outcome. The persuasive writing that resulted was impressive.

This session was intense and probably a bit static, but the learning was significant. Children learned that some questions don't have simple answers and it's OK to have a different opinion from your peers; also it's fine to change your mind as you learn more about a situation. They also learned that you don't necessarily just get on with a task you've been given if it doesn't feel right for some reason. They practised listening, persuading, and reflecting on their and others' points of view. They also practised concentration by sustaining their focus on one issue over a long session. By the end, children had quite strong opinions which they expressed through their persuasive writing. At the same time, they were protected against disappointment. By agreeing that the ultimate decision rested with the client, no one in the class could feel let down if their argument did not win the day.

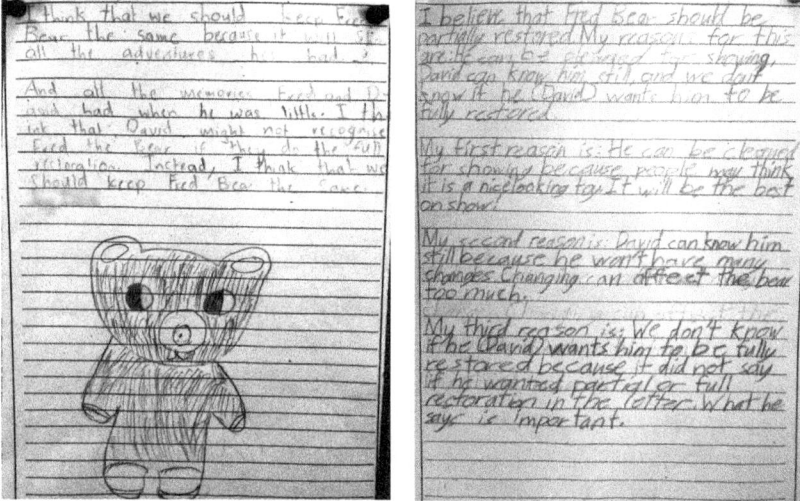

Figure 16: Example of persuasive writing

After writing to David, children heard back that he would prefer a partial restoration. Some members of the class phoned the restoration team to pass this on. Now that issue was solved, the class continued to work on their toy exhibits in time for the grand opening which, Melissa decided, would be staged in the classroom with parents invited. A big focus was the refining and publishing of the stories to accompany each of the toys.

Melissa asked me to spend a session with the class teaching the principles of storytelling, to help with the stories for the exhibits. I decided to teach some of the principles described by Aristotle: hook, climax, resolution, cause and effect, reversals, discoveries, complications, catastrophes, and detail. Detailed planning for this lesson, including curriculum links and a script of the teacher talk, can be found in a blog post (Aitken, 2012b). The episode began by stepping back from the world of our responsible team. I used Heathcote's "brotherhoods" strategy; inviting the children to consider for a moment just how many people over the years must have grappled with the same issue they were facing now—how to make a good story. Then, moving from facilitator to storyteller voice, I invited the children to imagine us travelling back in time to meet one of the very first people to consider this question: a man by the name of Aristotle. Donning a sheet to represent Aristotle's cloak, I mused aloud about the difficulties of writing an effective story and what I, Aristotle, had come up with to help with this challenge. Then I wrote out Aristotle's principles on pieces of scrolled up paper and one by one passed them "through time" to the writers of the future. Children reverently received the scrolls and pondered over the words written there:

- Hook to Climax to Resolution
- Cause and Effect = Logic
- Reversals, Discoveries, Complications, Catastrophes
- Detail—not just what happens, but why.

I came out of role again and we discussed what the different words and phrases meant. Children took responsibility in small groups to define the words on their piece of paper and were keen to check out the stories in the library corner to see if they could find examples of these features in their pages. Then each group shared back their discoveries to the class. Over the next week, as they continued to work on their exhibits, Melissa encouraged the children to use the features to enhance their own stories.

The experience culminated after 6 weeks. On the final day, the student teachers and I arrived at the school to find signage and posters around the school advertising the exhibition's grand opening. When we got to the classroom, the children were barring the doors. We were asked to wait until called for. Children had name tags with specific roles for the opening. Some were security guards, others were guides and receptionists, others were posted around the space with responsibility for particular exhibits. I asked one of the children what role the student teachers and I would be in today. They said, "You're the critics", and explained that

Figure 17: Participant in role as guard for the exhibition opening

this was the preview of the real opening, which would happen this afternoon for the parents. This shift of frame was interesting. Children had no problem seeing us as outsiders, though we had been members of the museum up to this time.

Eventually, we were shown into the museum and offered a map. The displays were set out in detail. Labels for the toys had been written out carefully. Some toys were represented in picture form, others were actual toys accompanied by a detailed observational drawing. There were notices to explain what was on show and each toy had a story to accompany it. Most noticeable to me was the way the children were talking about the exhibition, drawing on what we had done. One child spent time explaining to me how David's teddy was now partially restored: "The neck is a bit stronger but they didn't get round to sewing up the rip. We are quite happy with the job they did." All of this was imaginary; the actual bear was just as he had always been. I also heard another child explaining about the persuasive writing samples: "We needed to work out what was the best thing to do and we all had different opinions." Someone else was heard to say, "We got some ideas from a dude in a sheet about how to make our stories better." The children had created QR codes for each exhibit. When we scanned these, we were linked through to a video on the class website where each toy's story was read out by its author. There was also a play corner with toys for visitors to play with and a slide show telling the whole story of the toy museum and all the adventures we had together. Finally, at the end of it all there was a comments box for visitors to give feedback.

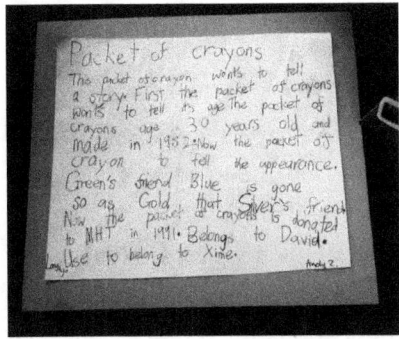 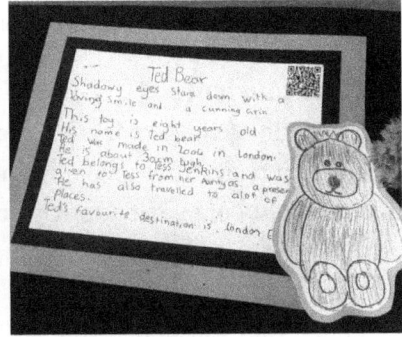

Figure 18: Toys and their stories

Once we had all been through the museum, one of the student teachers reappeared at the door wearing the hat that had been used to signal the role of David, the client. I heard children spread the word "David's here!" There was great excitement as they showed David around, even though the student teacher playing the role had already seen everything! The student teacher took the time to ensure everyone got a visit and a word of acknowledgement. While Mantle of the Expert is primarily focused on the process, rather than a polished product, the participants are motivated to produce quality work to meet the client's expectations. In this case, the client was evoked to see and praise the outcome of all the hard work. After David's tour, our group retired, leaving the toy museum still busy with visitors from the junior classes. That evening, the grand opening of the exhibition was held, with parents invited in as visitors. I'm sure they were impressed with their children's engagement and with the learning that had occurred. With the excitement of the opening, the Mantle of the Expert experience

Figure 19: Visits from other classes

was at an end. For the student teachers and me the ending was rather abrupt as it was the end of term and I was travelling overseas. However, Melissa took care over several days to lead the children through a process of reflection and closure to help them consolidate the learnings they had made and to move on from the imagined world.

Links to curriculum
This Mantle of the Expert was planned to provide authentic literacy learning in reading, in speaking and listening, and in writing. Children encountered complex texts with the commission, letters, and emails from the client. They also read and sorted labels, decoded daily agendas, and located Aristotelian features in stories. In terms of speaking and listening, they developed thoughtful questions for the bear, engaged in philosophical conversations on the ethics of restoration, reported to the insurance inspectors, and read their own stories with expression. As writers, they learned about features of effective storytelling and incorporated these into their stories which were drafted, refined, and carefully published and illustrated. They also produced thoughtful and considered pieces of persuasive writing which were presented using the conventions of formal letter writing. Other authentic writing carried out over the 6 weeks included filling in insurance claims forms, writing labels, creating reports, and designing name tags and signage— each of which carries its own formats and conventions. In every case, the learning occurred in authentic contexts with clear purpose and an awareness of the audience. While the focus was on literacy, the learning touched on a range of other learning areas including mathematics and statistics (calculating value and insurance), social studies (how people value cultural items in museums), technology (researching how toys have developed over time), and health and physical education (exploring attitudes to body image through the metaphor of the worn out bear). All five of the key competencies were also foregrounded at different stages of the experience.

Afterword
I have very warm memories of this Mantle of the Expert experience, particularly the level of buy-in exhibited by the children and the commitment, energy, and enthusiasm shown by the student teachers and

the classroom teacher. It was enormous fun and, I'm sure, educationally valuable. At the same time, there are several things I would do differently if I were to plan and teach this experience today.

Looking back at this Mantle of the Expert from almost a decade later, I'm very struck by its lack of cultural responsiveness. Other than mentioning the occasional local place name, the story could have been based out of any classroom in any country in the world—which I now consider makes it "tone deaf" from a cultural perspective. If I was planning this now I would actively look for a starting point to situate the imagined world within a local context. I'd be much more proactive about ensuring the identity and values of the responsible team embraced te ao Māori. In terms of the commission, I'd want this to encourage children to make connections with toys from a range of different cultures around the world and to value toys from their own family histories, not just the treasures of our wealthy white, male patron. I like how the plan successfully critiques the notion of value to include sentimental value as well as financial worth, but I'm concerned that cultural value was not included too. The plan as it stands normalises the experience of David with his well-off Pākehā childhood.

Back in 2012, my planning model was not as developed as the one shared in this book and I had not learned some of the tools for enhanced teaching. With these in mind, there are several ways in which the planning and delivery could have been stronger. Firstly, we didn't spend time consciously planning for the frame. We had some sense of our team's values and responsibilities but if this had been developed more consciously it would have given a shared reference point for the philosophical discussions about values. Neither did we plan for the children to embody multiple perspectives. The way we taught, children had the opportunity to adopt just one new perspective—as curators. They *encountered* other perspectives—the bear, other toys, toy owners, insurers, children responding to the exhibits, and so on— but they had limited opportunities to *inhabit* these. While the adults moved in and out of role frequently, the children hardly ever did. If I was teaching now, I'd use a range of drama conventions to ensure children could enter the imagined world more often. For example, when questioning the bear about his feelings on restoration, the children could have asked the questions not as themselves (within the real world) but as people from within the imagined world. They could have been members of the restoration team, or even other toys. This would have also given the task more coherence as everyone would have been inside the story.

Over time I have become more thoughtful about what's important in establishing the imagined world and how to enhance the poetic and aesthetic dimensions through signs and symbols. These days, I would not spend time negotiating the name of the museum but instead focus on the shared responsibilities, point of view, and values of the team. While the children clearly enjoyed the freedom to create their own desks, they responded from the point of view of enthusiastic children "play acting" as adults. So instead of drawing the whole desktop I might ask them to imagine something on their curator's desk that they look at every day that reminds them of the real importance of their work—and draw that. In 2012, I was new to Heathcote's notions of brotherhoods and the session where the children met Aristotle was a great opportunity to explore that strategy. However, that episode was probably the only one where the teaching took on an aesthetic dimension. Today I'd be looking for more opportunities to include the dimensions of dramatic imagination and poetic and reflective elements throughout. Finally, while I made some use of dramatic playing, we could have done more given the young age of the participants. We had a museum full of toys that had been on adventures so it would have been exciting to explore more of those together.

Senior primary—Shark Tank
Year level: 5–6 **Taught by:** Viv, classroom teacher Andy, and student teachers

Introduction
This Mantle of the Expert experience took place over 6 weeks during 2013, in the same primary school as our previous example. Once again, the teaching was part of a university course on Mantle of the Expert, so as well as fulfilling curriculum requirements for the children in the class, it was designed as an opportunity for student teachers to participate in planning and implementation. On top of this, it was a learning experience for Andy, the classroom teacher, who had never

used the approach before, and it was the subject of observation by a PhD student who was generating data for her thesis. The Mantle of the Expert adventure was sustained for 6 weeks, with the student teachers involved for one day a week and the classroom teacher continuing with activities between those visits. The student teachers and I recorded our reflections in the form of a blog (Aitken, 2013b). As with our previous example, I may seem to be describing a teaching situation few teachers could hope to emulate. So I'd stress again that while planning and teaching can be enhanced if collaborative effort and an extended timeframe are available, they are not a pre-requisite for success. As in our last example, this Mantle of the Expert experience could have been planned and implemented by a solo teacher or over a shorter timeframe.

The big idea/key learning objectives

There were several learning objectives for this planning. Andy, the classroom teacher, wanted to explore the curriculum areas of science and technology to draw in opportunities to decode complex texts. He also wanted to work with an ethical issue as he had heard positive things from a colleague who had used Mantle of the Expert to challenge her class to think about enviro-ethics (Aitken & Townsend, 2013). My objective was to meet these needs and to set up a "warts and all" example of Mantle of the Expert experience for students and teachers to observe. The additional presence of the PhD student making observations on the approach added a further dimension to the whole experience. I can't deny that this sense of being on show to all these observers played a part in my decisions, and not always for the better as we will see!

Key planning decisions

Planning took several months, and much was done in advance. The process was kept as simple and accessible as possible, to demonstrate for student teachers the planning model they would use in their assignments and to allow them opportunities for involvement in the teaching. The preplanning process is described in step-by-step detail in the next chapter, so the following narrative focuses on what happened in the classroom.

Before the Mantle of the Expert experience began, I visited the class on two occasions. I talked to the children in general terms about what we were planning to do; that we were going to spend 6 weeks together learning in a different kind of way, using our imaginations. I told them we needed to agree that we were important people with a special job to do and that for this to work we would need to interact with people, places, and objects that were imaginary. I used a range of simple drama activities to introduce some of the skills that might be required, including accepting others' ideas, agreeing to transform through imagination, and freezing key moments in time. I'm not convinced that such exercises are always necessary as a preparation for Mantle of the Expert, but it was useful for me to build relationship with the children, establish their social health as a group, and introduce the idea of embodied learning.

Implementation—the hook

The Mantle of the Expert experience itself began with the dramatic hook of a pre-rehearsed effigy presented by the student teachers. This was built up gradually. I started by asking the children to imagine a small bed with metal side rails and wheels. Where might the head and tail of this bed be? I spoke in a serious voice and slowed the pace right down, checking in to see if all the children were absorbed. Then I asked the children to imagine a young boy in the bed. At this stage, one of the student teachers took up the role of the boy, positioned as if using a remote control to operate a TV screen. I prompted the children to interrogate the body position, facial expression, and gestures of this figure, and they responded with comments like: "He doesn't look too happy", and, "What's a kid like this doing in a bed anyway? He must be sick." Next, I asked a second student teacher to move into her role and she took up the position at the foot of the bed as if making notes. The addition of this second figure promoted conversation about how annoying it would be to

Figure 20: The opening effigy

have the screen obscured and how their facial expression seemed to suggest a stern character. Or were they breaking some terrible news to the boy? Was he terminally ill?

Children were given the opportunity to question the figures in the effigy and the student teachers in role responded with information about the situation. Gradually, we discovered that this young boy, who loved skateboarding and riding his bike, had experienced breathing difficulties for many years and was now in hospital long term on an artificial respirator. We paused for a while to imagine and create the sounds that such a machine might make. Further questioning revealed that the boy was passing the time by watching action movies and playing computer games, which was fun, but he was very frustrated by not being able to participate in sports and activities for himself. Children were assured by the boy and the nurse that his condition was not terminal and that though he was feeling unwell, he was mostly bored.

Quite some time was spent interpreting the image and the activity gave the group opportunities to practise skills of inference, prediction, and argument while working with visual text and oral language. This opening hook engaged the children by presenting a world that was at once familiar and intriguing. Once I felt secure that the children were interested by the story of the boy's predicament, I started sowing the seeds for the responsible team that we would become. This was done through questioning. I invited children to discuss ideas about what could be done for this child. Who might be able to help? Whole-group discussion and a bit of steering from me led the children towards the idea of building an interactive computer game. One child offered the phrase "augmented reality" and this stuck, becoming a term we would use repeatedly over the next 6 weeks. By shifting my language towards more of an inclusive voice, I moved from discussing what *someone* might do to help this child towards what *we* would need to do as that team. And at some point, I asked whether they would agree to imagine themselves as people with expertise in such work—members of a company who had done this kind of thing lots of times before. There was enthusiastic agreement, and we were underway.

Suddenly, one of the children mentioned that it might be difficult to persuade the nurse they'd seen earlier to let us build something for the boy. This was a nice moment in several ways. It showed this child had bought in to the fictional world and that he accepted his position as someone who was going to act within that same fictional world. It also showed that he was taking the situation seriously and thinking critically about how we were going to achieve our intentions. From a drama point of view, he had raised a productive tension, which was very fruitful. When a child makes an "offer" like this—particularly one that promotes dialogic inquiry—it creates an opportunity for the teacher to detour into unexpected curriculum learning. So, we improvised a conversation in multiple pairs around the room, one person in role as the nurse raising objections, the other as a member of the company, attempting to persuade the nurse of the value of our product. Children appeared to have no difficulty with the complex idea that they were now embodying multiple versions of the same characters that had previously been played in front of them by two student teachers. They had moved from being positioned as onlookers, observing a presentation of the fictional world, to making meaning as participants within that world. After the activity, we shared back what we had learned about being persuasive and reflected on what would be most likely to convince the hospital of the benefits of our product.

Figure 21: Persuading the nurse

Deepening the learning

During the following week before the student teachers and I returned to the class, Andy worked with the children to build a shared sense of the world of their responsible team. Among other things, they mapped the company offices and came up with a company name, Augmented Reality Solutions. Andy was aware that part of the attraction for the children was the opportunity to use a subversive-sounding acronym ARS but he decided to let this pass. At the start of the next session, we started with a thank-you card written to the company from the father of the boy in the bed. The father's note said that the simulated environment had been a great success; the boy had benefited greatly from the opportunity to enjoy virtual adventures during his hospital stay, and the wrap-around environment was being left in the ward for other patients to enjoy in future. The father thanked the company for its excellent service, prompt communication, and high technical standards. This communication from a "fictional other" served a number of purposes: it shifted the element of time within the drama; it reinforced the work done the previous week; it hooked the children back in; and, crucially, it fed details into the back story of the responsible team, giving them a sense of accountability to high standards.

In this case, the hook that opened the Mantle of the Expert experience also served as a sort of mini-commission. Although participants did not spend time actually working on a wrap-around virtual environment for the boy in the bed, they did advocate for it, conceptualise what it might look like, represent and talk about the values of the company, and, just as importantly, they positioned themselves in imagination as people with a history of expertise in doing these kinds of things. The thank-you card was displayed on the company noticeboard under "past projects", to signify its place in our developing story. With this

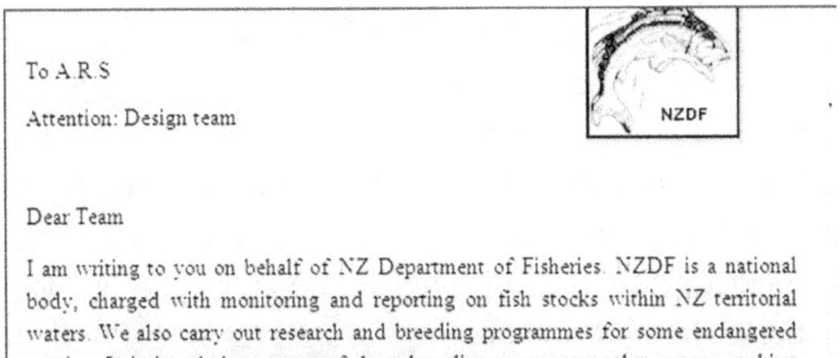

To A.R.S

Attention: Design team

NZDF

Dear Team

I am writing to you on behalf of NZ Department of Fisheries. NZDF is a national body, charged with monitoring and reporting on fish stocks within NZ territorial waters. We also carry out research and breeding programmes for some endangered species. It is in relation to one of these breeding programmes that we are seeking your assistance.

Our CEO attended a Government function recently, and heard the Minister for Health speaking about your Augmented Reality project in the children's ward of Hamilton hospital. After hearing about the success of that project and your skill and creativity in coming up with a solution for human patients we wondered whether the technology could be adapted for use in our work with marine animals. Specifically, we would like to commission you to produce a simulated environment for our shark breeding tanks.

Some background information: *Centrophorus harrissoni* (also known as the dumb gulper or gulper) is an Australian shark. It is sometimes found in New Zealand

Figure 22: Extract from the commission letter

experience of shared success behind them, the class was next introduced to the main commission. This time they received a letter purporting to come from a large aquarium in Wellington. The writer inquired whether the company would be willing to use their skills of creating simulated environments within the aquarium. Specifically, the request was to build a wrap-around environment for a breeding tank for a Dumb Gulper shark—a real endangered species which exists off the coast of New Zealand in rapidly reducing numbers. A productive tension was included in the letter, which said that the sharks had been found to eat their young in captivity. The client said that, to avoid this happening, the simulated environment needed to be of such high quality that the shark would be convinced it was in its natural environment out at sea.

We deliberately used dense language in the letter, providing an opportunity for children to meet one of the learning objectives and decode complex text. The commission letter was three pages long, and after it had been read out to them, children spent at least 45 minutes working together to decode what it was asking. The class was divided into groups and given a part of the letter to work on. This was an opportunity for grouping by ability, though children were not aware of this. The arrival of the letter was followed by a period of intense inquiry as the class debated what they'd need to know and do to carry out this commission successfully. Children recorded inquiry questions on a whiteboard and organised themselves into groups to address the questions. They carried out searches on their digital devices and reported back by sharing answers to the board and feeding back to a company meeting. An unseen complication arose at this point when one of the children searching for "Dumb Gulper shark" on a class iPad discovered the blog in which the student teachers and I were recording our experience of teaching the class. Fortunately, nothing had been written to compromise the research or give away the adventures to come!

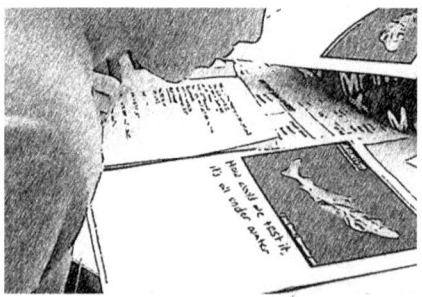

Figure 23 : Researching the Dumb Gulper shark

Some students became immediately interested in trying to complete the commission right away and started sketching designs for the simulated environment. While this level of engagement was positive, it was important to slow down and complexify their response. If children are accustomed to tasks being solution focused and short term, their instinct can be to jump in and try to provide a final answer, rather than taking time to explore the creative design process and grapple with underlying questions and issues.

Figure 24: Tank feeding system—initial concept design

What helped overcome this was having the focused inquiry questions on the board. I also invited the students to see the sketches as initial concept designs to be revisited as we found out more from the research.

Tensions

Over the following 6 weeks, the children in the class undertook a range of curriculum-based explorations related to tensions raised in the drama. There were many ways the learning could have gone, but we followed our original intention to focus on science, technology, and ethics. One early session involved an imaginary trip to Wellington to visit the aquarium where the shark tank environment was to be built. Preparing for the trip was an opportunity for action, as children packed their imaginary briefcases. This activity included some negotiation with one child who was quite keen to bring a handgun with him. After discussing the pros and cons, he conceded there was a danger of delay at the airport as the documentation was checked and a real danger of intimidating the client. I didn't tell him what to do but invited him to reflect for himself on the values of the company and what felt "right".

He was later spotted packing an imaginary wireless keyboard instead. All the children used drama to explore overcoming minor hitches experienced on their journey to Wellington.

Once we had "arrived", the imagined setting of the aquarium also provided opportunity to explore measurement: children spent time calculating the area and volume of the tank by marking it out on the classroom floor.

Figure 25: Carefully packing the briefcase

They did this as a whole group first, then each person wrote up the calculations in their maths books. As part of the imagined visit to the aquarium, I went into role as a shark expert named Wiremu. He was not the client, as he did not personally set the commission, but he was a figure dedicated to the wellbeing of the sharks and someone to whom they could refer questions about the shark's needs. Children seemed really engaged during the meeting with Wiremu and leaned in as he spoke about the difficulties of keeping these sharks in captivity.

Figure 26: Calculating the area and volume of the tank

Looking back, there were a few reasons why I chose a Māori male for the shark expert role. First, it was a way of making fictional other distinct from myself. Second, I was modelling how in drama we can play roles of people of different age, gender, and ethnic background to our real-life persona which is something we ask our participants to do throughout. Third, I wanted to introduce someone the children in the class could identify with. And fourth, I realise I wanted to counter stereotypical assumptions (about masculinity, about scientists, and about what it is to be Māori) that are so problematic in the real world. I think another reason for the choice was that I could see potential to explore perspectives on the issues that came up in the drama from a te ao Māori perspective. However, we did not really do this, which was a missed opportunity.

Figure 27: Shark expert Wiremu (teacher in role) explains requirements

Another key session involved hands-on science experiments. I wanted student teachers to see how teaching and learning shifts when a conventional task is reframed as part of a Mantle of the Expert exploration. So, the student teachers were asked to plan science experiments that could be introduced to the children as professional tasks for the tank design commission. They came up with a whole range of these. One explored the question of how we might filter the water from the tank through an experiment with sediment filtration. Another looked at pH testing as part of exploring how we could balance the pH of the tank to match that of the natural environment. A third considered how to account for temperature changes within the tank and what would be unsafe highs and lows for the sharks. The final experiment was about desalination, framed as a way of recycling the waste salt water from the tank. The student teachers set up the experiments as "stations" so that groups of children could rotate around the room and complete them in turn.

Figure 28: Science experiments—in sediment filtration and PH testing

Along with the familiar classroom challenges of time management and dealing with mess and breakage, the student teachers experienced an additional challenge—to present the instructions for these tasks while positioning students as expert adults. They did this very well and there was lots of evidence of children relating what they were learning to the authentic context provided by the imagined world. They discussed implications for the tank design and at the end of the session, recorded their findings. Andy helpfully backed this up by creating a text from Clive emphasising the importance of reporting back. Clive (our CEO in the imagined company) provided another fictional other for children to relate to, in addition to the father who wrote the letter at the start and Wiremu who ran the aquarium. However, Clive's position and therefore his function within the fiction was very different: he was a high status figure whose interventions kept everyone aware of the wider purpose for what we were doing, and accountable for the standards of our work. We could have used the client to similar effect.

Figure 29: Science experiment—in desalination

As well as science, the 6-week unit presented the opportunity to work in the curriculum learning area of Arts, in the discipline of Music—Sound Arts. To set up for the sound-based work, teacher in full role was used again. One of the student teachers went into role as Bruce, an expert scientist. He announced that a probe was being organised to head out to sea to collect samples from the shark's natural environment to help the tank designers reproduce the environment as accurately as possible. Students were asked what samples they wanted to receive. They answered with things like "water", "seabed sediment", and even "a sample of shark flesh—if it can be obtained without hurting the animal". Bruce also informed them that the probe would take sound samples from the area and the children agreed that this would be important, as a soundtrack would be necessary as part of the simulated environment.

Figure 30: A text from the CEO prompts deeper thinking

In the next session, Bruce returned with the news that, although the other samples were OK, the sound samples seemed to have something wrong with them. He used an iPad to play an audio clip with a mixture of natural sounds including deep sea effects, water, and whale calls and human-generated sounds such as grating noises and a sound like a motor or pump. Bruce was concerned that the pollution on the audio rendered the sound samples useless. This was an example of how dramatic tension can generate curriculum activity. The problem of the audio pollution set up opportunities for tasks that were both professional tasks for the tank designers and curriculum tasks appropriate to level for

Figure 31: Discussing the audio sample with Bruce (student teacher in role)

the children. Drawing on the learning objectives from the Music—Sound Arts area of the Arts learning area, the student teacher in role as Bruce took the children through an active listening task. He invited them to listen to the tapes with their eyes closed and identify the sonic qualities (pitch, volume, and timbre) of the sounds they heard. Then, working in pairs and small groups, the children set about using the class iPads to find and record samples of sound with similar sonic qualities. These were layered into new soundscapes using GarageBand software. In observation of the children's discussions it was clear they were taking care not only to complete the task but also to select and evaluate the sounds they were creating. The children were highly engrossed in this task, which could easily have been sustained for several sessions.

Figure 32: Exploring the sonic qualities of found sounds

Figure 33: Using GarageBand software to create a digital soundscape

Once again, the presence of the imagined world enhanced the learning for the children here and added purpose. This kind of composition task could have been carried out without the elaborate construct of the commission and the tension and perhaps the results would have been similar, but it's doubtful that the concern to mimic sonic qualities would have been so intense without the back story of the drama. The children's attentive listening was surely enhanced because the task carried a sense of importance and risk (for the baby sharks and for the reputation of the company). While completely risk free in the real world, every decision had significant implications within the imagined world the children had bought into.

As the discussion with Bruce continued, a chance comment from one of the participants opened up new and unexpected opportunities for deep thinking and collective problem solving. One of the quieter boys in the class raised his hand and said something to the effect of, "All these noises came from the seabed where the shark lives. So, what if these are the sounds the shark is used to? If we want to convince the shark it is still out at sea, shouldn't we include these sounds?" What a thoughtful challenge this was. It led to a fascinating discussion about what makes things "natural"—not just for sharks but people too. Is something natural because it is what we are used to, or is nature always what is there without human intervention? This child's question is an example of the rich critical thinking children are capable of, and how this is promoted in Mantle of the Expert's focus on complex, real-world issues and contexts. It also illustrates the sense of permission that can come from being positioned as competent within a genuine inquiry. Fortunately, in this case the student teacher was flexible and responsive enough to acknowledge the child's question, take it seriously and allow it to have a material impact on the direction of the inquiry. This moment also illustrates the power of the commission and the frame in Mantle of the Expert. After all, for these participants, this was not simply an abstract philosophical discussion: they had to reach a solution in order to be able to get on with the job at hand. Eventually, the decision was made to create separate tracks of the natural and unnatural sounds and conduct experiments so that both could be played to the shark and its responses noted.

The key tension in this Mantle adventure was introduced when the team was close to completing their commission. I went into role as Wiremu again and asked for a confidential conversation about something that was troubling me. Through questioning, children discovered that Wiremu was worried. He had found a letter revealing that one of the principal sponsors of the project was a shark liver oil manufacturing company and now he was thinking of quitting his job. After a bit of hasty discussion as to what shark liver oil is and how it is produced, children were invited to consider what might be the ethical implications of this revelation. Why did this make Wiremu concerned enough to consider leaving his job? Did this have repercussions for our own involvement? What difference did it make to the project if it was not about conservation of an endangered species but farming of it? The active strategy of a continuum was used so children could physically show their position on the issues, then a drama convention was used to make suggestions to Wiremu. The children stood in two lines as I walked through the middle holding Wiremu's hat. One by one, children spoke their advice as the hat passed by. The children took quite different positions on this issue: some advised Wiremu to leave on principle, while others encouraged him to think of his family and the financial implications of leaving his job. After I had left, Andy encouraged continued discussion and debate on this ethical tension for several sessions, which resulted in impassioned written position statements on the issues of animal testing and animal captivity. Eventually, the decision was made that the company would go ahead and complete the commission and then confront the client about the matter of sponsorship if they successfully won the bid for the job.

Figure 34: Teacher in role reveals the key tension

Outcomes

The final week saw class members preparing to feed back to the client. Groups took responsibility for different aspects, talking through the tank design, explaining the soundscape, reporting on safety and other aspects. For their last session with the class, the student teachers were asked to take on a collective role as the client

Figure 35: Presentation to the client on tank design

and the children presented their findings in serious tones, using heightened language. All groups chose to use dramatic conventions in their presentations, which shows that such conventions had now become part of the norms for communicating learning in this class.

Figure 36: Demonstrating how to change the filter for the shark tank

The Mantle of the Expert experience culminated with a light-hearted touch: students were invited to consider how company members would feel after their successful presentation at the aquarium, and how they might use their free time in Wellington to celebrate. Groups created a company photo album showing their perfect day. The images they created show how much these students had gained confidence in expressing their ideas through drama.

Figure 37: **Leisure time in Wellington.** Clockwise from top left: bungee jumping, coffee on the waterfront, paintball, and fighting over clothes in the sales

Links to curriculum

The children in this class made clear progress in drama, becoming much more confident in using their bodies, facial expression, and spoken language to develop and present ideas. The commission also provided opportunities for children to learn in science, with experiments in salinity, pH, temperature, and filtration all done in an authentic context. The work with recorded sound met achievement objectives in Music—Sound Arts, and there was a social science dimension in the discussions on ethics of shark liver oil manufacture. While we touched on technology with our design ideas for the tank, we would have needed to develop prototypes, carried out testing of materials, and so on to really have satisfied achievement objectives in this area. In terms of key competencies, the class worked often as a large group and in smaller groups, requiring them to stretch their capacities in *thinking* as well as *participating and contributing* and *managing self*. The commission letter exposed children to a complex written text that children were eager to decode. There was also a session in which we focused on calculating the volume in the shark tank, finding different measurements, and working as a team to reach a working estimate. In the ongoing teaching between our visits, Andy made some links to the Mantle of the Expert experience within his other teaching, though he chose to continue with his separate reading, writing, and maths programmes, rather than having the Mantle of the Expert extend throughout the school day. This had the advantage of maintaining class routines but probably also meant power relationships within the classroom were not renegotiated as much as they might have been.

Afterword

The planning and back story to this Mantle of the Expert were strong but there are several things I would do differently today. First, while there were periods of active, embodied learning, we also ran lots of meetings of our imagined company, in which talk was the dominant mode and things were pretty static. Over time I've moved away from this heavy reliance on the machinery of the company as I want to avoid setting up any assumption that corporate practices are the norm in adult human behaviour! My teaching was also limited in terms of the aesthetic possibilities. Transitions between activities were quite clunky and managerial and I could have made a lot more use of the storyteller voice. I was confident in only a limited range of conventions and did not know how to feed in Heathcote's six dimensions of dramatic imagination or the five levels of meaning-making. Now I think I'd be able to use those tools to charge the moments with more poetry and theatricality. Another confession: looking back at videos from the classes, it's clear that sometimes I dominated the classroom talk—something I'm still working on to this day!

The presence of the PhD student in the classroom added an interesting and unexpected dynamic to this experience, too. She only attended a handful of the sessions but whenever she did, I was very conscious of her presence in the room. Not being privy to her notes and reflections I found myself second guessing what she was writing instead of just focusing on the children's learning. I became concerned to accentuate drama for learning elements and on at least one occasion I forced this more than I would have done if no other adult were in the room. This was a great learning for me. As someone who often takes the role of researcher or evaluative visitor in a class, I got a taste of how it feels like to be under scrutiny and how easy it is to shift your focus and thereby distort your practice.

This Mantle of the Expert experience was more situated within a New Zealand context than the previous example, but there was a lot more scope for embracing te ao Māori perspectives. The figure of Wiremu could have been used to introduce stories and understandings from a Māori cultural perspective, which could have enriched the commission enormously. And not just that: if we had explicitly framed the company as a Treaty-based organisation, and included expectations of cultural considerations in the commission, this could have completely changed the starting point and the processes used to complete the commission. I'd love to re-plan and re-teach this Mantle of the Expert now, with these new perspectives. Another reservation is the lack of exploration around the ethical issue of funding. In retrospect, the light-hearted celebratory ending to our time together was out of tune with the seriousness of the "wicked problem" we had introduced. Andy did return to the matter for further discussion after the student teachers and I had left the class, but the implications were not fully explored or resolved. If I was to explore this context in a classroom again, I would want to acknowledge and problematise the ethical issues in a lot more depth.

Having said this, there was value in the experience for everyone concerned. As well as the children's learning, I was impressed with how the student teachers rose to the challenge of planning and implementing the science activities and participating in the various drama activities. Just as valuable were the reflective conversations and planning sessions we held between the in-school sessions. The PhD student got her data and classroom teacher Andy did a great job too—both in the planning and in his willingness to be flexible and responsive as things arose in the imagined world. Everyone, including me, benefited from his boundless energy and enthusiasm. Ten years on, Andy continues to explore Mantle of the Expert as part of his school's ongoing commitment to Dramatic Inquiry.

Objects of Significance

Year levels: 3–4 and 5–6 **Planned and taught by:** Viv, with support from Whakarongo, Materoa, Whitney, Atiria, and Kylie. Based on an existing plan by Trevor Sharp

Introduction

This Mantle of the Expert experience was planned and taught in a large multicultural primary school as part of a professional learning day for teachers in 2019. The planning was completed with input from professional development leader Whakarongo and colleagues from the school's partial immersion unit: Materoa, Whitney, and Atiria, along with another Māori staff member Kylie. The teaching described here consisted of two demonstration lessons based on the same planning but with different age groups. The lessons lasted 1 hour each, though these could easily have been extended to provide several weeks of cross-curricula tasks. I wanted to include this example in the book to illustrate how Mantle of the Expert can be used for a short learning experience—in this case, a single episode—and because I really wanted to include an example of planning that was more recent and more culturally responsive than my other narratives.

The big idea | Key learning objectives

The professional development of which this lesson was a part had two joint objectives. Alongside the deepening of knowledge and skills in Dramatic Inquiry, the teachers were also committed to teaching about New Zealand history, drawing on Hanly's *Critical Guide to Māori and Pākehā Histories of Aotearoa* curriculum programme resource (Hanly, 2017). Whakarongo requested a demonstration lesson to explore ideas from Unit Three of the resource, called *Two Worlds Meet* (Hanly, 2017). This unit looks at the experience of early European settlement in New Zealand from the perspectives of both Māori and Pākehā. There is a wealth of content that could be explored from this context and we had agreed to look at agricultural and trading practices. We wanted to use drama to highlight how different world views and perspectives played out during this critical time in our history. In particular, we wanted to present the first encounters between settlers and Māori as a meeting of two world views, each with their own technologies and belief systems. From a drama teaching perspective I hoped to be able to demonstrate: how to use frame distance for respectful exploration of culturally significant topics; how to work with the teacher compass to allow guided discussion and feeding in of facts; the importance of intrigue; and the use of the narrator or storyteller voice.

Key planning decisions

The planning process started as a solo effort and a partnership with the input of colleagues in the latter stages. Even though this was going to be just a short lesson, a great deal of thought went into my initial planning. I wanted to ensure the responsible team was framed so that participants had to think about agricultural and trading practices of the past from multiple perspectives. I followed the pre-planning steps (see Chapter 4) to think about who this team might be. The idea of a team of museum curators was rather obvious, and for a while I resisted it for this reason. But I found I kept returning to it as the most fruitful option. After all, museum curators have responsibility over handling, preserving, displaying, and explaining historical artefacts, and I had the hunch that a good way to access the historical material we wanted to explore might be through objects and their stories. I did some research into pre-European agricultural practices and discovered an array of intricate hand tools used in traditional Māori agriculture. I also discovered that the school's local region had enjoyed a significant trade in harakeke, with traditional harvesting methods used by Māori and mechanised methods introduced by settlers.

When thinking about other kinds of trade, I recalled an existing process drama plan written by my friend and colleague Trevor Sharp. Trevor's drama is based around a gold brooch made from the beak of a now-extinct huia bird. Participants interact with a teacher in role, and explore fictional diary entries and letters, to create the story of how the brooch came to be found hidden in a wall. There's a Mantle of the Expert quality to Trevor's planning, with participants positioned as museum curators, giving a sense of distance from the events. Trevor's original drama was written for Year 9 students and can be accessed online (Sharp, n.d.). The haunting image of that huia beak brooch has stayed with me ever since I first experienced this drama as a participant, and I was interested to see how we could draw on it again for this plan.

With only a 1-hour time slot, I knew we would not be able to take the cross-curricular exploration very far. What I hoped to do was to demonstrate to the observing teachers how we could build a sense of the imagined world quite quickly and, through intrigue and storytelling, build a sense of reverence and interest in the objects. I decided to work with three significant artefacts: the huia beak brooch, a carved kāheru digging tool, and a metal sickle like the one featured in an online photo of harakeke harvesting. Drawing on information from *Te Ara*, the online encyclopaedia of New Zealand, and Te Papa museum, I created one-page information sheets about each object and found an image related to how each was used. These were further edited after feedback from my teaching colleagues, resulting in the versions in Figure 38.

Then I started to work on my planning. I thought I would open the drama by inviting the children to imagine a space. Using Heathcote's six dimensions of dramatic imagination and a combination of a narrator voice and teacher-in-role voice, I scripted an opening to take us into the imagined world:

> Our adventure begins in a special place—a building where the past is as important as the present. Where we, the people who work here, the kaitiaki or guardians, deeply understand the importance of stories and

Chapter 3 Three New Zealand examples

Further information – Exhibit A

What is it? Huia Beak Brooch
How old is it? Made in 1900. So about 120 years old
What is it made of? Gold, steel, bird beak
What's its story?
This beak is from a huia bird. You don't see these birds today because they are extinct. Before Europeans arrived in New Zealand, Huia was one of the most important birds to Māori. They wore bird feathers as symbols of high status. Chiefs often wore the long white-tipped feathers or skins of huia.

When Europeans arrived, they also loved to wear animals, birds feathers and other ornaments. At this time there was a big fashion for wearing stuffed animals, birds, feathers and other ornaments. When people came to New Zealand, they wanted to express their feelings of belonging by using local flowers, birds plants and animals.

Maori traded feathers and birds with Europeans. Maori also took on ideas from European fashions and adapted them to suit their purposes.

We're not sure who owned this brooch but it was probably made by a jeweller for a young European woman. Perhaps it was a gift from her family. Something to be worn on special occasions such as balls or parties.

Over time, some birds, including the huia, died out as their forest homes were cleared for farmland. The last official sighting of a huia was in 1907.

Further information – Exhibit B

What is it? Kāheru – a light digging tool or spade
How old is it? About 100 years
What is it made of? Carved wood with shells for eyes
What's its story? We don't know who made this particular tool. The decoration suggests that it was used by a Māori tohunga (expert) to carry out special rituals.

Māori were farmers long before Europeans came to Aotearoa. They brought foods from Hawaiiki such as kumara, hue, taro and yams. They carried out a lot of research to find out how to grow food successfully in the New Zealand climate. Each Māori village was surrounded by gardens and everyone was expected to help out. Chiefs, families and children worked hard using lots of different tools.

The name kāheru applies to wooden spades. They came in three different shapes - short, long and triangle. Kāheru were not used for heavy work like digging but were useful for weeding and loosening the soil. The name 'kāheru' is also found in the name of a group of stars (Mata-kāheru). The constellation is the same shape as a short kāheru spade.

Farmers carried out rituals at planting time. Homage was paid to Rongomātane, the god of cultivated foods, to ensure good crops. Crops were stored in special buildings off the ground so that food would remain fresh.

When Europeans arrived they depended on Māori for food. There was no money yet, so Māori traded food for things they wanted, like nails and woollen blankets. Māori helped Europeans learn the skills to grow food for themselves. They tried to convince the new settlers of the importance of Rongomātane but not everyone understood. Europeans had their own tools and ways of doing things and Māori learned from these too.

Further information – Exhibit C

What is it? A sickle used for cutting flax
How old is it? About 100 years
What is it made of? Wooden handle with metal blade. Sharp on the inside edge
What's its story? We don't know who made this particular tool. We think it belonged to a family who worked as flax harvesters – like in the picture below

Harekeke or flax was used by Māori for many years before Europeans arrived – for food, clothing, mats, baskets, drinks, medicine and healing. It was very important for daily life. Traditionally, Māori cut, stripped and wove harakeke by hand. They performed rituals to thank the plant for giving its leaves. Māori were very careful of the plant and always left part of it to keep growing for the future.

When Europeans arrived in Aotearoa they could see how useful harekeke was. They ordered flax ropes for their ships, baskets, mats and other things. They were keen to get as much as possible. Mostly they didn't worry so much about the rituals and traditions.

There was no money yet, so Māori began trading flax for other things including muskets, (guns). Some Māori moved their whole village to live in areas like Waikato where flax grew really well. Some Pakeha and Maori went into business together. More and more flax was sent in ships to Australia and Britain.

After a while, people decided they needed machines to work the flax more quickly. It was usually still cut by hand, using a sickle. Big machines called flax mills were used to turn the leaves into fibres and bales. This was much faster, but did not take the same care as traditional approaches.

After a while plastic was invented and people didn't use flax so much. Harekeke is still used in New Zealand, but there are no more big flax mills. The last one closed in 1985

Figure 38: Information about the artefacts

95

treasures. A place where every day the folk of the town and the whole country come, young and old, to gaze and learn and wonder. We're in a museum but not just any museum, it's the main one for the whole country of Aotearoa. The treasures around us are treasures considered important for all and held here in trust for everyone in the nation to share. Right now, it's completely still in the museum. The lights in the main exhibition are off, because it's early morning and still very dark. Our ears pick up only the sound of distant traffic across the city. In a moment the lights will come on and the museum will open for the day. When is does, what might we see around us?

This script was designed to establish the elements of time and space for our imagined world, let the children know who they were within this world and build a sense of responsibility and intrigue. It also prompted participants to offer suggestions of what might be in the museum, and allowed me to check their level of engagement. The next part of my plan was to describe the early morning arrival of new objects at the museum. I decided to use the narrator voice again, this time to describe a courier van delivering parcels. Then I would slow down the pace by drawing the objects that had been delivered on pieces of paper. I had recently tried something similar in another classroom and enjoyed how children's engagement could be built from seeing the objects appear before their eyes rather than providing a photo or indeed the actual artefacts.

Once the objects had been manifested in the imagined world, my plan was to use the 'teacher compass' tool to support inquiry with a balance of free discussion and input of facts. I planned to start by encouraging the children to speculate on what the object might be, including using drama to show their ideas about the object in use (quadrant one). Then I would focus the discussion a bit through prompt questions designed to draw attention to the key features of the objects (quadrant two). Then I planned to feed in some factual information based on the information sheets I had written (quadrant three). And, finally, I would give the children an opportunity to consolidate what they had learned and think about implications for their exhibit (quadrant four).

I also realised I would need to introduce the crucial element of tension, always so necessary to successful drama. Without dramatic tension, we would need to rely on the children having an intrinsic interest in the task of understanding and describing the objects. While most teaching relies on that alone, a teacher using Dramatic Inquiry including Mantle of the Expert can also keep things interesting by introducing problems, challenges, or mysteries within the imagined world. For example, in Trevor's lesson, the sense of tension came from the idea that the owner of the brooch hid it through some kind of guilt or shame. For my own planning, I wanted to stick quite closely to the historical use of the objects. I also wanted to give the children some ownership, which Trevor's plan does in other ways. I decided to keep the tension quite open ended and asked the children to imagine that when they looked closely at their object, they discovered a tiny bit of damage. Here's the script I prepared for that part of the lesson, which shifts from narrative voice to facilitator voice:

> As the museum workers donned their white cotton gloves and began to examine the new objects in even closer detail, they noticed something significant. Some damage ... Now, as a group, you're going to have the power to decide what that damage is ... obviously it's not severe or we'd have noticed it when we opened the parcel. And it's not so serious that it stops the object being a treasure ... but something that shows us that once, some time in its past, this object has had something happen to it: accidentally or on purpose. Perhaps it's a hairline crack, some dirt, a chip or some other sign ... whatever it is, this tiny bit of damage has an important story to tell ...

To establish a productive constraint and encourage collaboration, I planned to hold back the pens, so that only when children had discussed and agreed could they add a mark to their picture to show the damage. From there, my plan was to encourage children to think about an exhibit that would tell the story of their significant object including how it was used, what it meant to people at the time, and what happened to damage it. The commission—from the owners who had lent the objects—would be to ensure that the exhibit told the story in all its complexity and with all perspectives respected equally. Once the children had shared ideas for their exhibits, I thought we could finish the lesson by bringing out photos of the real objects that had inspired the drama and discuss how these were housed in real museums.

I was happy with my planning to this point but knew it would benefit from the input of colleagues with knowledge of te ao Māori. I was cognisant of the fact that two of the objects I had chosen to work with were taonga, or at least the real-life versions would have been, and I did not want to assume that just because I could see them and read about them online it was OK to use them in a drama. I was mindful of the mātauranga embedded in significant objects and wanted to understand how contemporary museum curators would respect this. So, asking for help was about verisimilitude and making the experience authentic. On a deeper level, it was about my commitment to growing my understanding of culturally responsive or culturally sustaining practice. In the years since I'd taught the examples previous described, I'd become increasingly aware of the Eurocentric assumptions in my world view and therefore in my planning. I wanted to make a conscious effort to ensure Māori world views were represented in my teaching and this seemed particularly urgent where the content related to taonga. So, this was when I reached out to Māori colleagues for advice.

It was exciting to see how these teachers' knowledge and love of te ao Māori took the planning to a whole new level. The teachers suggested that, to ensure a sense of distance from any actual taonga and their real stories, it would be important to emphasise to the children that the objects within our imagined world are imagined too. This was useful guidance as without this I might otherwise have included real-life details of the objects that had inspired the drama. Also, since I planned to show photos of real objects at the end of the drama, I rephrased this part of the lesson to clarify that these objects were *like* the ones in our story without suggesting they *were* the same ones. This conversation was so useful in gaining new understandings about frame distancing in a cultural context.

Another key piece of advice was around the delivery of the objects. The teachers advised that, since two of the objects were living taonga, any museum would need to handle them with great care. They would have to be brought into the building with appropriate rituals: clearly my idea of a courier delivery did not fit the bill. We thought about how this could be done within the drama and Materoa offered to help by performing a karanga to welcome the objects. Another useful bit of feedback was in relation to the information sheets. The original encyclopaedia entry on the huia beak brooch focused its story on the final owner of the brooch—a Victorian woman—and I had copied this on to my sheet. But Kylie suggested that before talking about how the brooch was made and worn we "flip the narrative" and start with details of the bird (the true owner) and how Māori traditionally wore the feathers. This comment really brought home to me the ongoing issue of how Māori world views are often positioned in our cultural histories which was the very point we were trying to address in our teaching. I could see how this subtle shift in the language of the text made a significant difference to the balance of the historical narrative. Other advice included further information about the use of kāheru. Atiria mentioned that as well as being a ritual object, these are familiar everyday tools, still in use to this day. And Materoa suggested that both Māori and Pākehā would have made use of a metal sickle; a reminder not to think in binaries but to remember that the period of history we were teaching about is one where both cultures learned from each other and adapted technologies to suit their own purposes.

Implementation

The lesson was implemented twice. The first time was with a group of children from the middle school and the second time was later the same day, with a group from the senior classes. The teaching took place in the school's boardroom, an unfamiliar space to the children. It had been cleared of furniture apart from three tables. The groups of 12 children were selected by the teachers involved in the professional development who observed the sessions and participated in the final activity. Both sessions began with introductions and the "warm up your imagination" activity described later in the book. Then I sat with the children gathered close on the mat as I narrated the scene in the darkened museum. As I talked about the kaitiaki who work in the museum, I gestured to demonstrate to the children that I was including them in this description. For this group, many of whom were familiar with working in drama, this seemed enough to clarify the compact. On another occasion it may have taken longer to explain what was going on and more explicit signalling would have been appropriate. The children immediately came up with rich descriptions of what might be in the museum. Their ideas included maps, waka, an ancient book, paintings of landscapes, fossils, and dinosaur bones. I encouraged the children to describe where in the museum their items were, and they responded with details like, "just to the left of the main door" or "up there, high on the wall", or "in the big entrance hall across from the waka". With more time, these ideas could have been expanded and represented through drawings or a map, but for now we just needed to establish a sense of our role and the space we were operating in to allow us to step into the imagined world together.

The hook

I segued into the arrival of the objects with a storyteller voice: "There's a sense of excitement in the air as the workers of the museum gather. Today, they are expecting the arrival of three new treasures." With the younger group I wanted to foster a sense of playfulness, so I invited them to head off into the workroom and prepare the space for the arrival of three new objects. After a little hesitation the children started talking to each other and, through dramatic playing, began cleaning and rearranging the space. Before long everyone was playing at cleaning, wiping, sorting, and otherwise preparing. Next, I told the story of the arrival of the first object. This would become the sickle, though the children did not know this yet. It was signified by a blank piece of paper the size of a dinner plate. Drawing on the dimensions of dramatic imagination once again, I described the courier van drawing up in the basement of the museum, the doors opening, the courier checking her list and carefully unloading the object and wondering as she does so what new treasure this might be. Then, as I described the object being delivered and signed off, I carefully placed the piece of paper onto one of the three tables.

As mentioned earlier, colleagues had advised that the other two objects, the kāheru and the huia beak brooch, were living taonga so it would be appropriate for these to be accompanied into the museum by kāranga and tangi. So, at this point I invited children to turn their attention to the double doors of the boardroom through which Materoa appeared, dressed in a skirt and carrying the two other blank pieces of paper that would eventually come to signify the kāheru and the brooch. Materoa sang a karanga to welcome the taonga into the museum and to plead for the careful treatment and love of these items. There was a palpable sense of seriousness and ritual in the air at these moments. While it was not possible, or appropriate, to carry out a full pōwhiri, this use of ritual evoked the rites that would be carried out in such a context. And once Materoa had placed pieces of paper on the other two tables, I added these words: "The ceremonies continue for some time: there are visitors to welcome, kai to be shared, and stories to be told. It is a full and busy day."

At this point we paused to reflect and clarify what was happening. I noticed for some of the junior students there was still a little bit of uncertainty, so this was an opportunity to explain in plain language. While the use of aesthetic and ritual gives a sense of elegance and richness to a Mantle of the Expert experience, this doesn't mean you shouldn't give a straightforward explanation if this is what participants need. So, we talked as a group about what we were doing: who we were, who Materoa had been representing within the imagined world, and what the pieces of paper represented. Even with the explanations there was still a continued intrigue about what the objects might be. The children surmised: "It must be something important—and I'm guessing it's something from within New Zealand if it matters to Māori", and "Maybe the first box was something from outside New Zealand and that's why it came another way?" In both the junior and senior groups, it was particularly rewarding to see students with knowledge of te reo taking leadership and explaining to their peers what the words of the ritual meant: "Her words were a karanga—she told us we need to take care of these precious things." When I asked if the woman who had visited could trust us, the children replied firmly that yes, she could.

Figure 39: Examining the artefacts

Deepening the learning

I invited the group to don their (imaginary) cotton gloves and prepare their (imaginary) iPads to take notes as we moved across the room to begin examining the objects. Rather than dividing them up, I asked the children to watch and then stand beside the object that interested them the most. I also suggested that, as I drew, they were welcome to discuss with their colleagues what they saw and any thoughts they had about what this might be. One by one I started to draw the objects, pausing now and again without any comment, to leave space for discussion and conversation. I didn't take part in the whispered conversations, I just allowed the children to talk among themselves. Gradually, the three objects appeared and, without instructions from me, children gathered around and discussed in great depth what they were seeing. Their speculations were quite wide-ranging including wondering if the sickle was some kind of weapon, imagining the kāheru might be an oar or a spear, and questioning whether the brooch was a bow and arrow or musical instrument. In the junior group, I invited some of the children to show their initial ideas through a frozen effigy.

Then I started to provide information to focus understanding. Initially, I just gave the information that all the objects were around 100 years old. Then I fed in the details of what they were made of and provided a photograph related to their use. At each point, the discussion deepened. Finally, I introduced the detailed background information. I could have done this by reading or handing out the information sheet but at the last minute I decided it would be more engaging to use a teacher-in-role voice. I moved between each of the drawings in turn and spoke in role as the objects, telling the story of what I had seen and whose hands had created and handled me over time. Children in both groups listened to these stories in total silence, so I could tell they were engaged.

Figure 40: Creating the story of the huia beak brooch

With the junior students, the story was all the background they received. I gave out the information sheets and the children worked on their ideas for an exhibit of their object of significance. Then we shared our ideas back. One group, all boys, presented their ideas for their exhibit as a gallery of animatronics showing the different stages of the huia beak's life. This included the bird in flight, the hunter catching it, the jeweller creating the brooch, and the brooch being worn at a party. It was clear the children had clear ideas about the different stages of the object's journey. With more time we could have re-emphasised the idea of trade and asked for the exhibit to include this, too. Another group was still in discussion about their exhibit and didn't have anything to share back, so I suggested we work together to create an exhibit featuring the kāheru in use. The children and the teachers stood around in a circle and I asked the children to describe the scene they wanted to depict. It involved a group of Māori teaching European settlers about traditional agricultural techniques. As details were described, individuals from the circle could step in and say "I am ..." before taking up a frozen position in the tableau. I encouraged them to think of fine details they could add to the image; for example, "I am the kete. The villager will carry her kumara home in me." Some of the students made links to familiar traditional stories in their contributions, evoking a story about Māui in which he observes people tilling the soil in the underworld: "I am Māui, transformed into a bird, watching from a branch above."

We closed the junior session with a look at the photographs of real objects and a discussion about what we'd found out about history from the experience. One of the children commented that the session had been "really cultural" while another noted differences between the stories we had told and those his koro told him. It was great to see children making connections with their prior experiences in this way.

Figure 41: Discussing the real-world artefacts

The tension

In preparing for the seniors in the afternoon, my main goal was to ensure that I remembered to include the tension. The juniors had given their attention, been interested and engaged but did not develop a sense of concern or investment, so I wanted to see if we could build this with the senior group. The session started exactly the same way, with the ritual opening, the revealing of the items through drawing, and the adding of details through speaking in role as the objects. This time, however, I also remembered to invite the class to imagine that bit of damage on the objects. Sure enough this seemed to help children develop a concern about their objects and invest more in their position as experts. This, combined with the maturity and confidence of the senior group, resulted in more discussion and readier buy-in to the imagined world. Children were very willing to discuss and surmise about the artefacts and there was a pleasing intensity and buzz throughout the session.

As before, the children divided naturally into three groups to focus on the exhibition of one object each. As they moved off, the first group, working with the kāheru, went into dramatic playing mode and played through the process of creating the exhibit. It was interesting to notice how reverent and careful they were when they carried the paper object across to the part of the room where their exhibit was to be. They then had in-depth discussions about whether the taonga could be handled by the public. They wanted to give an authentic, interactive experience, with opportunities to enjoy and touch the rich carvings on the object but they were concerned that the person who donated it would not be happy if it were touched. When that group shared back with the rest of the class, we saw them in role as museum experts setting up for the exhibition. They told us there was going to be "a little play" about how the tool was used and a replica so that people could touch and feel the carvings for themselves.

Figure 42: The jeweller hands over the finished brooch

The other two displays focused on the moment from the object's life where the damage occurred. The huia beak group showed a sequence of events from the hunting of the bird to the selling of the beak to the jeweller and finally the moment when the wearer of the brooch stumbled and fell while attending a ball. Interestingly, the person depicting the wearer of the brooch held the paper against her body to signify wearing it. Those working with the sickle wanted to depict the moment when the sickle became damaged during the harvesting of a particularly tough piece of harekeke. Once again, we worked as a whole class on recreating that moment. I used the "five levels of meaning-making" to guide my questioning and the picture we created became more and more layered as children contemplated the actions, motivations, investments, models, and values at play and used these to add careful details. This took time, and left little opportunity for out-of-role reflection at the end of the senior session. All the same, I sensed the children were excited and animated as they left despite it being last thing on a Friday afternoon. One girl came up me as the children were leaving and said, "I wish museums were really like this. I'd want to go to our museum!"

Figure 43: Museum display on harakeke harvesting

Outcomes

This short lesson was designed as a demonstration for teachers of how drama could be used to explore different world views and perspectives from New Zealand's history. While the lesson did not go very deeply into this issue, I knew teachers would be able to take the starting point we had explored and create longer experiences in their classrooms, in which some of the subtleties of encounter could be explored more deeply. The objects we worked with sowed the seed of the big idea, which was that encounters between settlers and Māori were a meeting of two world views, each with their own technologies and belief systems. From a teaching perspective, I think we achieved our objectives in demonstrating how ritual and frame distance could be used to give a sense of respectful distance. We were reminded of the importance of intrigue, parsimony, and tension in building a sense of investment. Teachers also commented on how much opportunity children had for exploration and peer-peer discussion even though the teaching involved the deliberate feeding in of historical facts and information. I was pleased the session allowed me to model the teacher compass, the five levels of meaning-making and the narrator/storyteller voice (see Chapter 5 for more on these). I was also happy with my spontaneous decision to use a teacher-in-role voice to convey the stories of the objects. For me, though, the most significant learning of all was the benefit of planning in partnership with Māori colleagues. This is something I am committed to doing in my future practice.

Links to curriculum

These short sessions gave opportunities for students to explore the key competencies. Particularly foregrounded was *understanding language, symbols and texts*, given the visual language children were required to decode during the opening and with the use of the drawings. There was a lot of speculative *thinking* as well as cooperative planning in the creation of the exhibits, which required *participation and contribution* from all. In terms of curriculum learning areas, the lesson met the following achievement objectives for Social Sciences at level two:

- Understand how cultural practices reflect and express people's customs, traditions and values.
- Understand how time and change affect people's lives.
- Understand how places influence people and people influence places.
- Understand how the status of Māori as tangata whenua is significant for communities in New Zealand.

Working through Mantle of the Expert also meant students worked in the Arts learning area, specifically the drama strands of Developing Ideas and Communicating and Interpreting. Some literacy was also involved in the visual language explored, and in the process of inference, reading, summarising, and presenting ideas from the written texts.

Afterword
In comparison with the other case studies in this book, this example is the most culturally responsive, in that it consciously draws on Māori histories and world views and input was actively sought from Māori colleagues before teaching. A next step would be to work in partnership from the beginning of the planning process. It would also be good to progress from teaching generic histories of the sort explored here to developing local stories of specific significance to iwi. For example, in our planning discussions, Materoa mentioned a local pre-Europe pa site in the Waikato region that had been famed for its large gardens before being lost to land confiscation. With time to research, and in partnership with iwi, it would have been powerful to see Dramatic Inquiry used in service of a specific local story. There is so much potential in bringing together the strengths of Dramatic Inquiry with the unique stories and histories of Aotearoa New Zealand, and this example only scratches the surface of what culturally sustaining Dramatic Inquiry could look like. I'm excited to continue my work with colleagues from this school, deepening our shared understandings as we select contexts and ways of working that are responsive to the school's local curriculum. Our goal for the future is to create learning experiences for children across the school to explore the region's critical histories and cultural stories in meaningful and engaging ways. We see this as part of reconceptualising and reconsidering Dramatic Inquiry within a New Zealand context.

More examples
The table below shows some further examples of Mantle of the Expert experiences I have planned and taught over the past 10 years. I hope these, along with the detailed examples already described, give some sense of the diverse activities that can occur within a Mantle of the Expert planning framework. Some things to note: first of all, the table only gives the responsible team, client, commission, and some tensions; other core elements are not included in the interests of space. Secondly, you will see the first three examples do not involve a clearly

defined responsible team but rather a generic blanket role. This is because they were written for younger participants (more on this variation later in the book). Thirdly, several of these examples originally had clients with real-world names (including the World Wide Fund for Nature and the Hamilton City Council) but I have changed my practice on this aspect. These days I always choose a fictional parallel instead. Finally, setting out planning ideas in a table like this can make it seem like the experiences emerged fully formed or that they felt coherent at the time—not so! What's not shown is the trial and error and the mulling over of multiple options that went on, particularly at the pre-planning phase. As we will see, it's often not until after a Mantle of the Expert is finished that the story really becomes clear.

Chapter 3 Three New Zealand examples

Table 3: Examples of Mantle of the Expert experiences

Title and Age / level	Curriculum focus / key learning goals	Responsible team and Frame	Client	Commission	Key tensions What if…?	Enduring understandings	More information
Little Wild Thing New entrants Year 1.	Literacy (oral language, picture books), myths and legends. All Key Competencies— especially relating to others, participating and contributing.	Helpers who understand what it's like to be lost and lonely.	A lost baby monster / little wild thing.	Help the monster find Max (his friend from *Where the Wild Things Are* storybook) and to navigate his way back to Wild Things land.	Little wild thing is too scared to talk to people, having been screamed at by Max's Mum when he went to the house. Little wild thing is really hungry but doesn't like human food very much. Little wild thing can't remember his way home and is too tired to walk.	We need to be careful not to judge harshly on first impressions. The places we call "home" can be special for many reasons. It can be hard to build trust. There are lots of ways to travel from place to place.	
Animal helpers Year 1–2.	Literacy (oral language) health. All Key Competencies— especially relating to others, managing self, understanding language, symbols and texts.	Helpers who understand what it's like to be unable to manage everything by yourself.	An elderly person who loves animals but is starting to be overwhelmed by the number of unwanted pets dropped off at their lifestyle block.	Assist with the immediate care of animals and consider long-term options to improve the situation.	Some cages are overcrowded. There has been a mix-up with the pet food labels. The elderly owner agrees to put up a notice at the gate but doesn't know what it should say. One of the dogs attacks and injures another animal.	Living things need certain basic requirements to survive. Sometimes it can be hard to say "no" but it's important to know your limits. People use signs and other forms of text to share important information with others.	
Traditional story problem solvers Year 2.	Literacy (oral language, picture books). Learning Languages—te reo, Social studies— Traditional stories. All Key Competencies especially participating and contributing, relating to others.	Mediators who are good at seeing both sides of an issue.	Kaitiaki of the forest.	Mediate between Rata, who wants to cut down a tree for a waka, and Tāne Mahuta, the god of forests and birds, who keeps making it stand back up.	Rata can't understand why he shouldn't just help himself to a tree from the forest. Tāne Mahuta sends a message with some of the key words in te reo Māori. Rata is reluctant to meet or talk about why he needs the waka— but insists it is for something important.	People tell traditional stories for many reasons, including sharing life lessons or morals. People and events in stories may be different from us but we might also recognise things about ourselves. The words and actions we use to convey our ideas can make a big difference to how they are received by others.	

Title and Age / level	Curriculum focus / key learning goals	Responsible team and Frame	Client	Commission	Key tensions What if....?	Enduring understandings	More information
Playground designers Year 3.	Design—birds-eye view drawing. Science—Natural world. Maths, estimation and measurement, mapping. All Key Competencies especially understanding language, symbols and texts.	Children's Playground designers with a history of creating exciting and unusual "themed" playgrounds.	Local councillor.	Design a playground for installation in a local reserve, to attract visitors and inform them about the resident short-tailed bat population.	A local resident's group raise objections to the development. A report shows that some of our design could interrupt the bats' flight paths. A local tai chi group currently uses the park every morning and values it as it is. There's taniwha resident in the nearby river.	As humans we share our environment with many other species and our actions have a direct impact on their survival. People in a community need to negotiate to make the most of shared social spaces.	Teacher's blog: http://hnsmantle.blogspot.co.nz/
Diamond Demolition Year 3-4.	Maths—number and estimation. Science—Chemical testing.	Demolition workers who are famous for safe practice.	The owner of a disused wool scouring factory.	Demolish a large brick tower, saving the bricks for resale and calculating their value.	There are safety concerns about explosives. The site is polluted with chemicals. A memorial plaque is discovered revealing the site was the scene of a major industrial accident.	Human activities have lasting impacts on land and natural resources Old buildings are valuable for the stories they can tell about our past Places where people have lost their lives take on a special significance and need to be respected.	
Toy museum Year 3-4.	Maths—Calculation Social studies—Human histories.	Museum curators who specialise in toys and who understand how to handle things of value.	David—a rich man who has previously donated his collection of fantastic toys.	Set up an exhibit of toys with sentimental value.	We are asked to calculate the 'value' of toys in the exhibition for insurance purposes. We are told we can restore David's favourite old teddy to look like new, but he may not recognize it.	'Value' is about more than financial worth. People value things that bring back special memories. Significant objects deserve to be handled with respect.	Teacher's blog: http://vivadrama-toymuseummantle.blogspot.co.nz/
Truth tellers documentary researchers Year 5-6.	Social Studies—Animal ethics. Literacy—Persuasive writing.	Documentary researchers with a reputation for seeking out the truth.	A representative of the World Wide Fund for Nature.	Research for a documentary into feral horses in New Zealand.	We discover the feral horses are threatening highly endangered native plants. One of the people we have interviewed pressurises us to keep important information out of the documentary.	Truth can be contested—often there are many points of view on the same issue. Conservation involves a careful balance between different interests and competing species.	Case study described in Fraser et al. (2013)

Chapter 3 Three New Zealand examples

Title and Age / level	Curriculum focus / key learning goals	Responsible team and Frame	Client	Commission	Key tensions What if...?	Enduring understandings	More information
ARS - Augmented reality designers Year 5-6.	Music / Sound Arts—Soundscapes. Science—desalination, temperature, PhD, research into endangered species.	Designers of immersive virtual reality simulations with a reputation for helping people who cannot access the "real" experiences they value.	The head of a large research aquarium.	Design a wrap-around simulation for a shark tank, to convince endangered breeding sharks they are still in the deepest ocean and thus prevent them eating their young.	The probe we send out to record ocean sounds picks up a whole lot of sound pollution and is unusable. We discover the project is being funded by a shark liver oil company.	Any living creature in captivity deserves to have its essential needs met. There are many ways in which creatures, and people, can feel captured or trapped. There are always two sides to a moral or ethical dilemma and it can be hard to choose what action to take.	Teacher's blog: https://goo.gl/wfakLJ
Sing 4-U Year 9 Drama class.	Study of a theatre form—Melodrama. Devising.	A team of singing telegram performers with a reputation for creating classy, bespoke performances for every occasion.	The best friend of a wealthy man who wants to propose to his much less well-off but very well educated girlfriend.	Create a singing telegram performance to convince the girlfriend to choose her young love and reject the attentions of an older man who is blackmailing her father (to be rendered in the Victorian melodrama style).	The girlfriend is doing a PhD in Victorian melodrama, so we need to get the details right. We risk legal action from the older man's lawyers unless we can make our characterisations so melodramatic he doesn't recognise himself. Time is short.	People tell stories full of tropes and stereotypes which can be comic but are rarely accurate. People use performance in many different ways and for different purposes. Many aspects of our popular culture have their roots in historical practices going back hundreds of years.	
In your corner—defence lawyers Year 10 English class.	English Literature—Character study of Iago, in Shakespeare's Othello.	Team of expert defence lawyers with a reputation for taking on tricky cases.	Public prosecutor.	Build a case for the defence in the trial of "the beast"—a man with no friends and family who persuaded his close friend to kill his wife.	Evidence is incomplete and we need to piece it together. Key characters from the case are unwilling to speak.	Some people believe there is good in everyone – others that people can be "evil". Sometimes works of art written a long time ago can resonate in powerful ways with contemporary issues and concerns.	
Street theatre players Year 12 Drama class	Study of a theatre form - Commedia del Arte, costume design and devising.	Regional theatre company with a reputation for flexibility, cutting-edge political comment and working on a low budget.	Local city councillor.	Establish a weekly performance on a small wooden stage in the weekend town market, providing education and satirical commentary on current social events.	People we have depicted in the scenes are offended. We have only a shoestring budget to design costumes.	Theatre can take many forms and serve many different purposes. When using satire one needs to balance comic impact with humane treatment of other people. Some aspects of theatre making have changed over time, others are timeless.	

Title and Age / level	Curriculum focus / key learning goals	Responsible team and Frame	Client	Commission	Key tensions What if…?	Enduring understandings	More information
Education researchers Adult university students.	Master's level study in pedagogy - specifically Mantle of the Expert itself.	Education researchers with a reputation for making research accessible to classroom practitioners.	Freda from the NZ Ministry of Learning.	Conduct a literature review of peer-reviewed research literature and present our findings in an accessible way for teachers.	There is very little peer-reviewed research on Mantle of the Expert. The client puts pressure on us to "sell" the approach to teachers.	There are important differences between research, inquiry, and advocacy. Notions of rigour and trustworthiness are vital in research. Even authoritative texts should be encountered with a critical and questioning mind.	
Welcome agency Adults with intellectual disability.	Building confidence and self-efficacy.	Welcoming agency with experience helping new arrivals to a city find their way around and settle in.	Tronville City Mayor.	Work with a homeless person found living by the riverbank. Help them into independent living. Teach them everyday skills.	It turns out the person is from another planet. The new arrival's lack of understanding of basic skills leads to him being ostracised and picked on.	Sometimes people are treated as outsiders when they are different. People who are disadvantaged may need extra support to get a "fair go".	
Project managers Senior Ministry of Education officials from Bangladesh.	Project management in NZ secondary schools.	International project management consultancy team with a reputation for supporting big budget projects while always maintaining our humanity.	Head of international relations at the NZ Ministry of Learning.	Carry out an audit of online project management materials available to NZ secondary schools and report on fitness for purpose—with particular reference to an emergency building project in East Suvalu (a Pacific Island nation under NZ jurisdiction).	There are communities within East Suvalu who are not well served by current school provision. We discover someone from the East Suvalu education department stands to gain financially from sale of land for building work.	It takes courage to speak truth to power. People need soft skills just as much as technical ones when running projects that involve people. Some professional skills are the same around the world—others depend on culture	Slideshow of learning story here https://goo.gl/gh3rTq

Chapter 4

Planning and teaching in Mantle of the Expert

This chapter—the longest in the book—will focus on the process by which experiences like those described in Chapter 3 can be planned and implemented. To do this, I will return to the weaving metaphor offered by our opening whakataukī. Specifically, we will consider the weaving of korowai, which are literally "mantles": a form of kākahu, or cloak, adorned with hukahuka or tassels (Hetet, 2018). The idea of considering Mantle of the Expert through the metaphor of korowai was originally suggested by a teacher in Northland 10 years ago, and the imagery has been further developed through conversations with many teaching colleagues and input from expert weavers (see Acknowledgements).

Before moving on, it's important to acknowledge the depths of significance within this chosen metaphor. The process of weaving a korowai is steeped in tikanga and mātauranga well beyond the scope of this book. It is a sacred art, the knowledge of which resides with its practitioners. In research for this book I have gained some preliminary understandings but I have not even scratched the surface of true knowledge, which comes from years of practice. So, I wish to be clear that this chapter is not an effort to represent the art form of weaving with any authority, nor to appropriate this knowledge. The only focus is to explore Mantle of the Expert through the lens of a rich and culturally situated metaphor. Instead of privileging the perspectives of the Pākehā worldview in which the Mantle of the Expert teaching approach was created and is usually discussed, I wish to operate respectfully in a cultural "third space" (Greenwood, 2001) to see what new understandings can be formed by introducing imagery from te ao Māori. As the principles set out in *Tātaiako* (Ministry of Education & New Zealand Teacher's Council, 2011) remind us, engaging with, acknowledging, and validating Māori culture can illuminate teaching practice in New Zealand and offer new ways of thinking and understanding for the benefit of all. I've certainly found my understanding enriched by considering this metaphor and hope you will too.

Introducing the weaving metaphor

Metaphors are more than poetic devices or clever rhetorical flourishes. As Guy Deutscher points out in *The Unfolding of Language*, metaphors are all around us, not only in the words we speak, but also deep in our thinking:

> Far from being a rare spark of poetic genius, the marvellous gift of a precious few, metaphor is an indispensable element in the thought-process of every one of us ... we use metaphors not because of any literary leanings or artistic ambitions but quite simply because metaphor is the chief mechanism through which we can describe and even grasp abstraction.
>
> (Deutscher, 2005, p. 117)

Lakoff and Johnson (2003) discuss this further in *Metaphors We Live By*, showing how metaphors not only describe but also shape our understanding. Metaphors allow us to use things we know about our physical and social experience to think about and explain more intangible things. If I tell you that my day yesterday was "a trial" you get a different insight than if I tell you it was "a chore". The day itself hasn't changed, but the way I evoke it has. Metaphors don't only express our perceptions and actions, they shape and form them. If I tell you I was "blown away" by Lakoff and Johnson's writing, I am using metaphoric language. You understand that the descriptions are not literal: I was not blown away in the sense of being knocked off my feet by the movement of air. The words are chosen because they give a flavour of how the ideas in the book impacted on my mind (oh, look there's another one!). The metaphor of **ideas as physical forces** is evoked. Metaphors can be so hard to spot that Lakoff and Johnson adopt the convention of using capital letters to draw attention to them. In this discussion, I will use bold print **like this**.

Once you notice how ubiquitous metaphors are, you realise how much they shape our understanding. For example, if, instead of ideas as physical forces I chose the metaphor of **ideas as viruses**, this opens a whole different way of looking at ideas; how they spread, infect others, and morph into new things. The whole concept of what an idea is shifts. This is what Lakoff and Johnson mean by how we "live by" our metaphors. In this book, I'm interested in providing insight into something complicated—Mantle of the Expert. I'm evoking the context of Aotearoa New Zealand and our stories and experiences. For this reason, I find the metaphor of **planning and teaching Mantle of the Expert as weaving a korowai** really fruitful.

There are several reasons why a metaphor associated with weaving appeals as a way of illuminating the teaching-and-learning within a Mantle of the Expert experience. For one thing, Dorothy Heathcote worked as a weaver in Northern England before she became an educator. In *Three Looms Waiting*, Heathcote describes how the mill's owner funded her studies at theatre school but advised there would be "three looms waiting" when she returned (Smedley, 1971). And the weaving metaphor takes on additional resonance when we bring it into a New Zealand context where traditional weaving in a range of fibres is an art form used to create an array of objects and garments including kete, poi, whāriki and kākahu. As Puketapu-Hetet points out, weaving has practical uses but is also infused with creative and spiritual significance:

> Weaving is more than just a product of manual skills. From the simple rourou basket to the prestigious kahu kiwi, weaving is endowed with the very essence of the spiritual values of Māori people. The ancient Polynesian belief is that the artist is a vehicle through whom the gods create. Art is sacred and interrelated with the concepts of mauri, mana, and tapu.
>
> (Puketapu-Hetet, 1989, p. 2)

To use this metaphor not only locates us firmly within the cultural context of New Zealand, it also evokes the idea that teaching is a complex artistic undertaking with significant and even sacred responsibilities attached.

The metaphor of teaching and learning as weaving is already familiar within the education discourse in New Zealand. The entire early childhood curriculum *Te Whāriki* (Ministry of Education, 2017) is presented through an extended weaving metaphor and this imagery persists through *Arts in the New Zealand Curriculum* (Ministry of Education, 2000) too. Teaching and learning in the four arts—dance, drama, music, and visual arts—is characterised in terms of four interwoven strands: Developing Practical Knowledge; Understanding the Arts in Context; Developing Ideas; and Communicating and Interpreting. So, working with a weaving metaphor builds on how teachers in New Zealand already conceptualise teaching, particularly in drama and the other arts.

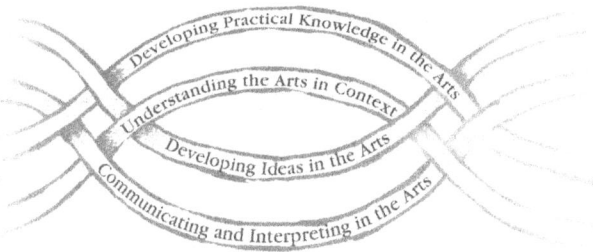

Figure 44: Strands from *Arts in the New Zealand Curriculum* (Ministry of Education, 2000, p.14)

With teaching and learning in drama already viewed this way, we can extend the metaphor to consider the special kind of weaving it takes to produce a Mantle of the Expert experience. Korowai are acknowledged as one of the most complex things a weaver can create (Hetet, 2016) and many would say that Mantle of the Expert is the most advanced and complex form of Dramatic Inquiry. And, just as not every drama is a Mantle of the Expert, not every kākahu is a korowai (Hetet, 2018). There are common methods for all kinds of kākahu: all are woven from carefully selected materials with a range of threads and colours used to generate patterns of significance to the creator and wearer. All include the use of tanikō and whatu stitches, and feathers and other flourishes might be used. However, it's the dark hukahuka, or tassels, that are the signature feature by which we can distinguish korowai (R. Hill, personal communication, 2020). In the same way, there are strategies and conventions that Mantle of the Expert shares with other teaching approaches and certain signature features by which we can distinguish it as unique.

The metaphoric parallels continue when we think about the underlying reasons for weaving. Anyone contemplating creating a full-sized korowai or any kind of kākahu needs to be open to growth in the cultural beliefs and philosophical values as much as the technical skills, since "weaving is not just about picking up practical skills, but learning the tikanga behind it as well" (Boynton, 2017). Tikanga for weavers is vast and includes: respect for ancestors and tradition; selection of materials; rituals for preparation; karakia and observing tapu; and many other considerations. Without claiming the same level of spiritual significance for the teacher of Mantle of the Expert, there are certain philosophical beliefs or paradigms that are assumed to be at the heart of the endeavour including: the importance of authentic relationship; the benefits of affective–cognitive learning; the embracing of complexity; the need to take multiple perspectives when forming understandings; and many more. In teaching, as in weaving, one could say that to focus on the technical practices of the approach without embracing these underpinning world views is to miss the true purpose of the practice.

Every Mantle of the Expert experience is different, just as each korowai is unique and represents both the weaver's and the wearer's identity and mana. "[The korowai is] regarded as a taonga tuku iko—a treasure handed down from generation to generation" (Ministry of Education, 2010, p. 12). They are often created and presented to acknowledge a significant achievement and are worn at a range of ceremonial occasions. Figure 45 shows korowai and other kākahu worn by students at their graduation, where the garments symbolise the wearer's achievement in reaching the culmination of their educational journey. To consider the korowai—this vivid and culturally familiar mantle—as a metaphor for teaching and learning in Mantle of the Expert symbolises the idea that teaching and learning is something woven with care and skill to serve a particular purpose and create something lasting and precious for others to benefit from.

Figure 45: Korowai and other kākahu worn at a graduation ceremony (photo by the author)

As with any metaphor, there are limitations to acknowledge, though on further examination, these also provide insights. First of all, Heathcote was keen to stress that "the Mantle is not a cloak by which a person is recognised. This is not a garment to cover" (Heathcote, 2009, pp. 1-2), while a korowai is both of these things: a physical garment and a way of recognising a person. However, to characterise it as "only" this would be to diminish what it represents, since "every korowai has a whakapapa, a story of where it came from and who the people were who brought it into being" (Te Rau Matatini, 2010, p. 24). In a sense, a korowai is itself a metaphor; a tangible manifestation of something beyond itself. The practice of weaving is endowed with significance far beyond creating the garment and the value lies not only in the finished item but also in the spiritual and cultural basis of the process. And this absolutely resonates with Heathcote's definition of Mantle of the Expert: "I use it as a quality: of leadership, carrying standards of behaviour, morality, responsibility, ethics and the spiritual basis of all action" (Heathcote, 2009, pp. 1-2).

Another potential limitation of the metaphor is that a korowai is generally created by one person and then presented as a finished object to be worn by another, whereas in Mantle of the Expert, the "cloak" of expertise and responsibility that develops around participants' shoulders is something that develops as a result of their own input as much as that of the teacher. On closer examination, again, this might not be such a mismatch. Perhaps we can say that in Mantle of the Expert teachers and participants are co-weavers, with the metaphoric korowai being the results of their collaborative efforts. Another way of looking at it would be to acknowledge that, in some senses, the recipient of a korowai does, in fact, collaborate towards its creation. They don't carry out the physical weaving but neither are they passive: they contribute the effort, commitment, grace, and energy for which the korowai is an acknowledgement. Similarly, participants in educational experiences are not passive recipients, but contribute their prior experiences and present energies to a process of ako with their peers and teachers.

Gathering materials

The weaving of a korowai begins with extensive preparation, and the same is true of weaving a Mantle of the Expert experience. Experienced weaver Te Kanawa reported that it generally took her 8 months to complete a korowai, the first 3 months being taken up in preparation (Te Rau Matatini, 2010, p. 39). Modern weavers may use a range of fibres, but traditional preparation involves harvesting and preparing harakeke, which has 60 different varieties, each with its own quality and strength (Puketapu-Hetet, 1989). Then there is teasing out the fibres, choosing dyes, selecting feathers or fur if these are to be used, preparing the hukahuka, and planning the overall design.

> Sometimes it is like a vision or a dream that comes to you, other times it comes together piece by piece until you have a picture of what it will look like ... What materials do I have at the moment? What do I need? Are any other people going to be involved? You will find when you start ... that [materials] will come to you, people will tell other people what you are doing and they will bring things to contribute to it. Other people will come along who will show you what to do. It's amazing how these things seem to happen at just the right time.
>
> (Te Rau Matatini, 2010, p. 42)

For the teacher planning a Mantle of the Expert experience, the process will also involve a lengthy process of gathering and researching, networking, and brainstorming. For the teacher, as for the weaver, the design process is thoughtful and deliberate, though not always predictable. Planning tools shared later in this book provide a structure to move through planning a Mantle of the Expert in a deliberate way, while other aspects will have a serendipitous quality; such as a chance conversation, picture, or news item that unexpectedly feeds into the thinking.

Whenu | Core elements

Once the weaver's preparations are complete, the weaving can begin. Generally this starts with laying out the key vertical threads—the whenu—to provide the fundamental integrity and structure. In a similar way, the Mantle of the Expert teacher starts by identifying key threads, or core elements, which are laid out as a foundation for the learning that will be co-created with participants. Below is a list of the "core elements" or fundamentals of Mantle of the Expert: those things that have to be planned by the teacher in advance and form the fundamentals on which the experience is woven. The list is displayed vertically to echo the image of whenu on a frame. We will come back to how these elements are planned for shortly but for now the important thing is the idea that planning begins by selecting and arranging certain threads in advance, and that these provide the integrity or underlying structure of the experience.

Ten Whenu/core elements to be prepared in advance:

- Fictional context
- Company/Enterprise/Responsible team of experts
- Frame/Backstory
- Commission
- Client
- Curriculum tasks framed as professional tasks
- Powerful positioning
- Drama for learning conventions
- Tensions
- Opportunities for reflection

For a weaver, the whenu will be much the same as for any other kākahu. It is the hukahuka tassels, prepared in advance to be introduced later, that mark this piece of work out as a korowai. With Mantle of the Expert, it is the core elements/whenu that give Mantle of the Expert its distinctiveness. These are what make it unique and allow us to distinguish it from other kinds of teaching, including Dramatic Inquiry approaches.

Ngā aho tapu | The sacred thread

The trickiest part of a korowai is the start. The first thread, which weaves the whenu together, is known as the aho tapu or sacred thread (the same term is used for the first line of the taniko border, too). This row is the foundation, it "requires a great deal of concentration as this is where the pattern is set" (Puketapu-Hetet, 1989, p. 4). The implication is that if this crucial first thread is securely in place, everything else will follow and hold together. In Mantle of the Expert, too, the teacher will often pay special attention to the opening "hook". If the start is right, this helps to ensure that the experience gets off to a strong beginning and the whole thing hangs together.

Aho | Interweavings

Having laid down the whenu or core threads and established the aho tapu, the weaver will start to work with the rest of the aho—the threads that run horizontally across the design and form the fabric of the creation. Aho are twined through the whenu using a binding technique known as whatu, with taniko to create borders and edges until gradually the fabric of the korowai emerges. As for the teacher, once initial planning is complete, they begin the process of introducing carefully selected activities that best allow participants to explore, learn, and develop understandings based on the pre-planned core elements. The carefully selected pedagogical aho are interwoven through the pre-planned core elements/whenu to create something with structure, strength, and integrity. Participants in the class also bring their own responses, perceptions, and reflections to contribute to the whole.

It is during the weaving process that the distinct qualities of what is being created will appear. For a korowai, the hukahuka tassels are introduced and with this the korowai takes its true form. With Mantle of the Expert, the defining features are laid down in the whenu/core elements. However, it is only when these are brought to life by the pedagogy that the Mantle of the Expert takes form. Many of the techniques, strategies, and conventions used in Mantle of the Expert are found in other teaching approaches, too, including other kinds of Dramatic Inquiry. Having said that, there are some which are more closely associated with Mantle of the Expert and can be called "signature pedagogies" (Shulman, 2005). I have identified a list of 10 pedagogies or aho which will be discussed in detail later. Notice that the list is presented horizontally, to suggest how they are woven across the whenu:

1. Keeping things safe and applying limits
2. Building relationships and fostering social practices
3. Taking on multiple perspectives
4. Questioning
5. Travelling in and out of worlds and through time and space
6. Introducing dramatic tension
7. Moving between teaching modes
8. Using drama strategies and conventions
9. Working with power: status, agency, and position
10. Encouraging critical thinking and reflection

Mahi whatu | Working the weave

The korowai weaver will use many hundreds of whatu to work the aho, creating effects, textures, and patterns in the emerging fabric. This can involve some thinking ahead to organise the threads so that certain patterns emerge or, sometimes, it might be that the design of the korowai emerges as you go. Hukahuka will be added, sometimes feathers will be used, and any bordering taniko designs will be incorporated. Some weavers will follow a pattern, while more experienced weavers may work without, drawing on their memories of designs that have been passed down for generations. As experienced weaver Rangimarie Hetet explained in an interview, "I know I prefer to do it without a graph—it's more interesting without. Because you have your pattern in your mind and you're building it up. Whereas if it's already there you already know what's going to happen" (Barclay, 1978). In a similar way, Mantle of the Expert may be taught by following a plan or by letting things unfold and trusting to experience. Either way, unexpected things can occur:

> Sometimes the korowai ends up different from what you had imagined at the beginning. Sometimes you start the journey then realise you need to go in a different direction. Sometimes other things in your life change or you end up with other materials, and your korowai reflects this.
>
> (Te Rau Matatini, 2010, p. 42)

Teachers, like weavers, know that, in the reality of the classroom, they will make new discoveries and change direction—sometimes creating something unexpected.

Ua | Hems and edges

Weaving a korowai, the work usually begins from the lower hem, with the decorative top taniko produced last. The garment needs to be inverted to see its finished form. The method for planning Mantle of the Expert outlined in this book is a bit like this, too, in that it works from the bottom up. As Heathcote put it, "the teacher can trust any Mantle to take to them to curriculum" (Heathcote, 1983), but you don't necessarily start there. Teachers will suit their planning to the level and curriculum needs of their learners, but the pre-planning process can feel "upside down" to teachers more accustomed to starting with curriculum and objectives. The process of "mapping" a Mantle of the Expert experience can have a backwards quality, too, in that often the last thing the teacher plans is the opening hook that will start the experience off. The same goes for participants working towards a commission: for them it is often necessary to start at the bottom, establishing the past history of the responsible team and building a sense of belief before turning to what the client has asked them to undertake.

Models and patterns

For a beginner weaver, it can be helpful to try out some smaller projects or other kinds of kākahu before tackling something as complex as a full-sized korowai (Hill, 2013). A first korowai may be a miniature; second and third attempts might look very much like those of a mentor. Similarly, the teacher will usually experiment with certain aspects of Mantle of the Expert before embarking on their first full-sized version.

A beginner teacher might try some drama for learning techniques or explore a "mini mantle" before they produce something original. Even then, suggested structures or patterns can be reassuring and later in the book you'll find suggestions for where to find good quality model plans and other advice for easing into using Mantle of the Expert. Whether following an existing pattern or creating a new one, no two korowai and no two Mantle of the Expert experiences will be the same. Each will be made of its own materials and each will tell its own story. But when a weaver works with attention to tikanga, the whenu, the aho, the whatu, and the taniko, if the design includes all these, and the distinctive hukahuka that distinguish a korowai from other forms of kākahu are in place, then we can consider the product of this process to be a korowai. Likewise, if a teacher plans with an awareness of the underlying principles and philosophies, attends to the core elements, interweaves the signature pedagogies, and incorporates inquiry, powerful positioning, and drama-for-learning modes in the process, then we can recognise the result as being an example of Mantle of the Expert.

The four stages of planning and teaching

For the teacher or the apprentice weaver, working from existing patterns and models is a great way to learn. Eventually, though, when you have tried out a few familiar patterns and adapted others' work, you will feel the urge to create your own. To help with this, I will now outline the planning process that was used to create the Mantle of the Expert experiences introduced in the previous chapter. The planning approach is characterised in four different stages and continues to draw on the metaphor of weaving. The first and second stages are carried out before teaching begins, while stages three and four happen once the teaching and learning is underway:

Stage 1. Laying out the whenu—pre-planning and research

Stage 2. Choosing the overall shape—mapping

Stage 3. Interweaving the aho—microplanning and teaching

Stage 4. Refining and defining—recording and assessment

There are a few things to acknowledge about the planning process outlined here. First of all, any description of planning as a set of linear steps is an over-simplification. The reality is you can expect the process to be creative, messy, and iterative—with all the frustrations and joys that implies. Secondly, the four stages outlined here are not the only way to plan for Mantle of the Expert. Alternatives can be found in Tim Taylor's *Beginner's Guide* (2016) and the various planning guides and handouts on the UK website www.mantleoftheexpert.com. One thing I've noticed in conversations with experienced colleagues is how everyone has their own way of assembling the elements that a Mantle of the Expert experience requires. These differences may be a result of the contrasting settings we work in and the unique ways we each learned about the approach. They are also an indication that Mantle of the Expert is not a "one-size-fits-all" programme with a recipe to follow, but a philosophy of teaching and learning in which individuals can find their own way. Please consider the process described here as a starting point for working out your own strategies.

Stage 1: Laying out the whenu—pre-planning and research

Like the korowai weaver, selecting and laying out the whenu, or vertical strands of their project, the teacher begins by attending to the core elements required for Mantle of the Expert. You may recall the 10 core elements discussed earlier. Here they are again—written horizontally this time for ease of reading:

- Fictional context
- Company/Enterprise/Responsible team of experts
- Frame/Backstory
- Commission
- Client
- Curriculum tasks framed as professional tasks
- Powerful positioning
- Drama for learning conventions
- Tensions
- Opportunities for reflection.

Like the korowai weaver, who may spend several months assembling materials, the teacher will benefit from exploring multiple possibilities before selecting the whenu, or core elements for a particular piece of work. The goal is to sift, select, and tease out potential planning material with care to build a good sense of the imagined worlds you will be operating in. This takes time and creative thinking.

The questions in the following flow diagram are designed to help you get your core elements in place. Supporting handouts are provided in the Appendix.

Figure 46: Pre-planning sequence

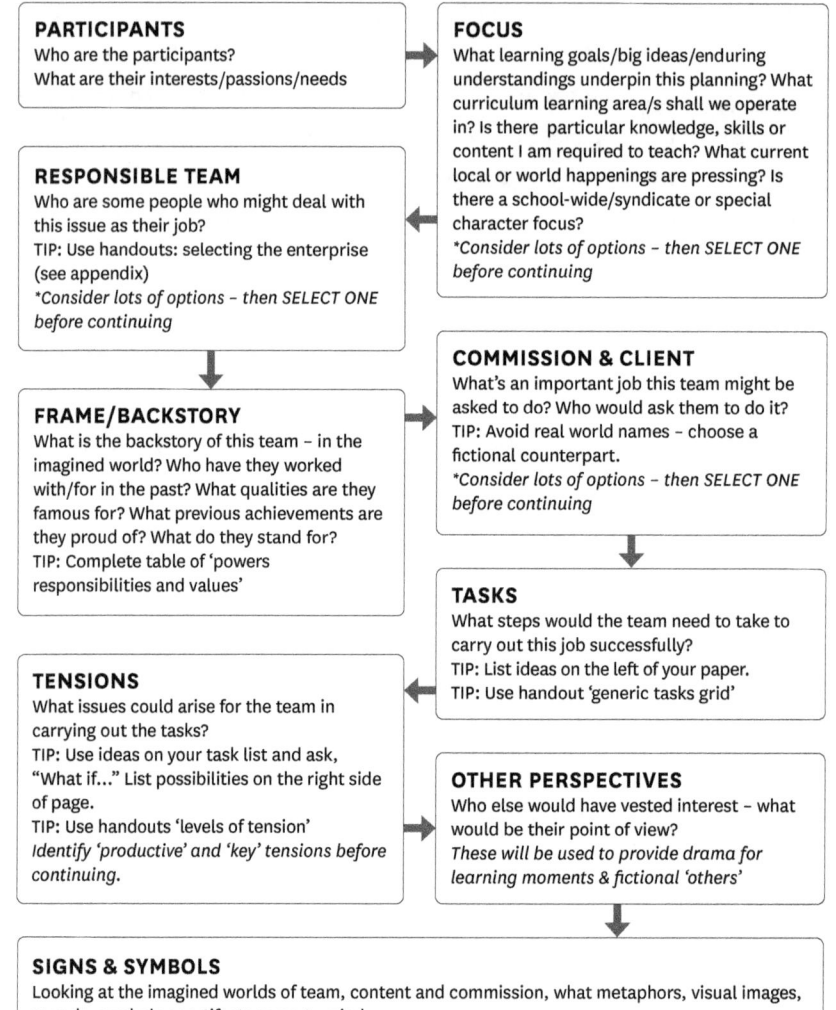

For more a dynamic version of this sequence, check out the "prezi" at the following link https://goo.gl/LERxg1

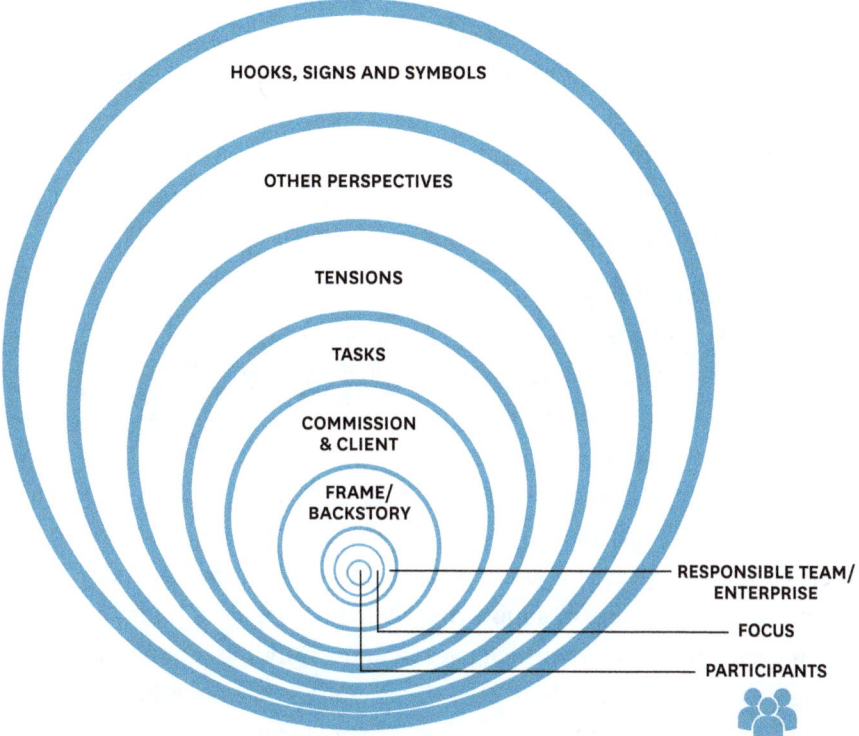

Figure 47: Pre-planning sequence—prezi version

In the prezi, the sequence of prompts is presented as a series of ever-expanding circles radiating out from a central point. Perhaps you can picture yourself, the Mantle of the Expert weaver, sitting beside a lake or pool, thinking about what materials you will use for your weaving and tossing a pebble into the water. As the ripples extend outwards, you'll consider a series of questions, beginning at the centre and moving out one circle at a time. Handouts and tips are embedded into the presentation.

Whichever diagram you work with, the best way to understand the pre-planning process is to have a go at it for yourself so I recommend having pen and paper to hand and responding to the prompts as you work though. That way, by the end of this exercise you should end up with a set of core elements/whenu from which your own original Mantle of the Expert could be woven. The process can take anything from a few minutes to a couple of hours and you can work through the process alone or in collaboration with colleagues.

With each prompt, or set of questions, you will be invited to come up with multiple responses, so try to write as much as possible. Sometimes you will be asked to select just one of your ideas to take forward. Try to resist the temptation to grasp the first idea and go with that. Keep thinking and exploring multiple possibilities. The more you allow your creative mind to get to work, the more likely you are to come up with unexpected and delicious ideas.

Pre-planning prompt 1

This first prompt is designed to help bring your participants to mind and think deeply about their needs and passions as a starting point.

> **PARTICIPANTS**
> Who are the participants?
> What are their interests/passions/needs

Write down as much information as you can to fill the page. Think about the age, gender, and cultural background of your class, what they care about, what motivates and excites them, and what works for them in supporting their learning. You might include achievement data or identified gaps in understanding, skills, or knowledge; or special needs here too. If you don't have much information about your participants, just write what you do know, or find out more by talking to other teachers. The idea is not necessarily that you will tailor your planning to the passions of your participants. It's more about taking time to acknowledge them and placing them at the heart of the planning. You will find that what you write here will "trickle down" into your later planning. There is no requirement to select one answer here. On the contrary, the idea is that your mind will keep all this information in the background as you continue to plan. Once you have written down as much information as you can think of, move to a new page and the next prompt.

Planning in practice: *In the Shark Tank example, planning began a couple of months ahead of teaching. The class was a mixed-ability group of 30 Year 5 children, around 10 years old. Class teacher Andy and I met to talk about the class and he had lots to tell me. Usually, I rely on the teacher's intuitions or assessment data for information about participants, but in this case Andy had conducted an exercise with the* *children where he asked them to write on sticky notes the things they most enjoy learning about, and what they wish they could do at school. So we used that data. Dominant themes were: animals, digital technology, and making things.*

Pre-planning prompt 2

The second prompt invites you to consider the curriculum focus, or learning goals for the experience. This is where you'll decide what content you will explore, or what aspect of human knowledge or understanding you and your participants will "operate" on together (Heathcote, 2009).

> **FOCUS**
> What learning goals/big ideas/enduring understandings underpin this planning? What curriculum learning area/s shall we operate in? Is there particular knowledge, skills or content I am required to teach? What current local or world happenings are pressing? Is there a school-wide/syndicate or special character focus?
> *Consider lots of options – then SELECT ONE before continuing*

To be clear, I'm not talking here about the specific learning intentions (LIs) that many teachers are accustomed to generating for planning. These will come later. What's required is something broader: the big ideas, curriculum learning areas, focus topics, or enduring or conceptual understandings that will underpin your planning. If you are lucky enough to be in a position to choose any curriculum learning focus, you might select something your learners have previously had little exposure to. If you are concerned at stepping into a curriculum learning area that is not a strength, you may find that planning in Mantle of the Expert provides you with the structure, authenticity of context, and tasks you need to feel confident.

Sometimes teachers resist selecting a focus in this way: those with a commitment to student-led learning may feel it's important to allow students to pursue their own areas of interest; and others may prefer to express their learning goals in terms of learning dispositions, mindsets, values, and competencies, not content focus. Certainly, we wish to foster student-led inquiry and we are fortunate in Aotearoa New Zealand that our curriculum frameworks foreground values, principles, and key competencies over content and subject knowledge. However, with Mantle of the Expert, you don't have to choose between the *how* and the *what* of learning, as the approach allows you to foster both, through inquiry within clear boundaries. Participants will have agency and lead the learning within a focused area of content.

If you are a specialist teacher you are likely to have learning goals from a particular curriculum learning area. You may also have specific assessments that participants will undertake and your planning may be geared around what is required for those. If so, write down the curriculum learning area or areas that will be your focus and any specific requirements for assessment within that. For specialist teachers planning collaboratively with others to support cross-curriculum integration, there may be a number of these content-specific goals from different learning areas to be considered in the one piece of planning. If so, record all of these here. More advice on planning for the specialist classroom can be found later in this book.

If you are planning for a generalist classroom, where the whole curriculum is taught, then in theory, you have the whole range of curriculum learning areas to choose from. In reality, however, most generalist teachers are not entirely free to choose a learning focus. Most have expectations to plan within curriculum priorities chosen by their syndicate or across the whole school, while some have special character qualities to consider. And schools will often have an expectation for how planning will begin: some start with topics like Matariki, the Anzacs, or robotics; others work from themes, such as sustainability or manaakitanga; some look at a big question or big idea, like "Who am I in the world?" or "What is a healthy lifestyle?"; while others develop enduring understandings, such as "human actions are having serious impacts on climate" and start there. If you are working within any pre-existing expectations, write these down and start from there. Even if you find yourself thinking of something that seems uncreative: "I have to do something on the rugby world cup", or "This lot need more on fractions", don't worry. Remember, you can rely on the Mantle of the Expert planning process to result in authentic cross-curricula learning experiences by putting the learning focus into meaningful, complex contexts. Fill the page with as many ideas as possible.

Before moving on, you will need to select just one from your list of ideas. Commit to it by highlighting or underlining it. Then, taking this idea, proceed to the next prompt. Remember, by choosing one learning focus, you are not rejecting the other ideas. Far from being wasted, you will find they inform and percolate through your planning. And, of course, should you decide you prefer a different focus later, you can always go back and select an alternative one to work with.

Planning in practice: *Andy didn't have any particular curriculum learning areas he was expected to teach, though he told me that for the term ahead the whole school was exploring the big idea of sustainability, so we wrote that down. We thought about what curriculum learning areas would align with the interests expressed by the children and science and technology were obvious standouts. After a good deal of thought, and listing possible ideas—including robotics, recycling, and electronics—we chose the focus of "rare or endangered animals" and crafted some enduring understandings we wanted children to grapple with, including "the actions of humans impact on the survival of other species". While we focused in on a particular learning area, the wider conversations about technology and sustainability were not forgotten. They surfaced again and played an important part in the planning later on.*

Pre-planning prompt 3

The next prompt is designed to help you with another core element or whenu of Mantle of the Expert, which is the selection of a fictional responsible team (sometimes a company

> **RESPONSIBLE TEAM**
> Who are some people who might deal with this issue as their job?
> TIP: Use handouts: selecting the enterprise (see appendix)
> *Consider lots of options – then SELECT ONE before continuing

or enterprise) for participants to be part of in the imagined world. Looking at the idea you chose from your previous page, ask yourself, "Who are some people in the real world who might deal with this issue as their job?" and "Who are the experts in this field?" This prompt question takes the broad topic or idea and conjures up a narrow and specific realm of expertise for participants to inhabit. I have learned it is important to resist settling on the first or most obvious possibility here. If something leaps to mind, write it down but then keep thinking: the most fruitful ideas at this point arise from thinking laterally. The planning tool, "Selecting the Enterprise", can really help with this process (see the Appendix). The handout gives a whole list of types of teams and will help you find a broad range of creative ideas. Challenge yourself to try and come up with at least one team per category on the handout. You should find the page quickly fills with multiple possibilities, each representing a different potential Mantle of the Expert experience. For the purposes of planning you will need to select just one of these. Then we can move on to the next prompt.

Planning in practice: *Taking the idea of "rare or endangered animals", Andy and I asked ourselves, "Who are some people from the real world who might deal with these issues professionally?" We had lots of ideas, particularly when we used the "Possible Enterprises" handout and we challenged ourselves to write down at least one idea for every heading. Ideas included people who breed special animals to go into space, people who run animal shelters, and those who run conservation reserves for native species. We tried not to jump on the first idea but let ourselves explore multiple possibilities. After a great deal of discussion, we settled on the idea of a responsible team that specialises in creating artificial environments for animals as part of zoo design. You can see how the children's interest in technology and animals played into this thinking. It also seemed to fit well with the school-wide theme of sustainability.*

Pre-planning prompt 4

This next prompt is designed to help frame the responsible team and provide a backstory to help you see the imagined team as three-dimensional, realistic, and complex. As explained in Chapter 2, framing helps

> **FRAME/BACKSTORY**
> What is the backstory of this team – in the imagined world? Who have they worked with/for in the past? What qualities are they famous for? What previous achievements are they proud of? What do they stand for?
> TIP: Complete table of 'powers responsibilities and values'

us understand how roles are played differently depending on points of view, responsibility, and other factors, so it's an important core element or whenu to get right at this stage of planning. Framing helps ensure the group has a shared perspective or point of view that goes beyond a simple job title or role. For example, imagining we are a group of archaeologists suggests some common skills, a shared language, and possibly some joint interests. But imagining we are archaeologists with a reputation for working in partnership with indigenous people, and a shared commitment to removing as little as possible from the site, deepens the bonds and brings an implied sense of responsibility and shared point of view (Bowell & Heap, 2013).

The frame helps establish the responsibilities the team will carry, what they stand for, and what binds them as a collective. The fictional teams in Mantle of the Expert are always experienced professionals with the highest ethical and moral reputations. They are not new at the job but have past experience; a backstory to be proud of. Some of this will be co-constructed with participants but there are aspects that you, as teacher, need to establish before the teaching begins. By establishing the history and ethical foundations of the fictional team at the planning stage, you achieve a number of things: first you are signalling the dispositions, mindsets, and values that are appropriate for real-world learning; secondly, you are ensuring your participants will have a way to see themselves in the fictional team. For, even if the specific expert skills of the team are unfamiliar, children can relate to transferable ideas such as being ethical and using sustainable practices; thirdly, and finally, framing at this point also helps you establish the "givens" of the imagined world, so that when you invite participants to step into it, everyone has a shared idea of what's going on and what's important.

The prompts invite you to think about what your chosen team might be famous for, what they might have achieved in the past, who they might have worked for, what they might be responsible for, and what they might stand for. Tim Taylor suggests three headings to help you go about this in a systematic way:

- **Powers**: The team's authority: its decision-making powers and circle of influence.
- **Responsibilities**: The team's duties and responsibilities to client, content and other people.
- **Values**: The team's beliefs and values: what they stand for, their professional code of conduct, and their belief systems. (Taylor, 2016, p. 120)

I've included a table in the Appendix to help you record your thinking under these headings in relation to your imagined team. To complete it, you will need to use your imagination based on what you know about expert teams in the real world. Better still, take time to research some real-world teams in the area of expertise you have chosen; this will help get a three-dimensional view of the profession. Having completed the table, you should have a much stronger sense of coherence between your responsible team and the imagined world they inhabit. You'll also have a sense of the capacities and the limits they will operate within. To express this in the language of Foucault, you will have negotiated the "habitus" your imagined team will be working within and the spaces for agency that your planning will open up.

Planning in practice: *In 2013 I didn't know about how useful a table of powers, responsibilities, and values could be. However, I was aware of the importance of framing, so Andy and I discussed what the professional team might stand for or specialise in. Given the children's interest in digital technology, we worked around to the idea that the team's speciality might be virtual environments. Perhaps our company might be famed for making zoo animals' experience as stress-free as possible through the use of digital technology such as projections, soundscapes, and simulations. This framed the team as having a responsibility for welfare and wellbeing. We also thought about how they might be asked to use sustainable materials in constructing their environments—thus framing them as having a responsibility for the natural world.*

Pre-planning prompt 5

This next prompt allows us to tease out two more whenu/ core elements as we decide on a commission and client. We do this by asking what important project in the imagined world

> **COMMISSION & CLIENT**
> What's an important job this team might be asked to do? Who would ask them to do it?
> TIP: Avoid real world names – choose a fictional counterpart.
> *Consider lots of options – then SELECT ONE before continuing

our responsible team might be asked to carry out and which individual or organisation might ask them to undertake it. You may find you've carried a clear idea from the start about what you'd like your responsible team to do. That's valid and you should write that down. But do take the time to consider other possibilities as well. The trick here is to remember the duality of real and imagined worlds and that you are planning for both. As teacher, you are planning for this group of learners in the real world but, just as importantly, you are considering possibilities for the expert team within the fictional world. In fact, at this point in the planning it can be useful to prioritise the group's fictional team identity over and above their real-world one. When choosing what the commission is and who the client might be, try asking yourself, "What's a project an expert team like this might be asked to undertake?" *before* considering, "Does this support what I want my learners to do?" It is in this kind of thinking that the difference between Mantle of the Expert and other project-based approaches to inquiry becomes very evident; you stop only thinking of the participants as learners of a particular age and ability level, and start also imagining them as responsible experts who are in demand for their skills and abilities. It doesn't matter whether your participants are aged 5 or 55, you can take steps later to ensure that activities are age- and level-appropriate. At this stage, what matters is to position them as competent, responsible, and capable professionals. In this spirit, it's also important to ensure that both client and commission are high stakes—which might mean they are high-status figures asking for an important job or might mean the client and commission have a strong emotional connection for the participants.

With Mantle of the Expert, unlike the commission model, both client and commission will be fictional. Your participants will not actually undertake a project in the real world, nor will a real individual or organisation be named as the recipients of this. In order to emphasise this, I also suggest you don't choose real-world entities for your imagined clients. When planning, you'll certainly find real-world examples come to mind, such as the World Wide Fund for Nature, NASA, the Ministry of Education, or your local city council. However, my very strong advice is to invent a fictional parallel to the real-world entities; for example, you could replace the real organisations listed above with fictional counterparts such as the Global Fund for Nature, the Pacific Space programme, the Ministry for Learning, or Tronham City Council. Many examples of Mantle of the Expert planning you can find online do use the names of real-world entities as fictional clients—including some I have written. However, I've deliberately changed my approach in recent times to reinforce the fictional aspect. You can read more about the reasons for this in the Cautionary Tales in Chapter 6, as well as advice about choosing an ordinary sounding name rather than going for something light-hearted.

Another thing worth considering is how to keep the fictional commission narrow. Being imaginary, the commission does not need to be limited by real-life constraints like budget, time, or lack of expertise or equipment. However, the more specific the commission is, the more focused the inquiry process will be—which in turn will deepen the learning across the curriculum. And, while it might sound counterintuitive, a narrow and specific commission will also enhance opportunities for ownership and agency from the participants, by providing the security of clear boundaries within which to collaborate, make decisions, and take action. For example, rather than thinking of the commission in terms of a broad sweeping responsibility such as "taking care of a sacred maunga", try to think of a time-bound project in a specific place with a distinct outcome, such as "designing a new visitor centre for the preservation society that takes into account this maunga's special character". Narrowing in the commission and client can result in totally different directions for the learning.

Once again, fill a page with possibilities. You'll find that each commission you think of will suggest a whole range of clients and vice versa. You'll also probably find yourself switching back to and reworking and changing the core elements you thought you'd already decided on. That's fine! Although this planning process is laid out in a linear step-by-step way, it's unlikely your thinking will work like that. Eventually, in this iterative back-and-forth way, you will come up with a company or responsible team, a frame, a client, and commission that seems rich and interesting and—importantly—makes sense within the fictional world.

Planning in practice: *Andy and I initially thought our company might be commissioned by a zoo, to create an enclosure for a baby white rhino, with the challenge being to make it seem to the animals that they are actually out in their natural habitat. We liked how this would take us into ethical territory by raising questions about whether captivity of animals is defensible, and whether being convinced one is free is different from actually being free. I have no doubt that a Mantle of the Expert based on creating a rhino enclosure would have engaged the children and created an effective Mantle of the Expert experience. However, at this point, one of the student teachers questioned whether the commission could be made more relevant to the local New Zealand context.*

We toyed with the idea of replacing the rhino in our commission with an endangered Hector's dolphin but then questioned whether we might have lost an edge of excitement in shifting from a bulky, strong animal like a rhino to a gentle creature like a dolphin. Someone suggested sharks and we went online to look at breeds of sharks found in New Zealand waters. That's where we discovered the Dumb Gulper shark—a real creature also found in some places off the coast of New Zealand. We decided the team could be asked to design an environment for captive sharks that is so realistic it convinces them they are still out at sea. So we finally had our commission. As for whom the client should be, we settled on the idea of a research aquarium run by the NZ Fisheries Department: an authentic-sounding, but entirely fictional organisation.

Pre-planning prompt 6

Having settled on a responsible team, client, and commission, the next prompt is designed to help with the core element of curriculum tasks framed as pro-

> **TASKS**
> What steps would the team need to take to carry out this job successfully?
> TIP: Write ideas in a list on the left of your paper.
> TIP: Use handout 'generic tasks grid'

fessional tasks. Don't worry yet about the sequence of these; remember, we are still at the pre-planning stage and just trying to gather materials that might be used in our weaving. For now, what matters is to ensure that everything the participants are asked to do during the experience makes sense as something the professional team would do. We don't expect participants in a Mantle of the Expert to do any task for its own sake or to meet curriculum requirements. Once again, this style of planning works best if you resist thinking of the tasks as things happening in a classroom in the real world. Instead, project yourself into the fictional world of expert team, commission, and client you have settled on and ask yourself, "What steps would this team need to take to carry out this job professionally? Where would they start? What materials and equipment would they need? Who might they need to talk to? Would they need to travel?" and so on. Stay playful and authentic to the fictional world you are creating and the learning in the real world will be the stronger for it. I suggest you write the list of tasks down the left-hand side of your page, for reasons I'll explain in a moment.

As you identify tasks the responsible team would need to do, be careful not to censor your ideas by thinking, "We could never do that in the classroom." The wonder of working in a fictional context is that nothing you could write at this point is logistically impossible, too expensive, or too time consuming. If your team needs to travel to the moon, raise a million dollars, gestate a baby killer-whale, or build a hadron collider—we can solve all that with the use of drama. It's just as important not to censor yourself on the basis that a task is beyond your learners' capabilities or that you don't know how your ideas fit with the curriculum. Trust that quality curriculum learning will emerge and be reassured that you can tailor the tasks to suit the age level and ability—that comes later. For now, simply focus on identifying as authentically as possible the professional requirements and the specific steps required to carry out the commission.

The only time you might need to censor yourself is if you get carried away and start listing things that go beyond the bounds of the commission. I remember doing this when planning a Mantle of the Expert about a specialist team of playground designers with a reputation for safety. This team was commissioned by the local council to design a bat-themed playground. I made a list of tasks including developing birds-eye view drawings, doing research into bat behaviour and movements, and advising on the location and installation of the playground. However, when I found myself writing that the team could offer advice on developing bat habitats in another part of town, I crossed that idea out as I realised this went beyond the range of tasks likely to be undertaken by playground designers. Keeping your team identity, commission, and client firmly in mind as you map out possible professional tasks will help you focus your tasks and make them more authentic. Remember, too, that in Mantle of the Expert we only ever ask participants to operate in ethical and legal ways—so your client, commission, and tasks should not involve anything criminal, underhand, or even vaguely dodgy. See Chapter 6 for some examples of the fallout from making this mistake.

You may find you can create this list of tasks with relative ease. Our brains are great at projecting into a fictional situation and imagining what we would need to do if we were someone else. And this is the very same ability that the participants will use once you are underway.

But if you do struggle—or want some additional ideas—there's another planning tool to help. The generic tasks grid found in the Appendix gives a list of the kinds of things all teams do when they are carrying out their business. The generic tasks are divided into four categories:

- tasks involving material resources
- tasks with social/cultural/historical dimensions
- tasks involving interactions within the team
- tasks involving interactions with the fictional world beyond the team.

Two quick comments about these categories. Firstly, for those of us teaching in the context of Aotearoa New Zealand, the cultural lens will be applied to all boxes, not just those identified in that category. If you look at the generic tasks listed, it's hard to see any that do not have a cultural dimension to them, assuming you are creating a fictional team that operates in a culturally sustaining manner—and why wouldn't you? Indeed, keeping cultural considerations in the forefront of your mind will assist you in generating many authentic professional tasks. For example, the responsible team may need time to develop culturally inclusive meeting protocols, consider tikanga at mealtimes, and incorporate te reo Māori in signage. A second thing to consider in a contemporary context is how many of the interactions listed on the chart will happen in virtual/digital spaces as well as face to face or in written form. The chart as written does not acknowledge this but if you keep in mind digital possibilities, you will come up with a whole lot of additional tasks for your list. After you have listed as many tasks as you can think of, we will move on to consider the next prompt.

Planning in practice: *Working together, the student teachers and I listed naturally arising tasks, using the generic tasks grid as a guide. We could see that shark tank designers would need to carry out research about the shark itself, gather and interpret data from the natural environment, and test things like water pressure, sediment, and light levels. They would need to understand volume and measurement to get a handle on the size of the tank as well as pH levels, temperature, and salinity to get a match between the natural deep-sea environment of the shark and the artificial one they wanted to create. They might need to* consider soundscapes to reproduce the sounds heard by the shark in its natural home and they would need to think about systems for feeding and dealing with waste. We also noted that they would need to use soft skills of interviewing and negotiation to speak to shark experts and our clients. And they would need to present their ideas both orally and in written form through plans and reports. We knew these professional tasks would need to be pitched at appropriate levels within the curriculum and we could already see how these activities could translate into curriculum tasks in Music—Sound Arts, and Technology as well as in the domains of science, maths, and literacy.

Pre-planning prompt 7

By now you have a lot of potential material to weave your Mantle of the Expert together. But don't stop yet! This next prompt is where we consider one of the most important elements in Mantle of the Expert, and indeed all dramatic activity—tension. In

> **TENSIONS**
> What issues could arise for the team in carrying out the tasks?
> TIP: Use ideas on your task list and ask, "What if…" List possibilities on the right of you paper.
> TIP: Use handouts 'levels of tension'
> Identify 'productive' and 'key' tensions before continuing.

Mantle of the Expert, as in theatre, TV, or movies, dramatic tensions keep things interesting and engaging. Whether it's a minor tension such as a new piece of information from the client, something major like an explosion at the factory, or something complicated and confronting like a betrayal by a member of the team, dramatic tensions in Mantle of the Expert create opportunities for authentic encounters with curriculum. They also allow participants to grapple with complexity, develop resilience, solve problems, and learn in an authentic, exhilarating, and safe way.

Some Mantle of the Expert practitioners prefer not to pre-plan tensions. They know issues will naturally arise as the Mantle of the Expert experience develops, and they trust themselves to respond to these in the moment to create productive learning experiences. However, there are several advantages to thinking through tensions in advance. For one thing, you might find yourself creating a curriculum task that requires resources such as science equipment, art materials, or a field trip. If you've planned ahead you'll have more time to ensure you have these prepared. Another advantage to thinking ahead is that you can distinguish between minor, productive tensions and more major ones. Having both kinds prepared is useful when scoping out the overall shape of a Mantle of the Expert experience.

One of the best ways to identify authentic tensions within the imagined world is to go back to all the professional tasks you have listed and, for each one, ask yourself, "What if ...?" If you've written your tasks on the left of the page, you can now ask yourself, "What if ...?" in relation to each task and write your ideas on the right. It's always delightful to witness teachers become storytellers and playwrights at this stage as they imagine the multiple tensions that could arise in the fictional world they have created. Tensions can arise from facing a small obstacle such as losing the car keys or pressures of time or minor miscommunications. Tensions can even be positive in origin, such as when a team is awarded a prize and is faced with the question of who should represent the company at the award ceremony. If you need help thinking of possible "what ifs" there's another planning tool to help—Heathcote's list of 12 levels of tension. Again, this can be found in the Appendix.

It can be tempting when planning tensions to get a bit carried away. Dramatic tensions, like real-life ones, are not limited to huge conflicts or problems. To ensure your ideas are realistic, keep the commission in mind throughout and include the subtle challenges: "What if we run short of time?" or "What if someone we need to interview is shy?"—along with the more significant roadblocks, like "What if someone on the team sells our secrets to the competition?" or "What if we accidentally injure one of the kiwi?" While it can be tempting, especially if you are a fan of action movies, to choose cataclysmic tensions—"What if the office buildings burn down?" or "What if a tornado strikes?"—these may well be less useful for your teaching. It's important to bear in mind that we are looking for tensions that the team has the wherewithal to solve.

When you have a page full of "what ifs", see if you can distinguish between two categories of tension in your list. First, there are those we might call "productive" tensions—the minor things that keep things interesting and challenging. And second, there are "key" tensions which would really challenge the responsible team. As the Mantle of the Expert experience unfolds, we will need lots of productive tensions, but only one or two key tensions. It's important that the key tensions confront the team in terms of their professional standards, ethics, and values but also that they are things the team has the capacity to withstand, overcome, and grow from. You could label the productive and key tensions and decide which you are most keen to include. While you will not use every one of the tensions you've thought of, you can now rest assured you have the basis for a series of episodes that will be engaging and educational for your participants.

Planning in practice: *In creating the fictional backstory to our commission we had already decided to introduce the idea that these sharks were known to eat their young in captivity, so we wrote this down as a "given" that was also a productive tension. Looking at our tasks and using the stem "what if..." and the handout, it was easy to come up with possible tensions related to the creation of a shark tank environment: What if there is a limited budget? What if the tank needs to be built in a hurry before the female gives birth? What if the shark becomes distressed as it is transported to the tank? What if the probe sent to collect samples from the seabed breaks down, or the samples from the sea are corrupted somehow? What if someone misreads the thermostat on the tank? What if it was discovered that the sponsors for the shark breeding programme were shark liver oil manufacturers? Some of these seemed "productive" and others major enough to constitute a key tension. We noted them all on paper, knowing they might not all be used but could all be useful for building engagement and leading to curriculum.*

Pre-planning prompt 8

We now reach the penultimate prompt, which invites us to consider the question of other points of view. This prompt is related to a fundamental principle of drama, that of walking in other people's shoes and empathising with things from their perspective. When you come to weave your Mantle of the Expert you will not only ask the participants to imagine they are a responsible team, you will also use drama strategies and conventions to explore many other perspectives on the issues at hand. This is an important counterpoint to the shared perspective of the

> **OTHER PERSPECTIVES**
> Who else would have vested interest – what would be their point of view?
> *These will be used to provide drama for learning moments and fictional 'others'*

team that you have established through framing, so it's worth having a think in advance about what some of those alternative perspectives might be. You might think of people directly impacted by the work of the responsible team; for example, the neighbours, people from a competing company, family members, or someone in the fictional world. Your thinking can also extend to non-human entities including the local wildlife or the mountain or river and indeed supernatural figures such as atua, taniwha, or patupaiarehe. Remember, too, to consider what vested interest might mean in cultural terms. For example, what perspective might local iwi have on this issue? What about a recent immigrant from another culture? With the power of drama we can also include perspectives from other time periods. Take a moment to include perspectives of ancestors and even future generations.

As before, there will be lots and lots of answers to these questions and you are encouraged to write down as many as you can think of. Remember to keep the commission closely in mind so that your ideas do not go off in too many directions. You won't use all these ideas in your planning but you will use some. And simply going through the process of bringing to mind these multiple perspectives will help you to flex your own "empathy muscles" for stronger drama teaching. As you write, you may find yourself once again revisiting your commission, or thinking of a really exciting new tension. This is all a rich part of the process of deciding which whenu you will lay down for your weaving. This part of the planning should be fun and creative, so enjoy it!

Planning in practice: *We could think of several viewpoints on the issue of captive shark breeding. We realised we could explore the shark's perspective on being captured and taken to a new home. Then there were the research scientists and aquarium staff, whose perspective would be different from that of our team. We'd also read in our research that some people use sharks' body parts for health products. Perhaps we could consider the motivations and perspectives of the producers and consumers of those products. All these perspectives gave us potential moments for the use of drama to build empathy in our planning and helped us thoughtfully complicate the picture. This was also where we considered cultural perspectives by raising the question, "What if local iwi have an objection to these sharks being bred in captivity?" If I was doing the planning now, I would not wait until the "other perspectives"* point in the process to consider te ao Māori perspectives, but would introduce these as part of the company identity and the "naturally arising" tasks.

Pre-planning prompt 9

The final prompt is to encourage you to identify metaphors, visual images, sounds, symbols, or artefacts related to the fictional world you have created. Images and symbols identified ahead of

> **SIGNS & SYMBOLS**
> Looking at the imagined worlds of team, content and commission, what metaphors, visual images, sounds, symbols or artifacts come to mind.
> *These will be useful to add artistry at different points including the 'hook'.*

time can be used during teaching to enhance the aesthetic and theatrical aspects of a Mantle of the Expert. Among other things, signs and symbols can be used to provide: a striking opening such as the pool of blood in Taylor and Edmiston's *The Mountain Rescue Team* (Taylor & Edmiston, n.d.); an image for the letterhead on the letter of commission; or an emotionally charged drama activity such as a doll being used to signify the presence of a missing child. Write down all the visual images, sounds, symbols, or artefacts that come to mind and don't discount any ideas. If you're stuck you could try doing an image search online based on key words from your chosen content, responsible team, client, or commission. There are no "wrong" answers here—what you end up using will depend on how the experience unfolds, so just let the ideas flow.

Planning in practice: *In 2013, when we worked on the Shark Tank planning, this final prompt had not yet been added to the diagram. In fact, it was added as a direct consequence of teaching the example because I realised how much richer our planning would have been if we had made more use of images, metaphors, and symbols. We must have done some of this thinking in an unconscious way, however, because I remember us discussing a human parallel to the kind of entrapment felt by the shark in a tank and coming up with the image of a person in a hospital bed which later became the image we used as our hook. If I was planning this Mantle of the Expert today, I might sketch some visual images such as a shark eating a smaller fish. I would note down words to evoke life in the deep sea—such as "darkness" or "pressure", and contrast them with words associated with life* *in a tank—"enclosed", "scrutinised". I would explore the way sharks are often feared in Western culture and the dominant symbols including the image of a single fin cutting through the water and the sounds from movie soundtracks related to sharks. I would also consider how sharks appear in Māori and Polynesian culture, where they are considered as guardians and the wearing of a shark's teeth in a necklace can provide protection. I would research traditional stories; for example, the one in which Maui places a shark in the sky to form the Milky Way. And then, during teaching, I would look for opportunities to incorporate these images within different activities.*

Summary of preplanning process

Having reached the end of this process, you can be reasonably confident of having planned for each of the core elements or whenu needed for a Mantle of the Expert experience. You should now have in place: a responsible team with a backstory; a client; a commission; some tasks; some tensions; and a sense of other perspectives that could be considered and reflected on. You will also have given thought to some of the metaphors, symbols, and other sensory imagery you might call on along the way. And because you have selected these core elements in a thoughtful way, you should find your material resonates with more authenticity than if you had rushed the process or settled on the first good idea. It is worth remembering that what we are planning here is not a unit or a lesson but a whole complex programme of learning that could take weeks or months. When you think about it that way, it's worth taking time to get it right!

Research

At this point, we are almost ready to move on to stage two, which is the mapping process. Before we do, however, there's another important step. You as teacher need to get to know as much as you can about the world of your commission and the body of skills and knowledge associated with the profession you have chosen for your responsible team. This means accessing appropriate real-world information such as dates, historical events, scientific understandings, geography, articles, images, links, and other information. For example, if your participants will be a team of boat builders restoring an ocean-going waka, you'll need to read a range of material on the topic of waka and also on the profession of boat building. You need to be well informed not because you are going to be the "sage on the stage" transmitting facts and information (though there will be times you do just that as we will see with the teacher compass). It's more about ensuring the imagined world you are learning in has detail, authenticity and accuracy. If this sounds onerous, don't worry. It's no different from any other form of inquiry where the teacher needs a broad familiarity with factual information that is fundamental to the work in hand. You'll probably find the research process interesting rather than laborious as by now you're invested in the imagined world yourself and you'll be surprised how many new tasks, tensions, and alternative perspectives arise based on what you read and discover. A final tip: As you hoard information, keep asking yourself, "what's really worth knowing here?" This will help you identify key learnings and enduring understandings to foreground in your teaching.

Planning in practice: *Andy, the student teachers, and I started gathering research material as soon as we knew the content world we would be working in. We created a shared Google Drive and loaded it with a whole lot of information related to the sharks. We found out how big they are and we located graphs of their declining population numbers. We located maps showing their habitat. We explored their physiology and biology and uploaded pictures. We looked at information about reproduction and we discovered that these sharks are highly prized by some people for their liver oil, which immediately rang bells for a possible tension in the drama. The real-world specifics helped us feel secure in the content world as well as giving us useful material for the commission and the professional tasks arising from it. And the more we discovered the more we found our own excitement and engagement levels building.*

Stage 2: Choosing the overall shape—mapping

Stage 2 of the planning process is where the teacher decides the overall shape the Mantle of the Expert experience will take and how it will be delivered over the available time frame. The thinking at this stage is akin to that of a weaver who, having laboured to select and lay out the threads, decides on the overall pattern for the korowai. The weaver will imagine how the finished korowai might look, choosing from the range of possible materials that have been collected, and selecting patterns and motifs to be worked into the weave. Likewise, the teacher will imagine the shape the Mantle of the Expert might take: what order to establish the responsible team and introduce the commission; how to set up and step in and out of the fictional worlds of client, commission, and content; which of the possible tasks and tensions to introduce; and how to bring the experience to a conclusion.

Not every practitioner has the need or desire to map in this way. Some would argue that mapping out a Mantle of the Expert experience contradicts the exploratory, co-constructed nature of inquiry that lies at the heart of the approach. For experienced practitioners, the only pre-planning required is to establish the responsible team, frame, client, and commission and an idea of how to open the experience. Such practitioners decide on a strong opening, then trust their abilities to co-construct the learning by bouncing off participants' ideas and doing some microplanning between teaching episodes. It's amazing to teach in this way and it is probably the ideal to aim for in terms of co-construction and student agency. However, it takes time to learn to listen deeply to participants, respond to their offers, and think on your feet. It also takes time to learn how to structure teaching episodes so that all the elements are established, an effective story arc is achieved, and deep learning is fostered at the same time.

So, just as the beginner weaver might find it beneficial to imitate a more experienced colleague's patterns, a beginner teacher in Mantle of the Expert may find it useful to copy a sequence that they know has been successful before. The image below gives a template that can be used to give an overall shape to the experience. The design is adapted from a style of planning used by Julia Walshaw at Bealings School in the UK, though her preference is to map the journey as it unfolds rather than creating a map in advance as is suggested here. The important thing to realise is that this map is always provisional and it's mostly there to provide reassurance for you, the teacher. As you gain in experience and confidence you will find you become more confident about deviating from the map and working with the participants to take unexpected directions. Eventually you can move away from mapping in advance and use the same format to record the journey as you go.

The template has been developed and used with students and teachers around New Zealand and I have used it myself on the majority of occasions that I have taught in a classroom. Often I'll draw my map by hand, as I like the sense of the document being personal, tentative, and evolving. Teachers around New Zealand have adapted the template in a range of different ways. Some use hand-drawn maps, others prefer online tools to create electronic versions. I hope you will find your method for creating a map that works for you.

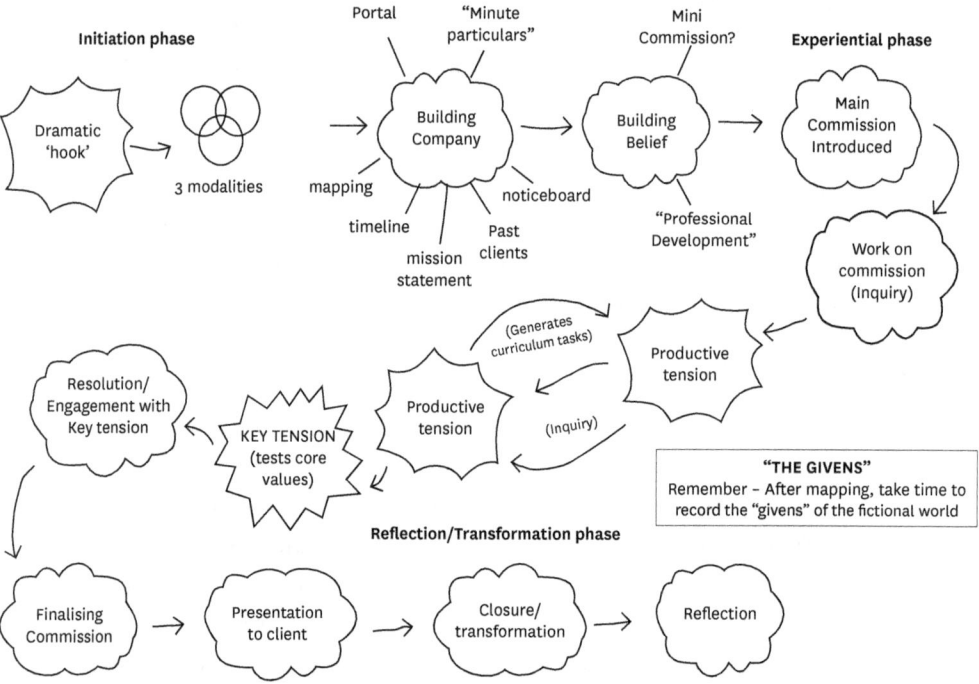

Figure 48: Mapping template

Using the template

You'll see the template shows a series of shapes, each of which indicates an episode of learning. The episodes are laid out with arrows between, to suggest a sequence through time. However, these episodes are not of a determined length: they might be a single activity, one lesson, or a series of these. Like beats in a play text or chapters in a story, an episode is defined not by duration but by where participants start from and where they end up. The teacher learns to focus on the purpose of each episode—for example, building participants' sense of commitment to the imagined world—and judges when the purpose of an episode has been fulfilled and it's time to move on. The different shapes used on the map indicate the quality of work in each episode—with pointy shapes being those with more tension, while softer cloud-like shapes suggesting episodes with less tension involved. Where the sequence gets to productive tensions, these are shown as a repeating cycle, indicating that, once a productive tension is resolved, it's time to introduce another one. One other thing to note is the "givens" box. This part of the template is provided so that the teacher can spell out the backstory of the fictional world: the team's history and any aspects of the content world that are non-negotiable. This is important when planning as it helps keep the activities narrow, focused, and aligned.

Using the template as a guide, the teacher can create their own map, filling in the shapes with specific details of tasks, commission, and tensions that were generated in the pre-planning notes in stage one. The template shows a single shape per episode as a minimum, but phases can be elongated by adding extra episodes. Links to key competencies and big questions can be made along the bottom of the page, along with links to anything else you wish to foreground in your planning. This might include a professional development focus such as the cultural competencies from *Tātaiako* (Ministry of Education & New Zealand Teacher's Council, 2011) or formal accountability documents such as *Te Whāriki* (Ministry of Education, 2017), *The New Zealand Curriculum* (Ministry of Education, 2007), your school's local curriculum or strategic plan, teacher inquiry questions, or required assessments.

While the finished map is linear, the process for completing it may not be. To return to our weaving metaphor, you'll recall that a korowai weaver will often work from the bottom hem of the garment upwards, finishing with the top border or taniko. Likewise, you may find it helpful to map your Mantle of the Expert experience by starting with the endpoint and working back through the tensions that will be introduced along the way. Often it helps to save the planning of your opening, or hook, until last. That way you have a good sense of the imagined world you are inviting children into and can choose how to introduce it creatively.

The narrative arc

Your map will serve as a unit plan overview by sketching out a sequence of possible tasks and activities. It also serves as a plan for the narrative arc of the experience. In Mantle of the Expert—as in a story, or a piece of theatre on stage, an improvisation, or a child's imaginary game with a friend—the layers of the imagined world need to be set up and agreed on, moved through, and then resolved in some way. O'Toole and Dunn (2002) describe how effective classroom drama has three phases—the *initiation*, the *experiential*, and the *reflection/transformation*—and suggest that if the teacher can move through these phases, they will produce a drama that has a satisfying sense of beginning, middle, and end. You see all three of these phases are embedded in the map, with suggestions of what needs to happen to fulfil each phase. Of course, the narrative arc proposed here is not the only—or even the most interesting—way to proceed: there are lots of other ways in which a successful narrative could be achieved. If you think about it, stories don't have to begin with "once upon a time" and end with "and they all lived happily ever after". They can start in the middle, they can start with a denouement then go back to explore how it was arrived at, or they can follow any number of other narrative structures. But here are some suggestions for a linear narrative arc.

Initiation phase

Opening with some kind of hook to arrest attention and intrigue the participants, the initiation phase is where the foundations are laid down and the core elements, or whenu, are gradually introduced. The teacher ensures that participants understand expectations, including the fact that we are working in an imagined world with certain boundaries and limits. Through dramatic episodes, the nature of the responsible team is clarified, including its frame and its backstory, and the client and commission are introduced. Time is taken to build a sense of investment in the imagined world and to ensure that all participants have bought in. This phase can feel quite teacher-driven as the teacher needs to focus participants and ensure that everyone gets a shared sense of the whenu. It may be characterised by a lot of whole-class activity.

Experiential phase

This is the longest phase of the experience and has two parts. The first begins when the participants positioned as the responsible team move into action and begin to tackle the commission. Working with increasing independence from the teacher, the participants begin to work through what's required to carry out the commission. As they do, they will respond to tensions; both naturally arising ones and others that are introduced along the way by the teacher. This phase can be much more participant-led and will include many opportunities to work individually, in pairs, or small groups—though it's always important to keep the whole group abreast of developments as they occur. For the teacher, this phase is about judging the times to introduce productive tensions and alternative perspectives, and facilitating deliberate acts of teaching to ensure participants are learning new skills and knowledge, both in key competencies and curriculum learning areas. The second half of the experiential phase begins once the teacher chooses to introduce the key tension which they will probably have planned in advance but—like a plot twist in a good story or play—will be unexpected to the participants. The key tension will be something that tests the team's values and resources. The experiential phase continues as the group is given time to grapple with and resolve the key tension in some way before finalising their work on the commission, and making some kind of presentation to the client.

Reflection/transformation phase

This final phase is focused on closure, reflection, and action in the real world. While participants will have been encouraged to reflect and think critically about their learning throughout the Mantle of the Expert experience, it's in this phase that they leave the imagined world for the last time to think about the implications of what they have learned. Real world parallels and the potential for real world actions are considered. The transformation aspect of the reflection phase can be a powerful coda to the cross-curricula learning that has taken place. The word "transformation" is used in the sense of making something new; this could involve some form of social action or intervention such as raising money for a charity or writing to a local MP. Or the transformation may involve some kind of creative work that expresses participants' new ideas or emotional responses to the experience. The purpose of the transformation stage is to consolidate the learning and deepen personal connection to the material. The idea of transformation is a little different from a celebration of learning where parents or others from the community might be invited in to see and hear a class present about their work. Though such learning celebrations can be really valuable, for the transformation aspect to be achieved, the learning needs to take a new form from what has been produced during the formal learning period.

Mapping in practice: *With the Shark Tank example, the first thing we thought about was the initiation phase, where the participants would need to build a sense of commitment to their team identity as virtual reality designers. We knew we would want to spend some time negotiating the physical space of the company offices, establishing the group's backstory, building a shared sense of the company's values, and other details. We discussed some strategies that I'd used in previous Mantle of the Expert experiences including having a staff notice board, creating a team logo, and a timeline and we included these in the first few episodes on the map.*

For the experiential phase, we decided when the commission would be introduced and what kinds of inquiry tasks would emerge from this. We looked back at the list of naturally arising tasks and our tensions and thought about how these could be woven in and what curriculum tasks could emerge as a result. In particular, we liked the pressure arising from the story of the mother shark eating her young. We could see that this would provide motivation for science experiments to ensure that the artificial environment exactly matched the under-sea one. We also incorporated the idea of the faulty probe and the need to reproduce the soundscape of the undersea world.

For our key tension, we chose the idea that the whole captive breeding programme was sponsored by a shark liver oil manufacturer. We decided roughly where in the 6-week sequence we could introduce this and added it to our map.

Having outlined the experiential phase, we looked at the reflection phase and ensured we had left enough time at the end of the experience to include some episodes providing closure and reflection. The final planning decision to be made was about the dramatic hook which would open the first session. We wanted an opening that would grab the children's attention, appeal to them and relate to their own lives, and sow the seeds for the ideas underpinning the commission. We knew we could start in a number of different ways—through an inquiry question, a drama convention, or dramatic hook by introducing the commission straight away. In this case, after some discussion of options we decided to enter through a drama convention.

We opted to hook the children's attention by showing a situation where the company had previously been successful. We thought about the company's expertise in wrap-around interactive environments and tried to imagine what some of their previous projects might have been. Between us we came up with the scenario of a child in a hospital bed whose illness meant they were no longer able to skateboard or experience the adventurous activities they loved. Wouldn't it be great to be able to produce a virtual reality experience for this person?

On reflection, I think this choice of dramatic hook was successful for a number of reasons. It was novel, and this grabbed the participants' attention. It also set the scene for the fictional world of the team, establishing the team's expertise and previous success. The fact that the fictional scenario involved a young person gave a degree of familiarity and connection for the participants, while the choice of a hospital setting introduced the idea that the team had a reputation for being caring and empathic. I realise, too, that we unconsciously drew on those earlier conversations about the ethics of captivity and the questions of human versus animal rights in these situations. By establishing that the company's previous work had been wrap-around environments for humans, this implicitly encouraged the participants to consider the needs of the sharks with the same attention as they would to meeting human needs.

At this stage, the pre-planning was complete and we were almost ready to start teaching. One final step was to make sure the "givens" of the fictional world were in place; those things that needed to be understood to ensure coherence of the backstory. In this case, this meant ensuring we were clear on the details such as where the real sharks are found, where the imaginary aquarium was situated, and the backstory about female sharks eating their young when they realised they were in captivity. This lining up of the "givens" is always important in Mantle of the Expert and even more important where there is a team of teachers, to avoid contradicting each other.

We noticed that our dramatic hook set up a backstory where the expert team had prior expertise in a slightly different area than that required by the commission. Though our initial idea had been that we were experts at animal environments, in the event we decided to change that and say the team was very accustomed to working with wrap-around virtual reality environments but had worked with human clients before. The commission, therefore, involved a new challenge in the fact that the artificial environment was for a different kind of creature. In this way, the commission was a step into unknown territory, not only for the class in the real world but also for the team in the fictional world. I realise this sidestepping is something I often do when I'm planning as it helps to account for the participants' lack of skills and knowledge in the real world.

Stage 3: Interweaving the aho—microplanning and teaching

At this point, the overall pre-planning and shaping for your Mantle of the Expert experience is complete. You have selected and teased out the core elements and laid them out in readiness. You have thought about the shape you wish the experience to take and you have created a map of where your journey might take you. You'll also have undertaken your own research into the content areas that are likely to be encountered. With all this careful groundwork in place, you are now ready to begin the teaching and learning process with your participants. Like the weaver of a korowai—who creates the fabric of the garment by taking the vertical whenu threads that were set up in advance and gradually binds another set of threads, known as aho, horizontally through them—the teacher takes the core elements laid out in the previous stages of planning and interweaves these with a series of consciously selected threads; in this case, pedagogical strategies. Weavers of korowai emphasise the importance of the aho tapu, the opening thread that binds the whenu to the aho. In a similar way, a Mantle of the Expert teacher is likely to put most thought and effort into planning the opening few sessions, to get the experience off to a strong start and ensure all the elements are in place.

Be prepared for the weaving process to be unpredictable. Any weaver might suddenly change their mind about patterns, bring in some new, unexpected materials, decide to shorten the length of the garment, or abandon the project. In the case of Mantle of the Expert, which is a collaborative and improvised process between you and your participants, implementation will be even more fluid. Some aspects of the imagined world may be pre-planned by the teacher, but the success depends on the buy-in, collaboration, and co-construction that happens moment to moment with participants. What was laid out on the map might easily take a different direction as new ideas arise, plans change, and your initial ideas are interrupted or, indeed, terminated. This doesn't mean that microplanning of individual lessons is a waste of time. Indeed, I recommend careful microplanning of each lesson you teach in Mantle of the Expert. Having a well-thought-out plan for each episode of teaching means that you are as prepared as possible, with an idea of where things might go and what tasks and activities you will introduce. With a good plan in place you will be more open to the unexpected offer, new possibility, or teachable moment. As for what to include within your microplanning, you will find that, in many ways, you are planning for the same things as any other lesson with an estimated time frame, a list of required resources, notes on transitions, and groupings. You'll probably find you can use whatever lesson planning format you're already familiar with. Some aspects may be different, such as detailed scripts for instructions or notes for moments where the storyteller, narrator, or teacher-in-role voice is to be used. When you've learned some of the tools described later in the book you will find you want to note these in your planning as well. And as a side note, if you are worried about consulting a written plan during your teaching, it's my experience participants have no problems with this, even when the teacher is in role. They understand that the plan is part of the classroom world and they don't read it as a sign or symbol of anything (other than evidence of your efforts to be an effective teacher).

With preparations complete, it's time for the teaching to begin, and the interweaving of aho to gradually build up the mantle of responsibility. Of course, it is impossible to describe every decision or action a teacher takes while implementing a Mantle of the Expert: there's no such thing as a manual for success in any kind of teaching:

> You can no more create a binder full of classroom practices that are scientifically proven to work than you can create a scientifically proven courtship and marriage manual. Yes, some practices are more likely to work more often for more practitioners than other practices are, and yes, some practices are probably not going to work most of the time, mostly. But there will always be outliers and exceptions, and there will never be guarantees. Never.
>
> (Green, 2018)

It's also important to note that the teacher will not only use the signature pedagogies of Mantle of the Expert for their aho. They will also draw on hundreds of different teaching threads that are common to many other teaching approaches; things like planning key questions, planning for deliberate acts of teaching, identifying learning intentions, strategies like "think, pair, share", thinking tools, reflection circles, and the wealth of pedagogical possibilities available with the use of digital apps and devices. Mantle of the Expert is not about discarding what already works in the classroom but building on these successes with new skills and artistry.

However, based on my own teaching, conversations with colleagues, and an analysis of Heathcote's writings, I have developed the following list of 10 aho or signature pedagogies within Mantle of the Expert. The list isn't exhaustive or final. However, if you can plan activities based on these 10 things, and can successfully interweave those with the core elements previously selected, this will go a long way to ensuring the work comes together with integrity.

1. Keeping things safe and applying limits
2. Building relationships and fostering social practices
3. Taking on multiple perspectives
4. Questioning
5. Travelling in and out of worlds and through time and space
6. Introducing dramatic tension
7. Moving between teaching modes
8. Using drama strategies and conventions
9. Working with power: status, agency, and positioning
10. Encouraging critical thinking and reflection

The list is framed from the point of view of what the teacher does, even though the participant is an equal partner in the process of teaching and learning that goes on. In practice, the aho listed here are rarely used in isolation; the teacher will usually combine them according to what's required to move the participants through the different phases. If you look back at the examples in Chapter 3, you may already be able to see some ways in which these aho were interwoven. So now we will look at each aho in turn, consider what each offers, and touch on how they might work together. After each aho, I will present snapshots illustrating a number of possibilities for how each could be used. The snapshots will come from a whole range of classroom scenarios, moving us beyond *Shark Tank* and the other examples we've focused on up to now.

Aho 1: Keeping things safe and applying limits

Setting up circumstances for the physical, social, and cultural safety of the class is fundamental to any teaching and learning experience. In terms of physical safety, particular attention is needed in Mantle of the Expert due to the active nature of learning, with participants using their whole bodies and all senses. The environment will be noisy at times and there will be different use of space, furniture, artefacts, devices, and other materials so it's important to establish ground rules for physical safety and maintain these throughout. Where a class is unaccustomed to working in Mantle of the Expert, the teacher can expect participants to take a while to adapt to new expectations. Even in classrooms where Dramatic Inquiry is familiar, the teacher may find themselves drawing on this aho to weave in activities that specifically focus on establishing and maintaining physical safety. Participants are also social and cultural beings, which means teachers need to be alert and responsive to anything that threatens safety in this sense—in both the real and imagined worlds. This means being mindful in the choice of content, support material, and references so that participants can recognise themselves and their world view in the material. It also means being conscious of tikanga and other social and cultural practices, which might have implications for furniture, group organisation, proxemics, touch, or eye contact.

Another consideration when weaving a Mantle of the Expert experience is emotional safety. All teaching depends on a trusting relationship between the teacher and the class and between classmates themselves. However, emotional safety has particular importance in Mantle of the Expert, where participants are asked to take risks in the real and the imagined worlds. The stronger the sense of safety already in place, the easier it will be to try Mantle of the Expert for the first time, though it's also true that the approach can be employed as a means to develop group safety. To enable this, the teacher can draw on this aho explicitly—by designing activities to establish and talk about emotional safety—or more subtly, such as being careful not to single out individuals to share when working in role. The aho will come through in reflection, too, since a teacher can't gauge emotional safety based on their own sense of what feels good, but must check in with the group early and often with questions such as, "How is this feeling?", "What's tricky?", or "What do we need to do to make this work better?"

Another aspect of emotional safety relates to the potential for drama to trigger emotions. This is particularly important when drama is used to explore difficult issues or sensitive subject matter, though even apparently innocuous activities can become surprisingly emotional, as in the case of the participants in the *Toy Museum* example who spoke in role as crayons about feeling undervalued and rejected. The power of the arts is that they provide ways to access and express human emotions and experiences and in drama, particularly when responding in role, we can experience intense empathy with another and also sometimes find ourselves stirring memories of past experiences from our own lives. The teacher needs to be aware of this and take steps to ensure participants are protected. Bolton's distinction between protecting from and protecting into emotion is useful here:

> I cannot stress enough how important it is for teachers to realise that because drama is such a powerful tool for helping people change, as teachers we need to be very sensitive to the emotional demands we make on our students. The notion of 'protection' is not necessarily concerned with protecting participants from emotion, for unless there is some kind of emotional engagement nothing can be learned, but rather to protect them into emotion. This requires a careful grading of structures toward an effective equilibrium so that self-esteem, personal dignity, personal defences and group security are never over-challenged.
>
> (Bolton, 1984, p. 128)

A key tool for protecting participants in this way is frame distance, where time, space, and relationship are used to provide distance from difficult or "hot" topics and this will be discussed in detail in Chapter 5. A degree of protection also comes from not spending too long in role and, where necessary, including a simple ritual to signify de-rolling, such as shaking the hands from the wrists or holding hands as a group and jumping back into "reality". Perhaps the most important principle for emotional safety is that participants must know they have the option not to participate in activities they feel uncomfortable with. This applies to any activity but is particularly important in role work. Participants need to know they can pull out if necessary and alternatives can be negotiated if needed. The need for emotional safety also extends to participants who join the group midway through a Mantle of the Expert experience, or leave it early.

Aho 1 in practice—some classroom snapshots:

- *Helen's Year 1 class has been working as "story detectives" solving clues and offering advice to characters from stories. The class has already explored a mix of European and Māori stories. Today Helen decides to introduce a story from Malaysia, which one of the class knows really well.*

- Ashley senses that emotions are running high after an in-role activity, so he invites participants to stand, shake out their hands, and sit together on the mat to talk about what they discovered.
- With the class working in small groups to create a frozen effigy, Cherie encourages participants to create a sense of connection between their bodies without touching heads or stepping over each other.

Aho 2: Building relationships and fostering social practices

This second aho is closely related to the first: it's impossible to foster relationship without considering safety as in the previous aho. The idea that relationship is core to effective teaching and learning is hardly new: it's at the heart of how we teach here in Aotearoa New Zealand, where our curriculum foregrounds social competencies and where the research of Bishop, Berryman, and others has demonstrated how relationship is the key to educational success, particularly for Māori (Bishop & Berryman, 2009; Ministry of Education, 2011a). At the same time, there are unique ways in which relationship and social practices can be fostered within the Mantle of the Expert approach. As has been noted before, participants are co-weavers. Teachers are responsible for the initial planning of the experience and maintaining control over the overall direction, but they depend on the participants as competent co-constructors with whom they will negotiate moment by moment to create the learning experience. With participants positioned as capable colleagues with a capacity for grappling with complex ideas, teachers will find themselves constantly opening spaces so that participants can fulfil this potential. The goal is to set up a reciprocal teaching and learning relationship founded on ako as everyone involved figures things out and builds understanding together.

The many moments of negotiation, co-construction, and reflection during a Mantle of the Expert experience mean participants and teachers will be constantly thinking about, discussing, assessing, and finessing their relationship. By working in and out of imagined worlds and in and out of multiple roles, teachers and participants can explore a whole set of new relationships with opportunities to interact in new ways; adopting different power positions and exploring language and actions that might otherwise not be available or permissible. Brian Edmiston puts it this way:

> One of the core reasons why as a teacher I use drama is because when we create an imagined world, we can imagine that we frame events differently so that our power and authority relationships are changed. A long-term aim of mine as a teacher is as much as possible to share power and authority with students. I want students to have more opportunities to use words and deeds to act appropriately but in ways that are often not sanctioned in classrooms. Additionally I hope that students' sense of their personal and shared authority will become more secure and more extended while at the same time more aware of others' authority. I want a culture to develop that is more egalitarian than most students expect walking into the room.
>
> (Edmiston, 2003, p. 225)

Meanwhile, Aaron, a participant in a drama group for adults with special needs gives the participant perspective: "In real life I'm a trolley collector in a supermarket. In the drama I get to be the manager" (Arts with Attitude, 2008). The chance to explore alternative relationship stances can be a real boon for teachers and participants alike, offering a chance to see and treat each other in a new way. This can be great for classroom management, especially if the existing relationships are strained in some way, and offers new assessment and research possibilities too (Aitken, 2012a; O'Toole & Dunn, 2002). In so many ways, the structures of Mantle of the Expert encourage a rethink of how teachers and participants talk to, think about, and act with each other. However, while the potential for a shift in the teacher–participant relationship is wired in, it does not happen by itself. The teacher will need to consciously draw on this aho during almost every activity, making shifts in use of language, routines, and ways of operating within the classroom to allow for a new relationship with participants to evolve.

This aho also refers to fostering relationship and collaborative social practices between participants. One of the core tenets of learning in Mantle of the Expert is how participants work collaboratively, as if they are a fictional team of experts responding to the commission from a client. It is this collaborative professional relationship that distinguishes Mantle of the Expert from other teaching approaches and makes it unique. Of course, Mantle of the Expert is not the only way to manifest a sense of collaboration: the teacher can build community by engaging in process drama, collaborative maths activities, kapa haka, science, social action projects, or singing. But with Mantle of the Expert, the difference is that every task or activity is collaborative and professional. Even individual tasks such as a piece of writing, a calculation of area, a drawing, or a science experiment are all framed as individuals' contribution to a collaborative whole. For participants to access the full advantages of the Mantle of the Expert approach, they need to engage in the social practices of a responsive team.

A successful team dynamic relies on the teacher setting up and sustaining the social practices to support collaboration within the class. Social practices are the accepted ways of behaving within a classroom. Teachers will already be familiar with establishing social practices such as silent reading after morning tea. If the routine is established, after a while children just know this is what happens and they get on with it. Other social practices might be less positive and less teacher-led but just as established in the participants' minds; for example, "whenever we get into line we push each other around". In Mantle of the Expert, there are some important social practices that need to be established and the teacher may need to spend time planning activities or working one to one with participants to cement these. These include: working as a whole class; working in smaller groups; collaborating to solve problems; compromising; listening; and give and take. Significantly, too, teachers will need to help participants adopt the social practice of agreeing that imagined things, people, and places can be treated with the same credibility and attention as things, people, and places in the real world.

Social practices are key to any Mantle of the Expert experience and do need to be taught. However, this is not to say that they need to be *pre*-taught. Indeed, Mantle of the Expert, and other forms of Dramatic Inquiry, can be a great way to introduce these social practices for the first time. In taking time to establish and maintain social practices, the teacher can help participants learn to be part of a social learning group—something that really matters if you subscribe to a social constructivist or sociocultural view of learning.

This aho involves the teacher planning activities and tasks that build and sustain the sense of a collective. This is achieved through language and framing. In terms of language, Heathcote (2007) discusses how the teacher shifts from an *I* voice: "I want you to ...", to a *They* voice: "What would people like this do about such a problem?" and, finally, to a *We* voice: "We'll have to move fast if we are going to make those changes before the deadline." So language is key to positioning and building the collective. Another key is ensuring that tasks and ongoing activities resemble the social practices of professionals in the real world. Rather than introducing something for its own sake, because "fractions are important" or because it's what we do at school and next week we're moving on to algebra, each task arises as part of the expected activity of the professional team. Thus a task related to fractions might be introduced something like this: "It looks like no one is going to be happy unless we find some way to divide the land evenly between them." The task is framed as something of importance for the collective within the imagined world.

The teacher will draw on aho 2 any time the sense of working collaboratively is lost; as in the *Objects of Significance* example, where children in their small groups needed to agree on how to present their exhibit. At these moments, it was important to pause and assert the social practice of collaboration, ensuring that any proffered ideas were taken seriously and negotiated in or out by the group. Rather than seeing disagreements as an annoyance or a problem, we can consider them as important opportunities to learn about kotahitanga: the art of finding a sense of unity and collective action even when we sometimes disagree. Participants in Mantle of the Expert do not come out of a 6-week experience believing themselves to be expert plumbers or insurance brokers, and to expect them to do this is to miss the point. But, if social practices are established and maintained well, participants will come away with relationships and ways of working together that will persist and serve them well, both in school and in life.

There's one more crucial dimension of relationship that cannot be overlooked and that's the participants' relationship with the imagined world. A key benefit of working in Mantle of the Expert is how participants can grow a sense of concern, investment, and eventually obsession with what matters in the imagined world (Downey, 2017;

Fraser et al., 2013). I used to believe this happened by itself as a by-product of the clever systems at work within Mantle of the Expert. Now, I can see there are many actions that a teacher can take to actively feed participants' sense of engagement. These include ensuring that participants have their interest hooked and maintained through moments of intrigue and tension, giving opportunities to grapple with tricky questions, allowing extended time to deepen understanding, revisiting key information in multiple ways, and demonstrating their own sense of passion, curiosity, enthusiasm, and concern through language and actions. In Chapter 5, we will learn about the "continuum of engagement"; a tool teachers can use to help gauge, sustain, and maintain participants' investment in the imagined world.

Aho 2 in practice—some classroom snapshots:
- *Maia works with her class to co-construct a mission statement for their team of archaeologists. She encourages participants to identify the words that will tell the world who the team is and what they stand for. Then she invites participants to create still images of moments from the team's history where one of their values was tested.*
- *Michelle is just finishing a busy day of inquiry and work on group tasks. She invites participants to think back to a part of their school day where they received help or advice from a peer. Everyone moves to stand or sit in the place where this interaction occurred and each person speaks about the difference it made to them.*
- *It's first thing Monday morning and one of the children in Leigh's class has taken the initiative to work at home creating a 3D walk through simulation of the company offices on his laptop. Leigh makes sure this participant has time to present it to the team for review and approval. The 3D model is compared carefully with the map previously created by the whole group and certain changes are negotiated.*

Aho 3: Taking on multiple perspectives

This third aho is perhaps more obviously a signature of Mantle of the Expert, since a key purpose for learning through drama is the opportunities it gives to walk in another person's shoes or consider an idea or issue from a range of different points of view. As Heathcote said, there are always multiple ways to look at something:

> When I think of a tree—I think of it in all different ways. I can be the tree, I can look down at the tree, I can be in the tree (like a bird). There's about 7 different ways of thinking about a tree and I can choose the one that works.
>
> (Heathcote, in Burgess, 1993)

Note that the intention is to give multiple perspectives, not just one other perspective. This was something I took a while to realise in my own practice. When I started out teaching in Mantle of the Expert I only ever asked the participants to take on one new perspective; that of the responsive team. Even this had its advantages: participants were included in the story and they could reflect on what was happening from the perspective of the team inside the action as well as returning to the classroom to "look in" at the action from their own point of view. However, in only ever expecting the participants to respond from one perspective other than their own, I was denying the many opportunities for participants to take on other roles within the imagined world.

If we only encourage participants to take on one other role during a drama, the danger is that we encourage them to think in binaries; comparing their own real-world point of view with the one they have taken on in the imagined world. If they adopt multiple roles, this encourages a view of the world as multi-layered, and subjective. Exploring multiple perspectives is not only about considering or even inhabiting different points of view, it also requires engaging in meaningful dialogue with them. Dialogue in this sense means much more than talk; it is an active interchange with others in which the objective is to take account of the other and build new meaning together, through what Edmiston calls "embodied dialogic imagination" (Edmiston, 2014). To achieve this, a teacher drawing on this aho will plan activities that allow for a number of different perspectives to be inhabited, and explored dialogically. Since the embodied dialogue is dramatic, the teacher will often do this by using drama strategies and conventions (see aho 8).

As a teacher thinking about how to draw in multiple perspectives, it can help to remember that these always exist at any moment, on any issue or idea, and also that they are found in both the real world and the imagined world. Within the real world of the classroom, the teacher can plan activities to foster dialogue at any point in the Mantle of the Expert journey to reflect on what is being learned and how the group is going. An example of this is the continuum used in the *Shark Tank* example, which was a way for participants to explore multiple perspectives on the ethics of shark liver oil. Other strategies include the "trading game" where participants move around a group, sharing their responses to a question asked by the teacher with the people they meet. After listening and before moving on they decide to either adopt what they've heard, make a change to their original answer, or stick to their first idea. They will then discuss their views with those around them, and might shift and change their position as their viewpoint changes. See Edmiston (2014) for more on this, and other strategies that can assist participants to reflect from their own and others' standpoints. As for activities that encourage dialogue with multiple perspectives in the imagined world, a whole range of strategies can be used here too. These include the teacher taking on a role, introducing "fictional others", or inviting participants to take up a role. We will see some specific examples when we get to aho 8. However it is done, the most important benefit of taking on multiple perspectives is that participants come to see beliefs, or "right answers" as provisional rather than fixed. This, in turn, teaches them that learning is always influenced by context and point of view.

Aho 3 in practice—some classroom snapshots:

- *Anaru wants to encourage the class to debate responses to a complex issue in the imagined world. He invites participants to step out of role and uses a "trading game" to encourage this.*
- *Lynne wants to encourage participants to consider the impacts of their play area designs on the inhabitants of the imagined world. She sets up a town meeting and invites participants to take on roles of local residents who have raised objections to the play area's development.*
- *Ray is supporting his class to find out how signatures were gathered when copies of te Tiriti o Waitangi travelled New Zealand in the 1840s. Drawing on historical documents and biographical details, he invites participants to imagine as accurately as possible the moment when one signature was added*

to the Manukau-Kawhia sheet on 28 April 1840. Groups create still images then compare them, noting how body language and use of space evoke very different versions of the same moment.

Aho 4: Questioning

Questioning is a fundamental aspect of any teaching approach:

Whatever the plan, strategy, or technique, effective teaching depends primarily upon the teacher's skill in being able to ask questions that generate different kinds of learning ... questions must draw on the wide learning possibilities inherent in the subject material; at the same time ... good, or effective, questions require the sort of vitality that challenges students to approach their learning creatively.

(Morgan & Saxton, 2006, p. 13)

A whole book could be written about questioning in teaching, and several have been. A favourite of mine, from which the quote above is taken, is *Asking Better Questions* (Morgan & Saxton, 2006); I recommend this text for any teacher looking for further professional development. Within Mantle of the Expert, the importance of thoughtful and effective questioning is further heightened as the teacher needs to manage multiple perspectives and multiple worlds, to take deliberate care with pace, aesthetics, and language, and to mark shifts in positioning. It's complex stuff, but in my work in schools around New Zealand, teachers often find the work within this aho is the most transformative in their professional journey.

There are many layers to questioning within Mantle of the Expert. First of all, we might refer to the big questions that underpin the planning, such as in the *Shark Tank* example, which revolved around big questions related to captivity and the rights and wrongs of creating health products from endangered animals. So, one way a teacher can draw on this aho is by planning activities where participants step back and reflect on these big questions and their responses to them. A second kind of questioning is when the teacher asks questions of participants. In Mantle of the Expert, as in other classrooms, this is likely to be the dominant form of exchange as the teacher continually prompts, extends, probes, and deepens participants' responses. Given its central importance, this is an aspect of teaching that is well worth consciously developing. Teachers can work on things like: including genuine questions where you don't already know the answer; reducing unnecessary or leading questions; and posing the kind of questions that promote higher-order responses. Michael Bunting (2006) has proposed a set of question stems to help with this, while Morgan and Saxton (2006) suggest a whole taxonomy of question types, each with its own subtleties of function, delivery, and purpose. It's well worth learning about these and practising their use in the classroom.

Another possibility for questioning, and one that is central in Mantle of the Expert, is where participants ask the questions. Sometimes these will be directed at the teacher, whether in the real world or in role, which means the teacher will need to consider whether, when, how, and what to respond. Again, Morgan and Saxton (2006) have some excellent advice on this. Among the range of choices available to a teacher in role, it can be useful to remember the power of a parsimonious response, where one holds back from giving too much information. This can help maintain intrigue and ensure participants have to work hard to understand and make meaning for themselves. Judging when to hold back and when to feed in information is something that comes with practice, though a tool like the teacher compass (introduced in Chapter 5) can really help.

Participants will also often question each other, both in the real world and in role within the imagined world. This is another version of the questioning aho that requires some skill from the teacher. Questioning is not just about the words we use but the use of voice, space, body language, status, and other factors. Given the potential for stopping, rewinding, and revisiting time, participants in a Mantle of the Expert can be encouraged to explore, discuss, and even trial different ways to form and deliver questions before the question is finally asked, as in the *Toy Museum* example, where participants considered Teddy's feelings when framing up their questions about his appearance. The safety of role also means that sometimes there are opportunities to ask difficult questions or have tricky conversations that call on participants to use their skills to thoughtfully draw out responses. Another useful strategy is to introduce a "truth button", or "truth serum", where someone from the imagined world is compelled to answer the question truthfully. This strategy works best where it is used with restraint; for example, by agreeing it's only available for one question. This encourages participants to think carefully about what form of question will get them the information they need the most.

At times, participants might have the opportunity to question fictional others not actually represented by someone in role, but still evoked in the imagined world. For example, they might question as part of writing to the mayor or constructing a survey for owners of pet dogs. This brings us to another important function of questioning, which is how it helps to develop critical thinking. Implicit in the notion of questioning is the possibility for critique and even challenge. Working in Mantle of the Expert opens up opportunities to question figures, systems, and organisations that might not occur in real life. In past research projects, this aspect of the approach—the way it encourages a respectful questioning of authority—has been a standout finding (Aitken, 2012a). The teacher using this aho can support participants to develop the language of critique by modelling provisional language such as "I wonder …" and "Might we …" and by including opportunities to question systems of authority including those used by the teacher.

Aho 4 in practice—some classroom snapshots:

- *Julie's class of new entrants is intrigued by the arrival of a letter from the monster they met yesterday. She builds tension and suspense by asking, "I wonder what's inside?"*
- *Arjun's class is working as detectives. Today they are interrogating someone suspected of stealing explosives from a demolition site. He tells them they have a limit of 10 questions they can ask and the children spend time debating and co-constructing these. Then a chair is set out in front of the group and the suspect is played by different members of the group taking turns to sit and answer in role.*
- *Rachel's class is preparing to present a written report to the fictional client. She introduces a letter from the client clarifying their expectations and asks the question, "What do they want from us?" The children use the letter to develop a set of criteria and carry out a peer-checking exercise, questioning each other to establish whether the report will fulfil requirements.*

Aho 5: Travelling in and out of worlds and through time and space

At first sight, this aho sounds more like something a character in science fiction would get up to than something for a teacher to consider in their planning. However, this aho is one of the most exciting signature pedagogies of Mantle of the Expert: with the teacher's help, participants can move in and out of the imagined world and can manipulate space and time in both those worlds. For the teacher wanting to tap into this potential, there are two key things to remember. First of all, learning in drama happens in "now-immediate time" (Heathcote, 2009, p. 1). That means that in drama we use our imaginations to agree that whatever is happening is happening now and happening to us. A second seminal idea is that you have two worlds to work in and between; the real and the imagined worlds. So, at any stage you can choose to pause the "now time" in one world and conduct yourself and the participants into the other. Operating in the duality of real and imagined worlds opens up all sorts of opportunities that are not available if we are only dealing with the lived reality of the classroom. These include deciding to stop, go back, repeat, reverse, or travel instantly from place to place. Some of these transitions will be decided in the mapping stage but many more will happen in the moment when the teacher senses it is right to make a transition to another world or to make some kind of switch in time for the next activity. Experienced Mantle of the Expert teacher Iona Towler-Evans describes it like this: "If the kids start going on about getting on board the ship—I start to think 'I'd better get them on this ship, then!' And I start to think about how I'm going to do it—either right then, or next time we meet" (Iona Towler-Evans, personal communication, 2017).

Although we have talked up to now about two worlds, there are, in effect, multiple layers within the real and imagined worlds of a Mantle of the Expert experience. There are also multiple times and multiple spaces available to explore within those worlds. Figure 49 gives an idea of this. The multiple layers apply to some socio-dramatic play and process drama too, but they are particularly pronounced in Mantle of the Expert, due to the presence of the client and commission. As the blue rings indicate, we can distinguish between two levels of the real world: one that lies beyond the classroom—the world of current events, history, politics, the news, festivals, and cultural occasions;

and one that lies within it—the world of routines, dynamics, relationships, passions, and needs particular to this group in this setting. Similarly, we can distinguish two layers in the imagined world: one that contains the world of the team—the office, the timeline, the business, its mission statement, backstory, culture, and ways of working; and the other that concerns the content—the physical, historical, cultural, geographical, and other information associated with what the client has asked the group to undertake. During a Mantle of the Expert experience, participants will step in and out of all these layers giving them opportunities to operate and reflect on the same focus from multiple viewpoints and perspectives.

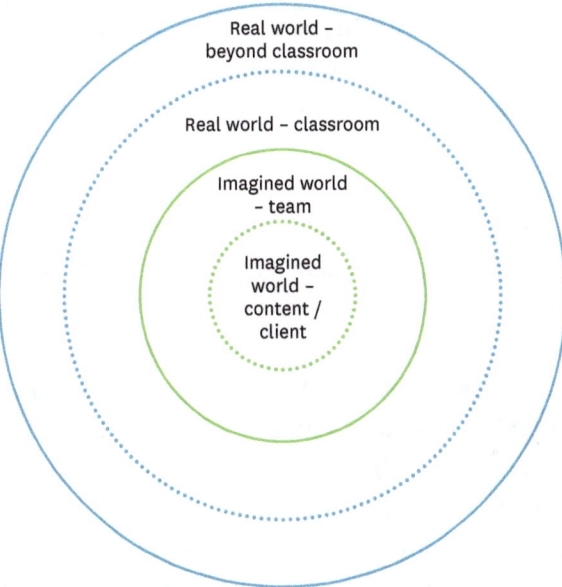

Figure 49: Layers within the real and imagined worlds

An important point here is the need for clear signalling to the participants about which world they are in and when a shift between worlds takes place. This signalling can be done through direct verbal instruction: "Right, for the next few moments we are going to take time to see things from the shark's perspective", or by indirect verbal implication: "If you'd like to join me in the boardroom, we have an important email from the client ...", or through non-verbal means; for example, by creating a setting and beckoning participants over to ritualistically it. I generally advocate being quite clear with participants about when shifts between different worlds happen—particularly when they are new to working in this way (see Advice and cautionary tales in Chapter 6 for more on this). As participants and teachers become more experienced, they can make the transitions between worlds quite subtle and elegant. Whichever way you go, always bear in mind that the main point is to shift perspectives and to ensure participants realise they are doing this.

Another thing to remember when working with this aho is that participants do not have to be in any of the fictional worlds for long periods. Indeed, teaching and learning in Mantle of the Expert is very rarely, if ever, about stepping into role for an extensive improvisation. Heathcote warned against this, and advised teachers to balance their time in role carefully with other kinds of teaching: "I decide when and why I shall leave role and become interrogator-leader. People assume that because I use role early, I mean to go on with it" (Heathcote, in O'Neill, 2015, p. 54). While this can seem counter-intuitive to teachers operating in a theatre paradigm, who might assume the role needs to be sustained, it can help to remember that the purpose of the drama in this case is not to create a product but to step in and out of a range of imagined worlds and gain different perspectives.

For some participants, moving between worlds takes practice. Teachers of juniors may find young children struggle to move out of the world of the content. Often they desperately want to stay with the story and talk to the teacher in role some more. This tendency can be helped by clear instructions and de-rolling rituals such as re-gathering participants on the mat. The inverse can be true for older participants, who may struggle to stay in the imagined world due to a sense of exposure or a feeling that working in that realm may be childish. Active resistance to role is unusual, and in Chapter 6 we will look at strategies to use if it does arise. In general, though, teachers can help reduce the participants' sense of exposure by making something or someone else the focus of the gaze: the teacher in role, a shared map, a set of photos, an artefact, or whatever. Teachers can also help by providing activities that involve practical doing, construction with materials or depiction of something tangible that creates a little more distance from the real-world self.

Having talked about moving between worlds, let's now look at the capacity to manipulate time and space within those worlds. In real life, time and space are linear and immutable but in the imagined world of Mantle of the Expert both time and space can be manipulated. Time can be paused, speeded up, slowed down, moved around, and revisited. Similarly, spaces and places can be created, recreated, exited, and re-entered. The table below sets out some of the possibilities. A teacher can shift time and space in any of these ways within any of the layers in the imagined worlds.

Shifts in time	Distant past, Recent past, Now, Near future, Distant future, Mythical time, Fast forward, Slow motion, Backwards, Rewinding, Looping, Parallel time
Shifts in space	Outer space, the natural environment, shared physical space, individual physical space, shared digital space, individual digital space, personal space, professional space, home space, intimate spaces, vehicles travelling between spaces, liminal spaces (spaces-between-spaces)

Figure 50: Exploring shifts in time and space

Experimentation with time and space is a nuance of teaching that takes a little practice but can be enormously liberating and productive. Learning to work confidently with the possibilities of this aho is like learning to be a storyteller. At the start, your tales might take place in a single setting, be told from the point of view of one character, and unfold in a linear way from beginning to end. As you become more confident you can make things more interesting by fragmenting the story, jumping around in time, moving between spaces and between worlds, and introducing different voices. This is not only a matter of being creative, there are also real learning benefits for the participants. A key reason we use Mantle of the Expert is to explore multiple perspectives and there's nothing like shifting around in time and place to ensure this occurs. Another benefit is how working in a fragmented way conveys the sense to the participants that there are no right answers nor fixed events, either within the imagined world or, by implication, within real life itself. Yet another handy thing about the capacity to manipulate time is how this can help account for the gap between the imagined expertise of the expert team and the actual skills and knowledge held by the participants. At any time, the teacher can pause the action and assist participants to build the skills required, before stepping back in to the now time of the expert team pursuing the commission.

Aho 5 in practice—some classroom snapshots:

- Mina's students have been working as a team of expert museum curators with a commission from Aucksea City Council to produce a waterfront exhibition about ocean-going waka. They step into the world of the content and travel to a time 1000 years ago when ocean-going waka were first built. Here they speak to an elder (teacher in role) who shares some insights into traditional approaches to navigation. On their return to the classroom world, Mina muses, "I wonder how people make this sort of voyage in today's world?" and a discussion unfolds.

- In Charles' class, participants are exploring the rushed moments as a team of conservation dog owners prepares to depart to hunt down an escaped kakapo. In the midst of rushing around, planning, and packing, they pause time to consider the range of thoughts going through the experts' minds at this time.

- Lisa's class is starting to work together as a mountain rescue team. Today she invites them to travel back in time to when the team was first formed. The group spends the morning learning basic first aid skills, with the episode framed as training from the team's past.

Aho 6: Introducing dramatic tension

You might be wondering why "tension" appears here as an aho when it was also on the list of whenu, or core elements. The thing is, just as there needs to be tension in both directions for a weaving to work, in Mantle of the Expert teachers need to give conscious thought to working with tension during both planning and implementation. In the preplanning stage, I suggested planning a whole range of possible "what ifs" that might arise in the imagined world, nominating some of these as productive and key tensions, and mapping out how they might be introduced to ensure a successful narrative arc for the experience. Once the Mantle of the Expert is underway, the teacher will need to work with those tensions by introducing them strategically at the right moment. And, as well as working with the pre-planned tensions, they will also respond to those that arise naturally within the drama. Note here that we are not talking about responding to the multitudes of everyday tensions that arise in any classroom, such as squabbles, misunderstandings, absent participants, or missing resources. Of course, the teacher and participants will need to cope with all of these, but the focus here is on tensions within the imagined world of the content and the responsible team.

Dramatic tension is central to drama. It impels participants into the task and makes it feel important. Over time, small children learn to introduce and respond to tensions in their play and it's this same capacity that grown-up playwrights, movie makers, and even advertisers use to increase the sense of urgency, enjoyment, and commitment in their creations. Role without tension is not dramatically satisfying: it can be interesting to "be" a pirate, watch a film about an astronaut, or see pictures of what's on sale at the supermarket. However, to really get our attention, we need something gripping to happen: the pirate is forced to walk the plank, there's an ignition failure, or there's a "limited one-time-only offer". Dramatic tension is what makes the imagined world exciting, intriguing, engaging, and fun and it has a number of benefits for learning, too.

A key benefit of dramatic tension is how it can open up curriculum learning, including deliberate acts of teaching in specific curriculum areas. Any productive tension requires some kind of action or task to be taken before the team can move on—and this action or task will be something that can be related back to the learning areas of the curriculum. For example, if the teacher reports to the team: "I've just heard from the printer that they can only do our logo design in two colours under the current budget—what are we going to do?" this opens up possibilities for exploring the use of texture, line, contrast, composition, weight, and shading in image making, which can be linked to learning intentions in visual arts. The skill for the teacher is to be alert to that link and ensure that deliberate acts of teaching occur at the appropriate level for the participants, as discussed in aho 7. In this way, the use of productive tension is like creating mini "problem-based learning" projects within the wider commission.

Grappling with tensions can also help foster deep thinking. This is true of all tensions, but particularly the key tensions. These are introduced so as to interrupt the progress of the commission, pull things up short, and make the team pause and consider their options. We saw this in the *Shark Tank* example, where Wiremu's revelations about the funding of the project forced participants to take stock and think about the best way forward. Working with tension like this allows participants to encounter problems in authentic ways, developing resilience and thinking skills. This sense of participants grappling with curriculum as they respond to tensions has been identified by teachers I've worked with as one of the most striking benefits for their learners (Fraser et al., 2012a). Of course, the teacher needs to employ key tensions sparingly. Too many experiences of being knocked off course and participants could lose traction and self-belief.

So, as part of working with this aho, the teacher will need to plan activities to introduce and work with the productive and key tensions that were planned earlier. Tension is inherently dramatic and vice versa—in fact, the two words are often used synonymously—so it makes sense to introduce tensions in a dramatic way. If you review examples of Mantle of the Expert both here in this book and elsewhere, you'll see that minor and key tensions are generally introduced through drama strategies. In the *Shark Tank* example, the key tension was introduced by the teacher in role, while in the *Toy Museum* experience, the key tension was revealed through a letter offering a full restoration of the bear. The *Objects of Significance* lessons didn't really include a key tension, more a series of productive ones such as discovering the damage to the artefacts and solving the problem of how to create an engaging display. It would be theoretically possible for a teacher to introduce tensions from outside the imagined world but even teachers new to the approach find it more natural to use drama strategies or conventions—like a letter or an overheard conversation—to introduce the tension in the now time of drama. When we come to aho 8, we will discuss drama conventions and strategies in more detail.

Even teachers who have clear ideas about the productive and key tensions they wish to introduce need to be open to working with unplanned ones as they arise. Not everything that occurs in a Mantle of the Expert journey can be predicted or planned. This is true of any teaching experience but becomes even more so when dealing with events in an imagined world and when one remembers the importance of positioning participants as competent collaborators. For a teacher wishing to generate possible tensions on the hoof, Heathcote's list of possible tensions, which was introduced in stage one, provides a useful set of prompts. Haseman and O'Toole provide another useful way of categorising tensions, with four main types: tension of the task—when something must be attained; tension of the relationships—positive and negative strains between individuals; tensions of mystery—incomplete or unknown circumstances; and tension of surprise (Haseman & O'Toole, 1987).

A shortcut to thinking up possible tensions as you teach is to use the strategy of asking "What if …?" just like we did when pre-planning. Say, for example, we find ourselves in an imagined world where there's a seal in the town's open air swimming pool. The first and most obvious question is "How did it get there?" But to raise productive tensions, we need to ask "What if …?" questions, like "What if it's hiding from a predator?", or "What if it doesn't want to come out?", or "What if it bites?" Often the difficulty is not in generating possible tensions but in knowing which ones are fit for purpose. Plenty of potential tensions could be unproductive in the sense that they might not be of benefit to the developing drama with this particular group. Some might undermine the fictional worlds as they have been set up so far—"What if the seal is actually a walrus?"—while others might be from an inappropriate genre—"What if Superman arrives and uses his superpowers to zap the seal?" Some tensions might not be age appropriate: "What if the seal is a metaphor for the fishing industry?", or they might be potentially upsetting: "What if the seal bites your baby brother's hand off?" As with any storytelling, or dramatic event, the teacher needs to screen potential tensions for what is productive and suitable. Anything introduced to the imagined world needs be sensitive to existing rules of that world, as well as being fit for context, purpose, genre, and safety.

The teacher is not the only one who will come up with tensions during a Mantle of the Expert. Participants will often suggest them too. This is because the approach is essentially improvisatory in nature. Mantle of the Expert doesn't involve an audience, narrative structures, rules, or fixed roles as in theatre sports games or TV improv shows. But it is improvisatory in the same way that children's dramatic playing is: participants are encouraged to put forward ideas as everyone creates a story together, making and responding to offers. With this in mind, the teacher will need to sift through offers made by participants and consider carefully how to respond. Sometimes an offer will be helpful and can be incorporated as a productive tension. An example of this can be seen in the *Toy Museum* example, where one of the children's comments about the crayons' low status grew into a set of monologues from different coloured crayons expressing existential angst. At other times, however, offers may be counter-productive, as in the *Shark Tank* example where one of the participants wondered about packing a gun in their briefcase. As teacher, I did not accept the offer, but used it to instigate a discussion about what the implications of that decision might be and what felt "right" within the givens of our imagined world. The teacher need not worry unduly that participants will "take over" and expect to dictate what the tensions should be. In general, unless they are out to deliberately subvert the event, participants understand that it is the teacher's job as the overall facilitator of the experience to filter offers in this way and select what tensions will be explored.

Another aspect of working with tension is where the teacher creates dramatic effect from moment to moment, using the dimensions of dramatic imagination, the techniques of voice, body language, and even technologies such as lighting, music, and objects to manipulate the mood of the experience. There are lots of ways to work with this kind of presentational tension, many of which are not exclusive to drama teaching. For example, when a teacher drops her voice to a whisper or uses an excited tone of voice to say "You'll never guess what we are going to do next ...", that is building tension. The same goes for introducing a scene through the dimensions of dramatic imagination, introducing mystery objects, setting a time frame for an activity, or making something into a game or competition. Parsimony, or deliberately holding back on information, is another example of this kind of tension. Any time a teacher adds interest, theatricality, complexity, or intrigue to a task we could say they are working with the aho of tension. Many teachers work in these kinds of ways without necessarily thinking of it as working with tension. However, by thinking of these techniques as part of the aho, the teacher in Mantle of the Expert can begin to use them in a more intentional and conscious way.

Aho 6 in practice—some classroom snapshots:

- Hine's class has been working on a technology-based commission designing night vision goggles. The client has specified that these are to be used in kiwi conservation projects. Back when she did her planning, Hine decided on a key tension in which it would be revealed that the goggles were also destined for military operations. Now it's time to introduce this problem to the team—so Hine starts thinking about what drama strategy and convention to use.

- Jane is using the storyteller voice to guide her participants into a moment from history. To build tension, she uses a hushed voice and describes the scene through the senses, drawing on the dimensions of dramatic imagination: light and dark, movement and stillness, sound and silence.

- Children in Alyssa's room are sharing still images of the expert team celebrating its success. One child notices a small detail: "That neighbour is angry about the noise—look at her cross face!" Alyssa responds to the offer by including it as a productive tension. She invites the class to consider the neighbour's perspective and a conversation with the neighbour is improvised in pairs.

Aho 7: Moving between different teaching modes

This aho is a complex one and will be something you will need to explore and practise over time. In some ways there are similarities between the use of this aho and the idea of moving between worlds discussed in aho 5, but there are crucial differences too, since different teaching modes can be employed in both the real and imagined world. Let's start by defining what a "mode" is. I'm basing my definition on the one offered by Brian Edmiston (2014). He describes modes of teaching *and* modes of learning but we'll focus on teaching modes only. Simply put, a mode is a particular way of going about something. If we use the literacy notion of "multi-modal" learning, we can say Mantle of the Expert is multi-modal in that participants can learn through moving, writing, drawing, the use of space, the use of gestures, the use of the body, and so on. Edmiston (2014) points out that teachers using drama often move through multiple modes in a single lesson. To give a simple example, a teacher who encourages participants to move around for the first part of an activity and then settle down to write has drawn on two different modes.

Mantle of the Expert teaching makes use of multiple different modes, not all of them dramatic. A teacher will certainly employ the drama conventions and strategies as described in aho 8, but will also draw on more traditional modes such as reading passages of text, making notes, doing experiments and trials, creating and testing models, drafting and redrafting, matching, labelling, repeating, memorising, and so on. The *Literacy Online* page of the TKI website describes the importance of "deliberate acts of teaching" including "modelling, prompting, questioning, giving feedback, telling, explaining and directing" (Ministry of Education, n.d.-b) and all of these have a place in Mantle of the Expert. Those new to Mantle of the Expert or enthused by the creative, dramatic aspects might assume that such traditional instructional strategies are ruled out. But in truth there's very little you shouldn't do in a Mantle of the Expert classroom as long as the task can be justified within the professional context of the commission. The approach is designed so that we explore curriculum in a holistic way, but the teacher needs to teach the skills, knowledge, and literacies associated with a particular curriculum learning area as these are encountered. In selecting the mode they want to use for a particular activity, teachers should not be afraid to employ deliberate acts of teaching to scaffold learning in whatever curriculum area is being explored.

As for how a teacher decides which mode to use, once again there are no firm rules about this—it's about meeting the needs of the participants in the moment. A teacher can simply bear in mind the range of modes available and endeavour to draw on the strengths of all of them. Fortunately, there are some rules of thumb that can help. Later in the book we'll look at a tool called the teaching compass that helps achieve a balance between open-ended and more teacher-directed modes. We'll also look at Bruner's triad of *enactive, iconic,* and *symbolic* forms of representation, since this aligns closely with the idea of teaching modes and provides a handy tool for sequencing. In terms of drama, another way of thinking about teaching and learning modes is to consider the difference between dramatic playing, projective play, and dramatic performance. As discussed in Chapter 2, all three of these forms of drama are familiar to children as extensions of their spontaneous dramatic play and their experiences watching theatre, TV, and movies. All have qualities that can be useful in a Mantle of the Expert experience, so let's look at them one at a time.

The dramatic playing mode is exploratory, open-ended, and enacted in "now time"; we agree to behave as though the things we are imagining are happening to us right now. Dramatic playing is generally unfocused with lots of fluidity between our real-world selves and the people we are being in the imagined world. It's also lived through together rather than being something prepared and shown to an audience. This mode can be really useful when exploring something new and generating new ideas, as in the *Shark Tank* example where everyone stood around the imaginary tank pointing and talking about the sharks swimming around inside. The teacher can prompt a shift into this dramatic playing mode at any moment in the same way that they might make an offer to enter into a child's imagination game: "I wonder what's in the garage? Let's take a look" or by using the narrator or storyteller voice: "And so the artillery waited for the order for the bombardment to begin." The teacher here is shifting into shadow role—remaining as teacher but signalling (through their words and also body language) that they have entered the imagined world. This implies an invitation to participants to step in too. The dramatic playing mode usually involves the whole class and is mostly done as a quick burst of improvised exploration rather than a sustained activity. It's all-in too, with no one "looking on" from the real world. Dramatic playing can be utilised with a smaller group provided the rest of the class is invited to adopt a watching role within the game; for example, "We'd better not all go into the clearing together. Can you lie down here in the bushes and keep watch?" Given that this form of play is associated with younger children, it is no surprise that dramatic playing is most often used with more junior participants, though it can be used with all ages.

Projective playing is where the teacher or the participants perform roles, but, rather than taking on full role with their whole body, they use objects or part of the body to perform indirectly. Examples include puppets, dolls, cutouts, hands, or objects. The examples in this book do not include many instances of projective playing, as I've only recently started to explore it in my teaching. There's a suggestion of it in the *Shark Tank* example where the participants were invited to speak as Wiremu's conscience, and rather than using teacher in full role, we had Wiremu represented by his hat. Other examples might be where participants improvise a conversation between two people, using their two hands to indicate who is speaking, or where a key moment from the imagined world is played out by setting up a scene constructed out of cloths and blocks. In a recent classroom drama based on the Māori creation story, I drew heavily on projective play by using simple puppets, cloths, and found objects to build a three-dimensional diorama of the story. This was valuable as a way of anchoring the turning points of the story and helping children learn the names of the different atua. Using projective play like this can bring a sense of magic and ritual to the storytelling and provides a sense of distance. This is particularly useful if you want to maintain a sense of reverence and to promote discussion and reflect on the action as well as being inside the story. Projective playing may be associated most with younger participants, but can be successfully used with all ages.

Dramatic performance is a more structured and controlled way of working with imagination and role. This mode can be distinguished from dramatic playing and projective playing in that it involves part of the class becoming an audience. Dramatic performance will involve a playing phase as ideas are explored and worked out, but when it moves on to preparing something for others to watch, it takes on the quality of dramatic performance. For participants working in this mode, there is a sense of focus and often more independence from the teacher. There's also a clearer distinction between the self and the role being played. Dramatic performance often makes use of drama conventions and compacts that give it an abstract quality; for example, by freezing time or listening in to the inner thoughts of a role. Working in the dramatic performance mode can be useful in all sorts of ways, including finding out more about people, exploring past situations—in the real or the imagined world—predicting future events, playing out conversations, reflecting, and evaluation. Dramatic performance can also be used as a way of rehearsing events or conversations that are then fed in to the imagined world. For instance, in the *Shark Tank* example, children rehearsed lots of different ways they might hold the tricky conversation between the company and the nurse to persuade her of the value of keeping the augmented reality simulator around the patient's bed. Working in dramatic performance encourages participants to think about the effective use of techniques such as voice, body language, and use of space, and the teacher might offer feedback and reflection on these aspects, though the main emphasis is always on the commission and the professional tasks being undertaken. This mode is probably the most commonly used with older participants and young adults.

Those familiar with process drama or drama for learning may be wondering why this isn't mentioned as a mode alongside dramatic playing, projective play, and dramatic performance. On closer examination, though, we can see that it's more a matter of quality and purpose: drama strategies and conventions can be used as part of dramatic playing, projective play, or dramatic performance depending on how much you wish to structure the experience and whether it's designed for an outside eye. In terms of modes, then, the teacher operating with Mantle of the Expert can move between student-led exploration and deliberate acts of teaching set up by the teacher. They can also shift between the enactive, symbolic, and iconic forms of representation and between dramatic playing, projective playing, and dramatic performance. Making full use of this aho is hugely complex and deserves thoughtful investigation. Over time, you will develop a sense of when to move between modes: you'll grow more familiar with the opportunities each one offers to make meaning; and you'll get better at matching modes to the needs of your participants. Every group will be different and every teacher will have their preferences and their strengths and it is this that makes each Mantle of the Expert experience unique.

Aho 7 in practice—some classroom snapshots:

- *Lin's specialist technology class is engaged in a commission to produce designs for portable cabins to be used as emergency housing for civil defence. The commission letter includes a requirement for them to be made of fire retardant materials. Lin includes several episodes in which testing takes place* in controlled lab conditions. During these episodes, explicit instructions are used to ensure the tests are conducted safely, and Lin gives a lecture to participants framed as "professional development", explaining what gives some materials their fire retardant qualities.

- Sefina's group are working as experts in animal transportation designing animal carriers for different endangered species. For the first episode, Sefina uses the dramatic playing mode, with the whole class in role as a team of rangers as they creep towards an injured Sumatran tiger. Next, dramatic performance is used as groups of children create photos of different moments from the successful capture, which are shared back to the whole class. After this, Sefina is concerned to include some symbolic learning, so—in role as head ranger—she thanks the team and invites them to complete the paperwork in which they need to log the job, identify all equipment used, and make a detailed record of the process and outcome.

Aho 8: Using drama strategies and conventions

Use of drama strategies and conventions is probably the most visible aho in Mantle of the Expert teaching and it is the thing that teachers most often ask for help with. To demystify things, it may help to remind ourselves that every teacher already uses a myriad of non-drama strategies and conventions every day—to organise the classroom, sequence activities, introduce new information, invite reflection, and so on. And they will continue to use these non-dramatic strategies and conventions when they use Mantle of the Expert. As for drama strategies and conventions, these are simply ways of getting things done within the special duality of classroom drama: signalling the presence of the imagined world, moving the teacher and participants in and out of role, exploring perspectives, introducing and exploring tensions, progressing the narrative, reflecting, creating aesthetic or artistic responses, and introducing new possibilities for dialogue.

It's also important to remember that the aho of using drama conventions and strategies is just one among many. I remember when I first started using Mantle of the Expert, I felt sure the secret to the whole approach lay in learning about as many drama conventions and strategies as possible. If I could just grasp the lot, I thought, I'd have the whole thing sorted. However, I've come to see that, for teaching to be fully successful, all the aho need to be interwoven. I've also learned to avoid seeing strategies and conventions as a collection of tools to be collected and mastered by the teacher or the participants. When I started out, I was hungry for descriptors, and couldn't understand why someone hadn't written a comprehensive list. Over time I noticed that there are no fixed or agreed labels. I also came to realise I only really understood a convention or strategy when I had seen it in action or experienced it as a participant. Slowly, it dawned on me that conventions and strategies look and feel different every time they are employed, depending on the context, the group, and the purpose. So instead of trying to collect them like tools in a toolkit, I started to see them as a set of principles to be reworked as the need arises.

If you read the drama education literature, you'll see it contains various definitions of what constitutes a "strategy" and what is a "convention". I'm about to use these terms differently from how they are used in other publications—including *The New Zealand Curriculum* and even my own previous writing! I don't wish to cause confusion, and as emphasised a few times, the definitions in this book are not "right" or "final". Be aware, this is a contested area as you seek to form an understanding that resonates for you and your practice. To be clear, in this book I'm using the word *strategy* very broadly, to mean any way of working in the classroom that is used to achieve a particular goal. As for *convention*, this is a tricky one. We actually have two quite different meanings within the same word: a convention is both a way in which something is usually done and it's an agreement between two parties covering particular matters. These are in fact quite different concepts and in Mantle of the Expert we need to talk about both. So, for the purposes of this book, I am using the word *convention* to cover the first sense of the word—a way in which something is usually done—and I'm introducing another word, *compact*, to refer to the agreement made at the time between teachers and participants about how the convention will work. Whether it is explicit or implicit, the *compact* is a unique agreement about how everyone will behave in light of how the imagined world is being set up and how the elements and techniques of drama will be organised. A compact might include: agreements about what's going on in the imagined world; whether participants will move into the imagined world or not; what objects or things in the real world will be used to "stand in" for things from the imagined world; how we will signal the start and end of the dramatic moment; and so on. This distinction between strategy, convention, and compact might seem rather picky, but I think it's a really useful way to consider how to use this aho.

Let's look at an example of how purpose, strategy, convention, and compact interrelate in practice. A teacher using a drama strategy or convention first thinks about the purpose of the next activity: for example, to bring in an historical figure from the imagined world. Then, the teacher chooses a dramatic strategy for how to achieve it. This could happen in lots of ways, but let's say the teacher decides to go into role. Next, the teacher needs to think about whether there's a convention, or familiar way of working with that strategy that could suit. For example, they might choose one of Heathcote's role conventions and decide to move into role as someone in a photograph (more on these and other conventions in a moment). The chosen convention will carry with it a compact—a set of agreements that will sustain the convention and make it "work". The teacher will need to decide whether participants can figure this compact out, or whether to make the terms explicit. Thus the planning goes through the following steps:

PURPOSE: To depict an historical figure from the imagined world.

STRATEGY: Teacher in role.

CONVENTION: The role representing someone in a photograph.

COMPACT: The teacher explains to the class that they're about to take on a role as someone in a photograph. This means they won't move around or speak and will act as if they can't hear or respond to anyone. The teacher will symbolise the role by sitting in a frozen position at a table (i.e., the elements of role and space will be foregrounded, but the techniques of voice and movement won't be used). The position of the teacher's hands and the direction of their gaze will indicate the presence of an imagined object on the table in front (in this case a typewriter). The teacher explains that they will be staying frozen for a few moments while participants discuss what they see.

Purpose, strategy, convention, and compact are nested terms, in the sense that any change a teacher makes in one of them will inevitably bring about a shift in the others. For example, in the example given above, the teacher could keep the same purpose and even the same strategy, but change the convention by playing the role within the convention of a documentary film clip. That version of the task would mean forming a different compact, with possibilities of movement and sound included. This example is a reminder that conventions and strategies are not "fixed" things, but constantly subject to adaptation as the situation requires.

Working with the definition of a convention as a "familiar way of doing things" reminds us there are a huge number of potential ways of organising our activities. Dramatic Inquiry is about bringing the real world into the classroom, and the real world offers countless familiar ways of working that can be co-opted as ways of working in the classroom. Many of the conventions used in a Mantle of the Expert classroom come from theatre and are associated with mime, soliloquy, use of mask, chorus, puppetry, tableau, and so on. Music and dance also offer familiar ways of working with composition and form that can be used in the drama classroom for arranging sounds and moving bodies. There are conventions associated with visual art where we can find paintings, friezes, photography, sculpture, and all the other ways of working with imagery. Then there's the media where we can make use of conventions associated with videos, news reports, documentaries, tweets, and so on. Every facet of cultural life has conventions associated with it, whether it be to do with food and eating, celebration, mapping, religion, or body decoration. Every expression of identity, selfhood, and culture carries conventions that can be useful in a Mantle of the Expert experience. In time, as these ways of working become familiar to the teacher and participants, they become familiar ways of working—or conventions—of the approach itself.

There are a number of books and handouts available to guide teachers in the use of conventions in drama teaching. See, for example, O'Neill and Lambert (1992), Bowell and Heap (2013), Neelands and Goode (2000), and Carey (1995). A glossary of some commonly used drama conventions can be found on the TKI website (Ministry of

Education, n.d.-c). Many of these sources use shorthand—one or two word labels to describe how conventions might be used; for example, we have "conscience alley" where participants form two lines and speak as the conscience of another person walking through. Then there's "freeze frame" where participants work in groups to create a frozen moment in time from the imagined world. Or how about "speaking thoughts aloud" where participants in role are encouraged to speak aloud the inner thoughts of a role. These are just three examples of many widely used conventions. It's already been noted that "mantle of the expert" is often included as a convention in these lists, which can be confusing! Thinking about conventions in terms of these labels is a useful starting point for many teachers and it can be helpful to have them presented in this accessible way. However, there are also some limitations in thinking about conventions like this.

One danger of working with labelled conventions is that the focus of the class might shift to learning the conventions rather than learning through them. Heathcote described her concerns about this tendency, referring to "the dreadful hot seating" which she said was to be "discouraged" due to its tendency to promote the "endless discussions which bedevil Mantles" (Heathcote, personal communication, 26 June 2010). While this certainly is not the message promoted by any of the authors listed above, it's important for teachers to avoid the trap of thinking of learning about strategies and conventions as the focus of the lesson. More on this in Chapter 6. Another concern that can arise from labelling strategies and conventions is that we can come to see them as fixed and to be used the same way every time. A clear example is the strategy of "teacher in role", sometimes abbreviated to TIR. Often, this term is assumed to mean the teacher will take on a full naturalistic role—one that talks and responds to the participants. This seems to imply that this strategy just carries with it one convention and one compact, where in fact there are many ways the strategy can be varied. The use of any convention depends on the purpose and strategy behind the convention, and the terms of the compact that will sustain it. So, while working with labelled conventions is a great start and I would encourage you to access lists and work with these, I would also encourage you to work towards a more nuanced awareness where purpose, strategy, convention, and compact are all considered so that strategies and conventions can be used flexibly to serve the wider learning purposes of the Mantle of the Expert experience.

For a more nuanced understanding of conventions, let's consider the list of 33 role conventions provided by Heathcote.

1. The role actually present, naturalistic yet significantly behaving, giving and accepting responses.
2. The same, except framed as a film. That is, people have permission to stare but not intrude. 'Film' can be stopped and restarted, or re-run.
3. The role present as in 'effigy'. It can be talked about, walked around, and even sculptured afresh if so framed.
4. The same, but with the convention that the effigy can be brought into life-like response and then returned to effigy.
5. The role as portrait of person. Not three dimensional but in all other ways the same as effigy.
6. The role as portrait or effigy activated to hear what the class is saying. This causes selective language.
7. The role as above, but activated to speak only, and not capable of movement.
8. The role depicted in picture: removed from actual life, as in a slide of role, a painting, a photograph or drawing. This includes those made by a class, as well as prepared depictions.
9. A drawing seen in the making, of someone important to the action, as on a blackboard.
10. A stylized depiction of someone. For example an identikit picture made by the class in frame as detectives.
11. The same, except made beforehand, so is a fait accompli.
12. A life size (cardboard) model with clothing (real) of role. For example, 'framed' as if in a museum or sale rooms. 'This is the dress worn by Florence Nightingale when she met Queen Victoria after Scutari.'
13. The same, except the class is dressing the model so as to see 'how it was' on that day when these events happened.
14. The clothing of a person cast off in disarray. For example,

remains of a tramp's presence, or a murder, and escape as in a highwayman situation.

15. Objects to represent person's interests. This works as above, but more intimate things can indicate concerns rather than appearance. For example, a ring of a Borgia.

16. An account of a person by another person in naturalistic fashion. For example, 'Well when I saw him last he seemed all right. I never dreamed anything was wrong.'

17. An account of a person writing as if from that person, but read by someone else. For example, a diary.

18. An account written by the person who now reads it to others, for example a policeman giving evidence or a confession. The role is present in this case but in contact through their writing as an author might well be.

19. An account written by someone, of someone else and read by yet another.

20. A story told about another, in order to bring that person close to the action. For example, 'I saw him open a safe once. It was an incredible performance. I'm not sure if he would assist us though.'

21. A report of an event but formalized by authority or ritual. For example, an account of bravery in battle on an occasion of the presenting of posthumous medals.

22. A letter read in the voice of the writer. This is an emanation of a specific presence, not just any voice, communicating the words.

23. The same, but the letter is read by another with no attempt to portray the person who wrote it, but still expressing feeling.

24. A letter read without feeling. For example, as evidence, or accusation in a formal situation.

25. The voice of a person overheard talking to another in informal language; that is, using naturalistic tone.

26. The same, but in formal language.

27. A conversation overheard, the people are not seen. Deliberate eavesdropping as in spying.

28. A report of a conversation, written and spoken by another.
29. A reported conversation with two people reading the respective 'parts'.
30. A private reading of a conversation, reported as overheard.
31. The finding of a cryptic code message. For example, tramps or spies.
32. The signature of a person found. For example, a half-burned paper.
33. The sign of a particular person discovered. For example, the special mark of the Scarlet Pimpernel. (Heathcote in O'Neill, 2015, pp. 76-76).

Heathcote published this list in 1984 and later expanded on it by and adding one further convention:

34. A coat of arms or initials placed upon objects denoting ownership. (Heathcote 2007; Heathcote & Whitelaw, 1985)

In her later version of the list, Heathcote included this reminder: "productive tension will always have to be a feature of such encounters … Careful framing or point of view and need must be attended to, otherwise class are merely entertained" (Heathcote, 2007). This fits with the notion of interweaving different aho, and could be rephrased as a reminder that aho 6 and aho 3 are closely interrelated with the one we are discussing.

The key thing to notice about Heathcote's list is that all the conventions are specifically related to role—hence the title "role conventions". In other words, they are all ways of bringing a person or perspective from the imagined world into life in the classroom. Heathcote put it this way: "All the conventions function as 'other' but in relation to people" (Heathcote, 2007). Instead of providing a set of labels for fixed and repeatable ways of working in role, Heathcote's conventions are offered as provocations that could be used in multiple ways and in any number of contexts.

Any of the role conventions on Heathcote's list can be used in three different ways. Option one is for the teacher to take on or evoke the role. Examples include: a teacher in full role; the teacher providing a coded message; or setting up a pile of important objects in the corner that evokes the sea. Option two involves the participants taking on or evoking the roles. For example, where the participants create an effigy in small groups or work in pairs to come up with a conversation overheard in the client's office. In option three, the role can be shared, with teacher and participants creating an image or a scene or otherwise taking on roles together—as, for example, the *Objects of Significance* example where everyone created a tableau of the exhibit. The decision on which of these three options to use will depend on the teacher's judgement about group safety and exposure. It will also depend on whether the teacher wishes to bring new information to the group.

If it's important for everyone to receive the same information—as in the *Shark Tank* example where everyone needed to hear the details from the under-sea probe—the teacher will need to take on the role themselves. If the aim is to prompt the group to create multiple ideas and responses, then the teacher will ask participants individually, or in pairs or groups, to step in to the imagined world and evoke the role. To stay with that point for a moment, the teacher does need to bear in mind how to take account of the multiple outcomes that might emerge from participants taking on roles. In the *Shark Tank* example, Heathcote convention 25 (voice of a person overheard talking to another) was used to improvise a conversation between the nurse and a member of the expert team trying to convince her to trial a virtual environment in her ward. In this case, some discussions concluded with the nurse being convinced, while others concluded with the nurse continuing to object. To avoid a sense of uncertainty, I reframed the conversations as provisional by asking, "What did we learn from that activity that will really persuade the nurse?" and then, in the next lesson, cemented the outcome by employing the strategy of a letter which confirmed that the virtual reality environment had indeed been built.

All the conventions on Heathcote's list, apart from the first, offer ways to work dramatically without necessarily using all the elements and techniques of drama that are employed in full-blown improvisation. For example, number 2—creating an effigy—places fewer demands on participants than actors feel when they create a scene in full role. Participants do not need to move, or speak, or maintain the action. They do need to consider tension, space, facial expression, and proxemics, among other things but this is contained within one focused moment in time. It is the deliberation and time taken to create the effigy that makes the work effective, rather than what it looks like. The other conventions, too, provide clever ways to create work that is abstract and non-literal: they reduce the demands for full-on acting while in no way reducing the level of thinking and creativity required to produce interesting work. And this is a key point about conventions. Their primary purpose is to set up circumstances where participants make meaning and think deeply. It's not only drama, it's also inquiry. Conventions can also be seen as key to making the learning social, since, through conventions, participants get into dialogue and exchange with each other, with the teacher and—in a sense—with the fictional others that are being represented. On its own, a convention is meaningless; only as a prompt for thinking and dialogue does it take on a purpose. So, the teacher needs to make sure that participants are actively speaking, dialoguing, and grappling with the ideas as they work. Another important aspect to bear in mind about these conventions is that they are often about constraining or only partially revealing information. For example: a photo presented to the class may be damaged; a letter may be found in fragments; or a person in role may only gradually reveal important information. This sense of mystery or intrigue is what builds participants' engagement and gives them permission to be creative. It is this aspect that makes conventions theatrical. It is also something that takes practice, even for the experienced practitioner.

So, how does a teacher know which convention to select? Well, if we think of conventions as "habits of practice" or "familiar ways of working" and if we consider that for each one there must be a purpose, a strategy, and a compact, then a teacher using one of Heathcote's role conventions might plan like this:

PURPOSE: To introduce a key tension.

STRATEGY: Letter.

CONVENTION: Letter read in the voice of the writer (Heathcote's role convention number 22).

COMPACT: The teacher invites participants to listen in as someone (in this case the client) writes the team a letter. The teacher adopts the body language of the client sitting at a desk and uses a formal tone and pitch to read out the words while typing on an imaginary keyboard. Before they start, the teacher reminds participants they are not in the room with the client and are unable to speak directly to them. They are asked to listen through to the end of the letter before reacting. As the teacher finishes speaking they press a button and a copy of the letter is projected on to the classroom's large screen.

Looking back at this description, and the list of role conventions, can you think of a way this teacher might fulfil the same purpose using the same strategy—the letter—but with a different convention? Can you sketch out the compact that might be in place for that? And how about if you keep the same purpose but use a different strategy—say, the teacher moving into full role —what convention could be used alongside that? Once we start to think of Heathcote's conventions list in this way, we realise how many possibilities it can generate. We also realise that the list could never be completed as the teacher will always find other possibilities depending on the purpose, strategy, and compact in each instance. For example, in my teaching, I frequently use emails, Skype calls, and avatars as ways of evoking role. These can be engaging for participants more accustomed to digital devices than hard copy letters. I used to worry that these were not truly role conventions since they were not included on Heathcote's list. Now, I realise they are, since they are ways of evoking people from the imagined world. Digital possibilities were only just opening up when Heathcote formed her conventions list, but her list was always updating and I suspect she would have acknowledged these examples over time. As the interplay of imagined and digital worlds continues to expand, I'm sure a whole range of new drama conventions will come to light. Remembering to think of conventions as provocations rather than a set of instructions will help us remain open to innovation and possibility when working with this aho.

The aho of selecting drama strategies and conventions will be used right from the start of a Mantle of the Expert experience. Take the opening of the *Toy Museum* example: here, the strategy was to use a narrated story, and the convention was close to number 15 on Heathcote's list—an object to represent someone's interests. In our example, the compact was that an object from the imagined world, in this case a toy, would be imagined by us rather than actually present. In the *Shark Tank* example, the opening strategy was to have student teachers in role using convention number 3, which then segued into number 7 when the figures in the scene were activated to speak responses to questions. Looking back at the other two examples, perhaps you can use Heathcote's list to identify the conventions used in each case. You can also see some of the ways drama strategies and conventions were used in the next phase to build a sense of investment in the imagined world. Examples included: representing the office space on paper; re-enacting moments from the team's imagined past; or creating artefacts to stand for objects in the imagined world. The commission, too, will usually be introduced by selecting a drama strategy and convention. In the *Toy Museum* example, the commission was introduced using the strategy of a letter, while in the *Shark Tank* example, the strategy was the same, but with the convention that the letter was read out in the voice of the writer. In *Objects of Significance* the commission was delivered through a combination of narrator voice and ritual.

Once the Mantle of the Expert experience is underway, drama strategies and conventions continue to be used to introduce moments of productive tension and to play out the resolutions of those tensions. This was something Heathcote emphasised in her own definition of conventions as ways of working designed to, "enable classes to get a grip on decisions and on their own thinking about the issues they are dealing with" (Heathcote, cited in O'Neill, 2015, p. 83). As the Mantle of the Expert journey nears its end, drama strategies and conventions will be used again to represent some kind of conclusion to the commission and the inquiry. You can see this illustrated in the examples described in Chapter 3. The conclusion, reflection, and transformation activities will also often have a dramatic element. It can be seen, then, that the aho of "selecting drama strategies and conventions" is used throughout the teaching of a Mantle of the Expert. As such, it is closely associated with other aho and may be inseparable from them.

This is particularly true of aho 3—"the taking on of multiple perspectives", aho 5 —"travelling in and out of worlds and through time and space", and aho 6—"introducing tension". These things are so inherently dramatic that the teacher is almost inevitably going to need to work with drama strategies and conventions to achieve them.

Different Mantle of the Expert practitioners will differ in the ways they approach conventions. If you use the structured planning process described in this book, you may pre-plan quite a few of the activities and conventions. You will have decided the overall direction of your Mantle of the Expert journey in the preliminary planning stage. Then, after you decide on the moments of productive tensions and the tasks that emerge from those, you can use the list of 34 role conventions as well as your own personal kete of preferred strategies—dramatic or not—to introduce the task to the participants. So, for example, during the preliminary planning for the *Shark Tank* example, one of the possible tensions was "What if there was a problem with the probe?" This led to a possible task around recreating the sound files. To introduce this, it seemed most useful to have a teacher enter the class in full role as the person in charge of the probe, so role convention 1 was used. The activity was planned something like this:

PURPOSE: To introduce key tension.

STRATEGY: Teacher in role.

CONVENTION: Teacher in full role—as actually present

COMPACT: The participants will be asked to agree that when the student teacher is wearing a tie, he will be representing a new person from the imagined world—a scientist called Bruce. We will interact with Bruce as members of the expert team of augmented reality creatives. We should think of ways to welcome him to our office.

If you pre-plan your activities like this, you can have quite a bit worked out ahead of time.

While carefully pre-planned activities like these can give a sense of security, you will soon find you want to work in a more spontaneous way, using conventions "on the hoof" in response to what is arising in the drama. This is what very experienced practitioners do all the time, and it gets easier with practice. The process begins by thinking deeply about the purpose: ask yourself what the fictional situation calls for and what the participants need before they can move on. For example, the lesson might involve speaking to a nurse from the battlefields of Gallipoli. Rather than going straight into role, the teacher might reflect that participants need a sense of the realities of her working conditions. With that purpose in mind, a strategy, convention, and compact can be set up to meet that need. For example:

PURPOSE: To paint a picture of the realities of a frontline hospital in Gallipoli.

STRATEGY: Teacher in shadow role.

CONVENTION: An account of a person writing as if from that person, but read by someone else. For example, a diary (role convention 17).

COMPACT: The teacher will use a small notebook, and will ask participants to accept this as representing the diary of someone involved in the battle, but not as a fighter. The teacher will ask participants to listen and imagine the life of the person who is writing. Participants will agree to imagine that the words spoken by the teacher are from the notebook. These will describe the sights, sounds, and smells on the ward as well as using some specific terminology from the period.

Where you need to think on your feet, a quick mental run through of "purpose/strategy/convention/compact" may help. Or, if in doubt, use a strategy and convention you are familiar with. Over time, you will find yourself internalising the general principles and you won't need to consult lists or plan in this kind of detail before you can start. Your participants, too, will become increasingly familiar with strategies and conventions the more they use drama. This means your compacts will become less and less ponderous. You may also find that participants themselves start to make suggestions—as when one of the children in a recent Mantle of the Expert I taught insisted that one of the fictional others from the imagined world should be present to watch our presentation to the client. The child realised I was not available to take on the role so they fetched the hat I had worn when in role, and set it down on a chair to watch, thereby evoking role convention 15.

Also worth acknowledging in this context is the idea of coherence. I've only recently cottoned on to this idea myself—following some professional development with Tim Taylor—so you may notice that many of the examples in the book lack what I'm about to describe. The notion of coherence involves making sure that the unspoken rules of a convention are followed carefully so that the decisions you make in the imagined world make sense and are consistent with things like logic, the laws of physics, and so on. For example, if you have chosen a convention where participants are creating a photo in a family album, it is somewhat incoherent if you suddenly decide the people in the photo have the power to listen to questions, answer, speak, and move around—that's not what photos do. If it suddenly feels important to speak to the person in the photo, the teacher *could* say, "I wonder what the people in the photo would say if only we could speak to them …" and, with that, the convention shifts from the people in role being in a photograph to something more akin to theatre where they represent the people from the photo. But this is shifting the convention simply out of convenience. For more coherence, and to maintain the dramatic tension implicit in the context, it might be better to stick with what is possible within the convention you have stipulated.

Another aspect of coherence is the idea that if some participants are in role, the others in the class should be too. To put this another way, the teacher should try to ensure that all participants are in the imagined world together, and that the givens of that world are consistently adhered to. For example, instead of "hot seating" where participants outside the imagined world ask questions of a figure from within it, Tim Taylor suggests that the questioners might also be given a role—for example, police officers, journalists, or concerned onlookers. Having done a lot of across-world "hot seating" in my time, including in examples described in this book, I have recently begun to follow Tim's advice and must admit I've found the resulting activities have a lot more integrity and depth to them. Taking a moment to invite the participants to take on a role—even a shadow role—lifts them into a different relationship with the person being questioned and opens up different status and language possibilities. Try it, and you'll see what I mean.

As teacher you can expect your use of this aho to be a little clunky at first, but as time goes on and as you and your participants become accustomed to the idea of conventions, you'll find they require less explanation. You and your class will also become attuned to working in more abstract ways and with increasingly sophisticated symbolism. For example, in the early stages of the *Shark Tank* example, participants were asked simply to improvise a conversation in pairs. There was no insistence on focused work and the role required only the voice with no expectation of movement or facial expression. In later episodes, with the participants more accustomed to drama, Andy and I were able to ask them to explore more abstract conventions including speaking from the perspective of the captive shark, or revealing the contrasting voices in Wiremu's head as he contemplated his ethical dilemma. With time and practice at drawing on this aho, you and your participants will become adept co-weavers until, finally, you will no longer experience the teaching and learning as a series of distinct activities based around conventions—it will be more fluid and intuitive than that.

Aho 8 in practice—some classroom snapshots:

- *Karin's class has been gathering information on the battle of Gate Pa. To make the process of sharing back information more interesting, she invites participants to step into role as soldiers from the 43rd British Regiment giving evidence at a military commission 5 years after the events. The compact is agreed that the teacher will pose questions in the voice of a critical and unsympathetic investigator. In response, participants have a few moments to consult their notes and prepare a written answer before nominating someone to step forward, stand to attention, and deliver the response.*

- *In Stan's classroom, participants are in role as villagers from settler times gossiping about a local scandal. Instead of a large-scale discussion where people might talk over each other, Stan invites participants to form groups with others to represent different households. Stan then takes on the role of a feral cat who wanders from house to house overhearing fragments of conversation. The compact is set up so groups know to speak up as Stan comes by and fall quiet as he moves on.*

Aho 9: Working with power: status, agency, and positioning

A key feature of Mantle of the Expert that differentiates it from other forms of teaching is the way a teacher works with power and positioning. For more on what these terms mean, see the theoretical underpinnings discussion in Chapter 2. It's a key premise of the Mantle of the Expert approach that participants are considered competent, capable co-constructors or co-weavers, and this is never set aside. Edmiston draws a useful distinction between teachers who only use "power over" their class as distinct from those who also explore using "power with" and "power for" the participants, which is always the aim in Mantle of the Expert (Edmiston & Bigler-McCarthy, n.d.). Here's how Elicia Pirini, a teacher from Tauranga, describes her experience of learning about power in Mantle of the Expert teaching:

> There's a difference between saying 'Here, you have my permission to take some power now,' and the kids understanding the power they already have within them. The kind of thing I'm talking about here is something I've only noticed within a Mantle (of the Expert). It's not a sudden shift or a gift from the teacher. It's a subtle process of growing into status ... evidenced in their body language and their side conversations with you and with each other.
>
> (Fraser et al., 2013, p. 142)

Working with powerful positioning is so fundamental to the Mantle of the Expert approach that it's already been included as one of the three teaching modalities alongside inquiry and drama. The reason working with power is also listed here as an aho is that there are specific actions and strategies the teacher can draw on from moment to moment within the implementation of a Mantle of the Expert experience. There are conscious strategies that can be used to rework power relationships, shift status, and create spaces for agency. These are signature pedagogies that can be practised and woven in to the process.

Within Mantle of the Expert there are always clear limits on participants' power: it is never a free-for-all. While Mantle of the Expert positions participants as co-constructors, opens spaces for agency, and gives authentic opportunities for ownership and agency, this is always within carefully managed limits. As the founder of Summerhill school A. S. Neill famously pointed out, there's a big difference between freedom and licence:

> As I understand it, freedom does not mean that the child can do everything he wants to do, nor have everything he wants to have. Yes, that simply stated, is the crux of the matter. Freedom, over-extended, turns into license. I define license as interfering with another's freedom. For example, in my school a child is free to go to lessons or stay away from lessons because that is his own affair, but he is not free to play a trumpet when others want to study or sleep.
>
> (Neill, 1966, p.7)

True freedom is always about give and take, and understanding how to work within the norms of a situation. Licence occurs when individual freedoms are over-extended to the point of impacting on others. Participants in Mantle of the Expert will never be granted licence to do entirely as they wish, either in the real world or the imagined worlds: both worlds depend on clear limits and expectations to function.

In the real world, participants are expected to operate within the social practices of the classroom: to be respectful; to work in collaboration with their peers; to share resources; and so on. Within the imagined world, too, there are clear limits set by the commission, the givens of the responsible team, and its backstory—including the context the team is operating in. This is why you can't pack a gun to visit an aquarium (unless you belong to a profession that uses a gun). The teacher's job when drawing on this aho is to ensure that clear limits, givens, and constraints are introduced, understood, and maintained. The teacher will use their own agency within the situation to set up limits and boundaries including safety protocols, the givens of the imagined world, and the requirements of the commission. Most of the time this will be done through co-construction, though on occasion the teacher may assert their authority and tell participants what's expected of them. A key part of this signature pedagogy is knowing when and how to exert authority when introducing limits and boundaries and creating a habitus for the learning to take place.

This insistence on clear limits is not because teachers in Mantle of the Expert delight in using power over their students, but always because of a desire to create spaces for agency. Sometimes, clear limits within the real world actually create more freedom in the imagined world. As Tim Taylor puts it, "one of the great things about Mantle of the Expert is how it can teach participants about the limits we all operate in—ironically by giving them far more scope in the fiction" (Taylor, personal communication, 2020). I like to think about learning as being like the flow of water in a river. If the banks are wide, the water meanders and runs slow and shallow. If the banks are close, the water flows more deeply, with increased energy and a clearer sense of direction. So it is within Mantle of the Expert. As teachers we can choose where to place the banks to control the flow of learning. We can plan for open-ended activities where the constraints of the task are set wide—as in the *Toy Museum* example, where children imagined playing with their favourite toy—or we might bring the banks in close to encourage a more dynamic flow—as in the *Objects of Significance* example, where the museum curators were encouraged to peer at one tiny detail on their artefact. Within the imagined world of Mantle of the Expert, constraint can be really productive.

Within a tightly focused task, participants have—ironically enough—more freedom to explore ideas, to ponder alternatives, to suggest different directions, and to come up with creative solutions. In the *Objects of Significance* example just described, the task was productively constrained by insisting that the damage was not visible to the casual observer. This encouraged the groups to discuss in even more detail what the damage might be and what the story behind it was. This task had coherence within the "givens" of the imagined world, in that more significant damage would have been spotted earlier. Also, narrowing the window of choice meant that participants went deeper in their responses; they were productively constrained into a position of power. And there was plenty of agency in their creative decisions, since what they decided had wide-ranging consequences within the imagined world. So one of the key ways in which teachers can work with this aho is to think about how they will set limits: to allow open-ended and free-ranging exploration or to keep things narrow and focused.

While the teacher maintains firm control over the limits of tasks, this doesn't mean they are authoritarian in their behaviour towards participants. Rather, there is a careful repositioning of participants in both the imagined world and the real world. Within the fiction of the responsible team, participants are framed as experts with authority and expertise. The tasks and activities they undertake are always those of competent, professional people. Powerful repositioning carries over into the real world, too, through the social practices developed there. The teacher signals and then maintains this repositioning by ensuring tasks are meaningful and by adopting a language and register that support the positioning.

One way teachers can start with this aho is to take care in their use of language in speaking to participants. Once we start to accept participants as responsible people who are colleagues and equals within the imagined world, we naturally begin to adopt inclusive language such as "What do we need to do next?" rather than "What should you be doing now?" We also adopt a respectful register even with direct instructions such as "If you wouldn't mind just checking …" Teachers have told me that, by making a conscious effort to see participants as high-status figures in the imagined world, they find themselves talking differently to participants in the classroom world, too. Our use of language is more of an indicator than a driver for shift in positioning: it's hard to force a shift in relationship by changing your way of addressing people, it requires a change of attitude first. Having said that, we have to start somewhere and language is a powerful tool. Positioning theory suggests that we can shift power with language, since every speech act we carry out subtly shifts and refines our roles and positions. With our modelling, participants, too, can shift their language register. In a previous book, I shared the example of a child who stayed behind after class one day to check in with the teacher with the words, "I fear I may have offended some colleagues today" (Fraser et al., 2013, p. 74). Here was a language register that would never normally have been adopted in the classroom, but which felt appropriate in light of the elevated language and respectful positioning that had been modelled.

Having said that powerful repositioning of participants occurs in both the real and imagined worlds, it's probably fair to say that the greatest opportunities to explore shifts in power take place in the imagined world, since the teacher must maintain an overall responsibility for the shape and direction of things in the real world. Within the imagined world there are endless opportunities for consciously shifting status positions, through the use of role. As we will see in Chapter 5, each time a teacher moves into role they have a range of registers or status positions available (Morgan & Saxton, 1987). Selecting and moving between these involves a conscious shift of position and language. The decision on which status position to choose will depend on what you are trying to achieve. And having explored multiple different stances, registers, and status positions, the teacher can also take time to invite participants to reflect and think critically about how power has been performed within their work, both in and out of role.

Aho 9 in practice—some classroom snapshots:

- Agnes has introduced the commission to her class in the form of a letter from the client. When she wrote it, she deliberately used language to match the professional status of the responsible team. Now she adopts another position, taking on the role of someone from the team who is confused by the letter and needs its meaning explained.
- Rawiri's class is working as a team of animators charged with creating stop-motion versions of culturally significant stories. They have created an image of the moment Mahuika loses her temper with Maui. As a productive constraint, Rawiri challenges the groups to think of one small head movement they could add to enhance the storytelling of that moment.
- Jonas wants to gather his class together for a discussion. Rather than using one of his traditional classroom signals such as clapping a rhythm, he tries a different language register, "Colleagues, could we gather for a moment?" It feels a little artificial and strange but he notices the children move quickly and quietly to the mat.

Aho 10: Encouraging critical thinking and reflection

Critical thinking and reflection are very visible signatures of the Mantle of the Expert approach, employed from the very first moments through to the end. The competency of thinking runs through all the other aho since each one depends on participants processing something—whether this is the social aspects of learning as in aho 1 and 2, exploring multiple perspectives and points of view as in aho 3, asking and responding to questions as in aho 4, negotiating the complexities of working in multiple worlds in aho 5, overcoming the tensions that arise in aho 6, engaging the mind through different teaching modes as in aho 8, or figuring out and shifting between different status and power positions as in aho 9. Teachers will draw on this 10th aho in combination with others throughout. From start to finish, participants will think in words and images, they will think through symbol and metaphor, they will think using their heads and their bodies, and they will think as individuals and as a group. As we will see, the circumstances to support thinking are almost "hard wired" into the design of Mantle of the Expert. However, this doesn't mean it happens by itself. The teacher still needs to set up opportunities and consciously reach for strategies that promote critical thinking and reflection. It's these strategies that are our focus here.

For a teacher trying to support critical thinking, one key strategy is to keep complexifying things. Critical thinking is about grappling with problems, and one way of categorising problems—the one favoured in medical literature—is to describe them as simple, complicated, or complex (Shuker, 2019). *Simple* problems are those in which one solution works every time. *Complicated* problems, while predictable, have multiple solutions that can be applied. With *complex* problems, on the other hand, the problem keeps changing as you approach it, requiring nimble, creative responses and a tolerance for trial and error. These are the very circumstances that Mantle of the Expert provides through the commission and the introduction of productive and key tensions. So, almost any time a "neat" solution or an oversimplified "right answer" is presented, the teacher can add complexity and make things trickier by slowing down, asking a question, introducing a dramatic tension, or using a dramatic convention to bring in another perspective. Some years ago a Year 5 student in a class working as documentary makers who had been charged with creating a fair and balanced story about Kaimanawa horses tugged at his hair in frustration and blurted out, "I just don't think there's such a *thing* as 'one truth' here ...!" which I took as a very good sign. Not because I enjoyed watching him suffer, but because I enjoyed watching him start to form an understanding of the complex ways in which the real world operates. Key steps a teacher can use to enhance complexity include slowing down, introducing tensions, questioning, stepping in and out of the imagined world, moving between roles, and using a strategy Heathcote called, "dropping to the universals"—which will be explained in Chapter 6.

A teacher wishing to foster sophisticated thinking is very much assisted by the fact that participants are working in metaxis—the dual awareness of the real and imagined worlds. First of all, moving into the imagined world provides opportunities to carry out mental practice of tasks and situations that might be encountered in real life. This is something psychology researchers have found can really enhance real-world performance, particularly if the mental practice is done with attention to detail (Driskell et al., 1994). In Mantle of the Expert, of course, this mental practice is embodied as well. And there are opportunities for it to be critical, too. At just about any time, a teacher can invite the class to pause the action in the imagined world, step back, and take stock—something we can never do in real life. This lets everyone rewind, replay, and fast forward time to reconsider key moments and play out multiple possibilities before making a decision and continuing with an agreed action. Augusto Boal once famously wrote, "Maybe the theatre in itself is not revolutionary, but these theatrical forms are without a doubt a rehearsal of revolution" (Boal, 1979, p. 141). Similarly, Mantle of the Expert participants experience an embodied rehearsal of behaviours and choices that can be applied in their real lives beyond the classroom.

Working in metaxis also sets up the conditions for meta-cognition. Having two worlds running at once means there is a sense of constantly "looking in" on the self and others in the imagined world, and "looking out" at the self and others in the real world. By drawing attention to this, the teacher can support participants to think about their thinking and be aware of their awareness; to operate on the meta-cognitive level. Through metaxis, Mantle of the Expert can teach important lessons about thinking itself, including that outcomes are not pre-determined and thoughtful actions and careful communication have tangible consequences. Participants learn that thinking itself is highly subjective and that in any situation there are multiple ways to think.

Another aspect of critical thinking that teachers can support is the conscious consideration of the power dynamics at play in a situation. This opens up possibilities for political, sociological, and ethical grappling, which is one of the things I enjoy the most about working in Mantle of the Expert. A teacher can prompt participants to reflect on power dynamics in the imagined world by inviting participants to consider how power is being performed within an image. This could be as simple as saying, "Point to the person in this picture who seems to you to have the most power. How do you know?" Reflections on power can be broadened even more with prompts such as, "Whose story are we hearing here?", "Who else would have a point of view?", "Which fictional others have power over others and where does this come from?", and, "What visible and invisible power systems are at work here?" Combine this with the potential for taking on multiple roles, as discussed in aho 3, and we have even more opportunities for developing nuanced and embodied insights into how power and ethics operate. From there, of course, links can be made back to real-world contexts. One of my favourite questions to ask participants is, "Does this sort of thing happen in real life?" which can lead to rich discussion on the real-world implications of the imagined action. Critical thinking about power can also be carried over to discussions about the real world of the classroom. By asking participants to consider their own interactions—who participated, who didn't, which points of view were aired, what helped the discussion flow, and so on—the teacher can encourage the group to consider who is advantaged and disadvantaged in their own dynamics. In my experience, the opportunity to explore and discuss and play around with power in the fictional context makes participants more alert to, and questioning of, power dynamics in the real world. They learn that communities of power depend on behavioural conventions, and this helps them reflect on those they see operating in the real world.

It can also be valuable to encourage participants to reflect on the learning process, including how they are making meaning. Whichever teaching mode you use, you can prompt participants to reflect on what they see and hear in their own and others' work, including noting the aesthetic and dramatic qualities. Given the emphasis on process over product, I don't suggest drawing attention to this up front in my instructions: I wouldn't say something like, "make sure you use really good gestures and facial expression", for example. However, I do think there's benefit in highlighting these as part of a response: "Notice that gesture and facial expression—what's that telling us?" is useful, since thinking about *how* we did what we just did will influence future choices. The "describe then interpret" strategy described in Chapter 6 is a useful tool for this. Another way to draw attention to meaning making is to use drama conventions to support interpretation—for instance, by inviting participants to step in to another group's image and speak in role from there. The use of drama strategies and conventions can also be used to prompt critical thinking on the learning process itself. For example, at the end of a recent session I invited participants to "mark the moment" by standing in a part of the room where they had a breakthrough or made a connection. I had previously only used this strategy as a way of working in the imagined world but it proved very useful as a prompt for thinking about our own process too.

Just like critical thinking, reflection is core to learning. The famous pioneer of progressive education, John Dewey, is often quoted as having said that "we do not learn from experience, we learn from reflecting on experience" and, while this exact quote is apocryphal (Lagueux, 2014), it is a pretty good summary of what he believed. Dewey did say this:

> The old phrase 'Stop and think' is sound psychology. For thinking is stoppage of the immediate manifestation of impulse until that impulse has been brought into connection with other possible tendencies to action so that a more comprehensive and coherent plan of activity is formed.
>
> (Dewey, 1938, p. 64)

If participants bring deliberation and consideration to bear on what they are doing or have done this will really help consolidate their learning; without it, they won't make lasting connections. It is valuable after any Mantle of the Expert experience to take time to "unpack" the learning process. Perhaps the simplest prompt for a teacher to use for this is, "So, what was tricky about that?" This goes straight to the "meta" level, encouraging participants to think about the challenge inherent in the task they just completed. And reflection does not have to wait until the experience is over; there is potential for fostering it at every point of a Mantle of the Expert experience. The teacher compass, described later in the book, is one tool that can help ensure reflection is given the time it deserves in every activity. For a teacher wishing to become more conscious in their support of critical thinking and reflection, it may be useful to have a set of prompt questions and activities prepared ahead of time. And be prepared to slow down:

creating the space for critical thinking and quality reflection is time consuming but the benefits for learning in using this aho make the effort very worthwhile.

Aho 10 in practice—some classroom snapshots:

- *Gio's class is fully engaged in an imagined world where they are advocates for a refugee family seeking asylum. Today they're meeting with a government official (Gio in role) to petition for consideration of the family's case. During the improvised meeting, Gio stops the action repeatedly so that participants can consider different options for what to do and say and so these possibilities can be rehearsed. At the end, Gio checks in with participants on what they found challenging about the process and what they've learned about speaking to people in positions of power.*

- *It's the end of an 8-week Mantle of the Expert experience in Luke's class, in which participants have been a team of farm advisers specialising in carbon sequestration techniques. The participants are asked to think of an appropriate ritual for closure and decide they will plant a (real) tree on school grounds. At the ceremony, Luke invites each person to write a six-word poem summarising their hopes for the world in light of what they have learned. The poems are written on slips of paper, read out, and dropped one by one into the planting hole.*

Stage 4: Defining and refining—recording and assessment

As the weaver works on their korowai they will spend quite a bit of time refining, trimming, and reviewing the work. When it is finished, they will look it over carefully to ensure it is coherent and neatly finished. In the same way, the fourth stage of creating a Mantle of the Expert experience is about the teacher defining what has been created and, in the process, making a coherent account of the whole. This is an important stage, since it is only when we pause to record, tell the story of the learning, and assess links to curriculum or other objectives that we get the full sense of what has occurred. Without this, the experience is left floating in the air; subjective, and somewhat intangible. With this stage, the learning "lands".

A teacher can use many different processes to story the learning. I recommend not waiting until the end of the experience but recording as it unfolds since many details get lost even after a few days have passed. Many teachers find an online blog useful: you can see examples of these on the Mantle of the Expert Aotearoa website and the UK website too. Blogging the experience can be helpful in a number of different ways:

1. During the Mantle of the Expert experience it allows the teacher to clarify thinking and decide on next steps.
2. It translates the lived, embodied experience into a commonly agreed narrative of "what's going on" in the imagined world—particularly important if participants are working in groups.
3. Teachers and participants can contribute to a shared telling of the learning story.
4. It serves as a repository for pictures, video clips, and other details, which can be dropped in alongside the text.
5. It can be shared with parents, colleagues, teacher aides, and other visitors to the classroom to help them get a sense of how the imagined world is unfolding and what learning is taking place.
6. It can be used to orientate participants who join the class midway through a Mantle of the Expert experience, and shared with anyone who misses a session or has to leave before the end.

Alternatives to blogs include creating a big book of the story of your Mantle of the Expert experience. This is often favoured in junior classrooms where the book can be shared and discussed before stepping back into the imagined world. Another option is to use the walls of the classroom to story your adventures. One teacher I worked with really enjoyed trying this approach: she loved watching the space gradually transform from a clean slate at the start of the experience to an environment that wrapped the story round the participants (Fraser et al., 2013, p. 138). Using the walls can be helpful when clarifying tasks or reflecting on the learning, as it allows the teacher to physically point out reminders of their shared journey so far. While the teacher is likely to lead the process, participants may also be involved in co-constructing the record. If you have the time, I have found it helpful to establish a rhythm of starting each day of a Mantle of the Expert experience with a reflection and joint storying of the previous day before continuing together with the next part of the journey.

Of course, part of recording the learning is assessment. Newcomers to Mantle of the Expert are often concerned about how they will assess the learning that has taken place. They soon find that, in many ways, their assessment does not change. Participants are still producing pieces of writing, carrying out experiments, and making presentations just as in the regular classroom, and assessments can be carried out on these in the usual way. Having said that, the shift in positioning that is so crucial to teaching in Mantle of the Expert may result in a bit of a rethink in assessment. As Mary James points out in her appeal for a new generation of assessment practices, any assessment should be congruent with what we truly value in teaching and learning (James, in Swaffield, 2008). So, if traditional assessment protocols are not fit for purpose, it may be necessary to come up with new ones, which are:

- Alongside learning, not an 'after learning' event
- Done by the community—self assessment, peer assessment and teacher assessment
- Of the group as well as the individual
- 'In vivo' studies of complex, situated problem solving—participation in authentic activities or projects
- Focussed on how well people exercise agency in their use of resources
- Captured and reported through narrative accounts and audio and visual media
- Portfolio style, assessment as inquiry
- Holistic and qualitative judgements not atomized and quantified

(James, in Swaffield, 2008, p. 31).

This list is a useful checklist for teachers to use when judging the value of existing assessment, or coming up with new forms.

There is space in a Mantle of the Expert classroom for traditional formative and summative assessment methods, though teachers may find themselves wanting to rethink the language they use. For example, given the framing of participants as experts it may feel a bit odd to be putting smiley face stickers and comments like "good job, keep trying!" on their writing—though participants generally understand that these comments belong in the wider classroom world rather than the world of the expert team. As for the traditional assessment tools that are used in the classroom, there is no reason these could not be applied to the products of learning from a Mantle of the Expert experience. The microplanning of individual sessions will involve the teacher identifying objectives within the curriculum learning areas, and these can be assessed in the usual way. To allow for the emergent or surprise learnings that occur along the way, you may also find it useful to look back at each session and retrospectively acknowledge how achievement objectives were met. There are two important things to bear in mind when linking back to curriculum. First, the curriculum level participants are working at may be higher than the one generally associated with the year group, since planning does not spring from a concern with curriculum level but with what is appropriate to the task at hand. Secondly, the teacher must use professional judgement to distinguish between activities that merely "touch on" curriculum areas and those that involve meaningful learning. Generally, assessment will relate to activities in which deliberate acts of teaching were involved.

Along with traditional assessment, there may be more of a focus on dispositional learning. Mantle of the Expert involves so much foregrounding of the key competences, teachers may wish to assess more in relation to these. My own strategy for this is to briefly jot down on sticky notes when I see an individual using one of the key competencies particularly well—or, indeed, struggling to do so. Over time these small notes can be collected together to create a set of data on each participant's progress in the key competencies within the larger group. This data can be included in reporting alongside the other assessment indicators.

Planning in practice: *When we taught the Shark Tank Mantle of the Expert, we were lucky enough to have Gay Gilbert, the deputy principal of the school, taking notes and photos of the experience. I then used these as the basis for a blog, written with some input from student teachers (Aitken, 2013b). Andy also carried out ongoing formative and* *summative assessments on artefacts of the children's learning such as the science experiments and their writing. Our particular blog was written with an audience of other teachers in mind, and gives a lot of background detail about the planning, etc. A teacher writing a learning story for her class, parents, and community would focus much more on the participants' learning and telling the story as it unfolds in the imagined world. See the Mantle of the Expert Aotearoa website for more examples of teacher blogs.*

Chapter 5
Tools to enhance teaching in Mantle of the Expert

So far in this book, we've seen how the teacher, like the weaver of a korowai, sets up certain key threads, or whenu, in advance and then creates the fabric of the learning experience by interweaving other threads or aho in collaboration with the participants. The next level of skill of teaching, as in weaving, is learning how to create patterns within the weave. Weavers learn over time how to select and place particular threads in a particular order, how to create borders and hems, and how to add the hukahuka and other flourishes to change the colour, texture, and feel of what is being produced. A teacher using Mantle of the Expert also learns how to employ the aho in certain ways to create effective patterns, and how to add flourishes to enhance the artistry of the learning experience. In this chapter, we will look at some of the ways a teacher can finesse their use of the signature pedagogies, or aho of Mantle of the Expert to make the work interesting and distinctive.

In the sections that follow, you will find some detailed advice on how you might go about selecting appropriate aho for each phase of a Mantle of the Expert experience. As before, these are not set in stone. Over time, you will find your own patterns and sequences that may be quite different from what is set out here. It's also worth remembering you will need to be discriminating about your choice of patterns. This section introduces 16 different tools, each with its own purpose. It would be impossible to use all of these at once. If a weaver attempted to work with all possible patterns at the same time, the results would be a big unsightly mess; the same is true for the teacher. I recommend trialling one or two of the tools at a time until you gradually become adept at picking them up when needed.

This section extends on information introduced earlier in the book. We'll be building on our knowledge of the 10 core elements, or whenu, laid down in advance (see Chapter 4, stage one) and the 10 aho that can be interwoven between these during implementation (Chapter 4, stage 3). We will also talk about the initiation, experiential, and reflection/transformational phases (Chapter 4, stage 2) and we will refer to the drama elements and techniques as defined in *The New Zealand Curriculum* as well as introducing Heathcote's six dimensions of dramatic imagination. For clarification of that terminology, you are encouraged to consult the glossary or revisit earlier chapters as a reminder. Many of the tools here are from Heathcote's 2009 keynote (Heathcote, 2009) while others are versions of teaching resources originally published on the UK website and used with permission (Abbott & Taylor, 2013). You'll notice each tool is presented in the form of a small prompt card. These can be photocopied and laminated to create a set for use in your classroom teaching.

Choosing an opening—three modalities

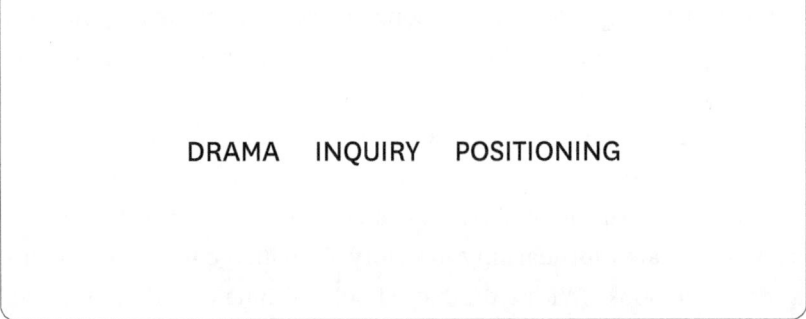

Figure 51: Three modalities tool

The first tool sets out three different ways you could start your Mantle of the Expert experience. There are several ways you can go about this. Tim Taylor describes his method as planning a sequence of five to six steps and he offers three helpful principles: "Principle 1: be subtle;

Principle 2: don't lie; and Principle 3: make it interesting" (Taylor, 2016, pp. 130-131). For my part, I suggest starting with a hook—something that will intrigue participants and draw them in to the imagined world. This is about creating the circumstances for interest and intrigue which, as Guy Claxton reminds us, are crucial to learning:

> From a functional point of view, emotions are general states of readiness to deal with broad kinds of threats and dilemmas. Fear is readiness to flee; anger is readiness to intimidate; sadness is readiness to withdraw and mourn; and 'interest' and 'intrigue' are the feelings that signal readiness to learn. Without some kind of emotional engagement, learning is slow and weak.
>
> (Claxton, 2008, p. 98)

Let's just clarify what we do and don't mean by the word "hook". If you only associate this word with contemporary fishing, it might seem an unfortunate image; as if the goal is to forcibly capture participants and reel them in to the imagined world whether they like it or not. That's definitely not the intention. Rather, we can look to Māori symbolism where the matau, or fishing hook, is associated with strength and safe passage. It is also closely associated with the forming of new terrains, as in the traditional story where Maui uses a matau to draw up the North Island of Aotearoa New Zealand. We can also look to music, where the word "hook" is used to describe the appealing introduction that draws you in to the song and sets the mood for what is to come. It's these connotations I invite you to consider as the hook for your Mantle of the Expert journey.

Looking back at the three modalities of Mantle of the Expert (see Figure 4 in Chapter 2), any one of the three can be chosen as the basis of your hook. You may choose to open your Mantle of the Expert using the drama for learning modality—in which case we can call it a "dramatic hook". With a dramatic hook a drama convention is used to conjure up a person, moment, object, or setting from the imagined world in order to entice participants to want to know more about it. All three examples in Chapter 3 began with some kind of dramatic hook: in the *Toy Museum* example, we had an imagined artefact, while the *Shark Tank* example began with an effigy gradually built up by student teachers in role and *Objects of Significance* began with the use of storyteller voice to establish a setting. A dramatic hook is a great choice if you think your participants will respond positively to a direct experience of the imagined world. You might choose to dramatise a moment from the world of the client, in which we come to see their need for help and assistance. Or you might dramatise something that shows the world of the responsible team in action. The possibilities are very wide and the process for planning is just the same as at any other point in the sequence: select a drama strategy, choose a convention, and establish a compact. A dramatic hook always has the purpose of providing clues about the imagined world you are inviting participants to enter, so you'll need to make it clear to participants that their job is to figure out what is going on. Remember to include some kind of tension, whether it's uncertainty, an intriguing facial expression, or some missing information. One of the most powerful things I have learned to do with a dramatic hook is to drip feed the information to participants. This builds intrigue and tension. Think carefully about the compact, since, with your hook, you are introducing the imagined world for the first time and the participants don't yet have any knowledge of the context. It's possible you can include them fully—as in the *Toy Museum* example—or it may be more appropriate to make the hook quite performative with participants sitting back to watch and interrogate, as in the *Shark Tank* example.

Another option is to choose a hook that invites participants into the Mantle of the Expert through the inquiry learning modality. Here, the teacher poses a provocative or juicy question or sets out a complex or wicked problem for the group to consider. Sometimes, a provocative question can be asked without too much preamble such as in the *Objects of Significance* example, where I wondered aloud what treasures New Zealand might hold in its national museum. While this question was not the initial hook, it could have been. Another option is to pose a question as a follow up to a shared story, as in Luke Willis's class, where he read a novel about an underground world and then pondered aloud: "I wonder what would actually be needed to sustain human society under the earth?" (Willis, 2013). Or, the inquiry hook might emerge from curriculum learning the class has already done. For example, in a class I visited recently, the children had become very excited about some learning they'd done in science, and the teacher wanted to move on to a Mantle of the Expert in which they created an interactive science exhibit for children. She did this by asking, "What do you reckon would be the youngest age a child could start to learn about the different states of matter?"

An intriguing inquiry hook doesn't only have to come in the form of a spoken question. It could be words written on a note or on pieces of a puzzle hidden around the room. Or the question could be posed non-verbally through an image—perhaps a photo, a video clip, or one of my favourites, a line drawing created on the whiteboard in front of the group. As with a dramatic hook, the teacher can build a sense of intrigue by drip feeding information and inviting participants to discuss what the images bring up. Of course, within the parameters of the planning process proposed in this book, the teacher has a purpose in mind. So, while the inquiry question is a genuine one and the discussion around it will honour participants' personal responses, the teacher will need to guide the discussion towards the focus they have in mind.

The third option is to invite participants into the imagined world through the powerful positioning modality. In this kind of hook, the teacher finds some way to consciously shift the power dynamics and appeals to the participants as high-status thinkers or experts in their field. This could be done in the real world as with the states of matter opening described above where my opening offer to participants was based on their recently acquired real-world knowledge of science. Or power dynamics could be shifted in the imagined world by setting up a task that displays the skills and attributes they will need for the expert team. For example, clues could be found and decoded that lead on to participants becoming a team of detectives. Alternatively, a positioning hook could be framed from within the imagined world by addressing the group directly as the experts and challenging them to respond in kind. The *Objects of Significance* example *could* have been launched like this, if, for example, I had started with a teacher-in-role voice and simply expected participants to work out who they were and what was going on. This would have been a risky move, however, and I would have been careful to stress that participants were not expected to respond in role right away. Personal experience has taught me that it can be counter-productive to expect participants to join in an imagined world before they have complete understanding of it. I have been a participant in Mantle of the Expert experiences where I was expected to improvise without full awareness of the context, which I found rather demanding and off-putting. This strategy should only be used with more experienced participants who can be expected to leap in willingly.

We've identified three possible types of hook: dramatic, inquiry, and powerful positioning. Sometimes, openings can be an elegant combination of all three. For example, Northland teacher Renee Downey used a photo of a fire-affected area of an Amazonian forest as an inquiry hook for a Mantle of the Expert experience looking at animal rescue. As soon as the children started describing what they could see in the image, Renee introduced a positioning dimension by addressing the group (who were very familiar with Mantle of the Expert) as if they were a team of people experienced in dealing with this kind of situation. Later in the experience, the same photo took on a dramatic quality when it became the basis for a mapping and planning exercise as the team prepared to enter the area. It's worth thinking about how images, drawings, notes, or roles introduced at the start might have an ongoing existence within the imagined world.

Whichever modality you decide to use to open your Mantle of the Expert, a key thing to consider is how you will connect the participants to the imagined world. Your goal is to find a point of connection between their real-world experience and enthusiasms and the imagined world and curriculum content you will be exploring. It is the choice of frame that provides a window to look through into an imagined world which is at once familiar and strange or intriguing. Bowell and Heap (2013) call this "the communication frame" and illustrate the concept very well with the example of a drama about cowboys. While many participants (at least in the UK or New Zealand) would have little or no direct experience of cowboy life, once they are framed as cowboys *who have lost their horses*, a point of connection is created (Bowell & Heap, 2013, p. 57). Any hook into a Mantle of the Expert experience requires some kind of familiar point of connection for participants, so this is a critical point to bear in mind when planning.

Setting up the imagined world—elements of drama

> ROLE   TIME AND SPACE   ACTION   TENSION   FOCUS

Figure 52: Elements of drama tool

Once you have begun your Mantle of the Expert experience, you and the participants will need to build a sense of the imagined world that you are operating in. Those familiar with process drama may use the term "building belief" for this important phase. You can also think of it as building commitment or concern, since it is imagination or affinity rather than belief that is being built. You will have made some broad decisions about the non-negotiables, or "givens" of the imagined world during your planning, so whatever you have pre-decided needs to be conveyed to participants and their buy-in needs to be earned. For example, you may have decided participants are going to become a responsible team with expertise in digital technologies. If so, you'll need participants to engage positively with devices and you'll need to develop a shared history of success in this area. The imagined world only becomes three-dimensional when it is fleshed out and further co-constructed with the participants.

Once again, there is no right way to go about this but if you are looking for a rule of thumb, it might help to look at the elements of drama and how children use them in their dramatic play. The five elements of drama, according to *The New Zealand Curriculum*, are: role, time and space, action, tension, and focus. The idea is that any drama needs these five elements in place so the teacher can use the tool above as a reminder of what's required any time they invite participants into an imagined world. While the elements could be introduced in any order, the sequence as written has merit, as it roughly echoes the way young children tend to set up their socio-dramatic play: "I'm a firefighter" (role); "I'm here in my truck" (time and place); "I'm driving along" (action); "Oh no—a fire!" (tension); "Let's put it out!" (focus). When building the imagined world in a Mantle of the Expert, the teacher can echo this sequence, starting with activities to establish the group's identity as a team before moving on to activities related to where they are and what they do. This then allows you to introduce the commission which will supply the action, tensions, and a sense of focus to the experience. Some tried and tested ways of working with role, time and space, and action in setting up the imagined world include the following:

Table 4: Suggestions for working with the elements of role, time and space, and action

Role	Who we are in the imagined world. Remember, it's the blanket role of the responsible team that matters most, not individual roles within it.	Letters to and from previous clients CVs, name tags Mementos from previous commissions Awards Home page of the team website Advertisements for the team Overheard conversations between people talking about the team
Time and space	Where we are in the imagined world. This includes the world of the responsible team and the client.	Plans of the office space Signs and information boards A timeline of the team's past history The company foyer The main entrance door
Action	What's going on. This includes the backstory of the responsible team and the client.	Revisiting key moments from a past commission Carrying out a mini-commission A visit from teacher in role as the client A story or account of a moment from the client's life Letters, reports, accounts, and commendations that add detail on the past actions of the team Introducing the main commission

Ideally, the 10 whenu, or core elements of the Mantle of the Expert, will be clarified for participants after the first few sessions. If this is not achieved, the teacher will need to spend time building and strengthening those aspects. Depending on the entry point, the early sessions of a Mantle of the Expert experience are often spent building a sense of affinity with the fictional world of the expert team. Once this has been established, the teacher can guide the students through the inquiry processes necessary to address the commission. As well as holding the commission as an overall goal, the teacher will hold in mind the narrative arc of the experience, introducing tensions to keep things interesting and allowing time for a sense of closure and reflection at the end of the journey.

Building commitment—continuum of engagement

> ATTRACTION—ATTENTION—INTEREST—MOTIVATION
>
> CONCERN—INVESTMENT—OBSESSION

Figure 53: Continuum of engagement tool

Heathcote's continuum of engagement is a tool that can be very useful for teachers at any stage of a Mantle of the Expert experience, including the early stages where commitment to the imagined world is being built. The tool is a reminder to plan activities with a view to participants' psychological experiences as well as the details of the imagined world. The version of the continuum shown here is adapted from Heathcote's original (see Taylor, 2018 for more on this). The continuum is based on the idea that the optimal psychological state for learning is one where participants are fully engaged or obsessed in their learning—akin to what psychologist Csikszentmihalyi has famously called a "state of flow" (Csikszentmihalyi, 1990). While most teachers will recognise this phenomenon, and agree that it is a great thing to aspire to in the classroom, it's not so easy to describe how to create, support, or sustain it. This continuum tool suggests a pathway. It reminds us that optimum engagement cannot be achieved unless participants are first attracted to pay attention. This can then build to interest and motivation, which involve more "buy in" than attention. Once participants are motivated their engagement shifts from being extrinsic (the upper level of the tool) to more intrinsic (the lower line of the tool). Then there is the opportunity to develop a sense of concern and investment in what is happening. This can eventually lead to a sense of being productively obsessed in the process.

The continuum tool can be used in a number of ways. It can be used at the planning stage as a reminder to plan activities designed to first attract, then interest, engage, and build investment. The tool is even more useful during teaching itself, as the teacher can observe the participants, gauging which level of the continuum they appear to be at and planning with an eye to the next. For example, if the teacher observes participants slipping back from being invested to just interested, they can focus on activities to build that sense of motivation and investment back up. While there is no simple recipe for the kinds of activities and tasks that will assist, we know attention is generally the product of something novel or exciting, while interest results from a sense of personal connection and perhaps also a sense of mystery or a puzzle to be solved. Concern and investment arises when we feel a sense of empathy with a person or thing and we have been part of decisions about it. True obsession takes time and arises from a strong desire to understand, practise, and get things right. Bearing these different qualities in mind can help teachers craft activities to support participants to move through the continuum.

An example of the tool in action can be seen in the *Objects of Significance* example described in Chapter 3. The initial opening of this lesson was designed to attract attention and engage the children. There was a sense of interest from the children but only the second time it was taught did we include an activity to foster participants' sense of investment; this was the point where they were invited to add some damage to the drawing of their object. This opportunity to contribute to the imagined world helped participants to build investment and thus a deeper commitment to telling the object's story. As for examples of motivation, concern, and investment there are flashes of these in the *Shark Tank* and *Toy Museum* examples where children did not want to stop working on some tasks and became intensely focused on fulfilling the requirements of the commission. For a more nuanced account of using Heathcote's continuum, see the sequence described by Taylor (2018).

Selecting drama strategies and conventions—enactive, iconic, symbolic

> ENACTIVE (1–4)   ICONIC (6–15)   SYMBOLIC (16–33)

Figure 54: Enactive, iconic and symbolic tool (for use with role conventions)

Drama strategies and conventions are woven in to every stage of a Mantle of the Expert experience. Earlier, we discussed how these can be selected based on the purpose, strategy, convention, and compact. This tool provides another possibility when working with Heathcote's role conventions. It's based on the work of Mantle of the Expert practitioner Allana Taylor (Taylor, 2009). She points out that Heathcote's role conventions align quite neatly with Bruner's theory of iconic, symbolic, and enactive forms of representation. Conventions 1–4 foreground the enactive in that they involve physical action and embodiment. Meanwhile, conventions 6–15 foreground the iconic, in that they involve symbols, images, drawings, or films (with a dash of the physical in conventions 6 and 7 where they come to life). Finally, conventions 16–33 are principally symbolic, in that they involve language, writing, maps, maths, music, and other ways of representing thoughts through language. Without wishing to over-simplify the conventions, which in fact all involve more than one form of representation, this tool may be useful when deciding which to use. If you want to extend a class to work with images and drawing this might encourage you to select a role convention from that part of the list, while if you are keen to encourage written language, this might be a prompt to choose from the "symbolic" category. Meanwhile if a class has been sitting too long, then you might decide to introduce an enactive activity. We'll return to this idea of working between the iconic, symbolic, and enactive shortly, with another tool to help with sequencing of activities.

Sequencing drama strategies and conventions—narrative, poetic, reflective

NARRATIVE   POETIC   REFLECTIVE

Figure 55: Narrative, poetic, reflective categories tool

Neelands and Goode (2000) suggest that drama conventions fall into three categories: those that are narrative, in that they help move the story forward; those that are poetic, in that they are used for exploring or deepening the aesthetics of the experience; and those that are reflective, in that they encourage participants to pause and think about the meaning that's being made. These three categories may already be familiar to New Zealand teachers as they were included in classroom drama teaching materials produced by the Ministry of Education (2006). If you are working with the labelled conventions often found in process drama, you may find that definitions of these include a note of whether they are narrative, poetic, or reflective in function. In the past, I created a set of conventions cards with this information included, and found it quite helpful as a way of thinking about which one to choose next. In reality, though, a teacher can use just about any convention for a narrative, poetic, or reflective purpose. So, rather than tying the categories to particular conventions, it may be more useful to consider whether your purpose is narrative, poetic, or reflective and to think about how you will work with conventions and strategies to meet this objective. The tool is also helpful in reviewing your planning, to help you realise if you're under-utilising one of these categories. At first, you're likely to focus on using conventions with a narrative purpose—moving the story along. However, over time you will develop more of a feel for the poetic and reflective moments too.

Working with signs and symbols—divisions of culture

War	Work	Workshop	Shelter	Health
Healing	Learning	Travel	Transport	Embellishment
Family	Child-rearing	Nourishment	Myth	Memory
Law	Punishment	Communication	Clothing	Commerce
Trade	Death	Leisure	Climate	Environment

Figure 56: Divisions of culture tool

As Heathcote was always keen to stress, "comprehending the remarkable range and subtlety of sign" is a crucial and sophisticated aspect of teaching in Mantle of the Expert (Heathcote, 2009, p. 14). Put simply, signs are things that stand for other things. Signs come in three types: icons—which have the direct appearance of what they represent (for example, a photo of somebody's face); indices—which represent something by direct association, like a frown suggesting concentration; or symbols—where the association is entirely dependent on convention, such as the red poppy traditionally used as a sign of remembrance on Anzac Day. We use icons, indices, and symbols all the time in daily life, whether we are making a shopping list, interpreting a friend's body language, recognising the meaning of traffic signs, navigating with a map, or listening to lyrics in a piece of music. And signing is core to literacy. The acts of reading, writing, speaking, and using body language—where letters, sounds, and gestures "stand in" for real concepts, ideas, and events—are all about signs and symbols.

Signing is a crucial skill for life and Mantle of the Expert is a great place to practise this. As in all dramatic play, the duality of real and imagined worlds in Mantle of the Expert means that signing takes on an additional layer of complexity. For example, a child taking an imaginary phone call by holding a wooden block up to their ear is practising signing. The block is accepted as a sign for "phone", with the imaginary phone standing in for a real one. In decoding the sign, the child has to work out which bits of phone behaviour will apply in this situation and which can be ignored; the fact that the phone does not emit the voice of the other person doesn't prevent the child accepting it as a symbolic substitute for a phone. It's all very clever.

All in all, it's well worth giving thought to the subtleties of signing in your teaching. When thinking about what artefacts you might introduce, create, or draw attention to within your Mantle of the Expert, the divisions of culture list can really help. The tool was developed by Heathcote from the work of Edward T. Hall (Hall, 1989) and was something Heathcote used actively in her own day-to-day teaching (Tim Taylor, personal communication, May 2020). The tool is designed to help a teacher think in more detail about the imagined worlds being created. Any imagined world will contain communities, which always organise themselves around certain cultural concerns. Selecting one of the divisions on the tool and teasing it out further can provide you with an array of signs and symbols that are appropriate for your planning. For example, when building the world of the responsible team you might look at the cultural division of "clothing", which might in turn spark an idea for an activity to create a team uniform or do an audit of protective gear worn out in the field. Moving to another division, say, "memory", inspires a very different set of possible tasks—perhaps a task based around digging up a time capsule that was buried in the 1950s when the company first began. The same cultural divisions can be applied to thinking about the world of the client and the world of the content providing a rich palette of possible colours and perspectives as you and your participants paint in the details of the imagined world. It's worth noting that, while Heathcote's tool is very valuable and effective for an Aotearoa New Zealand teacher, it was created with a Eurocentric world view, so may need revisiting and revising for the Aotearoa New Zealand context.

Hand-drawn pictures and words can be used to signify artefacts of significance within the imagined world. Carefully produced, these can have real aesthetic impact at every stage of the unfolding experience.

They can be used as a hook to start things off: an example I've used a few times begins with a careful drawing of a multi-storey building, to which I add a fence, a demolition sign, and finally curtains and a pot plant in one of the windows. Each of these signs layers in additional meanings and sets up a sense of tension and intrigue about the imagined world. Drawings and hand-written labels can also be used to represent items from the world of the responsible team, from everyday objects like phones, car keys, and filing cabinets to specialist equipment required by the expert team for the work at hand. As Heathcote reminds us: "These are the minute particulars of the mantle. Never to be ignored. Such signing creates the enterprise work and reminds all that we are colleagues, doing a grown-up job with ethics, responsibility, morality and spirituality—ie stewardship, honour and respect" (Heathcote, 2009, p. 15).

Drawing can also be a way to introduce new objects from the imagined world, as in the *Objects of Significance* example where three drawings on pieces of paper were used to signify the three new items arriving at a museum. In general, I recommend creating such drawings in front of participants rather than preparing them earlier: there's something magic about seeing a line drawing appear in front of your eyes and figuring out what you are seeing. Participants can also be encouraged to include their own drawings in their drama work. I experienced this recently while working with Tim Taylor and a group of teachers. Tim invited us to produce frozen images of scenes from Florence Nightingale's hospital in the Crimean War. As part of the picture, he invited us to consider where the light source was and to show any significant objects with a drawing. One group produced a drawing of a candle in a lantern held aloft and a cross to hang around the neck of one of the figures in the group—very simple objects. However, looking at these in the context of the wider three-dimensional image was a powerful invitation to really read the image as one might read a painting in an exhibition. The process helped us endow other parts of the image with significance that might not have occurred to us so readily without the use of the abstracted drawings. Because we'd created the pictures ourselves, we also had a sense of personal investment in the imagery.

Even though Mantle of the Expert is all about the imagination, it can be very powerful to include physical props, objects, and artefacts as signals. There are a number of ways in which real objects can be useful. Some younger participants benefit from working with concrete representations as a first step to imagining; for example, using a real phone to make an imaginary phone call before moving on to just gesturing with their hands. This can be helpful for participants on the autistic spectrum too. The same goes for marking the imagined space in some tangible way. If someone in your class struggles to buy in to an imagined space, a simple taped square or a chair and table may be helpful. And signs do not always have to be two-dimensional or crafted out of things in the classroom. Though none of the examples in this book used authentic objects, these can add a real sense of wonder and specialness. When most things are imagined, introducing something three-dimensional—especially when it is beautifully crafted or thoughtfully chosen—gives that object particular significance. Imagine the delight at unfurling a detailed facsimile map, handling a real fossil, or receiving a message in a real bottle.

Tangible objects can also be used to add historical authenticity. For example, as part of a Mantle of the Expert exploring the 19th century settler experience, the teacher might draw the blinds and light a real oil lamp before asking participants to write in role as someone who has just arrived in Aotearoa New Zealand on a settler ship. The sensory experience provided by the quality of light and the sound and smell of the lamp burning would provide valuable insights into the historical period as well as adding aesthetic impact to the task. And carefully selected objects can add a sense of ritual and seriousness, especially where they have symbolic importance. For example, a teacher might plan on concluding a Mantle of the Expert exploration of the history of Parihaka with an activity in which children speak in role as children who witnessed the events. To add even greater potency to this activity, the teacher could introduce a white feather (the symbol of the passive resistance of the people of Parihaka) and invite participants to hold this as they speak. While it is obviously difficult for teachers to make, borrow, or hire beautifully crafted props, documents, or clothing, it's well worth incorporating these where they are available.

Teaching in role—registers and positions

> ONE WHO KNOWS—INFORMANT—ONE WHO NEEDS HELP—IMPLICATOR
>
> LISTENER—SERVANT—APPRENTICE—DEVIL'S ADVOCATE

Figure 57: Registers and positions tool

Teaching in role—sometimes referred to with the shorthand TIR—is probably the most commonly used strategy in Dramatic Inquiry teaching, including Mantle of the Expert. There's lots about teaching in role in the theoretical and practitioner literature—including how it compares to acting—and it's well worth reading more widely if you're looking for advice or interested in deepening your theoretical understanding (Ackroyd-Pilkington, 2001, 2004; Aitken, 2007; Morgan & Saxton, 1987). There's more on teaching in role in Chapter 6 of this book where we'll look at the importance of clear signalling. But for now let's look at three different tools that teachers can use when they want to use the strategy of teaching in role.

We've already discussed the one tool in some detail: Heathcote's list of 33 role conventions. Whether you are new to teaching in role or have been doing it for many years, the list of role conventions supplies endless inspiration for experimentation and extension of your practice. It will help you shift the assumption that teaching in role is always about presenting a walking, talking, responding figure in full role. Heathcote's list reminds us that the role "actually present" is only the first of many options. Perhaps a more accurate definition for "teacher in role" is wherever the teacher takes on responsibility for embodying or evoking the role, using any of the 33 conventions. Under this definition, it would still be a form of "teacher in role" for participants to encounter a pile of discarded clothing or a cardboard cut-out of a figure, or even an encoded message. The more abstract conventions involve teaching "in role", in that it is the teacher who has imagined the perspective of a person in another world and left their signs for interpretation. As a teacher developing your practice and learning to create patterns in the weave, it is well worth experimenting with the full range of different conventions to explore ways to teach in and with role.

Teaching in role is about more than giving participants opportunities to engage with someone new: it's also about exploring the different power relationships and positions in that interaction. This is where the second tool can help. The tool is adapted from a handout on the UK Mantle of the Expert site and shows eight possible power positions that a teacher could take when in role, from the "one who knows" at one extreme through to the "devil's advocate" at the other. The table below expands on these eight power positions, giving an example of each and suggesting what response this would evoke from participants.

Once you've got the hang of thinking about position and register alongside role, there's a third tool you can use to add even more complexity and subtlety to the practice of teaching in role. This one involves considering the different *stances* you can take within each of these eight power positions. As Morgan and Saxton point out, any role and any position has a range of different possible stances within it. Simply thinking about whether to present a high-, middle-, or low-status stance can add countless further positioning possibilities (Morgan & Saxton, 1987, pp. 38–67). It's incredible to realise the multiple ways you can use role registers, status, and positions. Each variation supports participants to engage with new perspectives, new language registers, and new ways of processing and responding to the information at hand.

Table 5: Eight possible positions and registers when teaching in role (adapted from Morgan & Saxton, 1987)

POSITION	Relationship to group	Register	Example	Value within the drama
ONE WHO KNOWS	Someone important—with direct influence over the group.	"I am the one to be obeyed"	Teacher in role as the gang leader adamantly refuses to allow the bank robbers to use guns in the hold up.	Can be used to slow down the pace. Can prevent participants opting for "easy" or stereotypical solutions to complex problems. Prompts deeper thinking. Adds new, important information to the fictional world. Asserts teacher's authority.
INFORMANT	Someone with important information, which may be important to the group should they care to ask for it.	"Wouldn't you like to know …"	Teacher in role as a Parihaka local who can describe what happened when the village was raided—but will need to be asked.	Invites a questioning stance. Adds information and supports curious inquiry. Builds engagement—sense of earning the knowledge. Builds empathy. Invites participants to consider the act of questioning — how to go about it.
ONE WHO NEEDS HELP	Someone with no idea what to do next.	"I have no idea …"	Teacher in role as the lighthouse keeper's wife. Her husband and cat have gone missing and the light has not come on—she has no idea what to do.	Encourages participants to take charge of a situation within the imagined world (teacher still has control of the situation in the real world of the classroom). Prompts genuine responses and creative ideas. Engages critical thinking about the traditional teacher–student power/knowledge relationship.
IMPLICATOR	Someone aware of implications of different courses of action. The teacher presents these to the group and invites them to consider what to do.	"On one hand … on the other hand …"	Teacher in role as village elder points out that if the village banishes Maui for his trickery then justice will be served—but they will also miss out on using his superpowers for good.	Helps focus the class on what has happened so far in the drama and what might happen next. Helps prompt discussion (and possible exploration) of different courses of action. Helps build awareness that actions have consequences. Complexifies the right/wrong binary.

LISTENER	An interested listener—someone who is keen to hear the story of the drama so far.	"Tell me more …"	Teacher in role as the wolf's grandparent asks children (in blanket role as the wolf) to give their version of the story about blowing down the pigs' houses.	Prompts reflection in action. Can help participants consolidate what has happened so far in a drama. OR—it can help them take a whole new perspective on the story. Can help the teacher "take stock" and decide where the drama could go next.
SERVANT	Someone "in service" to the group. A helper who provides the resources (symbolic or actual) that allow them to put their ideas into practice—without providing the answers.	"I'll get you what you need …"	Teacher in role as personal assistant to a team of expert detectives investigating the scene of a monster invasion provides pens and paper for "monster profiling".	Helps position participants as competent. Supports inquiry—encourages participants to pose and pursue questions that matter to them. Encourages shifts in language register—from everyone.
APPRENTICE	Someone who wants to learn from the group.	"I'm keen to learn from you …"	Teacher in role as a beginner explorer asks participants (positioned as more experienced) for advice on what to pack for their first trip to Antarctica.	Allows teacher to conduct learning conversations with individuals and groups of participants (assessment). Helps the teacher position participants as competent. Encourages participants to grapple with incomplete understandings. Encourages participants to take a position, even if unsure.
DEVIL'S ADVOCATE	Someone taking a deliberately provocative stance on an issue.	"What about …?" Or "Go on—you know you want to …"	Teacher in role as head huntsman advises students (charged with taking Snow White into the forest and losing her) to "just kill her and get it over with".	Confronts participants with a point of view dramatically opposed to the one they are presenting in the drama. Builds engagement, through dramatic surprise and challenge. Encourages ethical thinking as participants have to justify and defend a more ethical position. Encourages critical thinking and appraisal skills. Allows opportunities to practise "speaking truth to power".

Working with the aesthetic—six dimensions of dramatic imagination

DARKNESS ⟷ LIGHT

STILLNESS ⟷ MOVEMENT

SOUND ⟷ SILENCE

Figure 58: Dimensions of dramatic imagination tool

This tool is really great for whenever you want to evoke an imagined world in detail. Heathcote's six dimensions of dramatic imagination listed here give the teacher access to the same artistic tools a director might use in a movie or a piece of theatre to create mood, set the tone, or draw attention to important moments: light and dark, stillness and movement, and sound and silence. While a theatre or movie director manipulates these dimensions through technology, the classroom teacher mostly does it through language (though if you have any of these technologies at your disposal, you can certainly use them). Here's an example of the six dimensions of dramatic action used to drop participants in to a moment within the imagined world. Imagine a teacher saying these words:

> As the villagers gather on the beach, the first rays of Te Ra are reaching over the crest of the hill, touching the clouds with golden light. The deeper valleys remain in shadow. Bright pohutukawa blossoms stir in the breeze and the expectant silence is broken only by the cries of hungry sea birds. All eyes are fixed on the sea...

Notice how these sentences evoke the scene by describing the light and dark, movement and stillness, and the sound and silence. In combination with a storyteller voice, the imagery creates a compelling invitation. Another example of the use of the six dimensions to open the imagined world can be found in the *Objects of Significance* example, which began with an evocation of the setting of the museum.

While the six dimensions of dramatic imagination lend themselves naturally to the storyteller voice, they are also very useful when working in the teacher-in-role voice or the facilitator voice. With the teacher-in-role voice, whether you're playing a low-status role such as a prisoner under interrogation or a high-status role such as a commander directing military action, you can draw on the six dimensions to give a richer, more sensory aspect to your improvisations: "It was pitch black when we started—lucky we had our headlamps ... I could hear Charlie's breath coming sharp and fast", or "We leave at dawn troops ... your orders are to proceed slowly and in total silence—is that understood?" At first you may find it helpful to script the words you will say, but in time just keeping the dimensions of dramatic imagination in mind will be enough to improvise the descriptions on the spot. This tool can be useful when you're using the facilitator voice, too. The six dimensions can help you form questions to ask about a photograph or indeed any image: "What does this shadow falling across the table tell us? What sounds do you imagine would be happening in the background when this was taken?" and so on.

The six dimensions of dramatic imagination are not only valuable for the teacher leading the experience. They can also be used to prompt participant reflection on the sensory details of an experience, whether from the real or imagined world: "Where were the moments of stillness and what did they tell us?" etc. And the same tool can be used to encourage theatrical aspects within drama for learning moments; for example, inviting participants who are working on a still image to include a drawing of whatever the light source is; having one group create a soundscape to layer over another group's tableau; or inviting individuals to add one carefully chosen movement to an effigy. A key to employing the dimensions of dramatic imagination is to use them sparingly and mindfully: as with the drama elements, it's sometimes the limitations and constraints that are the most productive.

Heathcote insisted that working theatrically was something teachers needed to consciously practise (Heathcote, 2009) and she suggested teachers flex their "signing muscles" by spotting the dimensions of light, dark, sound, silence, etc. within an existing text such as narrative poem. This is a very useful way to practise the skills needed for the more spontaneous moments that arise in the classroom situation.

By employing and drawing attention to the six dimensions, you will not only enhance the aesthetics of your teaching, you'll also model to participants how to create work that is aesthetic and appeals to the senses. As with drama conventions, it's not a priority to "teach" the dimensions of dramatic imagination, though you can do so. Over time, even just with modelling, you can expect to see enhanced imagery coming through in participants' own drama practice as well as in their drawing, writing, and oral language.

Supporting affective and cognitive learning—enactive/iconic/symbolic triad

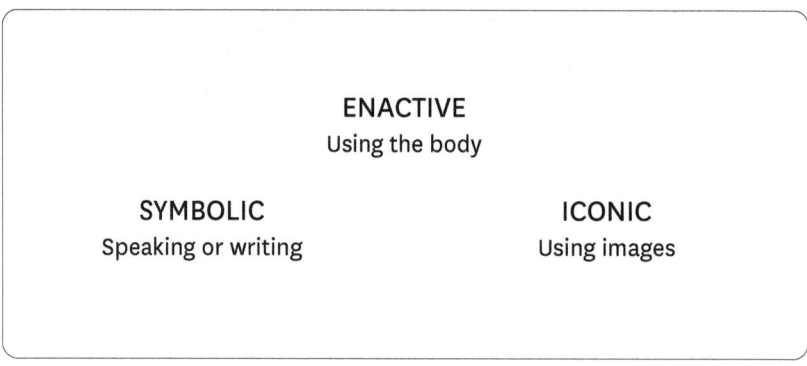

Figure 59: Three forms of representation tool

Bruner's three forms of representation have been mentioned a few times in this book and the tool above may be a useful visual cue to remember the three forms while teaching. As discussed in Chapter 2, Bruner's theory suggests that learners develop their understandings about the world by following a progression from action-based learning through the body to learning through images, drawings, and pictures to symbolic learning through language and writing. This progression can be really useful as a rule of thumb when planning and sequencing activities but Bruner's sequence shouldn't be regarded as fixed. Yes, the original theory of development implies a progression from the enactive to the iconic and, finally, the symbolic, but if you regard this as the only way to do it you may limit your opportunities. Sometimes it might feel more fruitful to move from iconic to symbolic and finish with the enactive. In practice, the best advice might be to keep Bruner's three forms in mind and be ready to shift between them when moving between activities and tasks.

Keeping a copy of this tool on hand in the classroom will nudge you to remember to move between all three forms of representation as you work with participants. It might also give you an idea for those moments when you're not sure what kind of task to offer next. For example, in planning a classroom drama on the Māori creation story recently, I wanted to create a sequence of activities where participants would explore the points of view of the brothers Tānemahuta and Tāwhirimātea disagreeing about whether their parents Ranginui the sky father and Papatūānuku the earth mother should be pushed apart. I didn't think of using Bruner's triad, so just used a role convention; asking children to listen with their eyes closed while I spoke as Tānemahuta trying to persuade his brother to listen. This worked OK and got the children's attention. However, if I had remembered the triad tool I could have started in the enactive form, with the participants asked to explore with their bodies the sense of being squashed and unable to stand up and move. Then, working in the iconic form, the children could be challenged to create an image of the brothers trapped in the tight space between their parents, perhaps using sheets of black paper. Then I could have moved on to asking participants to improvise a dialogue between the two brothers, which would take us into the symbolic. Without the triad tool to turn to I was limited to rehashing conventions I had used before. Turning to the triad would have opened up lots of new possibilities for really internalising and expressing the story through all three forms of representation.

While I have stressed that the teacher does not need to move through the three forms on Bruner's triad in any particular order, there is something to be said for planning so that participants are learning actively first, before moving into thinking through written or visual language. In my own teaching, I've found that participants tend to get more out of the experience if I set up some kind of active-feeling experience where they are encouraged to do something and feel something through the body before setting a task in which they think about and express the ideas through written or visual language. Another way to express this sequence is in terms of the affective and cognitive domains discussed in Chapter 2 (Bloom et al., 1956). For years I've described this as "affective to cognitive" learning, but, given that I'm usually talking about a practical, active experience as well as an emotional one, I suppose it should more accurately be termed "affective plus psychomotor to cognitive" learning, though that's quite a mouthful! The point is that it's often most powerful to explore a new idea by learning through the enactive first—doing and feeling—before moving on to learning by discussing, writing, or drawing what you've done and felt. Working from doing to understanding may seem counter-intuitive at first. After all, aren't we told as teachers that we must always be explicit about our intentions? And aren't we supposed to build on prior knowledge and experience and give the participants a chance to make links and clarify requirements before they engage in practical activity? But the two are not mutually exclusive: a teacher can still be explicit with participants about what is going to happen without sacrificing the affective to cognitive flow. A teacher who says, "Wow, I wonder what's inside this mystery box? Once we've found out perhaps we can sit down as a group and figure out what it all means", gives all the information usually contained in an explicit instruction without losing the opportunity for open-ended exploration through action.

Protecting into emotion—frame distance

PARTICIPANT—GUIDE—AGENT—AUTHORITY—SPIRITUAL GUIDE or PHILOSOPHER—

RECORDER—MEDIA   RESEARCHER—CRITIC—ARTIST

DISTANCE = TIME + RELATIONSHIP / METAPHOR

Figure 60: Frame distance tool

Mantle of the Expert can be a powerful way of learning about things that matter, including important, difficult, or emotionally charged issues. But any teacher using drama needs to be mindful of this potential and use it with care. How do we foster emotional connection and intensity without imposing experiences that could be overwhelming or triggering for participants, or indeed ourselves? Part of the answer lies in working with frame distance. Framing has already been discussed as a core element, or whenu, in planning. Put simply, frame distance refers to the size of the gap between the events in the imagined world and the emotions and responses felt by participants in the real world. Frame distance has a range of functions that include helping participants experience and learn about drama as an art form giving them experience of different points of view and deepening the aesthetic and poetic impact of the experience (Eriksson, 2011). Frame distance also helps to provide protection and safety. As already noted, this is not a matter of protecting participants *from* feeling, but rather protecting them *into* emotion (Bolton, 1984, p. 128).

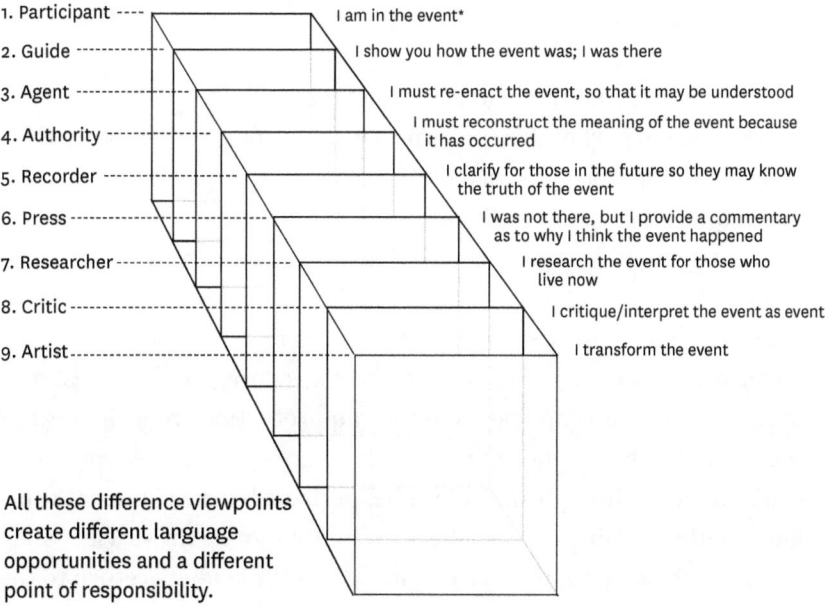

Figure 61: Role function in relation to frame distance (from Heathcote 2009, p.41)

Figure 64 shows how different role possibilities can be used to layer in distance from an issue or event. The diagram suggests nine role functions with each point of view or frame providing more distance from the content. Later versions included two further layers inserted half way along: priest/shaman/spiritual guide/philosopher; and media (Abbott & Taylor, 2013). Thinking about these different role functions can help at the planning stage, when choosing a responsible team or client, since different ones will have greater or lesser distance from the issue at hand. The tool can also be helpful during teaching where the teacher or participants will be stepping into role, by giving options for the different points of view that can be taken in relation to an imagined event, and by increasing or decreasing the sense of distance from it. This is particularly useful where the teacher wants to decrease the intensity and emotional "heat" to ensure safety. It's worth noting, too, that the more distanced roles contain within them the potential to step into and understand the less distanced ones. For example, an artist creating a sculpture to commemorate an historical event will need to empathise with those who were at the event and may even imagine themselves back into the event in order to do this job. This helps to explain how the responsible team in Mantle of the Expert works. Essentially, the team and the commission is one big exercise in role function and frame distance.

The second part of this tool is provided by Bowell and Heap in their book *Planning Process Drama* (2013, p. 80). They suggest teachers can provide distance from difficult topics through manipulation of two things: time and relationship. The example Bowell and Heap use is of a teacher wishing to explore World War I. To place the teacher, or indeed the participants, in role as soldiers in the trenches who are under attack would put them right in the centre, with no distance of time or relationship and therefore no protection from the heat of the issue. So the teacher might prefer to create some distance. This could be done through shifts in time; perhaps by travelling back to a few months earlier, as the soldiers excitedly sign up for service, or by travelling forward to many years later when the soldiers return to the site of the battle for a commemoration. Or a sense of distance could be achieved through shifts in relationship; instead of being soldiers under fire, they might be commanders issuing the orders, or medics waiting for the firing to cease so they can retrieve the wounded. This is very much the same idea as in Heathcote's frame distance diagram already discussed. Another option is to add distance through a combination of time *and* relationship. Options for this might include stepping into role as a journalist reporting on the battle a few days afterwards (a little distanced in time and a bit more by relationship), a member of the soldier's family waiting for news (some distance in time, very little in relationship), or a documentary maker creating a contemporary study of the battle for YouTube (lots of distance in both time and relationship). Used in combination, the frame distance tool and Bowell and Heap's reminders about time and relationship can be very useful. As well as providing multiple points of view, these shifts in distance can be used to help participants feel protected enough to explore and experience emotions.

As well as manipulating time and relationship, it can be useful to think about metaphor as another distancing device. As Bolton points out, all drama is already a metaphor in that everything that goes on in the imagined world stands in for real-world experience and, "its meaning lies not in the actual context nor in the fictitious one, but in the dialectic set up between the two" (Bolton, 1979, p. 128). We can make use of this by adding yet another layer of metaphor within the imagined world itself, thereby setting up another dialectic. For example, a potentially tricky topic like social prejudice might be explored through the metaphor of meeting and relating to a storybook monster or the potentially distressing issue of depression might be distanced by exploring through the metaphor of a black dog that follows someone around. When you think about it, fairy tales and children's stories adopt this technique all the time and it is often seen in process drama too. Working through metaphor allows participants to explore issues by implication rather than head on. This, in turn, can protect them against experiences that might trigger intense emotions or cause them to shut down. Peter O'Connor and colleagues have written about the importance of another level of framing, described as "double framing", which involves both working through metaphor and ensuring that participants are positioned within the fiction as someone with the capacities to address the issues at hand (O'Connor et al., 2006). Double framing is already one of the aims of Mantle of the Expert, achieved through the positioning of participants as members of a responsible and expert team. But the teacher can also reach for metaphor as an additional distancing device within individual episodes.

Frame distance can also be useful where you wish to protect or respect the content. For example, when dealing with culturally sensitive, sacred, or emotionally raw topics, frame distance might be employed as a matter of respect to the issues at hand. For example, I recently worked with a Pākehā teacher who was teaching her class about the Kingitanga movement. She wanted to introduce them to the processes used by Tainui when they go about selecting a new monarch. Her first thought was to go into full role as a member of the council seeking advice but she felt uncertain about this so instead she decided to work in a frame distanced way by inviting the class to imagine they were part of an imaginary kingdom—Urbana—with a leadership system that combined heredity and election of monarchs similar to that used in Kingitanga. After discussing with the class what they as citizens of Urbana would look for in a monarch, the children were invited to compare their processes and priorities with those of the real-world movement, including discussions with a real-world representative of Tainui iwi who visited the class and shared information. On this occasion, the teacher distanced not only through the metaphorical qualities of drama or the distance provided by role positions, but also by setting up a whole parallel situation. Participants never stepped into role as people within the Kingitanga movement but created their own movement and then drew parallels. This might seem counter to the idea of drama, which is all about "walking in someone else's shoes" but, as teachers, we must weigh the value of this against the danger of inadvertently "walking all over" other people's experiences, stories, or treasures. A light touch is required if we want to avoid diminishing or oversimplifying complex and culturally specific human experiences.

Balancing student agency and teacher leadership—the teacher compass

> 1) ENABLE EXPLORATION 2) ORIENTATE AND FOCUS
>
> 3) PROVIDE EXACT INFORMATION 4) CONSOLIDATE

Figure 62: Quadrants from the teacher compass tool

A teacher using Mantle of the Expert will make use of a range of deliberate acts of teaching including unstructured discussion, focused questioning, feeding in new information, and reflection. All four of these are important but it can be tricky to get the balance right. One tool that can really help with this—not just in Mantle of the Expert but in any teaching situation—is something we can call the circle of progression (Heathcote & Bolton, 1994) or teacher compass (see Figure 63). This circular diagram, originally developed by Lesley Webb and further developed by Dorothy Heathcote, Luke Abbott, and Tim Taylor, helps teachers maximise different kinds of thinking and inquiry within and between tasks (Heathcote, 2009). I've only learned how to use the tool properly in recent times and I feel like it's improved my teaching hugely. The full diagram shown below looks complex, but the principle behind it is quite straightforward. As the name suggests, the compass is like a navigation guide. The idea is that, for each new task, the teacher navigates the class through a sequence starting with quadrant one on the top left, moving through quadrant two on the top right, to quadrant three on the bottom right, and finally quadrant four on the bottom left. Each quadrant involves a shift in the way the teacher manages the interaction and inquiry (shown in the centre) and how participants behave (shown in the outer circle). Each quadrant builds on the one before, represented in the direction of the arrows. There is an overall progression within the cycle that moves from playful exploration to the making of choices into focused work and, finally, a careful consideration of what has been discovered and uncovered in the process.

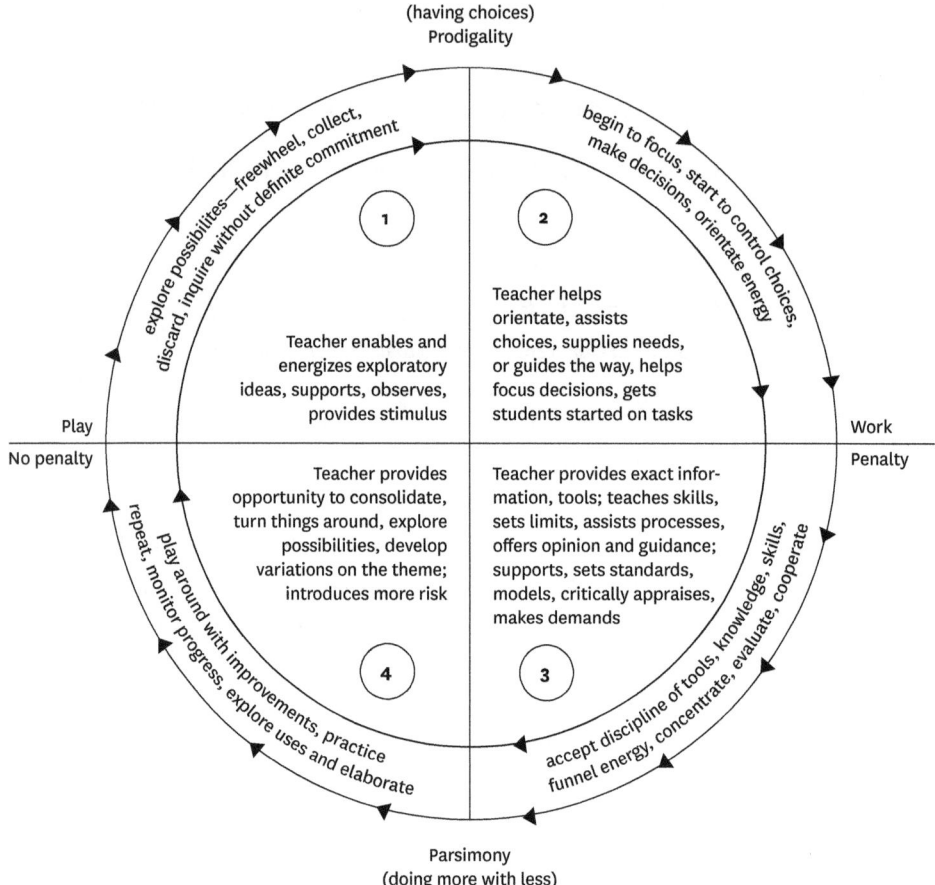

Figure 63: The teacher compass (Webb and Heathcote, n.d.)

In quadrant one, the emphasis is on playful exploration with little direct guidance from the teacher. Here the teacher's role is to support, energise, enable, and observe. This will look a little different depending on the activity. If you want to facilitate a class discussion about a photo, you might work in this quadrant by simply displaying the image and asking, "What do you make of this?" before pulling right back to allow peer–peer conversation with little or no teacher input. Or, if the activity is a practical, embodied one, such as imagining we are scientists packing a suitcase for a trip to Madagascar, you might begin with an opportunity for open-ended play by inviting participants to head off and search around their imaginary homes for their suitcases. The idea is to let this phase of exploration take its natural course before moving on to quadrant two.

In quadrant two, things become slightly more focused. The teacher helps participants with their thinking and organisation through carefully chosen prompts and suggestions. So, in the example of the exercise with the photo, the teacher might ask questions that draw attention to particular details on the picture, like: "How old do you think she is?", "Why do you think she's wearing black?", or "What's that lying on the table by her hand?" Or they might suggest a process by which participants describe and interpret what they see. For quadrant two in the suitcase packing example, the teacher might ask, "What's the weather like in Madagascar at this time of year?", or "What medications will we need?" Once again, this quadrant is worth spending time in and the teacher doesn't move on until it's been explored fully.

Quadrant three marks a distinct shift. Here, the teacher provides exact information, feeds in facts and knowledge, sets limits, and insists on standards. So, at this point in the photo activity, the teacher would feed in relevant information about the picture: who it is, the historical context and so on: "Mary Innes was in her forties when her husband died and left her with 10 children and a string of debts. Ten years later she had turned the family's fortunes around and created a successful brewery." The teacher might also bring attention to technical aspects including the play of light and dark within the photograph, the composition, vanishing point, and so on. For the packing exercise, the teacher might feed in very particular information; for instance, informing participants about weight regulations and any items that are prohibited in checked-in luggage. The teacher might also provide a tightly guided task such as inviting participants to choose the one thing they are permitted to take as a memento of their family. Again, time is taken to really explore this quadrant before moving on to the fourth and final one.

Quadrant four is about consolidating and bringing together what has been learned in the cycle so far. This is a time for stepping back, reflecting, and inviting participants to consider "So what?" and "Now what?" before moving on. In the case of the photo example, this might be where the teacher invites students to think back to their first impressions of the woman in the photo and consider what's shifted for them: "What aspects of Mary's life story are reflected in the image?" As for the packing activity, participants might be given the opportunity to rethink and explore possibilities including measuring, weighing, and re-discussing with peers before making a final drawing of the contents of their suitcase. If the task is part of a wider Mantle of the Expert experience, quadrant four is where the teacher will invite participants to think about implications for the commission as well as for their wider understanding of the world: "So were we right in our assumptions about business practice in the 1800s?" or "Are there parts of our commission we need to revisit?" This is also the place for reflections on understandings, including meta thinking about the learning process itself; for example, "What surprised us about ...?" or "What were the benefits and frustrations of doing this as a group?" The quadrant will conclude with decisions about action points and next steps.

I don't know about you, but before I got familiar with this tool I tended to work mostly in the second quadrant and probably did not give enough time to the other three. While I wanted to foster the sort of open-ended exploration and sharing of ideas of quadrant one, in reality I did not invest much time or energy in this. And I really struggled with the idea of the kind of transmission teaching found in quadrant three. In part, this was due to an idea that this kind of teaching was "wrong" and that students should be left to make their own discoveries through inquiry. Sometimes, frankly, it was because I didn't know that much about the issue or topic at hand. Now, I see things differently and I understand that within Mantle of the Expert pedagogy, it is part of a teacher's role to transmit, demand, assist, and appraise student's work—but only once participants have become interested and engaged. This realisation helps me to ensure I'm prepared. If I'm going to ask the class to discuss a photo, pack a suitcase, or anything else, I need to know enough about it to be able to feed in information and knowledge in quadrant three. And quadrant four serves as a reminder to taihoa, reflect, draw together the threads, take time, and ponder the next step; something I also tended to rush in my teaching.

My use of the teaching compass is in its infancy but already I have found it a powerful and transformative tool, and not just in Mantle of the Expert. Most of the case studies in this book were written before I was familiar with the tool but there is some evidence of it in the *Objects of Significance* example where the teaching moved from open-ended discussion and speculation, through supported questioning and revealing of exact information about the objects, to consolidation and decisions about action.

Varying delivery and elevating language—three teaching voices

> 1) FACILITATOR VOICE 2) STORYTELLER/NARRATOR VOICE
>
> 3) TEACHER-IN-ROLE VOICE

Figure 64: Three teaching voices tool

At any point in a Mantle of the Expert experience, the teacher has different voices they can choose to use when addressing participants. To clarify, we're not talking here about variations in the physical voice in terms of the tone, pitch, or volume, though these are of course critical in effective teaching. This tool relates to the different ways a teacher can "give voice" to their position within the duality of the real and imagined worlds. In this context, the teacher has three options available, as shown above. Each of these voices has its own purposes and each has benefits for teaching and learning. It takes a bit of practice to learn to use them but moving between the different voices can keep things alive, add variety in pace and colour, build intrigue, elevate language registers, and shift perspectives. Let's look at each in turn.

The facilitator voice will probably be the most familiar as it is the one we teachers use most of the time. It's the voice we use to greet: "Good morning room eight!" To organise: "Could you join me on the mat in 10–9–8 …" To establish expectations: "OK, today is going to be a challenge …" To explain: "You'll need to use the formula we practised last week." To instruct: "So, the address goes on the top right-hand side, like this." To question: "What do you make of this?" And to reflect: "What was something that surprised you today?" In terms of the duality of imagined and real worlds, all these examples of facilitator voice are firmly located within the real world of the classroom, but the facilitator voice can also be used to organise things in the imagined world: "OK, we're back in the story now and it's time to find out what Maui has to say for himself. I'll be Maui and you be the brothers …" The benefit of the facilitator voice, apart from its familiarity, is that it keeps things at arm's length so they can be negotiated, discussed, and reflected on. It allows the teacher to give clear, uncluttered instructions and to clarify details. Even where the other two voices are used, the teacher will often return to the facilitator voice to unify and refocus the class. The facilitator voice is probably the most adaptable of the three voices available and it is entirely possible to deliver an entire Mantle of the Expert experience without varying from it. However, to do so would be to miss the opportunity for richness, depth, and artistry offered by the other two voices.

The storyteller, or narrator, voice is situated in the imagined world, but above the action, as a sort of god-like figure or omniscient narrator, describing and overseeing events. This voice can be used in lots of ways. It could be used to feed in new information and details to help build the imagined world: "Once again it's a busy day at the office, with a buzz of eager expectation as the expert team gathers in the kauri-panelled boardroom to discuss the work ahead." Or the voice might introduce some new fact or knowledge related to the commission that the teacher wants participants to absorb: "And as Tama helped his father fill the gourds with water, little did he know that at that same moment, half a world away, another boy was helping his father to fill wooden barrels with fresh water to load aboard a ship. That ship's name was Endeavour …" The narrator voice is also extremely useful for efficiently transitioning from one time to another: "Come with me now as we venture back in time … it's early morning on a spring day in 1853 …" It can also be used as a way of issuing instructions, especially when accompanied by judicious gestures: "And so, the villagers gathered at dawn on the banks of the awa. One at a time they stood to speak and give their thoughts about what should be done with the young fugitive ..." Last, but not least, the narrator voice also serves as an efficient management device or focusing tool, by switching the mood of the class, attracting attention, and signalling that something significant is happening. I'm amazed at how often a class that is getting fidgety will become alert and interested again as soon as the narrator voice is used. And of course the teacher can always slip back to the facilitator voice if clarification is needed.

The function of the narrator voice is to switch the mood, and to model and encourage heightened oracy and vocabulary. This can present a challenge, of course, as the teacher needs to find a way and find the right words to weave an effective story. The "dimensions of dramatic imagination" tool described earlier (see Figure 61)can be a big help here. Early experiments with the narrator voice will most likely be scripted and read out word for word. But it's a skill that can be worked on and is worth practising for the way it builds the teacher's own oracy skills and, in turn, those of the participants. I've definitely noticed how the use of the narrator voice by the teacher prompts children to explore their own language in response, leading to more complex and lyrical language than might usually be heard in the classroom. Of course, this elevation of language is inextricably linked with powerful positioning—it can't be achieved unless the teacher honours the participants' thinking and input, so they feel safe to elevate their language.

The third voice available is the teacher-in-role voice (note the use of hyphens to distinguish this term from the strategy of "teacher in role"). The teacher-in-role voice is located right inside the imagined world and involves the teacher speaking or behaving as someone within that world. Now, as we have seen, teaching in role can involve the explicit, clearly signalled transition into full role. However, the teacher-in-role voice is more subtle than this. It may only involve a partial role, sometimes called a shadow or twilight role, and may only involve a short sentence or a single interaction. The teacher-in-role voice is often used as a way of sustaining the imagined world of the responsible team: "Colleagues, could we gather for a moment this side of the cordon. We've received an update from the police!" Or it could be a way of inviting participants into the imagined world as someone new: "Well, friends we made it on board at last and I'm glad to see the cabin space looks adequate." Another place you might find yourself employing the teacher-in-role voice is when responding to participants' work in drama: "Wow that guard looks pretty scary—we'd better keep our voices down. We don't want to wake him up." Similarly, once the improvised conversations are concluded, the teacher might encourage participants to share back using a teacher-in-role voice: "So, how did you get on trying to reason with our brother? He's always been unreasonable hasn't he?" There are so many ways the teacher-in-role voice can be used: to give instructions, question, manage behaviour, and press for reflection. The crucial difference between this and the other two voices is that the teacher speaks as someone within the fiction.

The benefits of using the teacher-in-role voice are similar to those of using the more fully fledged strategy of teacher in role. For one thing, it's engaging and novel, providing variety in classroom interactions. Also, it allows the teacher to make offers to participants from within the imagined world and respond to their offers too. And it's efficient, dropping everyone right into the story, saving time and bringing a sense of urgency and focus. Perhaps most importantly, the teacher-in-role voice allows the teacher to explore a range of different power and status positions, from high status: "Who are you people and what are you doing on my land?" to equal status: "Hmmmm, what do you think might be in that box over there?" to low status: "I'm completely stuck. What should we do?" The teacher-in-role voice requires quick thinking and creative responses from participants and for this reason it should be used with care, especially when participants are still getting used to working dramatically. The teacher must ensure participants are never confused or deceived.

It's exciting to realise that at any moment while teaching you could draw on any one of these three voices, knowing that each will take you forward in a slightly different way. While at first you may need to script the words you will use, over time you will get a sense of how to move between the different voices and what each contributes. Try keeping the list of three voices in mind or display the tool somewhere in your classroom. Then it's a matter of pausing each time you speak to decide which one you'll use next. Using this tool in combination with the "six dimensions of dramatic imagination" and the "five levels of meaning-making" (as per Figure 65) can really help you become more mindful of power dynamics and develop a more controlled linguistic and aesthetic tone.

Uncovering meaning—five levels of meaning-making

ACTION—MOTIVATION—INVESTMENT—MODELS—VALUES

Figure 65: Five levels of meaning-making tool

A number of times in this book we've touched on the idea of taking time—to reflect, to consider, to deepen understanding, and to grapple with complexity. This tool, from Heathcote, is a powerful way to help with that, providing a starting point for questioning or to prompt deep thinking at any time within a Mantle of the Expert experience. I first encountered this tool at the *Weaving our Stories* conference in 2009, when Heathcote shared these five powerful questions to ask someone in role:

1. What are you doing?
2. Why are you doing this?
3. What is it costing you?
4. Who taught you this?
5. What should life be for one such as you? (Heathcote, 2009)

I remember getting goosebumps as I wrote these questions down during the conference. It felt like we were being given a real gift—particularly question 5 which demonstrates Heathcote's skill with language. I still use the questions regularly, particularly where participants are in role within an effigy or scene. Placing a hand on a participant's shoulder and inviting them to answer these questions in role can encourage thoughtful meaning-making with any age group.

Participants don't need to be primed to answer the questions; the only requirement is that they have some understanding of the role they are depicting. The questions themselves scaffold the participant to uncover layers of meaning. Take the example of a Year 9 student I worked with a few years ago. We were exploring scenes from *Macbeth* and he was in role as a guard standing beside the body of the murdered King Duncan. He seemed quite casual about his role until we went through the five questions. His responses were: "I'm waiting for morning", "I'm just following orders—I don't get to ask why", "It's cost me my sleep—tonight and many nights to come", "They start us young at military school", and, "I should be … (pointing his spear at dead body) him!" His responses illustrate how using the five levels can prompt spontaneous responses with as much creativity and insight as the most carefully crafted monologue.

Having at first seen the five levels of meaning-making as purely a tool for questioning, I now see them as prompts for uncovering meaning in any situation. They can be used by the teacher to guide a group discussion, respond to a photograph, or reflect on the events that have happened in class that day. They can also be shared with participants as a tool for devising dialogue within a scene. Abbott and Taylor (2013) even suggest seeing them as steps to be used in structuring a Dramatic Inquiry. The point is that, whatever the context, the five levels can be used to support thinking in a gradually deepening process of uncovering meaning. For the tool to work, each level will generally need to be approached in order as each builds on the one before. To jump straight to the final one would be to expect too much of an empathic leap. But stepping through the levels in turn can have profound results. The first level—action—reminds us to look at what's going on. After that we can look at why this is happening—the motivation. Then we can consider the investment—what's at risk for those involved and what it is costing them in terms of energy, money, emotion, or time? After that we can go deeper and look at models—what life experiences, teachings, doctrines, or other influences have fed into this moment? And finally, deepest of all, we can try to understand the values—the core beliefs and principles at the heart of the matter. This is a powerful framework for critical thinking in all situations. I'm still learning to use this tool to its full potential and always make a point of jotting down

"Action—Motivation—Investment—Models—Values" on my planning so that I can refer to it during the lesson.

Encouraging critical distance—describe first, then interpret

```
DESCRIBE FIRST ...

THEN

INTERPRET
```

Figure 66: Two-step response tool

The next tool is a deceptively simple strategy for slowing down and deepening participant responses. I originally learned this two-step response process from a visual arts educator in an art gallery who taught it as a way to encourage children to examine artworks. I've found it works just as well within drama for responding to scenes, movement sequences, soundscapes, photographs, and other visual, sonic, or movement-based texts. The idea is to encourage participants to *describe* something in detail before they move on to *interpretation*. This encourages participants to take time to notice what they are seeing and hearing rather than rushing to assumptions based on first impressions. To help with describing, you could invite participants to use the stem, "I can see ...", or, "I notice ...", or, "I hear ..." Then, after the noticing is exhausted, they can move on to interpreting, with the stems, "I think ...", "It looks to me like ...", or, "Maybe it means ..." At first it can be tricky to learn what is a noticing and what is an interpretation, but that's the point of the exercise. Even a statement like "He looks happy" is really an interpretation. The challenge at the noticing stage is to describe what you see—what the face or body is doing—before moving on to identify how you are reading that.

This tool has several advantages. First, it encourages participants to tune in closely, paying attention to fine details they might otherwise have overlooked. The strategy also supports collective response: many eyes and ears together will notice more than those of one person observing alone. Another benefit is how, in articulating what they are seeing or hearing, participants need to grope for exact words: "I can see a pair of hands spread out wide, the palms are face up" or, "I can see a slight furrow on the forehead and the corners of the mouth are turned down." The strategy assists with critical literacy in that it draws attention to *how* the meaning is being made as well as what the meaning is. And, last but not least, it encourages deeper responses and interpretations. By holding off, slowing down, and drawing attention to detail in the noticing stage, the meanings that arrive in the interpretation stage are much deeper. This is a relatively easy strategy to explore and well worth a try to foster critical distance and creative thinking. I often hear participants coming up with interpretive comments that go way beyond anything that was intended by the creators of the work—which, of course, is fine. As this tool teaches us, creative work is not only important for what its makers intended, but also for the meanings people read into it.

Making critical connections—brotherhoods and otherhoods

> BROTHERHOODS—ALL THOSE WHO ...
>
> AND OTHERHOODS—WHOSE STORIES ARE WE NOT TELLING?

Figure 67: Brotherhoods and otherhoods tool

Another useful concept that can be drawn on while teaching is what I have decided to name "brotherhoods and otherhoods". The notion of "brotherhoods" emerges from Heathcote's practice and I've expanded on it with the word "otherhoods" to counter the obvious gender bias of the original. These terms are not easily defined, but the notion behind the tool is that human behaviour ideas, actions, or symbols are repeated across time, across cultural boundaries, across genres, and, indeed, across curriculum learning areas. To illustrate, in Alan Bennett's play *The History Boys* (2004) there's a moment where the teacher, Hector, hears a knock on the door and immediately responds with a quote from Shakespeare: "O villainy! Let the door be locked! Treachery! Seek it out." He then asks the boys to list all the instances they can think of where a knock on the door appears—in literature, sayings, or folklore. We could describe this moment as the teacher drawing attention to a "brotherhood of all those who knock on doors". And this is just what can happen within Mantle of the Expert teaching. For example, if participants are in role as 19th century European settlers about to step aboard the ship that will transport them to the Pacific, the teacher might pause for a moment and say, "As those in our story take this momentous step into the unknown, let us ask ourselves who else in human history—or, indeed, in books or films that we know—has taken a step like this?" Participants may respond with a range of suggestions from real-life explorers (Neil Armstrong, Tupaia, or Amelia Earhart) to pop culture figures (Mad Max, Batman, or an avatar from Minecraft). The benefit of this is that they come to recognise connections between actions of apparently disparate humans who have walked a certain path or crossed a threshold similar to the one they are now encountering in the drama.

Of course, we can question the sexism inherent in the word "brotherhoods" and suggest alternatives—a "community?" or "humanhood?" But to worry too much about the language is to miss the point, which is that, for teachers, there is huge value in recognising and drawing attention to moments that resonate across our historical, literary, and cultural memory. I love how this strategy of Heathcote's encourages thinking at the most profound level. Far from being a test of quick thinking or a snobbish display of literary acumen as it might appear from the Bennett play, working with brotherhoods demonstrates to everyone involved how learning is interconnected across historical time. It works against the hierarchies we usually set up between different kinds of knowing—high and low culture for example. Perhaps most importantly, it emphasises the commonalities within humanity and within curriculum. There's no question this adds depth and connectedness to other histories and cultural stories. At the same time, in the interests of critical literacy, I suggest it's equally important to consider those who don't fit into brotherhoods. Those whose stories don't tend to get told, who are regularly silenced, under-represented, or misrepresented across histories, stories, and mythologies.

Thinking about this, I've adapted the strategy and now try to also consider what I call "otherhoods". A teacher can draw attention to these by encouraging participants to think about those whose stories are *not* represented at threshold or other key moments. For example, in the case of stepping about the ship, the teacher might say, "As those in our story take this momentous step into the unknown, let us ask ourselves whose hidden and unrecognised efforts have brought them here …" or, "Whom have we focused on so far in our story and whose points of view have not been shared?" or, "Who, within our imagined world, is missing out on this opportunity—and why?" or perhaps, "Who might be opposed to the actions we are about to take—and why are the people in our story not listening?" In some circumstances, it can pay to focus in on groups known to be "othered" in mainstream narratives such as women, people of colour, children, or people with different abilities, and ask a question specifically related to them: "What does this moment tell us about the position of women at these times?" Of course, if you are keen to support this critical perspective taking within your teaching—especially if you want participants to represent these otherhoods accurately within their imagined worlds—you'll need to be ready to feed in accurate contextual information to avoid perpetuating the oversimplification or stereotypes yourself.

Marking moments of significance—dropping to the universals

> "OUR COLLEAGUE IS REMINDING US …"

Figure 68: Dropping to the universals tool

Like the previous strategy, this tool is all about marking moments and giving them weight and significance and, once again, its use is not limited to teaching in Mantle of the Expert. It can enhance any classroom interaction. What's different is that, rather than prompting new critical thinking, this tool is about noticing connections the participants make by themselves, and celebrating the wise and thoughtful things they say and do. Every teacher knows those moments where participants contribute something profound and meaningful. It's no surprise these arise in a Mantle of the Expert experience, since the approach sets up so many opportunities for grappling with complex ideas. The question is how to honour these. It can be tempting to praise or express amazement: "Wow, did you hear what Dan just said? Well done Dan, nice thinking!" When you think about it, though, this buries the participant's contribution in the teacher's response and values the contribution only in terms of its place in the classroom setting. Instead of this, Heathcote proposed teachers should acknowledge and give credit to participants' meaning-making in a more reflective way. So, for example, if a participant makes a comment that conveys insight or new understanding—something like, "This is really hard but it's also fun"—the teacher could pause and either echo the original statement or paraphrase it something like this: "Our colleague is reminding us that challenge can often be rewarding." A response like this acknowledges the participant's wisdom and reflects it back to the group in a way that doesn't overshadow the original contribution but instead gives it weight and significance beyond the classroom. The teacher is positioned as one who provides language to elevate the idea and gives it space in the classroom discourse. Heathcote called this strategy "dropping to the universals", implying that the teacher targets the deepest of meanings that apply across all of humanity. Another way to put this (if, like me, you're a bit uncomfortable with the notion of anything being "universal") is that the teacher highlights philosophical truths or enduring understandings as they emerge.

There are multiple benefits from this apparently simple tool. I use it often and it never seems to get stale. I appreciate how it explicitly reminds the participants of their position as collaborators within the teaching–learning relationship. I also like how it allows me to model elevated language and sets a tone for what is valued in the process of learning. I've noticed participants will often respond by adopting a similar language, addressing their classmates and teachers as colleagues and acknowledging the enduring understandings they are gaining from their peers. There's an old teaching adage that students will put their energies into whatever receives the most attention in the classroom environment. With this strategy, the teacher can ensure that time and attention are given to what really matters, so that everyone starts scanning for the value in what is being said and done in the classroom. Apart from anything else, this provides a rich and authentic source of assessment data. If we define assessment as seeking out that which matters most, then a tool like this can be invaluable. Any time a teacher or a participant drops in one of these statements about the enduring understandings being developed, this can be seen as powerful qualitative data about the learning that is going on. While I've only ever done this in an informal, formative way, I'm sure the tool could be used for more formal assessment with statements recorded in writing or captured on digital or audio files.

Co-constructing—principles of improvisation

> Responding to an OFFER
>
> DO: ACCEPT > EXTEND > ADVANCE
>
> DON'T: BLOCK, GAG, STALL, STEAL

Figure 69: Principles of improvisation tool

One final tool to help finesse teaching in Mantle of the Expert is this simplified list of the dos and don'ts of improvisation. I have argued throughout this book that Mantle of the Expert is an improvisatory form of drama: it depends on teachers and participants working together to build and sustain imagined worlds and storylines. There are whole books written on the subject of improvisation, which involves a complex set of skills well beyond what we are discussing here (Johnstone, 1992). However, the list above, adapted from Tourelle (1998) gives some of the central precepts. As the tool suggests, the basis of successful improvisation is the offer. Someone must make a beginning—a verbal or non-verbal action that introduces some aspect of the imagined world, sparks an idea, or begins a conversation. Examples in the context of Mantle of the Expert teaching could be as simple as handing someone an imaginary pen and paper and saying, "Sign here please", or as complex as setting up the whole classroom as a crime scene, framing participants as detectives, and inviting them to hunt for clues. Once the initial offer has been made, it's up to the other party or parties engaged in the improvisation to respond. There are some responses that will help sustain the imagined world and others that will get in the way. These are listed as dos and don'ts.

The dos on the list are subtle but critical to the success of collaboration in improvised drama. To accept an offer is to yield to the suggestion and the focus. In the example of the pen and paper, this might mean taking the imaginary pen and carrying out the action of writing one's name. In this simple action, the respondent has said "yes" to the offer and the idea is kept alive. Extending is about deepening the idea further, while keeping the same focus. For example, the person signing the paper might ask, "What about the back page?" or "It's done. Now tell me, what have I committed myself to?" Another option is to advance the offer. This usually comes after a few rounds of accepting and extending an idea. An advance involves making a new offer that will shift the focus in a new, but still appropriate, direction; for example: "So, I want to know what will happen to those in our town who refuse to add their names?" The onus is then on the improvisation partner to accept, extend, and advance this new offer and the improvisation continues.

Having established the dos, let's look at the don'ts. These are the responses that can impede progress. A block occurs when someone can't or won't buy in to the imagined scenario. In the example of the proffered pen and paper, a participant might block with, "That's only an imaginary pen!" Or an adamant "No way!" This stops the improvisation in its tracks. Note the difference between that response and something like, "No I'm not signing anything until you explain." This sounds like a negative, but it's not a block because the response actually accepts the offer and extends the idea. Slightly less terminal than a block, but still unhelpful, is the stall, where one of the participants questions or puts roadblocks in the way of the idea; for example, "Hold on, this pen's out of ink" or, "Why are you using your left hand? I thought you were right handed." A gag is a particular form of stalling in which a participant makes an unhelpful joke or looks for the comedy in the situation rather than honouring the idea: "Sign here you say? OK, how about this!?" [*grabs a real pen and draws a picture of a stop sign*]. This scuppers the improvisation and exposes the person who made the offer, leaving them to abandon the attempt or try to salvage things in some way. Another behaviour to avoid is the steal, where a participant responds to an offer with something intended to draw attention to their own idea rather than building on the focus: "Isn't my writing beautiful! I'm an expert in calligraphy you know. Let me tell you about my training …"

So, how can a teacher make use of this tool? First and foremost, it provides a lens through which to view classroom interactions. It provides a language to recognise and categorise responses—your own and those of participants. For teachers, the tool is a reminder to be alert to potential offers within what participants say and do, to sift through these and decide which to accept, extend, and advance. This can be tricky, since not every offer will be something you can work with. If you watch experienced practitioners in action, you'll notice their scrupulously ignoring some offers (which, as we've seen, is not the same as blocking them). Even more skilled is the art of taking whatever is offered, even the unhelpful or negative response, and reworking it into an offer to be extended. Heathcote was a master at this, as in one case where a group of children refused to take their coats off when she came into the room. Rather than assert her authority within the real world, her response was to reframe their action as an offer in the imagined world and say, "Oh I'm glad you've got your warm coats on—because today we're going somewhere very cold" (Johnston, 2017, p. 44). While blocking, stalling, gagging, and stealing do not necessarily derail a classroom drama experience, it can really help to recognise them when they arise so that you can work around them. Using the language of improvisation helps focus on the responses rather than seeing the person making the responses as either helpful or unhelpful. It's not just about understanding participants' behaviour: I've worked with a number of teachers who have seen this tool and immediately identified their own tendency to gag and steal within their dramas. Simply recognising this was enough to make them better at improvising and their teaching improved as a result.

As for whether to explicitly teach the principles of improvisation to participants, I have mixed feelings on this. Left to themselves, many children learn the principles of improvisation from a young age through experience with their socio-dramatic play and through the modelling of teachers and adults who play with them. This kind of inductive process is the ideal way to learn and a teacher can achieve a lot by simply modelling good improvisation themselves. The danger of teaching the principles of successful improvisation is that it might make learning in Mantle of the Expert look like an exercise in applying particular skills, which could damage the authenticity of the encounter. The principles of improvisation are not success criteria. Having said that, neither are they a secret to be withheld. From time to time, I have introduced the principles of improvisation to a group as part of a reflective discussion and have even encouraged practice through games and activities. However, this was only ever as an enhancement of the experience, to help us to understand, to theorise how we were working together. For younger participants, this can be a simple game of "Yes Let's" (Drama Toolkit, 2011) to remind them that saying "yes" to ideas makes things work better. Older participants might be interested in making links between what we are doing as the class and the way others in the real world—in this case, theatre makers—use improvisation in their work.

If all this talk of the craft of improvisation sounds rather daunting, it may help to remember four things. Firstly, all teaching and, indeed, much of wider life involves some sort of improvisation, in that everyone has to work out what to do from moment to moment and respond to other people, so improvising in drama is just an extension of this. Secondly, Mantle of the Expert is not all improvised, even if it might appear that way sometimes. Sure, if you watch videos of Dorothy Heathcote in action, particularly in her early work, you'll see her starting dramas with no preconceived ideas, what she described as, "going in like a gas cooker set at nothing" (Smedley, 1971). She was confident to simply respond to the offers made by the participants and let the experience unfold. However, she did not teach this way when she was working in Mantle of the Expert. In those cases, she had a clear plan and so should you. Mantle of the Expert is improvisation within a framework and that makes it much more manageable. A third thing to remember is that, while it can be daunting to watch a skilled practitioner in action, improvisation is a skill that can be practised just as you can practise and hone your skills in planning, questioning, or moving in and out of role. Tourelle (1998) offers a number of exercises that teachers could explore together during professional development sessions. And each day in the classroom offers another opportunity to practise: just be on the lookout for offers that can be considered and extended. Finally, it's worth reminding yourself that perfecting the art of improvisation is not the goal of Mantle of the Expert. It is a means, not the end. You and your participants will block, gag, stall, and steal from time to time and this will not mean the experience fails. Ultimately, what matters most is not how well you improvise but how deeply you and your participants care about the issues arising in the imagined world and how hard you work together to address the commission.

Chapter 6
Advice and cautionary tales

In the first five chapters of this book we teased out the strands of Mantle of the Expert, looked at the history and development of the approach, considered some examples of practice, identified a process for planning, and looked at some tools for finessing teaching. By now you have what you need to try weaving your own Mantle of the Expert experiences. The next step is to try things out for yourself. This chapter offers a few snippets of additional advice, tips, and cautionary tales from your fellow teachers who have already begun to use Mantle of the Expert regularly in their practice. As the whakataukī at the start of this book wisely points out, there is always value in reviewing what's been completed, to look at the good points and the dropped stitches. So, in this chapter, imagine yourself sitting round with a group of fellow weavers as they review their previous creations and share some words of wisdom, insight, caution, and advice.

Getting started

Giving it a go and learning through trial and error
When I asked experienced teachers from around Aotearoa New Zealand what advice they would give someone starting out in Mantle of the Expert, the most common response was to be brave, find a way, and have a go (Aitken, 2011). This sounds self-evident but may not be

straightforward. On a practical level, you may need to check in with your co-teachers, syndicate, or senior management to ensure you have their support. You'll need to work around issues such as pressures of time and existing commitments within the school timetable. You may find yourself putting up psychological barriers too. Actually, trying Mantle of the Expert may be rather daunting, even if you love the idea of it. You may have doubts about taking risks with power, using new forms of language, and employing artistry and creativity. You might worry about how participants will respond and whether you can manage their behaviour. Perhaps you are concerned that the planning process is beyond you. Or, if you're an experienced teacher, you may be unwilling to shift your existing successful classroom practice to make room for Dramatic Inquiry. Of course, these concerns are important but the best measure of whether something is worthwhile in your classroom is whether it's valuable for the participants. Remind yourself that it's normal to be nervous when you try something new. If it's important enough you will push through, gather the support you need, and make a start.

The next bit of advice is to start small. Introduce some drama-based activities or try teacher in role as part of a lesson and grow from there. Remember that, wherever you are at in your teaching journey you can start the process of exploring and improving your practice. Remember, too, that the moment you take a first step, try a new strategy, or use your first drama convention, you are as much a Mantle of the Expert practitioner as someone who has been using the approach for years. There's no external set of standards for you to achieve before you qualify as a Mantle of the Expert teacher, so don't worry too much whether you are "up to standard" or doing it "properly": other than deceiving children, there is very little you can get wrong. The only criteria to measure yourself by is whether you are engaging in ongoing learning and reflection, and whether your participants are experiencing enhanced learning experiences as a consequence of your efforts. Another important piece of advice is to realise that all learning occurs through trial and error. Don't expect things to be perfect first time and always remain open to learning from your mistakes. Remember that mistakes are the best, and sometimes the only, way to learn. This will help you avoid the temptation to dismiss the approach as "not for me" or "too hard" when challenges arise. Remind yourself that you are a learner alongside your participants and challenge yourself to build the same dispositions you look for in them: resilience, curiosity, critical thinking, and remaining open to new learning.

Warming up with preparatory activities

Teachers new to Mantle of the Expert sometimes feel they need to build skills, dispositions, and willingness in their participants before they start working with a class. This is an understandable feeling, especially if you have tried new things before and seen them fail. You may be concerned that your class will struggle to use imagination, participate in drama conventions, or accept a teacher in role unless you teach them how to do it. Certainly, the approach asks participants and teachers to behave and to think about the world, each other, and the learning experience in ways that may not be common in classrooms. However, it is worth remembering that most children have already built many of the skills required in Mantle of the Expert, through their play experiences. Even children whose life experience or disability means they may not have played as much as others, are often capable of working in imagined worlds once they are supported to do so. The same goes for teachers. You and your class already have the foundational skills required for success in Mantle of the Expert. It's just that you, and they, haven't used them in the context of teaching and learning.

You don't need to pre-teach the skills, but there are ways to support and scaffold children—and indeed yourself—to working in a new way. You might begin by setting up opportunities for children's play, using teacher in role, process drama, drama for learning, and then moving into Mantle of the Expert experiences, sometimes called "mini mantles". These have many of the features of the full version but are shorter; maybe just a single session like the *Objects of Significance* example described earlier. Of course you will need to compromise on some of the aspects that a full Mantle of the Expert experience would include: you won't have time for a strong sense of the client or the backstory of the team; you won't get to fully explore cross-curricula potential; and you'll only have time for one or two tensions to come into play. But you will have an opportunity to experiment with dramatic conventions and strategies and tools to build confidence. Practising drama for learning will not only prepare you for future teaching in Mantle of the Expert, it will also improve your overall teaching in lasting ways. By easing in like this you can glean which children need extra support, and identify resistance and uncertainty. Crucially, too, you can diagnose your own willingness to let children take a lead and you can become more confident in transitioning in and out of the imagined world, questioning, and other skills.

Drama games and activities can be useful to help flex the muscles of the imagination and establish the ground rules and understandings of working in imagined worlds. An online search will find hundreds of drama games you could draw on. However, be mindful in your selection. Many drama games are about competition, spontaneous comedy, practising particular techniques such as gesture or facial expression, witty dialogue, fast responses, and holding it together in front of an audience. These are great in their own way, but don't really align with what Mantle of the Expert is about. So look for activities that will introduce and reinforce the aspects of drama that are at the heart of the approach: working in imagined worlds; making and responding to offers in the fiction; building thoughtful dialogues; writing in role; taking drama seriously. Two activities I would recommend are the "Yes Let's" game (Drama Toolkit, 2011) which introduces the idea of accepting and building on offers, and the "Scarf Game" also known as "This Is Not A ..." (Dawson, 2019) which explicitly practises imagining objects as something else. Another activity I find beneficial is the deceptively simple "imagination warm up". In this, the teacher tells participants they are going to warm up their imaginations. First, everyone rubs their hands together to make them warm, and then the teacher asks, "So, where does our imagination live? Show me. What do we need to warm up, if we are going to use our imaginations?" This opens up fascinating conversations about where the imagination is located: participants will often start with the brain and go on to the heart. The teacher encourages the participants to justify and reflect on these choices, resulting in quite a sophisticated conversation about imagination. If you do want to use warm-up activities, choose examples like these that serve as a metaphor for how, or what, you will be learning. You can then refer back to them during reflective discussions.

Easing in through drama for learning and process drama

You can ease in to Mantle of the Expert by building some familiarity and confidence with the three different teaching modalities—drama for learning, inquiry, and powerful positioning—first. In my experience, most teachers in New Zealand feel fairly secure in leading inquiry learning, though you could deepen your understanding of this modality before starting on Mantle of the Expert teaching by reading about and trialling different approaches to inquiry learning. You could also work to practise powerful positioning by trialling new patterns of speech and structures for sharing power in your classroom. To be honest, Mantle of the Expert itself provides one of the best ways to practise these two modalities, so I'd suggest getting on with it if you want to work on inquiry and positioning. When it comes to the drama modality, however, many teachers do find it useful to spend a bit of time finding their footing with short exercises and dramas, moving into more extended experiences.

If you are keen to experiment with drama for learning, you will find drama conventions and the strategy of teacher in role can be woven in to just about any classroom activity. For example, as part of a unit of work exploring migration, you could introduce a story about an imagined family packing up to move to New Zealand, inviting participants to explore this story in parallel to the inquiry. Drama for learning moments could be included at different points; for example, speaking the family's thoughts as they say goodbye to friends in their home country or step off the aeroplane for the first time. You could try teacher in role to introduce different perspectives, maybe a friend from home who misses the family, or an unsympathetic immigration official. Teaching like this would give you the opportunity to try out some aspects of Mantle of the Expert such as: using drama conventions; moving between the facilitator, storyteller, and teacher-in-role voice; the use of tensions; and manipulations in time. You can practise these without the need to sustain a responsible team or work towards a particular commission.

One of the best ways to develop skills in the drama for learning modality of Mantle of the Expert is through exploring process drama. Mantle of the Expert originally grew out of process drama, so it's no surprise that's a good place to start. I recommend starting by trying out pre-existing lesson plans and you'll find lots of these available online and in book form, including Tanya Batt's *Imagined Worlds* (2001) for younger children, Miller and Saxton's *Into the Story* (2004) for primary- and intermediate-aged participants, and *Schemes for Classroom Drama* by Maggie Hulson (2006) for secondary teachers. Check out Ministry resources, too, including *Playing our Stories* (Ministry of Education, 2006), *Telling our Stories* (Ministry of Education, 2004), and the various plans available on TKI. These will give you models for a range of different strategies and conventions so you can build confidence without worrying too much about the cross-curricula aspects. When you're ready to start planning your own process dramas, check out the framework for creating process dramas from picture books, which is on the Mantle of the Expert Aotearoa website (Aitken, 2019). Many teachers have made use of this to create their own plans and build confidence and familiarity with teaching in role and some simple drama conventions. For a more comprehensive handbook on planning process drama, Bowell and Heap's book (2013) is a terrific guide.

Making use of existing planning

When you are ready to teach Mantle of the Expert, it can be very reassuring to start out by using existing planning rather than creating your own from scratch. This is certainly how most of your colleagues in New Zealand started. For my first attempt at Mantle of the Expert I adapted some planning produced by Julia Walshaw at Bealings School in the UK (Bealings School, n.d.). Another really good model plan is *The Mountain Rescue Team* written by Tim Taylor and Brian Edmiston (n.d.), which goes through the planning step by step including what the teachers were thinking and how they set up the various activities. Check out the Mantle of the Expert Aotearoa website and the UK website for more published examples of planning shared by generous colleagues. Do bear in mind that much existing planning comes from overseas, which means it is unlikely to be an exact cultural fit for the Aotearoa New Zealand context. Indeed, even resources produced here may need adapting for your setting and your local curriculum. If you do work with existing planning, see if you can spot the features we've discussed in this book. Ask yourself: Where are the core elements/whenu of Mantle of the Expert introduced? How are participants framed? Which aho/signature pedagogies does the plan draw on? Does the plan have an initiation phase, experiential phase, and reflection/transformation phase? What purposes, strategies, drama conventions, and compacts are used? What productive and key tensions come into play? Does the plan use teacher in role, and if so what is the status? You can start to build your own skills by spotting what went into the plan and how it works.

Adapting for early years and junior classrooms

Mantle of the Expert can be used within new entrant and junior classrooms and there are a few simple tips that can help you adapt for learners at this level. To start, let's think about the relationship between Mantle of the Expert and children's play. If you look at the Dramatic Inquiry framework in Chapter 2, you'll see Mantle of the Expert depicted as an extension of child-structured dramatic play. Many of the features of Mantle of the Expert are present in this kind of play, including opportunities for decision making, repositioning, experimenting with space and symbol, taking on multiple roles, and teaching in role to provide thoughtful complications and tensions. The crucial difference is that children's play is structured by the participants themselves rather than led by the teacher, and the teacher tends to take a supportive and responsive role providing provocations and responding to the play rather than guiding or leading it. Children's play generally has a lived through and spontaneous feel rather than being episodic. Young children tend to play in full role, or through projective play with puppets, dolls, or other objects rather than employing abstract conventions. Also, while it is naturally integrative, as children play with ideas from across the curriculum, any deliberate acts of teaching will tend to arise from the play itself rather than being planned in advance. In the schools I work with where Dramatic Inquiry is used across the whole school, there is often a focus in the new entrant and junior classrooms on promoting child-structured play rather than teaching fully fledged Mantle of the Expert experiences. The understanding is that learning through play in the early years will set some of the foundations in place for learning through drama and Mantle of the Expert in the middle and senior school.

That's not to say that more structured Mantle of the Expert-type experiences can't be used with new entrants and junior classrooms. Even if you are dedicated to a play-based programme, there may be times you wish to encourage learners to work as a collaborative group to explore a particular curriculum focus. You may have a group of advanced players who are ready for a more collaborative experience, or you may wish to scaffold your group to develop more collaborative and social skills. Drama for learning and Mantle of the Expert provide a great way to do this, with some amendments. The tips below are based on advice from Heathcote (2009) as well as anecdotes, planning ideas, and studies by new entrant and junior teachers around New Zealand and internationally (Allen, 2017; Baldwin, 2012; Batt, 2001; Edmiston, 2014; Otaika Valley teachers, personal communication, 2018).

- When thinking about your responsible team, avoid the formality of establishing a company. Giving the class a general blanket role as helpers is often enough.

- Don't worry about a complicated backstory for the team or spending time building the world of the team as you would with older participants. With this age group, work with the energy of socio-dramatic play.

- Be mindful of clear signals. Young children can be very caught up in imagination and it's easy to confuse or deceive them that fictional characters or events are real. This may feel magical but is in danger of diminishing their agency. It's also not ethical.

- Talk about "making a story" together rather than the more complex notion of building an imagined world. Signal the fiction by referring to "in our story …".

- Include lots of tangible symbols of the imagined world, such as drawings, objects and pieces of furniture. Encourage children to create things to add to the imagined world out of paper, found objects or playdough.

- Keep the dramatic moments straightforward. One way of doing this is making use of the dramatic playing mode (see aho 7) where the whole class takes on a blanket role and tackles a problem together in lived-through time.

- Some children may be able to manage pair work and small-group work with guidance, but, as a rule of thumb for younger children, stick to putting everyone into role together, "How are we going to feed all these kittens?" or as individuals, "Let's all be the giant, snoring fast asleep."
- Use teacher in full role and be prepared to sustain it through conversations with the group and also through periods of dramatic playing. This is a wonderful way to engage young children and will allow you to explore new power dynamics such as one who needs help.
- Don't assume you need to dumb down the drama. Continue to take the problems in the imagined world seriously. This will give curriculum tasks authenticity and urgency and encourage meaningful engagement and deep thinking from participants.
- Consider the use of puppets, masks (worn on the forehead, not over the face), dolls, or artefacts as alternative, low-stress but highly engaging ways to represent roles and evoke settings in the classroom. Teachers and participants can handle and move these around and speak through them in role.

Teaching in collaborative settings

For the most part, this book has given examples of Mantle of the Expert experiences taught within a single-cell classroom but for increasing numbers of schools today this is not how teachers work. With the development of Innovative Learning Environments and other flexible and collaborative settings for learning, more and more teachers are working in teams and with larger groups of participants. A clear benefit of this is the opportunity it brings for creative use of larger spaces and teaching as a team. For instance, I recently worked with 70 new entrant and Year 1 students and their teachers in a school in Christchurch where we set up a large classroom space to look like it had been invaded by a monster. In role as monster investigators, children moved through the space to search for clues. Teachers supported children to work in small groups to interact with the space and later the monster (teacher in role) who, it turned out, was the smallest Wild Thing from *Where the Wild Things Are* (Sendak, 1963) looking for his friend Max. The participants overcame their initial judgemental attitudes towards the monster, helped mediate with Max's mum, enjoyed a shared picnic, and collaborated in building a range of transportation options to get the monster home to Wild Thing land. The sense of excitement at working in a large group was palpable and the commitment and buy-in of teachers, along with judicious choice of drama conventions and strategies, meant that no one missed out on direct involvement. For colleagues working in settings like this, the success of Mantle of the Expert as with any other collaborative teaching, depends on careful planning and negotiation. When navigating between real and imagined worlds, teachers working together need to be clear on the roles they will take in and out of the drama, who would lead which part of the experience, and how the large group will be managed between them.

There can be many benefits in planning and implementing Mantle of the Expert as a team, rather than an individual. In planning, just like in imaginative play, two or more heads really are better than one, and you will find that bouncing ideas off other people deepens your thinking and fires your imagination. Without doubt, the most creative Mantle of the Expert plans have been those I've written with other people. It's also beneficial to draw on the different strengths and personalities of colleagues when working across the curriculum and in imagined worlds. As for teaching in a team, this too can be very successful. Of course, there are many styles of collaboration, from dividing up responsibilities for different aspects, to doing everything jointly. However you do it, you'll need to ensure everyone involved develops a shared sense of the imagined world, the team identity, the client, and the commission. Getting this right helps avoid the danger of taking off in totally different directions during the inquiry phase. To ensure the non-negotiable aspects of the experience are clear, you can expect a fair bit of whole-group activity in the early stages. It's also important to maintain an ongoing record of the learning journey so that common understandings are captured. This can be done digitally as well as through regular meetings with your teaching colleagues.

Another option in collaborative settings is to explore a rolling-role type arrangement (Davis, 2016; Heathcote, cited in O'Neill, 2015) where small groups take responsibility for different aspects of a shared commission. To achieve this, you'll need to establish a common client and commission then decide how different groups will share the commission between them. This could be something to try in settings where some curriculum is taught by specialists; for example, in design, technology, the arts, or science. In that case, the year group as a whole could be framed as a responsible team—say an event management company, with a shared client and commission—maybe a charity that wants to stage an intercultural sports tournament. After establishing the shared givens of the imagined world, different classes would then work with their specialist teachers to take responsibility for different aspects of the commission—one class working on marketing, another creating the schedules and scoreboards, and still another planning the catering for the athletes. For this to work, all the teachers involved would need to be part of the pre-planning process, so that, as a group, you have a clear shared sense of the company, the client, the commission and, just as importantly, shared agreements on the non-negotiable aspects of the imagined world. Once this is done, each specialist teacher can create their own individual "maps" and micro-planning to teach separately. Planning can include opportunities for artefacts, bits of writing and other evidence of learning to be shared between groups, and you might choose to finish up with some kind of shared experience to round things off.

Using Mantle of the Expert as a subject specialist

While it's true that the majority of Mantle of the Expert practice is currently taking place in generalist classrooms, recent research has shown its potential for specialist settings at primary, intermediate, secondary, and tertiary level too (Aitken & Edmiston, 2014; Downey, 2018; Dunne, 2015; Stoate, 2013). It's important to stress that Mantle of the Expert is not designed nor intended as a way to teach everything in the curriculum. Some things are best taught discretely and no one would suggest Mantle of the Expert as a replacement for specialist teaching at any level. Having said that, Mantle of the Expert can be used within specialist teaching in particular curriculum learning areas. We've just seen how it can be used by specialists in collaboration, across science and English, social studies and physical education, arts, and health, and so on. It can also be used by individual teachers to set up a meaningful context for teaching and learning in a particular curriculum area. For subject specialists keen to use Mantle of the Expert, the greatest challenge may be working around timetable constraints and gaining the support and understanding of colleagues in a high-stakes environment where assessment can tend to drive pedagogy. For those fortunate enough to work in settings that embrace quality teaching and learning and welcome innovation, here are some tips.

Subject specialists can use the planning process outlined in this book with some slight adaptations. Your learning focus will obviously emerge from the curriculum learning area you specialise in. Try to make your learning goal specific; for example, to learn about a particular scientific or mathematical concept, learn about a specific historical event, explore a piece of literature or artwork, undertake an art-making or performance process, acquire skills in an aspect of language, develop a technological response to a problem, understand the complexities of a health issue, explore a social science topic, develop a digital or coding skill, or whatever. Whatever your specific goal, identify this as the starting point and work from here. When it comes to framing, it will be important to think about the perspective you would like learners to focus on and include this in the planning. For example, if the curriculum focus is social sciences and participants are learning about Parihaka, you might wish to focus on the tactics of non-violent resistance used by Te Whiti-o-Rongomai and Tohu Kākahi. If the curriculum learning area is science, you might want to focus on the importance of density in floating and sinking or the scientific evidence for whether carbon-based life has ever existed on Mars. For mathematics, you might have the goal of understanding the patterns within algorithms for long division, and so on. If you are familiar with forming enduring understandings to guide your planning these can be very useful to record at this point. This will help you focus your planning to ensure goals are met, while allowing for holistic learning and connections to be made.

As a specialist teacher, when it comes to planning the professional tasks, you should still list all the tasks a professional team will undertake but, unlike a generalist who will embrace tasks from across the curriculum, you'll need to focus on those tasks that hit the mark for that particular curriculum area. When microplanning, choose tasks that involve deliberate acts of teaching with the curriculum learning areas you are focused on. You will find Mantle of the Expert is naturally integrative so you need to avoid drifting too far from your specialist topic. Even though you don't detour into other curriculum areas, even realising these detours would be possible is a healthy reminder that learning is interrelated and mutually dependent—that a specialist area has relationships with all other curriculum areas. Mantle of the Expert reminds us of the holistic humanity of curriculum, even if we don't explore every direction. Another thing to bear in mind when micro-planning is how to negotiate timetables: if your sessions occur weekly, you'll need to find ways to round off successfully at the end of each session and re-engage participants at the start of the next.

Another tip if you're working at secondary or tertiary level is that older participants often prefer not to hang around too long before getting on with the commission. Often they are more focused on assessment outcomes and want to be clear on how what they are doing in class will help with their results. In some ways this is unfortunate: in an ideal world all participants would focus on the learning journey itself, not only the outcome. And research has shown Mantle of the Expert can help them push past this tendency (Stoate, 2013). All the same, when you first start out you may want to consider using an inquiry or expert hook (see Chapter 5) to make clear connections to the content and introduce the commission quite early in the piece. Also, be prepared to stop and reflect with participants on whether they find the approach effective. One colleague who used Mantle of the Expert in her specialist theatre studies classroom used to negotiate with her senior classes by saying, "I want to try this way of working and I think you'll enjoy it. Give me two weeks, and we'll take a vote. If the majority doesn't like how we are learning, we'll stop and do it the old fashioned way" (K. West, personal communication, 2017). She found this was generally enough to convince everyone to give it a go and in 5 years she never had a group vote against using Mantle of the Expert.

As for whether participants in a specialist classroom will buy in and take the drama seriously, there may be some initial hesitation, but in my experience, if the teacher uses the pedagogical elements, conventions, strategies, and tools effectively, older students and adults become just as interested, engaged, and eventually obsessed as children in their learning. In an environment where outcomes are often the focus, your students may find the opportunity to emphasise process over product is a welcome change. And senior students benefit just as much as younger ones from being repositioned as experts. I'm reminded of an account by UK practitioner Debra Kidd whose class of senior students asked her to put them into role before a school exam as they felt so much smarter in role than as themselves (Kidd, 2011).

Taking account of specific learning needs

This book has focused on the planning and implementation of Mantle of the Expert in mainstream classrooms. If you are working with participants with recognised learning needs—and most teachers are in this position—you will need to be mindful of these needs in your planning and implementation. Of course, all learners are individuals so it's difficult to make sweeping recommendations, but one thing I would say is try to avoid a deficit view. It's too easy to assume that a participant with particular language, learning, behavioural, or other needs won't have the capacity for learning in imagined worlds. This is true of only a small number of people with extremely complex disabilities. It might be that you find it more appropriate to avoid the intricacies of full-blown Mantle of the Expert, so that what you try is more akin to dramatic playing, or simple process dramas, but if you don't give Dramatic Inquiry a go you won't know what your participants are capable of. Many teachers have stories of people who have shone in drama-based approaches when they would have previously thought they wouldn't appreciate or manage this way of working. In my own career, I have witnessed a child with elective mutism who was prepared to speak in front of the whole class when in role (Aitken & Cowley, 2007). I've worked with adults with intellectual disability who have found benefits in taking on high-status roles and solving complex problems in imagined worlds (Aitken et al., 2007). I've seen teenagers in an alternative education programme engage with a process drama with more buy-in than their teachers had thought they were capable of (Hamilton YMCA facilitator, personal communication, 2017), and I've seen a child with complex behavioural needs and learning delays taking an interest in the class commission, undertaking research, and sharing her findings with the class (Aitken & Townsend, 2013). These achievements only occurred because their teachers refused to take a deficit view and gave the participants a chance to engage to the best of their abilities.

Whatever the nature of the participant's learning need, start by asking yourself what they *can* do and build on this. One of the benefits of working in drama is that the teacher can give opportunities for existing strengths and passions to be expressed and incorporated into the imagined world. For example, one adult participant I worked with who had Down's Syndrome was very interested in a particular country music singer. Over the 5 years we worked together, just about every time we went into an imagined world, this participant would make suggestions inspired by this singer's life, her costumes, her moves, or the lyrics of one of her songs. I guess I could have seen my task as being to broaden her interests, but to me it was important to work with what she suggested. I did my best to weave in her offers and I think this participant experienced real pleasure working in an imagined world where her personal passion was given significance and framed in new ways.

Another suggestion is to find out teaching strategies that are already successful and include these in your Mantle of the Expert teaching. For example, when working with a group of Year 5 participants, all of whom were on the autism spectrum, I was advised by their teacher that they welcomed clear instructions and signals. So I devised very clear signals for when we were in and out of role and stopped to give explanations of why we are doing what we are doing. Another participant I worked with who is on the spectrum told me she found tangible indicators of objects and spaces within the imagined world very helpful. While others in the group could easily imagine making a phone call, she needed a physical something—not necessarily a phone—to hold in her hand to talk into. While she initially struggled to buy in to the idea we were going on an imagined trip into space, it became much easier once we taped out the dimensions of the space ship so she could "see" the edges of the vessel she was imagining. As a teacher, it's about finding out what already helps your participant learn and taking this with you into the imagined world. Parents, other teachers, support workers, friends, and the participant themselves can help you with this if you ask.

Where participants are speakers of a different language from the one you're using to teach, they may need additional support to understand what's expected of them in Mantle of the Expert. You could provide a short written explanation for the participant and their family about what is going on in the classroom and have this translated into their first language. You can do the same with the commission letter. Once the Mantle of the Expert experience is underway, the strong visual and embodied aspects of learning through drama can actually be very helpful to speakers of other languages but you will need to slow down and frequently check in with them. To reinforce understanding, try using visual images. It can also pay to have translations of key words or phrases prepared in advance and to encourage them to ask questions for clarification in their own language. With online translation tools now available on our devices, this becomes even easier.

What about working with participants with challenging behaviours? Again, each individual situation will be unique and complex. It is important, however, to remember that when working with someone for whom behaviour is a challenge, a primary goal is to foster the key competencies—*relating to others, participating and contributing,* and *managing self.* Mantle of the Expert can offer new and engaging opportunities for participants who have not responded well to school to achieve in this regard. It may be that the opportunity to be someone else in role provides an incentive to try different behaviour, so look for opportunities to support this. Perhaps you could recruit a participant with challenging behaviour to help with the introduction of a new tension or a piece of significant information. You can also look for ways to elevate their status within the imagined world of the team and ensure you accept and build on any "offers" they make where possible.

Mantle of the Expert has been shown to be an effective way of engaging learners for whom mainstream teaching is not working. In a survey of young people in the UK who attended an alternative education programme delivered through Mantle of the Expert, 100% of participants reported that they liked learning this way and would like to continue (Tim Taylor, personal communication, 2019). I'm sure this is partly to do with the novelty as well as the skill of the teachers involved, but it's reasonable to suppose they also appreciated being treated as capable and competent. Framing and positioning can be powerful ways to recalibrate a relationship, which is often the starting point for other kinds of change.

Sustaining professional learning

In the 10 years I have been supporting individuals and schools to use Dramatic Inquiry, it's been very evident that the most successful and sustained implementation happens where teachers have access to ongoing professional learning and support. It is possible to decide to use Mantle of the Expert all on your own but it is much easier with the support of like-minded colleagues with whom you can share practice, co-plan, and reflect. It's difficult to sustain professional learning alone, so one of the best things you can do is connect with others in your school or region through face-to-face contact or over social media. My advice for face-to-face support is to form groups of three people. Triads have three points of contact, which is stronger, more accountable, and more productive than a pair. Three people can keep each other accountable, make dates to meet, discuss readings and tools, and plan together without the difficulties of meeting as a larger group. If the triad is lucky enough to be in the same school, they can also visit each other's classrooms, share teaching inquiries, and carry out joint projects. As for wider contact, since 2009, an extensive informal professional learning community has developed around the country, with cluster meetings in Hamilton, Tauranga, Wellington, Auckland, and over Zoom. These are advertised on the website (Aitken, V., 2017). Cluster meetings provide valuable opportunities to talk honestly about recent experiences in the classroom, share planning and resources, and receive informal professional learning in a low-key way. At the time of writing, moves are underway to formalise this network through the forming of a trust with the goal of providing workshops, courses, and professional support in a more sustainable way. I hope readers of this book will be able to tap into the good work of this group in future. At present, the main way schools can access ongoing professional learning in Mantle of the Expert is by applying for centrally funded PLD through the Ministry of Education (http://services.education.govt.nz/pld/). As a Ministry-accredited facilitator, I have worked with schools to develop and deliver tailored professional development aligned to their needs as well as Ministry priorities.

Planning

Taking time to plan

The foremost advice for anyone planning a full-length Mantle of the Expert experience is to take time over the planning process. Teachers are busy people and time is precious but the more you invest in the pre-planning, mapping, and research stages the more you will be repaid when you are implementing the experience. Once you are underway, participants are engaged, the commission is in place, and you start introducing tensions, curriculum tasks seem to arise quite naturally and the whole thing unfolds very readily. However, this exciting feeling of flying along doesn't happen by chance. It takes commitment in the planning stages. Ironically, it's those very parts of planning that can feel like extras or trimmings that are the most important to take time over: establishing the backstory of the responsible team, avoiding the temptation to go with your first idea, ensuring the client and commission feel weighty and authentic, thinking of the multiple perspectives, and doing your research into the content. Planning in Mantle of the Expert is a creative process and the mind needs time to work creatively. Even experienced Mantle of the Expert teachers can fall into the trap of launching into a new term with something that doesn't quite feel right. Remember, a few extra hours devoted to building your own sense of excitement, commitment, and knowledge about the imagined world will pay dividends down the track.

Considering culture

For any teacher working in the Aotearoa New Zealand, cultural responsiveness (Berryman et al., 2018) or what some prefer to call cultural intelligence (Earley & Ang, 2003) or culturally sustaining practice (Milne, 2017) must be a key consideration. It is all too easy for a teacher to operate within the behaviours and world views they are familiar with instead of focusing on learning, understanding, and connecting with the ways their participants may see the world. There's a particular danger of this when working with the frameworks of a teaching approach imported from another country, as Mantle of the Expert has been. Here's a cautionary tale about how I came to recognise cultural bias in my own practice. Some years ago, I taught a Mantle of the

Expert experience in which children were a responsible team of playground designers who were commissioned to produce a playground for the local council down at the riverside. The site, on the banks of the Waikato River, was home to a colony of endangered short-tailed bats and the commission was to build the playground in such a way it would protect the habitat and encourage children and their families to learn about and respect the bats. Initially, I was planning to introduce a tension in which local iwi protested about the proposed playground on the grounds that a taniwha was believed to live at that bend in the river. This seemed like a delicious tension and I thought it would introduce participants to Māori perspectives and world views. However, on reflection, I realised that I was engaging in deficit positioning and tokenism: why should Māori perspectives only be introduced as a potential tension? Why wasn't I embracing this world view as a natural part of what was "responsible" within our responsible team? I was horrified to realise that I'd done this before in previous planning too. Far from operating in a culturally sustaining way, I'd been doing the opposite—positioning te ao Māori as other, or worse, as problematic. These days I am much more careful to start planning from a bicultural perspective in the first place. It is now a given in all my plans that the responsible team will be a Treaty-based organisation. This way, an engagement with te ao Māori and tikanga Māori is assumed to be part of what we do and who we are rather than something out there beyond the team. And if it's important for participants to learn about something from te ao Māori, I'll include this in the commission rather than as a tension. My journey into cultural responsiveness is ongoing and I'm sure my practice will continue to evolve. It's only through continued reflection on our cultural assumptions and biases that we can catch ourselves out and seek to make change in an ongoing way.

As part of recalibrating our cultural attitudes and assumptions, we desperately need more Mantle of the Expert planning based on our own contexts and history. As this book goes to press there are moves afoot to establish New Zealand history as a compulsory part of the curriculum. Many would agree that New Zealand history has not been taught widely or well in our schools to date (Fraser, 2019) and Mantle of the Expert provides an excellent way to do this better. Important work is starting to happen, as discussed in Chapter 7, and we are starting to see more resources on the Mantle of the Expert Aotearoa website written by Aotearoa New Zealand teachers and situated in our own cultural contexts and histories (see, for example, Tauranga, 2019). Plans like these allow participants to explore their own stories and see their own world views reflected. This is an important first step. We also need a bigger conversation about the inbuilt structural assumptions of Mantle of the Expert itself, and how these might or might not support effective relationships and culturally sustaining practices.

While we are waiting for more culturally specific planning to be developed, the majority of plans you'll find online as models are from the UK. This means, inevitably, they are Eurocentric in their concerns and contexts. Many are based on teaching about figures and events from European history—the Great Fire of London, the Vikings, Kindertransport, etc. Or you'll also see imagined worlds that draw on European traditional tales—troll hunters, fairytale problem solvers, Hansel and Gretel, The Selfish Giant—or European stories of adventure and danger—Pirate Rescue, Dinosaur Island, Mountain Rescue. A small number have been written on international topics—The Olympics, Deserts—but, on closer inspection, you'll find the client, commission, and context usually have a strongly Eurocentric orientation, unsurprisingly, since they were written for and by UK-based practitioners. I don't wish to put you off using this international planning, but it is important to consider how we adapt these overseas resources to make them more appropriate for our contexts. As I said at the start of this book, most Aotearoa New Zealand teachers are accustomed to reworking overseas resources in some way. Often you'll find you can take the overall shape of the Mantle of the Expert experience and use it to explore an Aotearoa New Zealand story, event, historical figure, or context. Or you will find sequences of strategies and conventions that you can adopt and rework into new planning. Here are some points to consider if you wish to adapt planning for a local context.

Chapter 6 Advice and cautionary tales

Table 6: Adapting planning from overseas

Themes	Considerations for Aotearoa New Zealand teachers
Traditional tales	Many European folk tales are well known in Aotearoa New Zealand and are part of the tradition here. However, instead of working only with European traditional tales, why not explore traditional tales from te ao Māori—particularly local stories associated with your iwi and location—and take the opportunity to work with significant stories from other ethnic and cultural groups in your community too.
History	While there is lovely international planning available on world history, children in this country also need the opportunity to learn about significant events, people, and movements from our own past including tribal histories, the suffrage movement, land wars, Tangata Rongonui, pioneer and immigration stories, and much more. Luckily, more and more resources are being published to support and inform teachers in their planning. Check out Tamsin Hanly's curriculum programme resource on Māori and Pākehā histories (Hanly, 2017), the materials produced under the Ministry of Education's Ngā kōrero o nehe project (Ministry of Education, 2019), as well as the guidelines found in *Te Takanga o Te Wā* (Ministry of Education, 2015).
People and society	Ours is a country of five million people with a unique historical and cultural context. Check planning carefully to ensure it reflects the reality of individuals, communities, and life here. This will be in small details such as the choice of names for people and places in the imagined world—and also more holistic things such as social and cultural norms. For example, while we officially still have the Queen as our head of state, we have a very different relationship to the monarchy from what's implied in UK planning. And we don't have the same historic assumptions about class and social structure. Within a Māori world view the notion of "self-hood" is not individualised, but is a collective thing—strongly embedded in whānau and iwi connections. Human relationships are considered in terms of whakapapa which ultimately links people to the atua and thus the land, sea, sky, wind, nature and the cosmos.
Outdoors and adventure	As a set of islands set in the Pacific Ocean, we have our own distinct geography and topography and our own relationship to land. First and foremost, there's cultural significance associated with our natural landscapes, particularly mountains, lakes, rivers, and oceans which have ancestral significance for Māori. Secondly, the physical experience of travelling through our country is different from anywhere else in the world. We have vast empty distances, volcanic activity, earthquakes, and geothermal areas, none of which are likely to make an appearance in planning from other countries. As a result, the notion of what constitutes adventure or danger in this country is different from what might be found in a UK plan: venturing into the backcountry on a 5-day tramp, climbing a mountain, or fighting a bushfire in this country is a very different proposition to rambling, climbing, or firefighting in a UK context. Even apparently everyday activities such as driving between cities, preparing for adverse weather, or ensuring access to emergency services all have a very different flavour. If using a story of adventure or exploration, think about how these perspectives can considered from the start and integrated throughout.

Animals and plants	Aotearoa New Zealand has its own unique flora and fauna and what counts as a prized wildflower or a cute wild animal in the UK may well be a noxious pest in our country. Before making use of existing planning about a "woodland", a "bear sanctuary", a "zoo", or a "pet shop" be mindful of the fact that this country has no native mammals other than bats and that many creatures, including snakes, are prohibited altogether. The same goes for plants: asking children to imagine planting out bamboo as a windbreak for native planting would not strike the right note for a New Zealand classroom! Find out what species of plants, birds, and other wildlife are precious to your local area and focus on those instead.
Cultural practices/ cultural divisions	Te ao Māori and tikanga Māori have a unique status within New Zealand's multicultural society, and this influences the rituals and practices that we consider a normal part of life. Important occasions such as welcomes, celebrations, births, and burials as well as day-to-day practices like meals, visiting someone's home, or holding a meeting have distinct social practices that may not be reflected in planning from overseas. In Heathcote's "divisions of culture" planning tool (Heathcote, 2009), she lists 25 aspects of cultural life—*war, healing, family, law, trade, work, learning, child-rearing, punishment, death, worship, travel, nourishment, communication, leisure, shelter, transport, myth, clothing, climate, health, embellishment, memory, commerce* and *environment*—and suggests every community will have its own distinct activities and attitudes related to each of these divisions. The tool was designed for teachers to use in creating an imagined community. It might also be useful when adapting planning from one cultural context to another, since every one of those cultural divisions will be different in the New Zealand context.

Trusting the process to take you to curriculum

Dorothy Heathcote once commented, "the teacher can trust any Mantle to take them to curriculum" (Heathcote, 1983) and this is a good thing to bear in mind when planning. Of course, there may be times when you need to steer your planning in a particular direction: if you're a subject specialist or if you are planning something to fit with a particular school-wide focus. For others with more flexibility, it can be very liberating to keep an open mind and see where the planning process leads you. It may open up meaningful learning opportunities you did not foresee. Earlier in the book I quoted Graham Aitken's suggestion that an important part of teaching is to beguile participants into areas of curriculum they might not otherwise have thought of going (Aitken, G., 2017). In Mantle of the Expert, the teacher, too, can be beguiled by allowing curriculum learning goals to arise as an authentic consequence of the commission. For example, when planning the *Shark Tank* experience, Andy and I did not initially foresee possibilities for Music–Sound Arts exploration. We arrived at that curriculum area through a sort of reverse engineering beginning with the commission (in this case, the augmented reality shark tank environment), then the professional tasks required to fulfil it (including sending a probe to take samples), and finally the tensions that might arise (what if the audio collected by the probe was polluted with other sounds?). Only at this point did we think about classroom tasks to address this tension and how they could be tailored to the appropriate curriculum level. That's how we came up with the level two Music–Sound Arts activity of matching sounds and creating soundscapes on GarageBand. Planning in Mantle of the Expert is something like the backward design planning model of Wiggins and McTighe (2005) in that it encourages teachers to start with the big picture and work backwards to the details. The difference with Mantle of the Expert is that, instead of having to think of tasks through which to approach the enduring understandings underpinning your teaching, you can trust the core elements to provide a framework and a set of tasks in which the understandings are given purpose and focus.

You may be surprised at the array of novel and interesting tasks that arise even if your starting point does not seem too interesting. I recall at one teacher's cluster meeting we set ourselves the challenge of planning from the most uninteresting starting point we could think of, just to see what would happen. Someone suggested "dried vegetables" as a very uninteresting topic, so we worked with that. Before long the group had used the list of possible enterprises to think of a number of exciting possibilities including enrolling participants as a team of experts in desiccated foods, with a commission from a space agency to create nutritious meals that would be prepared and eaten on an international space station by astronauts from all over the world. Our "boring" topic quickly opened up exciting professional tasks such as measuring the nutritional value of food after freezing with liquid nitrogen, discovering how liquids and solids behave in zero gravity, researching the food and flavour preferences of different cultures, and writing instructions in a range of different languages. This planning experiment showed us we could trust the planning process and tools of Mantle of the Expert to open up authentic, purposeful, and engaging curriculum from any starting point. It was also a reminder that there is no such thing as a boring topic: everything in our universe has the potential to be fascinating if it is located in an interesting and authentic context, which a well-planned Mantle of the Expert can provide.

Weighing up when to use the commission model

As mentioned in Chapter 2, the commission model is a variant of Mantle of the Expert in which participants are engaged to undertake a real-world commission, usually (though not always) with a real-world client. With its focus on bringing about actual impact or change in the real world, Heathcote's commission model shares many of the objectives of social inquiry projects found in social science education (Wood, 2013) and the hands-on environmental action projects promoted in technology science and education for sustainability (Department of Conservation, 2017). It's beyond the scope of this book—and the expertise of its author—to discuss the commission model in much detail, but for those readers who might be considering it, here are some notes on how the commission model differs from Mantle of the Expert and some thoughts on when you might consider this alternative.

At first sight, the commission model seems really similar to Mantle of the Expert and indeed it does involve many of the same core elements. The key difference is that not all the core elements are situated in the imagined world. There are various ways you might go about a commission model experience. Here are some examples:

> A group of Year 3 students is commissioned by the board of their local hospital to design a real-world multisensory garden walk for blind and partially sighted patients on hospital grounds. A scale model of the site is marked on the classroom floor and drama conventions and strategies are used to simulate visits for planning, soil testing, and planting and to fast forward into the future to imagine how future users will enjoy the fully grown garden. Hospital managers are invited to the school to view the plan and hear the students present their case.

> A Year 7 art class works as a team of experienced designers with a commission to create a design for a mural which will be installed on a real wall within their school grounds. The commission comes from the

school board but is framed as part of a fictional inner city rejuvenation project with a fictional client. Painting is completed by the students, assisted by a real-world professional painter.

A group of Year 12 students work with their technology teacher to design and build a real-world drone with the capability to deliver a small package of a specified size and weight. The teacher co-constructs the brief with input from the local civil defence manager, who supplies information about how such a drone could be employed during a natural disaster. Drama is used to explore multiple imagined scenarios. Students share their final design with the civil defence manager along with a report about its potential uses in the field.

As this list shows, in the commission model approach, the commission is always situated in the real world. However, other core elements may or may not be. Usually the client will be from the real world but it's also possible to use a fictional frame, as in the second example. As for the responsible team, it's up to the teacher whether participants are framed within an imagined world as team of experts with a fictional backstory or whether they work on their commission solely as their real-world selves. Note that each one of these examples involves some level of engagement with an imagined world and the commission model always involves the use of drama strategies and conventions within the teaching episodes. Without this, the experience would fall outside of our definition of Dramatic Inquiry.

While the differences between Mantle of the Expert and the commission model may seem minor, the focus on a real-world commission makes a significant difference to planning. The teacher will need to begin by choosing a real-world commission and a client to work with and will need to think carefully about whether participants are to be framed in a fictional team. They'll also need to decide what an appropriate "product" will be and negotiate this with the client and indeed the participants. The commission should extend and challenge the participants without being too overwhelming. One way of managing this is to negotiate a product that isn't the final and full completion of the commission. For example, the product may be a design or report, or sometimes professionals may be used to see a commission through to completion, as in the first two examples given above. Once the experience is underway, operating in the real world necessitates planning for real-world eventualities: following budgets, sticking to time frames, accessing the right materials, observing safety protocols, meeting legal requirements, and so on. While participants will take responsibility for some of these, the teacher still needs to take oversight as part of their professional duty of care. Teachers also need to protect participants from exposure, since there is a lack of frame distance to tasks and everyone involved is aware of the real-world consequences. The teacher will need to plan carefully to ensure a focus on the process as well as the product.

In the commission model experience, the orientation is always towards the real world—what is going on *out there* beyond the classroom. This makes a difference to the overall "feel" of the experience and provides food for thought. Throughout this book, including in its title, I've made the case that when it comes to learning, particularly for young people, working within the real world is not necessarily better or more authentic than working within the imagined. I've also argued that the imagined world allows participants to do things that cannot be achieved in the real world of a commission model experience, including moving backwards and forwards through time and space, rewinding and trying things again, operating with a limitless budget, exploring what happens when laws or safety rules are broken, tackling difficult or perilous tasks, solving complex ethical issues, holding difficult conversations, responding to emergencies, travelling into space, and much more besides. In the real world, very few of these are possible or safe, for the simple reason that reality is subject to the constraints of laws, physics, and the social habitus of the classroom. At its best, however, the commission model can still achieve the benefits of an imagined experience by using the power of drama to extend meaning-making and imagine possibilities within the real world commission.

So, when is the commission model the right choice? Iona Towler-Evans, an experienced user of the approach, reports particular success with disaffected participants or those with a strong prejudice against working in the imaginary realm of drama (Towler-Evans, 2020, personal communication). The commission model might also be appropriate where participants identify a real-world issue that they want to address, or are approached by a real-world client from their community. Sometimes the real world just insists on being addressed. For example, some years ago I was part of a project where a teacher was planning to use Mantle of the Expert to explore natural disasters. During the planning process, an actual tsunami struck Samoa and so this teacher made the decision to shift to a real-world social action project in which the class would work to equip a real school in the village (Fraser & Deane, 2010). I don't think the teacher used the commission model, as she didn't use drama strategies and conventions during the unit. However, these could have been included as a way to rehearse key moments, explore multiple perspectives, visit imagined versions of the real places, and even introduce and explore imagined tensions. Of course, the line between fiction and reality would need to be navigated carefully so as to avoid compromising the real-world integrity of the project and to ensure fictional aspects did not trivialise or sensationalise people's real-life experiences. It would take an experienced and sensitive teacher to manage this but I'm sure it could be done.

The key attraction of the commission model is the opportunity it brings for connection with community outside of the school. There is something appealing about an approach that encourages real-world action, given our world's urgent need for change on sociological and environmental issues. We have a curriculum that promotes active citizenship, and the opportunity to achieve real social action may feel like an exciting way to go. And it's also true that being accountable in the real world can give a sense of focus and raise the stakes for quality work. Participants may feel additionally motivated by the opportunity to make something tangible or take action with a lasting impact. Certainly, they will have opportunities to learn real-world lessons. Heathcote's commission model has not been sufficiently explored within New Zealand or internationally and, like all forms of Dramatic Inquiry, it has great potential in the right context.

Finding alternatives to real-world names

One thing I have learned about planning in Mantle of the Expert is to avoid co-opting the names of real-world people, companies, or entities for use in the imagined world. It may seem harmless to ask participants to imagine they are working for NASA, the Department of Conservation, or the Ministry of Education and certainly I spent many years doing this as I know Heathcote did and other experienced practitioners still do. However, I have now changed my practice on this front, having encountered a few issues that brought home the value of fictionalising. First of all, if participants have any sense of confusion about whether what they are doing is real or imagined, real-world names can add to this. Hearing that, "the Department of Conservation has asked us to do this …" or even, "We're imagining the Department of Conservation has asked us to do this", carries more danger of confusion than if participants are told the commission comes from an imaginary entity such as the Department for the Protection of Nature and Culture. In a world where young people clarify their understandings through online searches, it will only take a moment to discover that there's no such department in real life. The same goes with discussions participants may have back at home.

As well as protecting the participants, the use of fictional names also protects you as teacher from any accusations of misrepresentation or defamation. This may sound over-cautious, but consider this newspaper article from the *Southland Times* in 2010, which describes how then Minister of Education Anne Tolley was angered when her name was included along with a "fake" ministerial letterhead in a creative writing exercise:

> Education Minister Anne Tolley is outraged and police are involved after a letter was circulated claiming school hours would be extended. Year 5 and 6 pupils at the school near Invercargill were given a letter in class stating school hours would be extended by an hour next year, as teachers did not have enough time to 'implement the New Zealand Curriculum'. The Beehive banner used on ministers' press statements was on the letter, which was apparently signed by Mrs Tolley. One parent said others she had spoken to found it distasteful and were angry that it might be a 'disguised effort to sully Anne Tolley's name with parents and students for political gain'. 'It can't be a coincidence that this happens at a time when pay talks are failing and National Standards are a sore point with many teachers,' she said. She had received an email on Tuesday to say the letter was fake, and a 'springboard for a piece of persuasive writing,' she said. 'We appreciate you playing along and keeping this to yourself,' the email

says. Yesterday, principal Sharon Livingstone said the letter was a 'mistake' and was not meant to go home to parents. It was part of a creative writing exercise and children were not told it was fake as teachers wanted the reactions to be 'authentic'. 'In hindsight it wasn't a good idea. It should have been done differently.'

(Crayton-Brown, 2010)

In this case, the offence was compounded by the fact the imagined world was unsignalled: the teacher wanted children to think the letter about extending school hours was real so that responses would be more authentic. However, the letter could still have caused upset even if it had been used in a clearly signalled Mantle of the Expert context. Since reading about that story and others, and reflecting on the ethics of using real names, I have always opted for fictional parallels any time I'm referring to a real person or organisation. This is easy enough to do when planning and I would always recommend it.

Keeping things ethical

When selecting a responsible team, client, and commission in Mantle of the Expert it is imperative that you set things up so that participants will inhabit ethically sound positions and carry out morally upright activities. This piece of advice may appear to go without saying, but the repercussions of getting this wrong are so potentially damaging that they are worth spelling out. Theoretically, it would be possible to create an imagined world where the team are experienced pranksters with a history of picking on defenceless people, or assassins, or crime magnates. However, this would breach one of the tenets of Mantle of the Expert, which is that it gives participants an opportunity to operate as their best selves and to rehearse the kinds of actions they might carry out in the real world. Parents, communities, and governments have an expectation that education will offer guidance on how to make the world a better place, not a worse one. This is not to say we must never touch on difficult or contentious issues, or never explore what motivates people to trick others, break the law, kill, or whatever. However, the form of Mantle of the Expert with its invitation to adopt an imagined position of expertise over a sustained period should be handled with care and respect for the common good. Teachers have got in serious trouble for getting this wrong. In 2010, a teacher in Australia was sanctioned for setting students a homework task in which they were to pretend they were terrorists planning a chemical attack on an Australian community:

> The task included choosing the best time to attack and explaining their choice of victims and what effects the attack would have on a human body. 'Your goal is to kill the MOST innocent civilians in order to get your message across,' the assignment read. Principal Terry Martino said he withdrew the assignment as soon as he heard of it. 'The teacher, who is relatively inexperienced, made a well-intentioned but misguided attempt to engage the students in an assignment on contemporary conflict and how beliefs and values influence the behaviours and motives of individuals,' Mr Martino said in comments provided by the state Education Department. Mr Martino said the highly regarded teacher was not promoting terrorism but just made a mistake.
>
> (Associated Press, 2010, n.p.)

The teacher in this case was not using drama, but even in a writing task the adopting of such a point of view was deeply troubling for his students and their families, particularly those who had been affected by terrorist activity in the past. Had the students been framed differently as journalists, artists, or investigators, this teacher could have engaged the participants in the important learning he was looking for without these issues arising. For teachers using drama, where learning is embodied and participants walk in the shoes of the figures in the imagined world, careful framing takes on extra importance. Use the frame distancing tool (see Chapter 5) and protect your participants and yourself.

Avoiding light-hearted names

Another lesson I learned the hard way on my journey into Mantle of the Expert is that it's generally best to avoid light-hearted or comic names for people or organisations in the imagined world. Tempting as it may be to adopt a comical facial expression or funny costume when going into role, to call the client at the bank "Mr Red. E. Cash" or to introduce a forestry company called "Choppemups" or "Slash and Burn Ltd" with an amusing piece of clip art to use for a company logo, I suggest thinking hard before doing so. Yes, Mantle of the Expert should be fun and using this kind of language does feel playful. It also puts a sense of distance between the classroom and the imagined world which helps reduce the possibility of deception. But is it the right kind of playfulness and distance? As Eriksson has pointed out, too much distance is as much of a threat to successful drama as too little (Eriksson, 2011). Remember, Mantle of the Expert is an improvisation so participants will respond to the tone that you set with your offers. If you model an interest in comic effect and go for the gag, this is exactly what participants will think they should do too. A teacher going into role with a funny wig or glasses can expect to evoke laughter and light-hearted responses. A letter with an amusing logo or clever pun will do the same. If we want to encourage thoughtful engagement and critical thinking then it is better to opt for names and imagery that signal this. One exception to this rule of thumb might be when you are working in an imagined world which has magical or storybook elements, such as advising the tooth fairy what to do with the excess teeth or helping Elmer the toy elephant settle in at school. If the givens of the imagined world include fairytale or fantasy elements, then more light-hearted signals may be appropriate.

Focusing learning with a narrow commission

One of the great advantages of Mantle of the Expert is the way it focuses inquiry and provides a clearly bounded field for exploration. The focus of a defined commission enables deep learning in authentic contexts and encourages the class to work as a collaborative group with a sense of shared purpose. Teachers often tell me how much they value this feature of Mantle of the Expert, even those who previously assumed inquiry had to be student directed and individualised. Those forms of inquiry have their strengths, of course, but for some they also have their limitations. I remember one teacher describing how she found it hard to ensure meaningful learning in individualised inquiry once her students headed off in multiple directions (Elicia Pirini, personal communication, 2012). Another confided that "I've done a lot of inquiry learning ... but there is often one group that is a bit off, not quite bought in" (Parkes, cited in Fraser et al., 2013, p. 114). Mantle of the Expert allows for deliberate acts of teaching in curriculum as well as spells of individualised investigation: "With Mantle ... they self-select the tasks and buy into their own goals" (Parkes, cited in Fraser et al., 2013, p. 114). Another benefit is that everyone is working towards the same shared goal. If a participant gets carried away by personal interest in something beyond the commission, the teacher can return to the commission to check what the client asked for. The commission isn't set in concrete and could be renegotiated if there is good reason, but it does provide a set of parameters to bound the task and keep things collective.

To ensure you play to the strengths of Mantle of the Expert's particular approach to inquiry, it can help to make sure you keep your commission as narrow and specific as possible. Far from limiting your learners, a narrowly defined commission will encourage commitment to the imagined world and opportunities to dive deeper into curriculum. Consider the difference between this broadly expressed version of a commission: "A team of expert wildlife transporters is brought in to help clear animals from the scene of an Australian bushfire" and this more detailed version:

> A team of expert wildlife transporters is brought in to conduct an initial trapping and treatment exercise in the immediate aftermath of a bushfire. There are known to be multiple animal fatalities at the scene, but these will be dealt with by other groups. The transportation team will be brought in for 5 days, during which they are asked to focus on the trapping and treatment of three of the larger marsupial groups—kangaroo, koala, and wombats—each of which has different diet and needs for survival. Individual animals will need to be assessed and treated for any injuries at the scene before being sedated and placed into a crate for transportation by air to the wildlife recovery centre 800 km away.

Far from narrowing possibilities, a detailed commission brims with possibilities for curriculum learning. It feels authentic and urgent and invites detailed and specific action where a more vague set of instructions permits a more shallow or casual response. Producing a narrow and specific commission like this comes with practice. It really helps to think of what would happen in a real-world context: think about what a real team of experts would be asked to do and the level of specific detail they would be likely to need. Remember to keep the requirements of the commission reasonable to the time frame and resources your imagined team has available.

Of course, the full details of a commission will not always be revealed in one go. Often, the team will receive an initial request, setting out the general terms of the commission, followed by a letter or conversation to give further detail. Or the terms and conditions might be negotiated between the team and the client. Eventually, though, everyone should understand exactly what their commission entails.

Conducting research into content and the professional world of the team

The importance of research has already been mentioned in Chapter 4 but I'm repeating it here as it comes up so often when supporting teachers with planning. As a teacher using Mantle of the Expert, it's not enough to "wing it" with little curriculum knowledge, or decide that you will learn alongside your participants. You need to allow time during planning to build up your own skills and knowledge, both in terms of the content your participants will be exploring and in terms of the responsible team they will be inhabiting. When planning for the *Shark Tank* example shared in Chapter 3, Andy, the students, and I needed to read all we could about Dumb Gulper sharks as well as finding out about the realities of running an aquarium. Researching the content enabled us to feel secure about what we were teaching—an essential whether you are a specialist teacher or a generalist—while the research into the responsible team allowed us to gain a sense of the terminology belonging to that professional context. Often, researching the world of the team will provide additional ideas for professional tasks and tensions to enhance the drama.

The essential importance of research as part of planning is not something Heathcote necessarily made explicit in her writing about Mantle of the Expert but I think that is because she just assumed teachers would do it, as she always did. It may sound like quite an old-fashioned view to say that you need to start from a broad base of skills and knowledge of content and context. It's not just so you can impart skills and knowledge to participants in a transmission mode—though you might do that from time to time. It's more about making sure you have the right ingredients to draw on when you're mixing the recipe for the imagined world. If the content and the context feel real and exciting to you this will help you successfully sustain participants' interest, establish an appropriate language register, and feed in critical information. With the wealth of material available on the internet, research is not an onerous task and you should find it interesting and exciting to fill out your planning in this way. For many teachers I've worked with, it's this step that really brings their planning to life and gives them a place to stand within it.

Including other perspectives

When I first started using Mantle of the Expert I knew the approach was drama based but tended to assume I had taken care of this aspect by putting participants in role as members of the responsible team. I went in and out of role a lot, using teacher in role, but I did not give participants many opportunities to take on roles in the imagined world beyond their team identity. Looking at the first two examples in Chapter 3, I can see this tendency in the planning. I knew that to foster critical thinking and empathy, participants needed to encounter other points of view, including those who might be affected and impacted by the team's actions. I was sensitive, too, of the need to avoid an unquestioned collaborative mindset, lest I trained participants to take on a corporate identity. But I tended to think it was enough for participants to encounter alternative perspectives and think about them as a team. Over time, I've come to think that it's necessary to actually embody these different perspectives through role; to go beyond merely encountering other perspectives to moving, speaking, thinking, and acting as other people. This is much more likely to challenge and dislodge the "group think" of the team's collective identity. Yes, it's vital for participants to build a sense of commitment to their expert team identity, and there's great value in the teacher taking on roles to introduce new perspectives. However, if a class only experiences the commission and the various events of the Mantle of the Expert journey from the perspective of the team, the danger is they will privilege that perspective over the others. If there's one thing we need to foster in today's world, it's the idea there is not just one way of looking at things. So, these days, I make sure participants are given lots of opportunities to step out of their team position and take on roles within the imagined world.

To avoid the same blindspot about the use of role in Mantle of the Expert, I advise being mindful in your use of the language in relation to the responsible team. It might help to think of the team identity as first and foremost a position rather than a role. Of course, participants imagining themselves to be experts are in role, but being a member of the responsible team is mostly about playing a version of oneself: participants don't need to adopt a new name, take on characteristics, or act a part in any way. The chief function of the responsible team in Mantle of the Expert is to position participants in powerful ways: the role aspect really only arises because this takes place in an imagined world. I find it helps to think of team identity as a position and reserve the term "taking on a role" for activities where a specific drama convention or strategy is used. This will include times you use drama conventions to ask participants to step into full role as team members; for example, imagining themselves at the opening of a new exhibit or interviewing a suspect at a crime scene. But making this distinction between role and position reminds us there are always myriad other roles available that can take participants beyond their team position to consider other perspectives.

Working with the mythological

I would like to offer a few thoughts on including mythological elements in your Mantle of the Expert planning. Please note, I'm not using the term "mythological" in any disparaging sense but as a way to refer to people, places, things, or ideas that are not a tangible part of our world but are nonetheless familiar from fables, stories, religion, or traditional tales. First of all, it's important to acknowledge a distinction between mythological elements that form part of people's spiritual and cultural belief system and those that do not. Examples of the former might include things like gods, taniwha, angels, patupairarehe, ghosts, or spirits. We understand that these are to be handled with sensitivity because we acknowledge that, for some people, these things do have a reality in our world albeit in an unseen, intangible form, and are significant or sacred. On the other hand, there are other mythological elements that carry little or none of that kind of significance. Examples might include unicorns, superheroes, wizards, and Pokémon characters. These have a more playful connotation, as they are assumed to be located firmly in the realms of story, fantasy, popular culture, and magic. Of course, how individuals categorise these things will differ according to world view: some would disagree with the way I've categorised my examples. As a teacher, you will need to judge how the mythological elements you want to work with should be categorised, based on your world view and the context in which you are teaching. Once you've reconciled which category your mythological elements are situated in you'll be in a position to think about how to work with them.

When it comes to the sacred, or culturally significant, there is a clear argument for making space for these in your imagined world: after all, if they are acknowledged and important in the real world of your classroom, shouldn't they also be included within the imagined world of your Mantle of the Expert experience? You may worry that certain things are just too sacred or culturally significant to be explored in your planning. However, before ruling anything out, you might want to explore the use of frame distancing techniques and alternative role conventions. Increased frame distance can be a way of keeping interactions respectful and appropriate for your context. For example, if you are teaching in a special character Christian school then introducing teacher in role as God might feel inappropriate, but the chance to hear from a monk who has been grappling to understand God's commandments might hit just the right note. This is an example of increased frame distance. Similarly, you may decide it doesn't feel right in your teaching context for the class to receive a visit from someone in full role as Māui, Te Rā, or Papatūānuku. If so, try using one of the more abstract role conventions, so that participants overhear the culturally significant figure or receive a message from them in some other way. The goal is to find a way to introduce culturally or spiritually significant aspects in a way that matches how they are experienced in the real world of your context. A combination of frame distance and careful consideration of role conventions can help with this.

What about introducing the more playful mythological elements of magic, fantasy, or digital characters? Young children in particular can be very enthused by such elements, so it can be very tempting to include them in your Mantle of the Expert planning. On the whole, though, I'd advise against it, at least within the world of the responsible team. It may sound fun to decide to have a time machine in the corner of the room, or accept an offer from one of the children who suggests the group all have access to magic wands, or to liven things up by announcing that the boss has decided everyone can ride to work on dragons. Unfortunately, it can also be really problematic. For one thing, whatever you include in your imagined world will become a given of that world and therefore needs to be taken account of for the duration of the experience. If you suddenly decide to have magic wands, this brings up all sorts of issues: where they are stored; how they are charged; whether other people such as the client might have them too; what the protocols are for use; and so on. These will distract from the commission. More importantly, if you were hoping to operate in an imagined world that parallels the real one, you've blown it! Sometimes Mantle of the Expert is about creative storying in a fantasy world, but more often it's about participants grappling with real-world issues in authentic ways. Allowing for things like time travel, superpowers, or magic may be fun and engaging but undeniably reduces opportunities for authenticity. If the imagined world of the Mantle of the Expert experience runs to very different rules from the real world, this allows for short cuts and solutions that would never be possible in real life. Instead of grappling with complex issues and rehearsing how to tackle wicked problems, participants indulge in escapism. That's not always a bad thing: we may sometimes plan Mantle of the Expert experiences specifically to enjoy this feature, but as teachers we need to be conscious we are making this choice.

Lest you think I'm a total killjoy, I do have one suggestion for embracing fantasy elements, which is to include them in the *client's* world. To give a few examples: participants might be contacted by the tooth fairy to help decide what to do with the vast collection of teeth; Elmer the patchwork elephant's mum might look for advice on how her son, a talking elephant toy, can cope at school among the human children; a teenage superhero might seek guidance on whether, when, and how to tell their parents about their superpowers; an alien newly arrived on earth might request a detailed breakdown of the compounds that make up carbohydrates and a description of how they are broken down in the body; or an online avatar might ask for advice for designing a new home within their Minecraft village. In all these scenarios, participants can enter into an imagined world in which other people (or animals or things) have magical or superhuman powers, without having those powers available personally. This is one way of bringing mythology, fantasy, or magic into the teaching and learning relationship without undermining the learning potential that comes from grappling with issues in the real world.

Teaching

Moving beyond the surface features

As you embark on the implementation of a Mantle of the Expert experience, it's worth reminding yourself of your purpose in choosing to teach this way. In the novelty of exploring something new it can be easy for participants and teachers alike to get caught up in the surface features of the teaching modalities and lose sight of the deeper reasons for using them. In terms of inquiry, at the surface level this is represented by the commission, which spells out exactly what participants need to tackle. Remember, though, it's not about how quickly this can be achieved. The inquiry process is about grappling, questioning, and overcoming instances. As a teacher, you can support this by problematising, questioning, and introducing tensions. As for the drama, participants might get caught up in the surface features of this too— what it looks like, who can demonstrate the most convincing character, or who can be smartest or funniest in role; who can demonstrate the most interesting facial expressions, the most interesting use of levels and so on. Through your own modelling and the way you set up tasks, you can gently steer participants towards the real value of drama for learning: taking on multiple perspectives, developing empathy, and exploring and making meaning through the body. The third modality, powerful positioning, is most readily represented in the presence of the responsible team. It's important to help participants build a sense of commitment to this but, once again, beware of getting caught up in the surface features. It's easy to get carried away with the enactment of being in a company with things like business cards and briefcases, and sitting in proper chairs or holding proper meetings. Remember, though, the real purpose of repositioning is to share power, not to train participants in how the systems of power currently work in our corporations and businesses! To move the class on from reproducing the artefacts and trappings of power, focus on activities that express and strengthen the expert team's responsibilities, skills, values, and attitudes.

Avoiding deceit

This piece of advice is something I feel very strongly about. It's the one thing I would express as a hard and fast rule about Mantle of the Expert that everyone should follow. Simply put, any time you use drama, you should never present something that's happening in an imagined world as if it is real. I don't think there's any teacher who would say they want to teach through deception, yet it's a surprisingly easy trap to fall into and even find yourself defending. Teachers sometimes think it's more exciting, or more impactful not to let on about the imagined world; they worry it will somehow spoil the fun, diminish the magic, or reduce the authenticity of an experience if they tell participants that what they're doing is not real. However, this attitude is misguided and even potentially dangerous. Let me illustrate in more detail, with a cautionary tale about my first experiment with teacher in role.

When my daughter was about 10, I was invited by her teacher to do some drama with her class. I decided to take on the role of a character from a book the class had been reading together. It was all about spies. As the teacher finished the story, I would appear in role as the spy chief and tell the class they had been selected to be trained as special agents. This would start an interactive adventure where they would solve mysteries, solve clues, and eventually track down an enormous horde of gold, to be divided equally between them. This was an exciting opportunity to teach mathematics through an imagined world. Except back then I thought it would diminish the impact if I told the class who I really was. I thought they'd be more likely to buy into the story if I framed it as a real-world mission. In the event, as I learned the hard way, the opposite was true. I appeared in the classroom in full role (and full costume—right down to a special plastic spy chief watch), introduced myself, and announced the mission. The children were certainly intrigued. But they did not leap enthusiastically into action as I thought they would. Most simply froze: they couldn't make sense of what they were seeing. No frame had been offered so they were searching for some way to understand this strange experience. About a third of the class said, "You're not a spy chief!" and started to discuss all the reasons it was impossible. Another third turned to my daughter and said, "Wow, you never told me your Mum was a spy chief." And about a third completely bought it: they really believed that they had been chosen to do some kind of special training as spies. None of these responses actually set up the relationship to the imagined world that I was seeking.

Far from enhancing the experience, my failure to signal the imagined world had the opposite effect. None of the participants went into a state of metaxis—that dual awareness of real and imagined worlds which, as we have seen, sets up the safe no penalty zone required for learning. I had not offered participants a new role or power position; they were invited to do this spy training as themselves, a group of 10-year-old children. As Brian Edmiston states:

> When we create an imagined world, we can imagine that we frame events differently so that our power and authority relationships are changed ... I want students to have more opportunities to use words and deeds to act appropriately but in ways that are often not sanctioned in classrooms.
>
> (Edmiston, 2003, p. 225)

By not signalling my own shift in role, I made no steps to shift the power dynamics. In fact, the only thing that had happened in terms of power was that I, as an adult visitor to the class, had asserted my authority over the situation and played a trick on them. I'd caused confusion and distracted attention from the maths tasks, which were the real point of the exercise.

Aside from being hard on the participants, I hadn't set myself up for success either. By appearing in full role, I had to sustain my spy chief persona for as long as I was in class with the children. I couldn't pop out of role to adopt the facilitator or narrator voice; instead, I was forced to try to keep the role going whatever happened, including when the dental nurse came into the room or the bell went. Eventually, the teacher had to stop things and clarify who I was and what the point of the exercise was. This caused some disappointment among those who had been convinced they were going to be secret agents, but at least it allowed everyone to understand the rules of the game so they could get on with playing it. Sadly, by failing to signal drama I had perpetuated the idea that "just pretending" is somehow more disappointing than something being real. How much simpler it would have been to have proved that wrong from the start: introducing myself to the class out of role, explaining the situation, establishing the compact, and then using the tools of drama to capture interest, intrigue, and build commitment to our shared endeavour. All in all, I had failed to follow the number one rule of drama which is, as John O'Toole and Julie Dunn so succinctly express it, "the teacher who trusts the power of drama does not need to use deceit" (O'Toole & Dunn, 2002, p. 6).

Mixing up drama with deceit is an easy mistake, and one Heathcote herself made in her early experiments with Mantle of the Expert, as her biographer describes here:

> She had been asked by John Fines and Ray Verrir of Chichester to use drama to interest primary school pupils in Elizabethan architecture ... Dorothy had not previously met the children and she asked John and Ray to provide a wheel-chair for her ... she had already written them a letter to say that she was thinking of purchasing this house but needed their advice in their role as experts on how it needed adapting ... They learnt a good deal about architecture but the trouble was they had been conned ... no one had made it clear to them that they were all role playing. John explained to me afterwards that when they learnt that it was only role-play the children were very angry and didn't want to trust John and Ray again.
>
> (Bolton, 2003, p. 133)

As Heathcote discovered, any pedagogical benefits of unsignalled role are soon undermined by the fact that it is a breach of trust. I'd go so far as to say it's a breach of the values underpinning the New Zealand teachers' professional code of ethics: whakamana, manaakitanga, pono, and whanaungatanga (Education Council, 2017). Can we really claim that misleading participants is part of a high-quality, respectful, ethical, and collaborative teaching relationship of mana enhancement? How would we feel if the shoe was on the other foot, and our participants presented something to us as a real-life issue when it was really made up? I think we'd be likely to call that a prank or a lie and be really concerned. I know I'm being very uncompromising here. Some would argue that it's a matter of degree; that a teacher needs to weigh up the educational benefit of their actions and if participants learn something valuable it may be OK to frame something fictional as real. However, after exploring this at some length in my research (Aitken, 2008) I'm clear about my stance. To my mind, whether in a theatre, a classroom, on the street, or in any other setting, a dramatic event requires the awareness and consent of all parties and a shared agreement about how to participate to sustain the event. Without that awareness and agreement, you might have something interesting going on—it might even be educationally worthwhile—but it isn't drama and it isn't ethical.

Signalling the imagined world

Having made a case for ensuring participants are aware they are doing drama, let's look at how you can go about this. There are actually lots of ways, from the overt to the subtle: you could sit participants down and explain exactly what is going to happen; you could beguile them into the imagined world using a storyteller voice; or you could signal with a dramatic hook such as an artefact, a drawing, or a person in role. While I've argued passionately for the importance of making participants fully aware, this doesn't mean I'm opposed to subtle ways of going about it and the more accustomed you and your participants are to working in drama, the more subtle your signals can be. However, for a novice teacher, or for someone working with a new group, it might be a good idea to signal the presence of the imagined world in quite an explicit way. The process doesn't have to be elaborate. Don't feel you have to leave the classroom or use elaborate props or costumes: in fact, these are really counterproductive ways of signalling and it's harder to move in and out of role as I discovered when I was the spy chief. Here's a simple three-step transition that can be used when a teacher wants to signal the imagined world. The example given here is for teaching in role, but the same steps could be used to set up the ground rules for any role or drama convention. These three steps are particularly recommended when participants are new to drama. This transition takes place in the classroom in front of the class:

> Step 1: Tell them what is going to happen: "In a moment, I'm going to take on a role." Pause—check understanding. Clarify if necessary.

Step 2: Tell them how they will know. Declare and demonstrate the signal: "You will know I'm in role when ..." Examples might include, "I'm wearing this hat" or, "I'm sitting in this chair" or, "I'm carrying this kete." Pause—check understanding. Model a couple of times: "Hat on—who am I? Hat off—who am I now?"

Step 3: Spell out the expectations and the compact: "For this to work you need to accept me in role. You'll be able to talk to me and I'll answer as if I am really X." Pause—check understanding.

Note the third step is not phrased as a question like, "Do you think you can agree to behave as if I am X?" This is not a negotiation with participants. If you simply wish to establish the ground rules for an activity then it is more authentic to state your expectations directly.

Once these three steps have been followed, the teacher is as secure as they can be that participants understand what is going to happen and what is expected. Participants are much less likely to disrupt the drama by challenging or questioning the activity. This is not to say they will all instantly work with it successfully. You can expect them to giggle, or laugh, and find it a little strange. You can expect some to push back and test the boundaries of the new relationship. When this happens, try not to write off drama as "not for me" or "not for this class". Instead, consider it just like any other skill you bring in to the classroom and allow everyone time and practice to become familiar and comfortable with it. Once participants understand the strategy then you will no longer need to be so explicit with your words and can try more subtle signalling.

Using de-rolling rituals
Just as it's important for participants to know when they're moving into the imagined world, it can also help to mark the transition back out again. To clarify, I'm talking here about where drama conventions are used to step into full role, not so much about the roles participants take on as members of the responsible team. I used to spend time on transitions in and out of the team—everyone putting their lanyards on and off, or stepping over an imagined line into the world of the company—now I don't see this as necessary. As discussed earlier, the function of the responsible team is mostly to do with repositioning

participants and we don't need to undo that at the end of an episode or session. The one time we might de-role from the team is when the Mantle of the Expert experience as a whole comes to a close. At that point, some kind of ritual to decompress and reflect on the experience can be valuable. Mostly, though, de-rolling is used after moments in the experience where participants have entered into full role as someone from the imagined world, particularly if the experience was emotional or intense in some way. For example, let's say participants have been invited to pair up and go into role as neighbours gossiping about a troubled family. A clear signal for when it's time to stop helps mark the end of the exercise and releases participants from the emotional state, mindset, body language, and spoken register they've adopted during the activity.

The de-rolling signal you choose will depend on how deeply participants worked in role. It might be as simple as a shift in your tone of voice or a quick click of the fingers. You might ask everyone to shake their hands to shake off the role. Or, for a more fully embodied transition, you could ask children to turn around twice and sit down, or move to another part of the room, or join hands and jump out of the story, or even go for a run outside and come back in as themselves. In general, the more deeply embodied the role was, the more embodied the de-rolling ritual may need to be. It's not just a matter of shifting the pace. Sometimes participants can get a bit stuck in role, meaning they don't quite let it go. I remember one new entrant teacher describing how, after working with the story of the three little pigs, she had a room full of big bad wolves until she invited children to shake off their wolfiness and come back to the mat as themselves.

Do be mindful of the difference between de-rolling and other activities that actually deepen role. I once participated in a process drama where I got quite stuck in role (we were playing miners trapped in a mine collapse which triggered associations for me with a real-life mine disaster that killed my great-grandfather). I felt rather sombre and asked the facilitator if we could do something to de-role. He agreed we should, and set up a task involving writing letters to the figures in the story. This only took me deeper into difficult emotional territory and I had to quietly remove myself from the room as a way of de-rolling. I guess this is a reminder of the emotional power of drama and the importance of safety protocols. As a teacher, we can't be sure what will come up for individuals, so it may be good to remind participants they can use de-rolling rituals to step out of role if needed.

Maintaining the grace element

Another important idea to bear in mind at all times in our teaching is what Heathcote called the "grace element". Simply put, it's about avoiding the temptation to demonise anyone, whether they are a role within the imagined world, a member of the participant group, a real-life person from the world outside the classroom, or a historical figure. It's this grace element that Sandra Heston is talking about when she notes how Heathcote's lessons always involved "a dialectical process which turned the potential for evil into the potential for good" (Heston, 2012, p. 8). Though a simple enough idea, it can be quite hard to maintain the grace element in practice. It is human nature to stereotype or at least categorise people, particularly those with different beliefs from our own (Haidt, 2013). It's particularly tricky to remember to present people in a compassionate light when working in an imagined world. After all, we have a long tradition of storytelling and play filled with "goodies" and "baddies" and other useful archetypes. However, Mantle of the Expert seeks to offer a more nuanced take on humanity than the simple triumphing of good over bad that is the function of such stories. If we are truly to explore multiple perspectives and empathise with different points of view, this must extend even to those who appear to be disagreeable, criminal, or bad.

What does maintaining the grace element look like in practice? It could be as simple as consciously avoiding stereotypical presentations when teaching in role. Heston quotes an example from a lesson in 1983 where Heathcote went into role as someone committing a robbery, and her first words were, "Eh, isn't this a marvellous building to break into? Have you noticed the architecture?" (Heston, 2012, p. 8). Rather than fall back on a stereotype of the uncultured robber trope, Heathcote introduced a grace element where the role showed an appreciation for aesthetics and design. This made the role more three-dimensional and encouraged empathy and curiosity rather than simple judgement of the robber's action. A teacher can work to maintain the grace element any time they notice the group slipping into a one-dimensional view of someone in the imagined world. A simple prompt like, "I wonder what drives someone to behave this way?" encourages everyone to discuss and access their capacity for empathy. Maintaining the grace element is not about denying culpability and it's not about planning Mantle of the Expert experiences where people only do good things. What the grace element does is remind us that people—even very misguided people who do awful things—have humanity within them if you look deep enough. This is an important message for people to sit with in the 21st century where every day we see the consequences of humanity's inability to tolerate difference and the preference for demonising and othering.

Overcoming uncertainties about teaching in role

Teachers new to classroom drama can feel hesitant to try teaching in role. There can be a whole lot of reasons for this. Sometimes it's due to a fear about how students may react. If you've never tried teaching in role before you have no idea whether the children will accept the idea of working in this way. What if they don't get it? What if they resist the role? Worse still, what if they reject the whole thing outright? It may have taken some time to build your sense of authority with this class and you might not want to risk that by suddenly presenting yourself as someone else—particularly someone of a lower status to the children. No one wants to be laughed at or be made to look foolish. Teaching in role means taking a risk and that is bound to make you feel vulnerable. If so, remind yourself that learning is always about taking risks and stepping outside our comfort zone. It is what we ask our learners to do all the time—so why wouldn't we model that to them? Some teachers are hesitant because of their own negative experiences with drama in the past. If this is you, it may help to tell yourself that by using drama differently you're helping ensure participants in your class have a more positive time than you did. Sometimes the hesitation is due to a private sense (even on an unconscious level) that drama is somehow a dodgy or unimportant activity. Western culture has a long standing distrust of role-taking due to associating it with being somehow fake or untrustworthy behaviour (Barish, 1981). We all need to beware of this kind of unconscious bias. Teaching in imagined worlds and moving in and out of role is a challenge but that's because it's a specialist pedagogy, not because it's a dodgy or unworthwhile thing to be doing! As a teaching professional, I urge you to judge teaching in role or any new teaching approach based not your own comfort level or cultural biases but how effective it is at supporting learning. Some of your colleagues around Aotearoa New Zealand who are most hooked on Mantle of the Expert would never have imagined they would be teaching in role but now can never imagine going back.

Ironically, it's those very things that make us nervous to take on a role that are the whole point of the exercise. Teaching in role allows you to step away from your established power relationships and offer a space for participants to experience a new kind of agency. Even if your existing relationships with children are as effective and productive as they could be, you only have a limited range of possible stances open to you in the real world: authority figure, friendly face, mentor, coach, adviser, and perhaps a few more. In an imagined context, you can explore power stances that are not generally available to a teacher, including one who needs help, devil's advocate, the victim, the flawed hero, the uncompromising boss, the bumbling apprentice, and so on. And in doing so you'll open up a wider range of stances for the children to adopt: the helper, the advocate, the supporter, the wise adviser, the speaker of truth to power, and so on.

Here is some advice drawn from conversations with Kiwi teachers that should help set you up for success in teaching in role.

- Make yourself accountable: Include teaching in role in your planning documentation or teaching goals. Tell a colleague you're going to try it and set yourself a deadline. Otherwise, it may be too easy to put it off.
- Get support: Ask an experienced colleague to help you with your first in-role experience. They may even be prepared to come into the classroom with you and help with the transition into role.
- Go for a serious role: Avoid a lighthearted name or comedy costume. Instead, choose a role that participants will empathise with.
- To begin, try a low-status rather than high-status register: "One who needs help" is a great way to start. Again, this fosters empathy and encourages participants to take things seriously.

- Remember the importance of tension: Use the role to introduce a problem or issue from the imagined world.
- Play it safe: Avoid really contentious or upsetting themes until you are familiar with how to use frame distance to protect yourself and participants.
- Think about coherence: While it's always possible with the power of drama for participants to interact directly with someone from the imagined world, is there a role you can give the participants too? For example, if you're planning to take on the role of a farmer wondering how to keep her cows out of the river, you could ask participants to imagine themselves as a group of fellow farmers, or perhaps journalists or district council officials. Each of these would carry a different position and register and you'll be surprised what this adds to the experience.
- Script: If you will be speaking in role, think carefully about the words you will use and write them down. Consider "holding back" on information—just give enough to be intriguing.
- Consider other drama techniques too: We convey a sense of role through body language, gesture, and movement as well as voice. So think about how you will use these.
- Rehearse: Have a practice beforehand. If you are going to speak in role, rehearse the words you will say. You don't need to memorise them—but it will help you feel and sound more convincing if you're not "finding" the words spontaneously.
- Keep it short: Just a quick step into the imagined world is enough for a first go.
- Keep it simple: No need for complex props or costume or a virtuoso performance. You don't need to leave and re-enter the room. And no need to work without your scripted plan.
- Be honest: As mentioned elsewhere, it's important participants understand what's happening. Try the three-step transition or find another way to be clear about the compact.
- Invite response and reflection: When you come out of role, give participants the opportunity to respond to what they saw, heard, and understood as well as what it was like to see you go into role.

Dealing with resistance to role

A key reason teachers may hesitate to try teaching in role is due to doubts about whether students will buy in to the role. And it's a valid concern. While many participants will become fully engaged right away, leaning in to listen and respond to the teacher in role, others might giggle, or laugh, and find it a little strange. Just occasionally, some may test the boundaries of the new relationship you've offered them by resisting the role or even rejecting the role altogether. In my experience, this happens very rarely. So the first piece of advice is not to assume that resistance or rejection will occur. Instead, approach it as you would any other new skill the participants need to learn: give them time and opportunities to become familiar and comfortable with it.

Once you've decided you will try teaching in role, there are several things you can do to help participants understand and buy in. First of all, you can explain the rules of engagement and make your expectations clear, as described earlier. By doing this, you avoid the element of surprise or deceit, and signal to your class that this kind of thing is a part of normal classroom activity. By explaining the rules of the game, you make it more likely participants will get on with it. Often, it's this figuring out process that causes the most disruption. Secondly, remember you can and should pull out of role if necessary. If you've clearly signalled the role, you are protected: you can step back out, reiterate your expectations, renegotiate if necessary, and then give it another go. This is much more likely to succeed, and much safer for you and the participants than attempting to stay in role and bluff your way through opposition. Remember, this is not a performance and there's no pressure to ensure "the show must go on". In fact, it's a feature of process drama and Mantle of the Expert that participants spend more time out of role than in it. So, if you need to, pull out of role, discuss, and reset.

What about when participants laugh? Responding to giggles is a matter of judgement for the teacher in role. If it is only one or two who giggle and if it seems more important to progress the drama—for example, if you are bringing an important message from the client or introducing a key tension—you might overlook the laughter and push on with the drama, trusting that the giggles will gradually subside as the participants engage with the tension. Or, you could pause the drama, step out of role, and take the opportunity for a discussion about the tricky feelings that come up in drama work. Be careful of your language here. Rather than telling a participant off for laughing or resisting a role, try asking them what's going on for them: "It's tricky isn't it? Tell me more about that laughter." Acknowledge that it does feel strange at first to work this way and suggest to participants that if they can work out how to use their imagination and work with you within the drama then interesting things might happen. I remember hearing one teacher say to her class, "I've got the feeling that just the other side of that giggle is something really interesting. Let's see if we can move on and find it!" This was a lovely way to appeal for focus without telling off or demeaning the participants.

Sometimes, despite your best efforts and clarity, participants will resist the role. This could be because they don't understand or it could be because they enjoy the opportunity to subvert the usual authority structures of the class and joke with the teacher. It's sometimes hard to tell the difference. Either way, you can use the same response to manage resistance in a positive way. In this scenario, transcribed from a video taken during the *Shark Tank* example, I was in full role as Wiremu and one of the participants (we'll call him Alex) resisted the role:

Alex: Ha ha—I didn't know Wiremu wore lipstick and earrings!

Teacher: I'm just going to stop for a moment and come out of role.

[Removes signal prop—a hat]

Teacher: Now, someone just raised something quite important. Alex, can you repeat what you said a moment ago when I was in role.

Alex: It doesn't matter.

Teacher: I think you were telling us it's tricky to imagine me as Wiremu?

Alex: Well you're *not* him ... You're not even a man.

Teacher: Alex is quite right, isn't he? I'm not really Wiremu am I? That's exactly what 'taking on a role' means. Like I said before, for this to work we all have to agree to use our imaginations. And as Alex points out, that can be tricky ... So, perhaps there is something else I can do to help you with that. What do you think, Alex?

Alex: Maybe use a deeper voice ...

Teacher: OK, let's try that. I'll put the hat on and use a deeper voice and you remember to work with me as if I'm Wiremu. Ready—here goes.

[*Goes back into role ...*]

In this example, Alex was familiar with the teacher in role strategy and I think he was resisting the role as a way to explore his agency in the situation. He was grinning broadly as he spoke and looked a bit embarrassed when I came out of role and asked him to repeat himself. I could have reprimanded him but instead used it as an opportunity for discussion about drama techniques and how these help us work with someone in role. If you read the interaction again, you can see it would be just as appropriate for the teacher to respond this way to a student who was resisting the role through genuine confusion about what is going on. Either way, with this approach, the teacher can assert their authority, clear up any confusion, maintain the mana of the participant, and re-confirm the expectations and the compact.

Avoiding the temptation to pre-teach

When you first learn about Mantle of the Expert and want to introduce it to the class, you may assume participants need a whole lot of coaching in the new skills required before they can get started. However, deciding we need to pre-teach participants things like "freeze frames", "hot seating", or "taking on a role" is antithetical to a key principle of Mantle of the Expert, which is that learning happens in a context. Think about other classroom strategies you use, like think–pair–share, mind-mapping, or a whole-class brainstorm. The first time you introduced these, did you explain how the strategy worked and practise it first, or did you simply include it as a part of the flow of the lesson, with just enough explanation to help everyone learn the rules? The best way to learn is by doing, and children soon adapt to a new strategy or indeed a whole shift in culture once it is explained and modelled to them. Take it from me as someone who has spent this whole book struggling to describe embodied learning in words, you stand a much better chance of explaining a convention in context! It's easy to see drama conventions as a list of discrete tools and this idea is reinforced if one visits a specialist drama classroom and sees posters with lists of labelled conventions on display for participants to learn and memorise. But this is not the priority in Mantle of the Expert. It is not important that participants know or can name the conventions they are using. It only matters that they engage with the issues in the imagined world and the commission and we help them solve it. In Mantle of the Expert, like in process drama or socio-dramatic play, it's about learning *through* the conventions, not learning the conventions themselves—there's an important difference.

Using manipulations in time

Earlier in the book we learned how time can be manipulated in Mantle of the Expert: the teacher can invite participants to move back, forward, rewind, revisit, slow down, and speed up time. Here are a couple of tips for ways this can be really helpful in managing your classroom. If you like, these are conventions, not of role but of the element of time. First, a way to overcome the gap between participants' actual knowledge and the idea that within the imagined world they are framed as experts. Teachers often wonder how they are supposed to help participants build up specific skills and knowledge required for the commission when, according to the story, they're already highly experienced. One answer is through manipulating time. At any moment, you can pause and travel back to a time in the team's history when they first learned whatever this skill was. Taylor and Edmiston's *The Mountain Rescue Team* (n.d.) includes a good example of this where the participants go back in time to "revisit" the day they did basic first aid training. Framed as their earlier selves, participants can layer in necessary understandings without losing the powerful positioning or coming out of the imagined world. Indeed, the shadow awareness of connection between what they are doing and an expertise in their "future" gives participants a really clear sense of purpose and a clear imperative to understand.

In a similar way, time can be manipulated to account for the practical and temporal challenges of the commission. Often, participants have only a few weeks to tackle a commission that in the real world would take much longer. And just as often, they will be working on something well beyond their real-world capabilities. Rather than simplifying tasks, running out of time, or abandoning the commission, the teacher can create a ripple in time to transport participants to the future where the commission is completed; perhaps with a visit to the opening ceremony, or an overheard conversation between the appreciative client and a friend. Of course, manipulations in time should not be used as a short cut to avoiding curriculum. Participants need to grapple meaningfully with the commission and complete tasks they have been set. However, many teachers find it enormously reassuring to realise they don't need to push participants to complete the whole commission in real time. Completion can be signalled by some kind of version or a component of the whole: a scale model, a report, a prototype, a presentation, or whatever. And if time is short, they always have the option to flash forward to an end point to round off the experience.

Keeping the sense of a team

When I first started teaching in Mantle of the Expert, I had the idea I needed to give participants particular roles within the imagined enterprise, which I usually thought of as a company. I assumed participants would need to know who they were in the fictional team—a bit like casting for roles in a play or setting up a role-play activity. It seemed to work: participants got quite excited about becoming the security team or the research arm. For them it was like a pretending game. I thought working in small groups would give a sense of structure for dividing up aspects of the commission and I thought it would be useful to have all the different professional teams interacting with each other. What I hadn't realised was that, by giving the class a whole lot of different professional roles, I was essentially setting up multiple Mantle of the Expert experiences, with each group framing the commission differently. I noticed it was hard to get into the professional roles in any depth, especially since this wasn't a rolling role where there was a specialist teacher to work with each group separately. I noticed groups tended to play act their professional roles, rather than working as themselves in an expert position, and I found groups tended to get competitive rather than working collaboratively. I also discovered it was difficult to justify the tasks I wanted to introduce: why should the security guys be part of designing the new visitor centre when they were more invested in their cameras and eye scanners? I realised that, by having multiple professional teams, I was emphasising the power relations within a corporate structure rather than exploring collaboration. So, over time, I learned to take a different approach. I now set up the class as one responsible team, rather than thinking of it as a company or an enterprise (the language makes a lot of difference), and I plan for everyone to take the same blanket role as members of the same team on the same footing. Within this, I can invite participants to break into groups to consider different dimensions of the commission—including security, research, or those other aspects—but participants always maintain a shared identity as a group and a shared commitment to the commission. As I've said before, membership of the team is not really about role so much as positioning: being seen and seeing yourself as competent and capable. It's also about framing, and the importance of shared point of view. Partly so we can collaborate, and partly also so we can question and critique our collective view.

Working with fictional others

There are so many valuable things that can be achieved in Mantle of the Expert by introducing a "fictional other" from the imagined world who represents a different perspective to that of the group. The most obvious example is the client, whose purpose is to serve as an agent for the teacher within the fiction (Taylor, 2016, p. 58). In a sense, each time participants go into role they adopt the perspective of fictional others too. However, what I'm talking about here is a more strategic introduction of a fictional other introduced by the teacher for a particular purpose. For example, the team might be informed that someone within the responsible team (an invented person—not one of the actual participants) has breached security, stolen the trade secrets, leaked important documents to the media, or been otherwise incompetent or lacking. This creates a challenge, or tension, for the team to unify around. Alternatively, the fictional other might present some critical new information for the team to respond to, as in the *Shark Tank* example where Wiremu revealed his ethical problems with the funding behind the commission. Or the fictional other might be used as a way to teach or assess skills. In her science-based Mantle of the Expert, Carrie Swanson used a range of fictional others including an incompetent senior scientist and potential candidates for lab positions whose science experiments needed to be double-checked by the responsible team to see who should get the job (Swanson, 2017). In this case, the fictional others were people, but examples could also include entities such as a panel, a lobby group or an institution, or supernatural figures such as patupaiarehe or atua. Depending on which role convention is used, the fictional other could be embodied or simply evoked. Using fictional others has the real benefit of encouraging participants to consolidate their identity as a team as they pull together to work out a collective response to the challenge or perspective presented by the other. And, since fictional others only exist in the imagined world, their mistakes, lapses in judgement, amazing achievements, instructions, or high expectations can be responded to without the consequences that would arise from singling someone out in the real world. Having said that, fictional others always need to be treated with respect, with the "grace element" maintained.

Ensuring curriculum is taught in depth

It's in the nature of Mantle of the Expert that you and your participants will inevitably encounter many curriculum learning areas within the imagined world you are exploring. To ensure meaningful engagement in curriculum, it's important to carve out time and resources to allow for deliberate acts of teaching. It's not enough to claim you have taught visual art by creating a quick poster, or consider that you've "done some maths" by mentioning volume or diameter. Skimming the surface in this way devalues the true potential of the approach. To enable quality cross-curricula teaching, it is necessary for the teacher to take time to construct challenging tasks and to understand the context, knowledge, skills, literacies, and signature pedagogies of different learning areas. As we've said, you can trust any Mantle of the Expert to lead you to curriculum, but once you're there you need to set up camp for a while and really explore. For example, planning for the *Shark Tank* example took us naturally to the curriculum area of science. Once there, we set aside a full day for hands-on experiments in which the signature pedagogies of science—making hypotheses, testing, recording, and comparing results to theory—could be practised. At that point, science teaching needed to take priority, and all other aspects, including the aesthetic and the dramatic, took a back seat for a while. It's not that the aesthetic and dramatic disappeared completely—concerns about the client and the ongoing tensions remained a driving force—but for a while at least, science learning was foregrounded above all. Similarly, once we moved on to exploring Music—Sound Arts, Andy ensured that time and resources were committed to learning in that area of the curriculum by encouraging the class to experiment, explore, imitate, and therefore learn meaningfully in the Developing Ideas strand. For Mantle of the Expert to be used effectively within a generalist classroom, this is an important balancing act. In a sense, the teacher needs to navigate not only between the real world and the imagined worlds but also the worlds of different curriculum content, literacies, and pedagogies.

True integration involves meeting achievement objectives in a range of different learning areas. To ensure that curriculum is taught properly, stay mindful of the commission at all times, and beware of leaping into teachable moments that go beyond the terms of the commission. A group of children framed as scientists observing the looping movements of the monarch butterfly caterpillar might well create a dance piece based on their data, but for this to make sense within the Mantle of the Expert frame, the activity would need to be framed as part of the science team's performative research methods and not simply an opportunity for the class to move and create. Much incidental learning may be legitimate—(what learning isn't?)—but a key feature of the Mantle of the Expert approach is that all curriculum tasks are framed as professional tasks for this team of experts so keep coming back to that. Multiple cross-curricular opportunities will arise during a Mantle of the Expert experience and you can't possibly hope to go deeply into all of them. However, for those you do choose to pursue, it's important to consult the achievement objectives in the curriculum, plan accordingly, and take note of how well participants meet the objectives. Remember, assessment is not only about making judgements on student learning; it also helps you as teacher gauge whether your attempts to deepen the learning within a particular curriculum area have been successful. The teacher compass, discussed earlier, will help where there is explicit content knowledge or skills you want to help participants develop.

Including participants who come and go

This final piece of advice relates to meeting the needs of participants who arrive late or leave early from a Mantle of the Expert experience. In the realities of classroom life, this is a major issue. I don't think I've ever taught a group where every participant was present throughout. There are lots of reasons why: participants get withdrawn from class for periods of targeted support; people get sick; families have tangi and weddings; sports teams and cultural groups have rehearsals or go away for trips; families shift to a new area and their children leave one class mid-way through a term and join another; and so on. Behavioural challenges, school refusal, and other attendance issues may also come into play. Any interruption of schooling can cause setbacks for learning (Ministry of Education 2011b) so the last thing we would want to do is add to that by throwing participants into the deep end into a confusing new experience or abruptly curtailing something that has not yet reached its resolution. During the 2-year *Connecting Curriculum, Connecting Learning* project in which five classes were observed using Mantle of the Expert pedagogy, it was found that the only participants who reported being disengaged where those who had missed part of the experience, particularly the building of the expert team (Fraser et al., 2012b). As Mantle of the Expert depends so much on a shared, collaborative group experience, we need strategies to take care of those who, for whatever reason, move in or out of that group.

For those who are suddenly dropped into a Mantle of the Expert experience midway through, there are a number of things you can try. It may be important to take time to explain to the participant and their whānau that the class is learning through their imagination. Telling the story of what has happened so far in the imagined world can be helpful: use a storyteller voice and the rest of the class can assist by illustrating key moments with drama. If you have been keeping a good record of your learning, as advised in Chapter 4, this can be shared with the new arrival and their family. Without drawing undue attention to the newcomer, it may be appropriate to create a reason within the imagined world for why this person has just joined the team. Perhaps the team decided we needed someone with new skills and expertise. Perhaps they have transferred from another office.

Participants themselves may have suggestions for taking account of this new person and ensuring they enter as a highly regarded member of the team. A classroom buddy can also be selected to work with the newcomer, with their job framed as part of the responsible team's practice of manaakitanga. You may be particularly concerned about new arrivals who are speakers of other languages than the one in your classroom, but, in my experience, the embodied, visual nature of the learning can be an advantage rather than a disadvantage as they figure out quite quickly what is going on. In the *Shark Tank* example described earlier, we were amazed by how quickly a Korean student slotted in with what we were doing even though it was his very first day at school and his first week in New Zealand. With the help of another participant who gave him translated instructions, he was able to successfully imagine himself packing to go on a plane and visiting the shark in the aquarium with his peers. While I'm sure he struggled with some of the spoken dialogue, he joined in fully with the science experiments and excelled in the creative music composition task, matching and mixing sounds on his iPad.

For those who have to unexpectedly depart from the group, or who miss a chunk of the action, many of the strategies already suggested will be helpful. I have found that participants themselves will often take delight in inventing reasons for their departure that sound authentic within the imagined world. In the *Shark Tank* example again, we had one student who was picked up by his mother from the class to attend a family wedding. He proudly announced that he was off on a special mission and would be back to report to us later. On his return a week later, the group put aside time for a meeting to report back to him how the commission had progressed in his absence, while he enjoyed the opportunity to share an imagined story about what he'd seen in his time diving with great white sharks in Australia. Where a participant departs and is not going to return it could be good for the class to stay in touch or at least send a letter at the culmination of the experience in which they recount what happened. In this way, participants who were part of the journey benefit from relating and reflecting on it and the participant who left the journey gets to experience a sense of how it ended. Of course, this won't always be possible but for me this is part of repositioning participants so that all are treated as competent co-constructors and inhabitants of the imagined world.

Chapter 7

Looking to the future

As we approach the end of this book, I hope you feel a tapestry of understanding about Mantle of the Expert beginning to form in your mind. Chapters 1 to 6 have focused on the "what" and "how" of Mantle of the Expert: offering definitions; some theory and context; a guide to planning and implementation; and some tips and advice. In closing, we will turn to the bigger question of "why", and consider Mantle of the Expert's place in the New Zealand education system now and into the future. We'll look at the priorities for 21st century education and see how well Mantle of the Expert aligns with these. We'll consider the challenges to overcome if Mantle of the Expert is to secure a lasting place within New Zealand schools and we'll look at the work that has already begun.

Mantle of the Expert: A teaching approach for our times

Here in New Zealand, as in every country around the globe, teachers, academics, policy-makers, parents, and young people are engaged in an urgent conversation about what 21st century education should look like. Humanity is facing unprecedented challenges to its own survival, including an unsustainable population explosion, the climate crisis, globalisation, growing economic disparities, diminished natural resources, environmental degradation, an ageing population, a loss of social cohesion, and a rise in cyber dependency, all of which have urgent implications for education (World Economic Forum, 2020). At the time of finalising this chapter, the additional crisis of the COVID-19 pandemic has added a further layer of uncertainty and turmoil. How do we educate future generations for a future so uncertain and unpredictable? While it is daunting to consider how we might prepare the next generations to cope with and address these existential crises, it's also crucial we bring our best energies to the task. Andreas Schliecher, director for education at the OECD puts it this way:

> The demands on learners and thus education systems are evolving fast. In the past, education was about teaching people something. Now, it's about making sure that individuals develop a reliable compass and the navigation skills to find their own way through an increasingly uncertain, volatile, and ambiguous world ... A generation ago, teachers could expect that what they taught would last for a lifetime for their students. Today, schools need to prepare students for more rapid economic and social change than ever before, for jobs that have not yet been created, to use technologies that have not yet been invented, and to solve social problems that we don't yet know will arise.
>
> (Schliecher, cited in Fadel et al., 2015, p.1)

The challenge is also an opportunity, and Mantle of the Expert can play its part in preparing future generations to cope, adapt, and problem solve in the way Schliecher describes here. Mantle of the Expert experiences can offer a safe place for trial and error in which participants take responsibility in situations of uncertainty and practise finding ways forward where outcomes are unknown. The scenarios in Mantle of the Expert may be imagined, but these learnings are real, so that participants "flex their muscles" in the difficult skills of responding to complex and evolving problems. Mantle of the Expert also emphasises collaboration and compassion for others, so that the "navigation skills" most necessary for an uncertain future are practised not just individually but also within a context of shared responsibility, collaboration, and empathy for others.

Another priority for 21st century education is to respond to the rapid burgeoning of technology, including digital devices, the internet, cyber networks, and artificial intelligence systems. In just a few decades, digital technology has transformed the ways we store, develop, access, and process information and this has huge implications for how we teach and even what we think learning is. Whereas in the past teaching focused on developing content knowledge, in the digitally connected schools of today, facts and information are readily accessible at the push of a button or a verbal command. While it's an oversimplification to say that learners don't need to know things because now search engines "know everything" for them, it's certainly true that a world of pervasive digital content changes the priorities for learning. We now need to teach people to be discriminating in their engagement with online material; to use and adapt information to solve problems; and to think laterally, critically, and creatively. And we need to teach them how to use what they know to bring about action in the world with compassion and respect for others and for the environment. Again, Mantle of the Expert offers a really good way for participants to develop these skills. The framework of client and commission provides a focus for information gathering and an opportunity to make the most of online resources. At the same time, the use of drama encourages multiple perspectives and the ongoing reflection process encourages a healthy and critical questioning of information sources and uses. At the time of writing, the period of enforced lockdown in response to the COVID-19 pandemic has focused teachers' attention on new ways of delivering Mantle of the Expert experiences through digital platforms. While in its early stages, we are already seeing exciting potential in this form of delivery, with high levels of engagement from teachers, participants, and whānau (Aitken, 2020; Aitken & Downey, 2020; Aitken et al., 2020; Taylor, 2020).

Advances in technology have not merely changed how we store and use knowledge information, they've actually transformed how we think about and value that knowledge and information. The democratisation of information in the 21st century has seen a significant move away from specialisation—where individuals or groups devote themselves to developing skills, knowledge, and expertise in a particular field—to a more generalist approach, where knowledge and skills are shared more widely. Schliecher claims the process has gone even further:

> The world is also no longer divided into specialists and generalists. Specialists have deep skills and narrow scope, giving them expertise that is recognized by peers but not valued outside their domain. Generalists have broad scope but shallow skills. What counts increasingly are the *versatilists* who are able to apply depth of skill to a progressively widening scope of situations and experiences, gaining new competencies, building relationships, and assuming new roles. They are capable of constantly adapting and also of constantly learning and growing, of positioning themselves and repositioning themselves in a fast-changing world.
>
> (Schliecher, cited in Fadel et al., 2015, p. 2)

As we increasingly value versatility, we begin to think quite differently about skills and knowledge and the best way to learn them. Instead of seeing understanding as being simply a process of breaking complicated ideas into small parts (though this is still important) we start to value other things, like the ability to pull together meaning from multiple sources, to see things from different perspectives, to embrace complexity and inconsistency, and to innovate and create new ideas and solutions. Again, it's an oversimplification to say that education has completely ignored this in the past: there have always been innovators and lateral thinkers and there have always been educators who have valued and supported them. But it's fair to say that versatility and creativity are becoming more and more of a focus in 21st century learning, which has significant implications for teaching and learning.

Properly implemented, Mantle of the Expert can be used to develop both in-depth subject specialism and versatilism. The terms of the commission and deliberate acts of teaching can support explicit teaching. Indeed, while it might seem counter-intuitive, operating in an imagined world can teach participants a great deal about what being a real-world specialist entails. Going through the gradual process of committing to their place in a responsible team teaches participants that developing depth of skill takes time. At the same time, by encountering the challenges of the commission and responding to the different tensions that arise, participants learn the importance of being flexible and adaptive with one's expertise. As for practising repositioning and shifting of roles, both things mentioned by Schliecher as vital skills for the versatilist, we have seen that Mantle of the Expert consciously includes both of these as signature pedagogies.

Given the world we need to prepare our young people for, we must consider how well the current education system does this and what needs to change. In a presentation that remains the most frequently viewed TED talk of all time, Ken Robinson argues the current Western school system was developed on a 19th century model as part of the industrial revolution, designed to provide workers for factories (Robinson, 2006). The result, he says, is a system that emphasises academic skills and content knowledge delivered through sedentary methods. Robinson claims that the paradigms underpinning this model are no longer fit for purpose given our rapidly changing relationship with information, technology, the world of work, and the natural environment:

> Our education system has mined our minds in the way that we strip-mine the earth for a particular commodity. And for the future, it won't serve us. We have to rethink the fundamental principles on which we're educating our children.
>
> (Robinson, 2006)

He calls for a rethink so that creativity, learning to learn, and embodied active approaches are prioritised and normalised:

> We know three things about intelligence. One, it's diverse. We think about the world in all the ways that we experience it. We think visually, we think in sound, we think kinesthetically. We think in abstract terms, we think in movement. Secondly, intelligence is dynamic. If you look at the interactions of a human brain ... intelligence is wonderfully interactive. The brain isn't divided into compartments. In fact, creativity—which I define as the process of having original ideas that have value—more often than not comes about through the interaction of different disciplinary ways of seeing things.
>
> (Robinson, 2006)

Mantle of the Expert aligns really well with the aspirations Robinson expresses here. It's an active, sensory approach to learning that deliberately incorporates embodied, iconic, and symbolic forms of learning. And it is creative, both in the sense that it works with the aesthetic, and in the sense that participants have opportunities for original ideas of value, given their responsibilities within the imagined world.

In the book that preceded his talk, Robinson offers a new set of more organic metaphors for schooling and gives examples of schools that have been reshaped along those principles (Robinson & Aronica, 2015) He suggests education needs to fulfil the following key purposes:

> Personal: Education should enable young people to engage with the world within them as well as the world around them.
>
> Cultural: Education should enable students to understand and appreciate their own cultures and to respect the diversity of others.
>
> Social: Education should enable young people to become active and compassionate citizens.
>
> Economic: Education should enable students to become economically responsible and independent.
>
> (Robinson & Aronica, 2015, pp. 45–53)

Used to its full potential, Mantle of the Expert can support these priorities. The approach is all about engaging inwards and outwards, understanding and respect, and rehearsing what it takes to become active and compassionate in the real world. And, while some may resist the "economic responsibility" label lest Mantle of the Expert be seen as training for a life in business, the approach certainly does offer opportunity for learning about economic responsibility in its broadest and most holistic sense.

Another conception of 21st century learning, similar to Robinson and Aronica's and more fully developed, comes from the Centre for Curriculum Redesign (CCR). This consortium of teachers, academics, policy-makers, futurists, entrepreneurs, and others, analysed and synthesised the features of successful curriculum design from around the world including New Zealand to come up with a "four-dimensional" model of education for 20th century learning (Fadel et al., 2015). The competency-based framework comprises three overlapping dimensions—skills, knowledge, and character—within a fourth dimension, meta-cognition. The model is represented by the following diagram:

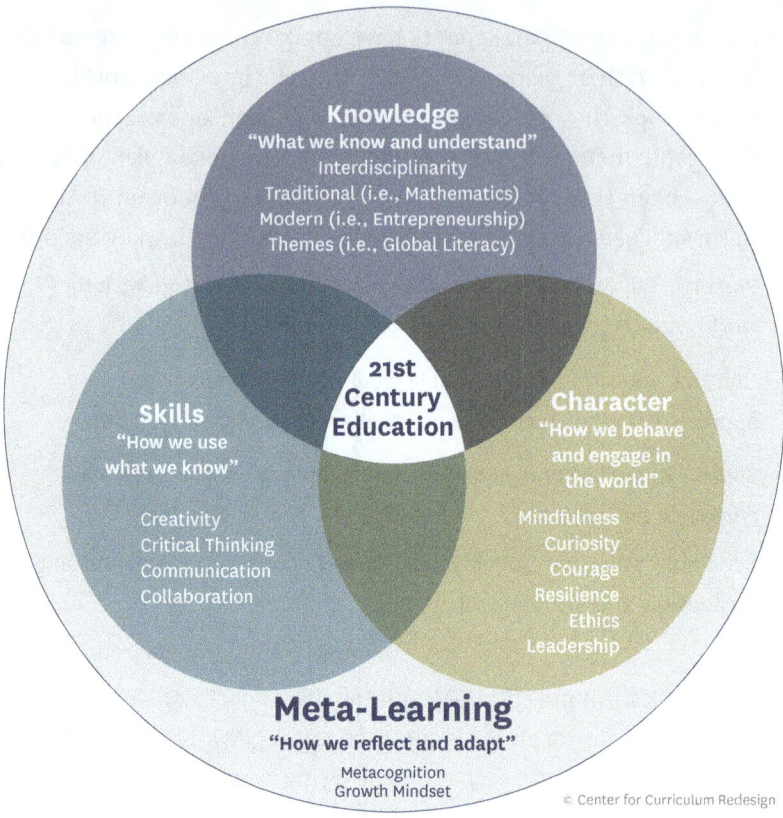

Figure 70: Four-dimensional model of curriculum from
The Centre for Curriculum Redesign (Fadel et al., 2015, p. 43)

The alignments between the goals of Mantle of the Expert and the ideals of 21st century education as represented in the CCR model are striking. Every aspect of what we have learned about in this book can be seen within the four domains of this framework. The core elements/whenu of commission, client, responsible team, and the rest sustain learning in the three dimensions of "knowledge", "character", and "skills", while the teaching modalities—drama for learning, inquiry, and powerful positioning—ensure that these three domains overlap and interrelate in meaningful ways. Meanwhile, the duality of real and imagined worlds provides a site for learning in the fourth dimension of "meta-learning".

The authors of the four-dimensional model acknowledge that it focuses on the "what" of education, rather than on the "how" (Fadel et al., 2015, p. 101). They don't specify which approaches schools should use in delivering the curriculum, arguing that this will be context dependent. They do, however, stress that classroom practices need to match the school's content and education goals and suggest, "these activities often go beyond didactic lecturing, into project-based learning, inquiry learning, debate, design, performance, expedition, sport, contemplation, and play" (Fadel et al., 2015, p. 102). Again, these are just the kinds of activities that Mantle of the Expert employs, confirming that Mantle of the Expert is one possible "how" for the "what" presented in the four-dimensional model.

Other commentators and researchers have reached similar conclusions about the requirements of a 21st century curriculum and have been more willing to propose what kinds of teaching will best support these goals. In the quest for what he calls "deep learning" Michael Fullan calls for new pedagogies to support "the six Cs":

1. **Character education**—honesty, self-regulation and responsibility, hard work, perseverance, empathy for contributing to the safety and benefit of others, self-confidence, personal health and well-being, career and life skills
2. **Citizenship**—global knowledge, sensitivity to and respect for other cultures, active involvement in addressing issues of human and environmental sustainability
3. **Communication**—communicate effectively orally, in writing and with a variety of digital tools; listening skills
4. **Critical thinking and problem solving**—think critically to design and manage projects, solve problems, make effective decisions using a variety of digital tools and resources
5. **Collaboration**—work in teams, learn from and contribute to the learning of others, social networking skills, empathy in working with diverse others
6. **Creativity and imagination**—economic and social entrepreneurialism, considering and pursuing novel ideas, and leadership for action. (Fullan, cited in Fullan & Langworthy, 2014, p. 49)

Fullan's list is a close match to the Centre for Curriculum Redesign's model discussed earlier and it's a good description of what Mantle of the Expert at its best can achieve. Indeed, one teacher recently commented to me that, "It's almost like Fullan wrote his six Cs with Mantle of the Expert in mind!" Meanwhile in their book on arts-rich learning, Gibson and Ewing argue that arts experiences offer four additional and much-needed Cs: curiosity, connection, compassion, and courage (Gibson & Ewing, 2020). Of course, no teaching approach in and of itself guarantees certain outcomes; everything depends on how teachers use it and how participants respond. But the structures, strategies, and potentials of Mantle of the Expert certainly align well with the priorities implied here.

There's a strong alignment between the features of Mantle of the Expert and what Fullan and Langworthy identify as effective new pedagogies for the 21st century (see Table 7).

Table 7: Effective vs ineffective new pedagogies (Fullan & Langworthy, 2014, p. 45)

Effective New Pedagogies (High Levels of Pedagogical Capacity Needed)	Ineffective New Pedagogies
• Establish students and teachers as co learners • Long-term deep learning tasks; cross-curricular; complex, interdependent tasks • Deep learning tasks have clear learning goals and clearly defined measures of success • Give students control and choice suited to their level, gradually building students' capacity to manage the learning process • Continuous, effective feedback; formative assessment towards the learning goals • Identify and use digital tools and resources to support deep learning tasks and to help students master the learning process. Analyse progress data to inform changes in teaching and learning strategies	• Too much student autonomy • Short-term tasks for one unit or lesson; not multidisciplinary • No clear learning goals or ways of measuring success • Give too much control and choice to students before they have skills to structure their own learning effectively • Ineffective feedback or only summative assessment at end of task • Use digital Tools and resources only to deliver content and track progress, but not to inform changes in teaching and learning strategies

Mantle of the Expert, taught well, allows a teacher to avoid all the things listed in the "ineffective" column. As for the "effective" column, it might seem that Mantle of the Expert runs counter to the recommendation that students have control and choice over the learning process. As has been noted a number of times in this book, Mantle of the Expert is not student-led, in that the teacher chooses the content and facilitates the episodes in terms of adding tensions, introducing activities, and so on. However, as we've seen, the planning process begins by taking account of participant interests, and there is plenty of room for participants to take control in managing the learning process once the inquiry is underway, so one could argue this feature earns a tick for Mantle of the Expert too. Until recently, I would have said there's room for improvement in how digital tools, resources, and data are used "to deliver and track progress" but the recent experience of teaching during lockdown has taught me there's plenty of potential for the approach to be used in this way. One area yet to receive proper attention, at least in my own practice, is the need for alternative models for assessment to value and track dispositional learning as well as content knowledge. As Fullan notes, this is something many new pedagogies are grappling with (Fullan & Langworthy, 2014, p. 9).

It's interesting to note the summary table doesn't mention the importance of students following their own passions or offering participants real-world applications for their new knowledge, though these are both things the authors discuss at length elsewhere in their book (Fullan & Langworthy, 2014, pp. 5, 7). They do, however, suggest that personal passions can only be found and formed through skills development and experiences and that a core role of the teacher is to "help students discover and sort out the experiences that best suit them" (Fullan & Langworthy, 2014, p. 5). This sounds to me like a phase in which Mantle of the Expert could be valuable. As for real-world learning, as we've seen, there are really good reasons why Mantle of the Expert does not involve carrying out the commission in the real world, but if we wish to take Fullan and Langworthy's suggestions on board, there are certainly possibilities available, including: using a "flipped" classroom model, with lots of time for self-directed experimentation; making opportunities for real-world social action in the transformation phase; or mixing it up by using the commission model from time to time.

Overall, then, it looks like Mantle of the Expert is a strong "fit" with the ideals for 21st century pedagogy. This is reassuring and very useful. It's good to know we can justify and advocate for the approach by drawing on studies like these, and we should do so wherever possible. At the same time, we must never forget the aspects of Mantle of the Expert that aren't mentioned in the wider literature on 21st century pedagogy, but which are crucial to the potency of the approach. For one thing, there's the way Mantle of the Expert is rooted in the child's familiar world of play and imagination. This is a quality that we adults may not give enough credence to, though research into play, gamification, and learning in alternate worlds is starting to be taken more seriously (Carroll et al, 2006). Perhaps in future, learning through imagination and the power of metaxis will earn a place in the list of indicators for highly effective pedagogies. Another special quality of Mantle of the Expert not mentioned in Fullan and Langworthy's list of effective pedagogies is the fostering of empathy, or what Gibson and Ewing call "compassion" (Gibson & Ewing, 2020). Even more than other arts pedagogies, Mantle of the Expert explicitly encourages everyone to bring their best selves and to acknowledge the grace element in the other. With humanity's increasing propensity towards populism and intolerance, highly attuned empathy may be one of the most compelling requirements for 21st century learning. Another aspect not rated in the effective pedagogy checklist but central to Mantle of the Expert is its aesthetic dimension; things like sustaining learning within a compelling narrative arc, the strategic use of the six dimensions of dramatic imagination, care and attention to language, the integration of symbols and artefacts, shifts in register and position, and dropping to the universals; all the aspects that give the approach its artistry. Mindful teaching in Mantle of the Expert is about giving space and expression to what is beautiful in our world, which could be seen as another vital purpose for education.

Where's the evidence?

We now have more literature than ever before on what helps people learn and how the human brain works, yet we still struggle to clarify what an effective education system could look like. For one thing, the education literature is so vast that it can be hard to be discriminating. I recall a conversation early in my career with a senior research colleague who said that, in education, one could find evidence to back up pretty much any claim one wanted to make. We need to do better than simply cherry picking studies to back up our opinions. So should we focus on what has been shown to be effective through verifiable evidence to a scientific standard? Well, yes and no. Scientific research can turn up really important information, such as the now well-established idea that the best way for the brain to learn is to build on prior knowledge (Ausubel, 1968); the importance of learning over time through distributed practice (Thomas, 2016); and the value of explanatory questioning techniques such as learners explaining to themselves how they are learning something (Roediger & Pyc, 2012). As solid evidence-based practices like these emerge, we must consider how they can be incorporated into Mantle of the Expert pedagogy as a way of improving practice. The problem, of course, is there are so many variables in teaching that, while things can be shown to be effective, it takes a long time to build up a body of evidence for "what works". The creators of the four-dimensional curriculum model shared earlier make a similar point:

> Some may argue that there is not yet enough scientific evidence to conclude that all of the dimensions and elements of the framework ... would truly benefit humanity if they were taught well. After all, science has not yet proven beyond a reasonable doubt that they would. There is a danger in believing in a false dichotomy about scientific fact— either science has 100 percent proven something to be true, or we are unable to say anything about it at this time. Even well-established scientific concepts such as evolution are currently suffering from this kind of false critique, with some people believing that since it hasn't been 'totally proven' it may as well have been proven false.
>
> (Fadel et al., 2015, p. 104)

We don't as yet have enough specific, evidence-based research into Mantle of the Expert but there is some. The small number of qualitative research studies that have been conducted here in Aotearoa New Zealand, including my own, have found promising signs of increased engagement, improved oral confidence, benefits for writing, and other positive outcomes where Mantle of the Expert was used (Aitken, 2012a; Downey, 2018; Dunne, 2015; Fraser et al., 2013; Stoate, 2013; Swanson, 2016). And there's a wealth of research evidence to suggest that the kinds of active, embodied, engaging, relational, purposeful learning experiences that happen in a Mantle of the Expert experience are optimal for learning. More work is needed to build a reliable evidence base for Mantle of the Expert but the indications are good.

While there is a need for more formal evidence of Mantle of the Expert's effectiveness, we don't need to wait for that evidence to be in place before we get started with using it. As Fadel et al. point out, there's a difference between innovation-led evidence—in which something is tried out and honestly tested to see how good it is, and evidence-led innovation—in which formal evidence from previous trials is required before anything new is tried (Fadel et al., 2015, p. 105). Mantle of the Expert is perfectly positioned for further investigation of the innovation-led kind and we can all contribute through ongoing investigation and honest assessment of our practice. As we go through this process, we must remain open to new ideas from research, including things that contradict what we think we know. And we must distinguish trustworthy peer-reviewed research from inquiry, opinion, dated ideas, or pop psychology. Lethaby and Harries use the term "neuromyths" to describe a number of ideas that have been discredited by research but still pop up in teacher's thinking (Lethaby & Harries, 2015). These include things like planning differently for "left and right brain" learners, or males and females, or people with different "learning styles". In the ongoing conversation about how to improve education, we all need to be alert to what we can learn from research and mindful of our human tendency to oversimplify, confirm bias, overclaim, and misrepresent findings.

Priorities for 21st-century education in Aotearoa New Zealand

Here in Aotearoa New Zealand we face the same existential, epistemological, technological, and research challenges as the rest of the world. On top of those, we have some additional drivers for change arising from our own unique environmental, societal, and cultural context.

As one of the last places on the planet to be settled by humans, this country has a rich and unique ecology that needs preserving and understanding. Just as unique is our identity as a multicultural country built on bicultural foundations. Our history of colonisation and our evolution as a Pacific nation all have a part to play in shaping what we want education to look like in Aotearoa New Zealand in the 21st century, while the Treaty-based partnership between tangata whenua and the Crown means te ao Māori has a particular importance both in terms of the content we teach and the ways that we teach it.

In terms of what we teach, every teacher I encounter says they would love to teach more about Aotearoa New Zealand's history, geography, local flora and fauna, traditional stories, and so on. I think they feel inhibited by their own lack of knowledge and by a shortage of quality resources. So it's up to those of us with a commitment to Mantle of the Expert to create local resources and build teacher knowledge so that the strengths of our teaching approach can be used to teach things that matter in our context. However, it's also up to teachers themselves to fill the gaps in their knowledge so they can commit to planning based on the local contexts, historical events, environmental issues, picture books, and traditional stories that are most applicable to their local region and their school. With a wealth of easily accessible online information and more and more resources becoming available, this is something we can all commit to doing better. It takes a bit of time and energy, but the results will be worth it.

Of course, cultural responsiveness is about much more than *what* we teach. It's about *how* we teach and how we *relate* to those we teach. There is a lot of debate about what culturally responsive teaching and learning entails. Some question the term culturally "responsive", preferring to describe "culturally intelligent" (Earley & Ang, 2003) or "culturally sustaining" (Milne, 2017) practice. Personally, I like the notion of "culturally sustaining" practice as it puts the emphasis on the experience of the learner rather than the actions of the teacher. As Berryman et al. (2018) point out, "culturally responsive pedagogy is understood and implemented in many ways" and "some of what is done in its name may appear quite differently to our learners" (p. 3). Berryman et al. caution against focusing only on those aspects of cultural practice that teachers themselves identify as important:

> We have often observed that, in their efforts to respond to a student's culture, teachers fall into the trap of essentialisation in which they, as the professional and adult, determine what that culture is or isn't, often by picking up the pieces that are most easily identified and they can make sense of. In schools this often plays out as bilingual signage, charter statements that acknowledge Te Tiriti o Waitangi, the use of pōwhiri to start the school year, or the ubiquitous kōwhaiwhai patterns around the whiteboard.
>
> (Berryman et al., 2018, p. 6)

They continue:

> Shifting the focus from being responsive *to* the culture of others to developing and being part of cultural relationships *with* others, legitimates the aspects of culture that are less tangible but fundamental to the identity and wellbeing of all people. These are the things that lie beneath the surface ... such as expectations, thought processes, perceptions, notions of self, and values.
>
> (Berryman et al., 2018, p. 6)

Appealing for a culturally responsive pedagogy of relations aligned with the metaphor of mana ōriti, Berryman et al. stress the importance of trust, respect, and dialogic spaces in which students and their whānau are engaged at every level. It's important to consider what these more deeply embedded aspects of culturally responsive sustaining practice mean in the context of Mantle of the Expert.

Right at the start of this book, in discussing the elevator pitch for Mantle of the Expert, I made a case for how it can resonate with metaphors from te ao Māori such as ako, whanaungatanga, manaakitanga, kotahitanga, rangatiratanga, mōhiotanga, māramatanga, and tuakana–teina. Of course, as with all elevator pitches, this was an oversimplification. Just because Mantle of the Expert puts an emphasis on relationships, power sharing, and reciprocal teaching and learning this doesn't mean it's automatically culturally responsive. Equally, just because it's an imported pedagogy with inbuilt colonial assumptions, this doesn't mean it can't be used in a culturally sustaining way. It's teachers who make the difference, no matter what teaching approach they use. A few years ago I would have said that Mantle of the Expert is culturally neutral and can be used anywhere in the world. Now I consider this a dangerous oversimplification. Whether we like it or not and whether we are conscious of it, teachers are always playing out cultural assumptions and dispositions when we plan and teach. As Bolton (2007) points out, it's all too easy for drama to be used as a platform for ideology or a tool for political ends, and we should avoid the temptation to assume it can do only good or to slavishly adhere to it, or any other teaching approach. If Mantle of the Expert is to have a future in this country it will need to be deconstructed and reconceptualised in a way that works within and for the unique bicultural and multicultural contexts of our schools. This journey has begun and the culturally situated metaphors and examples offered in this book are a small part of these explorations, but they are only a small step and there's a long and fascinating journey ahead.

I've been inspired by colleagues around New Zealand who have started the crucial conversations with their communities about whether, and how, Mantle of the Expert can support their priorities and develop culturally sustaining practice. The results of these conversations have proved really fruitful and the methods used might be useful for other schools to adopt. For example, in a recent 18-month-long TLRI project at Otaika School in Northland, teachers focused on looking at how the practices of Dramatic Inquiry aligned with their values and culture as a school (Downey, 2017). The process they followed was something like this:

1. Parallel professional development in Mantle of the Expert and culturally responsive pedagogy.
2. Classroom trials. Ongoing discussions and reflections with whānau and community.
3. Developing a visual metaphor based on the school's existing values statement and the new learnings developed in 1 and 2.
4. Strategic planning to sustain and support those priorities for their school.

By following this process, Otaika School came up with a unique visual and conceptual metaphor that worked for their own school. In this case, it was an image of a kauri tree, with a ruru representing the school's values nested inside it. The green leaves of the tree symbolised the aspects of their teaching in Mantle of the Expert that teachers considered were most culturally responsive, while the yellow leaves represented additional measures or conscious actions the teachers would need to take to further grow their practice to be more culturally sustaining for participants. This process resulted in a metaphor that was unique to that school and that the teachers and community felt a connection with because they'd created it. This living metaphor will now be embedded into the school's strategic planning and used as a device for ongoing reflection and professional development. In future, the metaphor itself can be altered and amended to reflect everyone's shifting understandings and priorities.

A similar process of professional development and working through metaphor is now being followed by at least three other schools as they develop local curriculum with a dual commitment to Dramatic Inquiry and cultural responsiveness. While the process they follow will be similar, the outcomes will look different for each school—which is exciting in itself. And the outcomes will not be fixed, either. This is a process of ongoing learning, growth, and development with partnership as a key goal. School leaders and senior management need to support the process with time and funding and, of course, whānau and student voices are central to this process so that the process is owned by everyone and relationships of care and connectedness are at the forefront.

Here are some questions for teachers in New Zealand to consider as we work to develop a more culturally responsive approach to planning and teaching in Mantle of the Expert. Any one of these could be used to spark conversations between teachers, schools, and communities:

- How do we know Mantle of the Expert is the right "fit" for our community? How do we bring whānau and community into dialogue about our reasons for using it?
- How do schools support staff to build knowledge and skills in culturally responsive pedagogy/culturally sustaining practices alongside Mantle of the Expert?
- How can the prior knowledge and expertise of Māori teachers, students, whānau, and other community be honoured through enriched planning in Mantle of the Expert, without taking advantage?

- How do we work with frame distance as a way of showing respect for historical figures/atua, etc., and what other cultural implications arise with particular drama strategies and conventions?
- How do we need to rethink the existing planning tools; for example, the circles of the pre-planning model and the generic tasks grid and others to recognise our cultural contexts?
- How do we need to update our planning models to ensure Māori world views are included and not othered? For example, making it a "given" for the responsible team to work in consultation with tangata whenua and to conduct itself as a Treaty-based organisation?
- How do we work more with the culturally situated stories and histories of Aotearoa New Zealand?
- How can all teachers learn about and draw on metaphors, concepts, and language from te ao Māori—not as a tokenistic "mining" of information without reciprocation, but as a means of situating understandings and knowledge in a culturally situated way?
- How can we incorporate te reo Māori within the written and spoken language of our imagined worlds and within our planning and support literature?
- How can we ensure Mantle of the Expert is balanced with other teaching approaches to meet the needs of all learners?

These are exciting questions to debate. And at the same time, we need that bigger conversation about the inbuilt structural assumptions of Mantle of the Expert itself, and how these might or might not support effective cultural relationships and responsive pedagogy. The challenges raised by Berryman et al. are a good starting point and their table giving indicators of effective cultural relationships—whanangatanga, whakapapa, kaupapa—and responsive pedagogy—wānanga, ako, and mahi ngātahi—needs to be considered alongside the six Cs and the four-dimensional curriculum as core to 21st century curriculum in New Zealand (Berryman et al. 2018).

Those who advocate for an overhaul of education in line with 21st century priorities acknowledge that change is difficult. The authors of the four-dimensional model discussed earlier advocate for a staggered approach:

> Progress will be staggered. When renovating a house, it is important to drastically change only one section at a time, while living in the other sections. In trying to change a large entity like the education system, we must understand that it will not happen all at once. Both the *what* (standards and assessment), and the *how* (curriculum and professional development) need to change over time.
>
> (Fadel et al., 2015, p. 37)

Fadel et al. position themselves as focusing on the first two "rooms of the house" and driving for change in standards and assessment, with the intention of effecting change from there to curriculum. For those of us at the coal face—teachers, school leaders, and professional development facilitators—it's more productive to focus on change from the other direction and address curriculum, pedagogy, and professional development. This was something Heathcote herself advocated when she wrote, "Should it be seriously adopted as a system our schooling would change. There is no reason why a 'Mantle (of the Expert)' school could not be administered within the portals of the nineteenth century model which most schools operate in" (Heathcote, 2009, p. 3). Even with a system operating on the industrial paradigms described earlier, there have always been teachers who emphasised more progressive values and worked more creatively.

Here in Aotearoa New Zealand, we have a significant history of progressive education, beginning with esteemed figures such as Sylvia Ashton-Warner (1908–1984) and Elwyn Richardson (1925–2012) who fostered arts-rich, experiential learning and their legacy has persisted even through to the market-driven reforms of the 1980s (Mutch, 2013). Ings (2017) has commented that the resilience and creative thinking that Kiwis like to proudly call our "number 8 wire mentality" should not be claimed as an innate characteristic, but recognised as the product of an education system that fosters these attributes. Ing's point is a good one, though we mustn't forget that the education system in New Zealand has also included punishment, disgrace, and disadvantage for some learners, particularly Māori. Our urgent challenge is to find ways to sustain the ideals of progressive education while addressing and redressing these historical injustices.

It is not the place of this book to politicise Mantle of the Expert. I would argue that good pedagogy has a place in any system and the strength of the approach transcends politics. However, the agency of teachers is always dependent on the political climate within which they are operating. So, as we consider the future, much depends on how education policies and priorities play out in our country. It is encouraging to note that even when there was a political shift away from progressive ideals in the 1980s and 1990s—with the National Standards era of the late 2000s—New Zealand teachers and communities continued to find ways to sustain their ideals. As Mutch noted in 2013:

> The New Zealand system has been able to embrace progressive educational ideals and keep them alive in the face of on-going, and often unwarranted, criticism. ... without decades of committed and conscientious educators, who have managed to win and hold the respect of generations of students and parents these ideals could have been lost under a tide of market-driven reforms. It is heartening that parents and school boards of trustees have felt the need to support teachers when the values and principles the system is built on come under threat. It is this collective dedication to the children and young people of today and tomorrow that gives hope that progressive ideals will continue to underpin educational practices in New Zealand for many years to come. (p. 112)

There have always been what Ings (2017) calls "disobedient" teachers willing to go into bat for progressive ideas in education. In the last few years we've seen more of a shift back towards these ideals and away from neo-liberal paradigms and the accompanying focus on assessment. This change in political climate has opened a space where teachers and communities are freed up to consider what matters in education and focus again on progressive ideals. O'Connor points out that the focus on assessment still persists in some settings: "Although the standards have gone in name, their ghost still hangs over classrooms restraining both what and how things are taught and measured" (O'Connor, 2020, n.p.). Nonetheless, with innovations in technology and access to information Heathcote could never have imagined when she created the approach, with the dedication of teachers, with investment in professional development, and with support from Ministry and senior leadership, I believe we in New Zealand are better positioned to make the most of Mantle of the Expert. The schools I am working with are determined and inspired to do just that.

Where to next?

As this book has recorded, there has been a steady growth in interest in Dramatic Inquiry in New Zealand over the 20 years since Heathcote's first visits to the country. Alongside a growing body of scholarly work, there are now hundreds of subscribers to the Mantle of the Expert Aotearoa website, mostly teachers who are using drama in their teaching to some degree. At least seven primary schools in Northland, Auckland, Hamilton, the Bay of Plenty, Wellington, and Christchurch have embedded Dramatic Inquiry into their local curriculum, with some teachers using it as their main approach to curriculum. Informal networking takes place through cluster groups in centres from Northland to Christchurch and there are regular workshops, conference presentations, and other professional opportunities. All of these are publicised on the Mantle of the Expert Aotearoa website (www.mantleoftheexpert.co.nz). Anyone reading this book who wishes to connect with other teachers, visit classrooms, get support with planning, or access resources will find a supportive and easy going community ready to welcome them. Schools looking for more sustained and targeted professional development can apply for centrally funded professional learning from the Ministry of Education to work with an accredited facilitator. This is probably the most effective way to support change at a school-wide level.

To date, much of the networking between schools has been voluntary and informal, which has been both a strength and a limitation. The advantage is the strength of relationships and the low-key nature of sharing. The disadvantage is that groups come and go and people get spread rather thin. So, as the book goes to press, there are plans underway to formalise things somewhat and try to ensure a sustainable support network for teachers. A small group of experienced teachers is forming a charitable trust with the goals of providing online support, courses, and face-to-face support into the future. It will be important to do this in a spirit that maintains positive relations with Mantle of the Expert practitioners in the UK and elsewhere, and with the existing subject society Drama New Zealand. Another priority is to ensure that any organisation is committed to culturally responsive/culturally sustaining practices and walks the talk of the pedagogy in terms of power sharing, emergent leadership, and empathy. It's likely that Mantle of the Expert will morph and change in the future as it is woven and rewoven by the weavers here in Aotearoa New Zealand. This is just as it should be, and was as Heathcote wanted it. The final words of her 2009 address will serve very well as the final words for this book, too. They are a reminder of how we need to proceed; to honour the core foundations of this most elegant and fascinating teaching approach, and at the same time make it our own:

> There are many variations and adaptations available to us teachers, but Mantle (of the Expert) is the neatest most elegant way I have yet found to bond specific learning within the praxis of drama. We don't have to copy each other's ways of working—but the drama structure must be our honoured inspiration.
>
> (Heathcote, 2009, p. 25)

Further information and support

Mantle of the Expert Aotearoa website: www.mantleoftheexpert.co.nz.
Mantle of the Expert UK: www.mantleoftheexpert.com

Appendix

Four handouts to help with pre-planning

Handouts 1, 3, and 4 are adapted from Heathcote (2009). Handout 2 is adapted from Taylor (2016).

1. Selecting the enterprise

Selecting the enterprise to provide mandatory controls and access to selected curriculum	
There are 11 kinds of enterprise, each of which engaged a different type of client, and thus different demands are made upon the thinking, language and research skills of the teacher and students in particular, attitudes and point of view vary but never the need of standards and responsibility.	
Serving enterprices	Bank, library, hospital, fire station, post office, rescue & emergency, disaster services, transport & haulage, recycling, sports centre, travel agency, activities & adventures centre, catering, entertainment, exhibitions, events, fitness & health, gardening & landscaping, safety consultants, etc;
Manufacturing & agriculture	Factories, a dairy, a bakery, fashion house, herb garden, cards, building, engineering, a farm, naval, architects, etc;
Charitable	Red Cross, Greenpeace, National Trust, English Heritage, homeless shelters, etc;
Nurturing circumstances	Hospice, orphanage, gene of blood bank, safe house, library, council office, etc;
Regulatory situations	Police stations, tax and immigration offices, prisons, law courts, armed forces, housing authorities, customs and excise, harbour authorities, fire safety, flood protection, border authorities & immigration, environmental agencies, etc;
Maintenance enterprises	Plumbers, electricians, joiners, archivists, stone masons, security, building restoration & conversion, excavation, demolition, house clearance, housing developers, housing association, salvage & reclamation, etc;
Arts establishments	Theatre, photographic studios, film makers, art gallery, ballet and dance companies, museums, craft workshops, architects' business, authors & illustrators, set & costume designers, animators, sculptors, etc;
Training establishments	Any learning programmes related with human endeavours. The students would plan the training not function as students come to learn.

Chapter 7 Looking to the future

Investigation, Research & education	Historians, archaeologists, palaeontologists archivists scientists, curators, conservation, heritage, museums, visitor centres, exhibits, criminologists, private investigators, accident & incident investigators, crime scene investigators, missing person, etc;
Animal & Wildlife	Animal rescue, vets, zoos, wildlife parks, SPCA, dogs homes, animal welfare & protection, grooming & training nature reserve animal sanctuary, etc.
Personal Services	Advice & support, conciliation & mediation, financial services, care of the elderly or disabled, etc.

2. Building the frame/backstory

Building the frame/backstory for your responsible team

Insert the name of your responsible team here		
Create a fictional backstory: Who they have worked with in the past, what they are famous for etc.		
Powers *The team's authority: its decision making powers and circle of influence* *Note also the limits on that power – what the team CAN'T do.*	**Responsibilities** *The team's duties and responsibilities to the client, the context and other people* *In NZ, include here responsibilities under to Tiriti o Waitangi*	**Values** *The team's beliefs and values: what they stand for, their professional code of conduct, and their belief systems*
Find out about how teams/professional organisations like this operate in the real world and record relevant information (use next page too)		

3. Generic tasks grid

Generic Tasks Grid

A list of the types of tasks/activities used in Mantle of the Expert

Purple – Material resources of the team
Green – Social/cultural/historical dimensions of the team
Red – Interactions with people within the team
Blue – Interactions with people outside the team

Places	Buildings & Structures	Portals & Barriers	Utilities	Working Environments
Landscapes, maps, models, aerial views, scene of events, environment	Company HQ, rooms, cellars, attics, sheds, outbuildings, fences, garages, bridges, plans, architectural drawings	Entrances & exits, doors, gates, fences, walls, gate-keepers & security guards	Heating, plumbing, lighting, disposal, re-cycling, re-using, reducing, waste	Sound, space, resources, human interactions, access to food & water, shops, message boards
Planning & Preparation	**Equipment Machinery, Material & Resources**	**Transport**	**Maintenance & Repair**	**Building Security**
Plans of action, means of entry, lists, procedures, things to consider – materials, equipment & resources, problem solutions, maps and schemas	Vehicles, special machinery, computers, cameras, safety, specialists equipment, clothing – suits helmets, boots, gloves	Ways of travelling to work, vehicles used by the co., car parks, garages, air-strips, helicopter-pads	Maintaining & repairing: equipment, machinery, buildings, structures, enclosures	CCTV, codes, procedures, guards, dogs, fences, towers, safes, ID cards, card-readers, scanners, keypads, passwords/numbers
Safety	**Preserving & Protecting Information**	**Protocols & Procedures**	**Customs**	**History/Possible Futures**
Emergency procedures, evacuation, fire-drill, emergency exits, first ait, communications, use of fire extinguishers & other equipment, health & safety regulations	Archivies vaults, safes, encryptions, codes, access procedures	For effective working, for meetings, for dealing with people at & out of work, for working safely, dealing with dangerous situations, dealing with complaints, rotas, timetables	Entering the building, celebrating success, welcoming guests/new employees	Timeline, journal, photos, diaries, videos, photographs, letters, artefacts, memories, memorials, dreams/nightmares, hopes, plans

Appendix

Meetings	Employment	Jobs	Training & Staff Development	Induction For New Employees
Meetings for: making decisions, sharing information, planning next moves. Meeting with: clients, customers, bureaucrats	Job descriptions, job adverts, tendering, sub-contracting	Areas of responsibility, special duties, collaborative possibilities	In-service presentations, demonstrations, simulations, videos, training manuals, booklets, posters, exams	Presentations, demonstrations etc, by existing employees
Human relations	**Health & Well-being**	**Comfort & Refreshments**	**Internal Communications**	**External Correspondence**
Agreed practices & values, support for employees' families, crèches, wheelchair access	Work/life balance, questionnaires, exercise, health information, medical care, first aid, medical emergency procedures	Cafeteria, drinks machine, fruit/water at work, staff room, toilets, showers	Messages, notes, meetings, e-mails, circulars, phone calls, text-messages, incident board, mobiles	Letters, e-mail, fax, phone calls, cards, postcards, video/text messaging
Providing Information	**Presenting Information**	**News**	**Advertising**	**Displaying**
Writing reports, making films, giving interviews, making presentations & displays, taking photographs	Website, reports, business cards, power-points, leaflets, books, posters, films, display boards, guides, manuals, signs, photo albums	Dealing with the media: newspaper, TV news, radio, magazines. Preparing press releases, interviews, briefings	Promotion, activities/products, posters, letters, leaflets	Wall displays, slide-shows, short-films, posters, leaflets, exhibitions, photos, awards, past accomplishments, website
Portfolio	**Company Identity & Values**	**Gathering Information**	**Cataloguing & Recording**	**Client/s**
Company portfolio, history, past work, personnel, booklet, website	Logo, slogan, poster, co. sign, website, letterhead, flag, motto	Researching using: the internet books, video, interviews, newspaper, museums, libraries, DVD, TV, databases	Films, photographs databases, folders, archives, store rooms, vaults, filing-cabinets, incident books, journals, log-books, diaries	Profiles, pictures, personalities, background family, company history

4. Levels of tension

Levels of tensions in order of subtlety

Level	Category	Examples
1	Danger named by not controllable – apprehended presences which threaten	• The danger of the 'watcher' who is know to be there but cannot be located – human or animal • The seen watcher/s – soldiers, gods, witches, guardians etc. Not benign presences.
2	Dangers known in advance	The quest • In the face of an enemy • To find something • To release someone/something and protect them into escaping (this involves being in a place which is forbidden!)
3	Duty in the face of distraction	Territories which daunt and are unpredictable as to their challenged and properties e.g.: • Ruins • Wastelands • Caves • Water (The head must sustain imagery to create territory)
4	Herculean tasks – extremely difficult or dangerous; requiring an enormous effort	Extra effort required due to e.g: • Time • Climate • Dangerous loads (all require inherent pressures to be built in)
5	Danger from guile	Threats of possible betrayal e.g: • Judas in the garden of Gethsemene • Spy infiltration
6	Threats from stupidity	Foolish carelessness such as • Losing something • Forgetting critical information
7	Pressures from timing limitations	Threats of time impacting on activity e.g: Vampire activity that is curtailed by daybreak • Bomb defusing – urgency to complete before it blows
8	Pressures from sickness	Different kinds of impairments cause by e.g: • Wounding • Accidents • Traps of various kinds

Level	Category	Examples
9	Breaks in communication	Difficulty of connection with others e.g: • Failure of messages • Failure of technical resources • Lights falling
10	Missing of misread signs	Inability to understand what something means – or a failure to notice something of significance • *A missed clue* • *A misunderstood clue*
11	Breakdown in relations	Personal or professional differences which threaten support systems
12	Loss of faith in some companions	Honourable betrayals – losing trust in those you thought you could depend on

Additional tensions (some are part of the 12 levels above)
- Missed appointments
- Limitations of space
- Mazes
- Requirements to be silent
- Requirements to leave no evident
- Impenetrable codes/messages/other language
- Something mislaid
- Missing the road/path/signs
- Too many choices
- A blocked exit
- Disguised entrances
- Expected guide or helper is helpless/boud/dead/asleep/hurt/late
- Something important is not sufficient (not enough rope/ladder too short)
- Expertise is essential but leader unable to lead
- Broken up messages (e.g., phone contact poor/damaged papers)
- Conflicting messaged or evident

No matter which level of tension is invoked, it must be clearly foreshadowed and contracted PLUS the power to resolve be possible but not easy – it has to be fought for during the process of the action.

References

Abbott, L. (2007). *Mantle of the Expert 2: Training materials and tools*. Essex County Council.

Abbott, L., & Taylor, T. (2013). *Mantle of the Expert resources: Resources for using Dorothy Heathcote's imaginative-inquiry approach to teaching and learning*. https://www.mantleoftheexpert.com/wp-content/uploads/2019/05/RFH-Resources-pack-FINAL.pdf

Abdul Samat, N. (2016). *'In this class automatic my words come out': Implementing process drama in two Malaysian English language-learning contexts*. Doctoral thesis, University of Waikato, Hamilton. https://hdl.handle.net/10289/10820

Ackroyd-Pilkington, J. (2001). Acting representation and role. *Research in Drama Education: The Journal of Applied Theatre and Performance, 6*(1), 9–22.

Ackroyd-Pilkington, J. (2004). *Role reconsidered: A re-evaluation of the relationship between teacher-in-role and acting*. Trentham Books.

Aitken, G. (2017). *Called to teaching at 15*. Interview with Kim Hill. Radio New Zealand National, 30 September. http://www.radionz.co.nz/national/programmes/saturday/audio/201860647/graeme-aitken-called-to-teaching-at-15

Aitken, V. (2007). The relationship managers: Towards a theorising of the teacher-in-role/student relationship. *Journal of Artistic and Creative Education, 1*(1), 86–105.

Aitken, V. (2008). Pedagogical learnings of Borat for make benefit glorious community of drama teachers: What teachers can learn from Borat about frame, position and power when working in role. *New Zealand Journal of Research in Performing Arts and Education: Nga Mahi a Rehia, 1*. http://www.drama.org.nz/?p=394

Aitken, V. (2011). *Teacher survey responses* [Unpublished data set]. The Underground online: New Zealand teachers' use of face-to-face and online support networks in the ongoing implementation of Mantle of the Expert—a pilot study. University of Waikato, Hamilton.

Aitken, V. (2012a, July). When you've been doing it as long as I have: Repositioning children through role based strategies in classroom research. IDIERI 7 (International Drama in Education Research Institute), Limerick, Ireland. Also presented at *IDIERI 7: The NZ Papers*, University of Waikato, Hamilton 28 November.

Aitken, V. (2012b). Penultimate visit to room 17. *Toy museum with juniors*. Blog post, 22 August. http://toymuseummantle.blogspot.com/2012/08/week-5-21st-august.html

Aitken, V. (2013a). Dorothy Heathcote's Mantle of the Expert approach to teaching and learning: A brief introduction. In D. Fraser, V. Aitken, & B. Whyte, *Connecting curriculum, linking learning* (pp. 34–56). NZCER Press.

Aitken, V. (2013b). *Six week MOTE adventure at HNS*. Teaching blog. https://hnsmantleadventure2013.blogspot.com/

Aitken, V. (2014). Risking heuristics: Towards a classification of the features of Mantle of the Expert through the metaphor of the korowai. *Drama Research: International Journal of Drama in Education*, 5(1), 2–19.

Aitken, V. (2016). 'Te Aho Tapu: Precious threads in Mantle of the Expert'. *Te Aho Tapu* symposium, Rototuna Junior High School, Hamilton, October. https://1drv.ms/p/s!ApyDz8naiP7igg9mXzCxGdzr27nx

Aitken, V. (2017). The mantle underground: A case study in informal school–university partnership. In R. McNae & B. Cowie (Eds.), *Realising innovative partnerships in educational research* (pp. 169–179). Sense. https://mantleoftheexpert.co.nz/research/11-viv-aitken-final-october-18-formatted/

Aitken, V. (2019). *Drama from a picture book*. Blog post, 8 October. https://mantleoftheexpert.co.nz/drama-from-a-picture-book-taniwha/

Aitken, V. (2020) *Dramatic Inquiry and home learning*. Zoom presentation hosted by Drama New Zealand's Reaching the Edges: Networks of Expertise Project, 1 May. https://docs.google.com/presentation/d/1ILCjHGqSq-S_VNqoQZWnaMw4fUcdUnSr2vI6QY_KBvQ/edit?usp=sharing

Aitken, V., & Cowley, S. (2007). Safe to speak? A teacher's story of one child's apparent 'liberation' and 'transformation' through the security of role. *Waikato Journal of Education*, 13, 211–220. https://researchcommons.waikato.ac.nz/handle/10289/6191

Aitken, V., & Downey, R. (2020). *Dog squad: A Mantle of the Expert-inspired learning adventure*. Zoom presentation hosted by Drama New Zealand's Reaching the Edges: Networks of Expertise Project, 5 May. https://docs.google.com/presentation/d/1VpA8mnjDoa0lDiCw_jx5kx35at6KECWBfxWQIP6V738/edit?usp=sharing

Aitken, V., Downey, R., & staff from Hillcrest Normal School, Hamilton. (2020). *Dog squad: A cross-curricula learning adventure for home learning*. https://docs.google.com/presentation/d/1r1f6o5FgtPQXrZp-4B1JRtB-hvaoCZcPVeKisGgFpAs/edit?usp=sharing

Aitken, V., & Edmiston, B. (2014). *Dramatic Inquiry in teacher education: Preliminary findings from a recent project using Mantle of the Expert at University of Waikato*. [Conference presentation]. Spicing up Teacher Education. TEFANZ (Teacher Education Forum of Aotearoa New Zealand) Conference, Hamilton, 8–10 July. https://mantleoftheexpert.co.nz/research/

Aitken, V., Henshilwood, D., & Boyd, M. (2007). *'In my twenty-five years at Warner Brothers ...' benefits of high status roles for adults with intellectual disabilities in a process drama approach*. [Conference presentation]. NZ Association for the Study of Intellectual Disability Conference, Wellington.

Aitken, V., & Townsend, L. (2013). Searching for the truth/s: Exploring enviro-ethics. In D. Fraser, V. Aitken, & B. Whyte, *Connecting curriculum, linking learning*. NZCER Press, (pp. 57–82).

Allen, L. (2017). A glimpse into Mantle of the Expert. Blog post. https://numberagents. blogspot.com/2017/08/a-glimpse-into-mantle-of-expert.html

Arts with Attitude. (2008, April 20). In Attitude TV. TVNZ. https://www.youtube.com/watch?v=ey5NaSo6GwU

Associated Press. (2010). Australian teacher set terrorism plan homework. *Independent*. 25 August. https://www.independent.co.uk/news/world/australasia/australian-teacher-set-terrorism-plan-homework-2061388.html

Ausubel, D. (1968). *Educational psychology: A cognitive view*. Holt, Rinehart and Winston.

Baldwin, P. (2010). Drama is an elephant. *Drama Magazine: The National Drama Magazine of Professional Practice*, 17(2), 15–18.

Baldwin, P. (2012). *With drama in mind: Real learning in imagined worlds*. Continuum.

Barclay, B. (1978). *Ahu mahi Wwatu Māori*. Pacific Films: Ngā Taonga Sound & Vision. https://ngataonga.org.nz/collections/catalogue/catalogue-item?record_id=69704

Barish, J. (1981). *The antitheatrical prejudice*. University of California Press.

Batt, T. (2001). *Imagined worlds: A journey through the expressive arts in early childhood*. Playcentre Publications.

Battye, S. (2010). Dramatic reputation echoes in classrooms. *Education Review*, 1(3), 46–47.

Battye, S. (2016). Drama for learning: Mantle of the Expert makes its mark. *Tomorrow's Schools Today NZ*. https://www.tstnz.com/teaching-resources-and-health-information-for-teachers/arts-drama-for-learning-mantle-of-the-expert-makes-its-mark/

BBC News. (2017). Students' Richard Burton diary film to get premiere. BBC News website. http://www.bbc.com/news/uk-wales-south-west-wales-40415305

Bealings School. (n.d.). *Diamond demolition*. Video recording. https://www.mantleoftheexpert.com/video/diamond-demolition/

Bennett, A. (2004). *The history boys*. Faber & Faber.

Berryman, M., Lawrence, D., & Lamont, R. (2018). Cultural relationships for responsive pedagogy: A bicultural mana ōrite perspective. *Set: Research Information for Teachers* (1), 3–10.

Bishop, R., & Berryman, M. (2009). The Te Kotahitanga effective teaching profile. *Set: Research Information for Teachers*, (2), 27–33.

Bleaken, S. (2012). *Hikoitanga tapuwae o te hunga ke To take a walk in another's shoes: Using process drama to teach the underlying principles of restorative practice*. Master of Education (MEd) thesis, University of Waikato, Hamilton. https://hdl.handle.net/10289/6486

Bloom, B., Englehart, M., Furst, E., Hill, W., & Krathwohl, D. (1956). *Taxonomy of educational objectives*. Longmans.

Bloom, B., Krathwohl, D., & Masia, B. (1964). *Taxonomy of educational objectives: The classification of educational goals. Handbook 2: Affective domain.* Longman.

Boal, A. (1979). *Theatre of the oppressed.* Pluto Press.

Bolton, G. (1979). *Towards a theory of drama in education.* Longman.

Bolton, G. (1984). *Drama as education: An argument for placing drama at the centre of curriculum.* Longman.

Bolton, G. (1985). Changes in thinking about drama in education. *Theory into Practice,* 24(3), 151–157.

Bolton, G. (2003). *Dorothy Heathcote's story: Biography of a remarkable drama teacher.* Trentham Books.

Bolton, G. (2007). A history of drama education: A search for substance. InL. Bresler (Ed.), *International handbook of research in arts education* (pp. 45–62). Springer.

Bowell, P., & Heap, B. (2013). *Planning process drama.* Fulton.

Boynton, J. (2017). *Weavers' hui focuses on teaching tikanga.* Radio New Zealand National. http://www.radionz.co.nz/news/te-manu-korihi/342105/weavers-hui-focuses-on-teaching-tikanga

Brook, P. (1995). *The empty space: A book about the theatre—deadly, holy, rough, immediate.* Scribner (reprint edition).

Bruner, J. (1966). *Toward a theory of instruction.* Belkapp Press.

Bunting, M. (2006). *Questions, questions, questions!* http://www.mantleoftheexpert.com/studying/articles/Michael-%20Questioning.doc

Burgess, R. (1993). *Pieces of Dorothy: A new biographical documentary.* [Video] Newcastle University Archive. https://vimeo.com/14360472

Carey, J. (1995). Resources pull out: Drama conventions a quick planning guide. *Drama,* 4(1), 29–32.

Carroll, J., Anderson, M., & Cameron, D. (2006). *Real players? Drama, technology and education.* Trentham Books.

Claxton, G. (2008). *What's the point of school? Rediscovering the heart of education.* Oneworld.

Crayton-Brown, K. (2010). School apologises for fake letter. *Southland Times,* 27 August. http://www.stuff.co.nz/national/education/4063280/School-apologises-for-fake-letter

Csikszentmihalyi, M. (1990). *Flow: The psychology of optimal experience.* Harper Collins.

Davis, S. (2016). *Learning that matters: Revitalising Heathcote's rolling role for the digital age.* Sense.

Davis, S., Simou, P., Wales, P., Kulik, J., Hatton, C., Kennard, J., Mooney, M., & Nicholls, J. (2014). The water reckoning—learnings from the international Rolling Role project. In P. Bowell & C. Lawrence (Eds.), *Heathcote reconsidered: Conference* echoes: Keynotes and presentations from the proceedings of the National Drama International Conference 2013 (pp. 89–112). National Drama Publications.

Dawson, K. (2019). 'This is not a …' Drama Based Instruction Network. University of Austin, Texas. https://dbp.theatredance.utexas.edu/content/not-0

Department of Conservation. (2017). Tools for environmental action. Online teaching resources. https://www.doc.govt.nz/get-involved/conservation-education/resources/tools-for-environmental-action/

Department of Education. (1986). Dorothy Heathcote in New Zealand. Drama as a medium for learning. Videocassette. Wellington.

Deutscher, G. (2005). The unfolding of language: An evolutionary tour of mankind's greatest invention. Metropolitan Books.

Dewey, J. (1938). Experience and education: The 60th anniversary edition (A. Hall-Quest, Ed.). http://ruby.fgcu.edu/courses/ndemers/colloquium/experienceducationdewey.pdf

Doppelt, Y., Mehalik, M., Schunn, C., Silk, E., & Krynsinski, D. (2008). Engagement and achievements: A case study of design-based learning in a science context. Journal of Technology Education, 19(2). https://doi.org/10.21061/jte.v10i2.a.2

Downey, R. (2017). Enhancing writing outcomes for Māori students through the application of Dramatic Inquiry within culturally responsive practice. Teacher-Led Innovation Fund Final Project Report. Ministry of Education.

Downey, R. (2018). The sustainability of inquiry skills developed through Mantle of the Expert: A case study on the impact of a Dramatic Inquiry pedagogy on a group of students as they move on to intermediate. Master of Education (MEd) thesis, The University of Auckland.

Drama Toolkit. (2011). 'Yes Let's' game. https://www.dramatoolkit.co.uk/drama-games/item/improvisation/yes-lets

Driskell, J., Copper, C., & Moran, A. (1994). Does mental practice enhance performance? Journal of Applied Psychology, 79(4), 481.

Dunne, S. (2015). Using a Mantle of the Expert approach to build professional expertise in interior design. Master of Education (MEd) thesis, University of Waikato, Hamilton. https://mantleoftheexpert.co.nz/wp-content/uploads/2019/02/Dissertation-final-draft.pdf

Dweck, C. (2006). Mindset: The new psychology of success. Random House.

Earley, P., & Ang, S. (2003). Cultural intelligence: Individual interactions across cultures. Stanford University Press.

Edmiston, B. (2003). What's my position?: Role, frame and positioning when using process drama. Research in Drama Education: The Journal of Applied Theatre and Performance, 8(2), 221–229.

Edmiston, B. (2010). Chapter 5. Dramatic Inquiry: Imagining and enacting life from multiple perspectives. In R. Beach, G. Campano, B. Edmiston, & M. Borgman,

Literacy tools in the classroom: Teaching through critical inquiry, grades 5–12 (pp. 69–89). Teachers College Press.

Edmiston, B. (2014). *Transforming teaching and learning with active and dramatic approaches: Engaging students across the curriculum.* Routledge.

Edmiston, B. (2016). *Core elements and pedagogical dimensions in the Mantle of the Expert approach.* Unpublished handout for teachers.

Edmiston, B., & Bigler-McCarthy, T. (n.d.). *Building social justice communities: Using drama to make power more visible.* https://www.mantleoftheexpert.com/resources/reading/

Education Council. (2017). *Our code our standards: Code of professional responsibility and standards for the teaching profession.* Author. https://teachingcouncil.nz/sites/default/files/Our%20Code%20Our%20Standards%20web%20booklet%20FINAL.pdf

Education Review Office. (2017). *Otaika Valley school report 15/12/2017.* https://www.ero.govt.nz/review-reports/otaika-valley-school-15-12-2017/

Eriksson, S. (2011). Distancing at close range: Making strange devices in Dorothy Heathcote's process drama: Teaching political awareness through drama. *Research in Drama Education: The Journal of Applied Theatre and Performance, 16*(1), 101–123.

Fadel, C., Bialik, M., & Trilling, B. (2015). *Four-dimensional education: The competencies learners need to succeed.* Centre for Curriculum Redesign. https://curriculumredesign.org/our-work/four-dimensional-21st-century-education-learning-competencies-future-2030/

Foucault, M. (1977). *Discipline and punish: The birth of the prison.* Allen Lane.

Foucault, M. (1980). *Power/knowledge: Selected interviews and other writings 1972–1977 by Michel Foucault.* (Trans. C. Gordon et al.). Pantheon.

Fraser, C. (2019). *Push to teach New Zealand history in schools becomes more desperate.* Newshub story and video, 24 April. https://www.newshub.co.nz/home/new-zealand/2019/04/push-to-teach-new-zealand-history-in-schools-becomes-more-desperate.html

Fraser, D. (2000). Curriculum integration: What it is and is not. *Set: Research Information for Teachers,* (3), 34.

Fraser, D., Aitken, V., Price, G., & Whyte., B. (2012a). Inquiry learning, drama and curriculum integration. *Set: Research Information for Teachers,* (3), 32–40.

Fraser, D., Aitken, V., Price, G., & Whyte, B. (2012b). *Connecting curriculum, connecting learning: Negotiation and the arts* [Summary report]. Teaching and Learning Research Initiative. http://www.tlri.org.nz/sites/default/files/projects/9281_summaryreport.pdf

Fraser, D., Aitken, V., & Whyte, B. (2013). *Connecting curriculum, linking learning.* NZCER Press.

Fraser, D., & Deane, P. (2010). Making a difference: Agents of change through curriculum integration. *Set: Research Information for Teachers*, (3), 10–14.

Freire, P. (1972). *Pedagogy of the oppressed*. Penguin.

Fullan, M., & Langworthy, M. (2014). *A rich seam: How new pedagogies find deep learning*. Pearson.

Gain A. (2002). Toward a Theory of Social Practices: A Development in Culturalist Theorizing. *European Journal of Social Theory*, 5(2), 243–263. doi:10.1177/13684310222225432

Gain, P., Maubach, C., Morin, R., Locke, M., & Charmin, J. (2018). *Orff level one module 1 booklet*. ONZA.

Gallagher, K., & Jacobson, K. (2018). Beyond mimesis to an assemblage of reals in the drama classroom: Which reals? Which representational aesthetics? What theatre-building practices? Whose truths? *Research in Drama Education: The Journal of Applied Theatre and Performance*, 23(1), 40–55. https://doi.org/10.1080/13569783.2017.1396209

Garrett, S. (2001) Wild Things *NZADIE Journal* 25, 67.

Gibson, R., & Ewing, R. (2020). *Transforming the curriculum through the arts*. Palgrave Macmillan.

Goffman, E. (1959). *The presentation of self in everyday life*. Anchor Books.

Goffman, E. (1986). *Frame analysis: An essay on the organisation of experience*. Northeastern University Press.

Grace, P. (1993). *The trolley*. Viking.

Green, P. (2018). Why what works doesn't work. Curmudgucation blog post, 12 December. http://curmudgucation.blogspot.com/2018/12/why-what-works-doesnt-work.html

Greenwood, J. (2001). Within a third space. *Research in Drama Education: The Journal of Applied Theatre and Performance*, 6(2), 193–205.

Greenwood, J. (2009). Drama education in New Zealand: A coming of age? A conceptualisation of the development and practice of drama in the curriculum as a structured improvisation with New Zealand's experience as a case study. *Research in Drama Education: The Journal of Applied Theatre and Performance*, 14(2), 245–260.

Haidt, J. (2013). *The righteous mind: Why good people are divided by politics and religion*. Penguin.

Hall, E. (1989). *Beyond culture*. Knopf Doubleday.

Hanly, T. (2017). *A critical guide to Māori and Pākehā histories of Aotearoa: A curriculum programme resource*. http://www.criticalhistories.nz

Harré, R., & Langenhove, L. (1999). *Positioning theory*. Blackwell.

Harré, R., & Moghaddam, F. (2003). *The self and others: Positioning individuals and groups in personal, political and cultural contexts*. Praeger.

Haseman, B., & O'Toole, J. (1987). *Dramawise*. Heinemann Educational.

Heathcote, D. (n.d.-a). *Working with tension*. http://www.moeplanning.co.uk/wp-content/uploads/2008/04/working-with-tension.pdf

Heathcote, D. (n.d.-b). *Establishing procedures and implementing the style and possibilities for developing standards and progression*. https://www.mantleoftheexpert.com/wp-content/uploads/2018/01/DH-MoE-Establishing-Procedures.pdf

Heathcote, D. (1983). *Education through drama: Planning with Heathcote*. [Video recording]. Insight Media.

Heathcote, D. (1984). Signs and portents. In L. Johnson & C. O'Neill (Eds.), *Dorothy Heathcote: Collected writings* (pp. 70–78). Stanley Thornes.

Heathcote, D. (2002). *Contexts for active learning: Four models to forge links between schooling and society*. NATD Conference. https://www.mantleoftheexpert.com/blog-post/dorothy-heathcote-four-models-for-teaching-learning/

Heathcote, D. (2007). *Drama conventions list*. http://www.mantleoftheexpert.com/wp-content/uploads/2009/02/conventions-list-dh-revision.pdf

Heathcote, D. (2008). *A letter from the patron of Drama New Zealand*. http://www.dramanz.decanker.com/wpcontent/uploads/2009/11/DHeathcote.pdf

Heathcote, D. (2009). *Mantle of the Expert: My current understanding*. Presented at the Weaving our Stories: International Mantle of the Expert Conference, University of Waikato, Hamilton. Transcript available from https://docs.google.com/document/d/1ugZEpTfm2nopG7L3k681hgj6f9qQHr1fTHaov1u05xg/edit?usp=sharing

Heathcote, D., & Bolton, G. (1994). *Drama for learning: Dorothy Heathcote's Mantle of the Expert approach to education*. Heinemann Press.

Heathcote, D., Johnson, L., & O'Neill, C. (1991). *Dorothy Heathcote: Collected writings on education and drama*. Northwestern University Press.

Heathcote, D., & Whitelaw, M. (1985). *Notes on signs and portents*. http://www.mantleoftheexpert.com/wp-content/uploads/2009/12/conventions-notes.pdf

Heick, T. (2018). *What is Bloom's taxonomy? A definition for teachers*. Teachthought blog post, 11 December. https://www.teachthought.com/learning/what-is-blooms-taxonomy-a-definition-for-teachers/

Heston, S. (1993). *The Dorothy Heathcote archive*. Manchester Metropolitan University. https://web.archive.org/web/20060823171033/http://www.partnership.mmu.ac.uk/dha/hcheston.asp

Heston, S. (2012). Dorothy Heathcote: Larger than life teacher who placed drama at the heart of education. [Obituary]. *Drama*, 18(3), 3–11. http://www.nationaldrama.org.uk/wp-content/uploads/sites/5/2014/07/Drama-18.2-web.pdf

Hetet, V. (2016). *Rauaroha—the journey of a korowai*. Ako Aotearoa website, 14 January. https://ako.ac.nz/our-community/tertiary-teaching-excellence-awards/rauaroha-korowai/ (previous page no longer live).

Hetet, V. (2018). They're not all korowai: A master weaver on how to identify Māori garments. *The Spinoff*, 26 April. https://thespinoff.co.nz/atea/26-04-2018/theyre-not-all-korowai-a-master-weaver-on-how-to-identify-maori-garments/

Hill, R. (2013). *Making your first small korowai*. Soft Systems.

Hopkins, E. (2017). *Helping young people discover town's secrets with Richard Burton's diaries*. Blog post. https://www.hlf.org.uk/about-us/news-features/helping-young-people-uncover-town%E2%80%99s-secrets-richard-burtons-diaries

Hulson, M. (2006). *Schemes for classroom drama*. Trentham Books.

Ings, W. (2017). *Disobedient teaching: Surviving and creating change in education*. Otago University Press.

James, M. (2008). Assessment and learning. In S. Swaffield (Ed.), *Unlocking assessment: Understanding for reflection and application*. Routledge, 20–36.

Jeffers, O. (2013). *The day the crayons quit*. Philomel Books.

Johnston, C. (2017). *Disobedient Theatre–Alternative ways to inspire, dramatise and play*. Bloomsbury Publishing.

Johnstone, K. (1992). *Impro: Improvisation and the theater*. Routledge, Chapman & Hall.

Kidd, D. (2011). The mantle of Macbeth. *English in Education*, 45(1). https://doi.org/10.1111/j.1754-8845.2010.01083.x

Krathwohl, D. (2002). A revision of Bloom's taxonomy: An overview. *Theory Into Practice*, 41(4), 212–218.

Lagueux, R. (2014). *A spurious John Dewey quotation on reflection*. https://www.academia.edu/17358587/A_Spurious_John_Dewey_Quotation_on_Reflection

Lakoff, G., & Johnson, M. (2003). *Metaphors we live by*. University of Chicago Press.

Lethaby, C., & Harries, P. (2015). Learning styles and teacher training: Are we perpetuating neuromyths? ELT Journal, 70(1), 16–27. https://doi.org/10.1093/elt/ccv051

Miller, C., and Saxton, J. M. (2004). *Into the story: Language in action through drama*. Heinmann.

Milne, A. (2017). *Colouring in the white spaces*. Keynote at #Ulearn17. Core Education ULearn discussion group. https://edspace.org.nz/blog/view/27082/ann-milne-keynote-colouring-in-the-white-spaces

Milne, A. A. (1926). *Winnie the Pooh*. Methuen.

Ministry of Education. (n.d.-a). *Project-based learning*. http://elearning.tki.org.nz/Teaching/Future-focused-learning/Project-based-learning

Ministry of Education. (n.d.-b). *Deliberate acts of teaching*. Literacy Online: TKI website. http://literacyonline.tki.org.nz/Literacy-Online/Planning-for-my-students-needs/Effective-Literacy-Practice-Years-1-4/Deliberate-acts-of-teaching

Ministry of Education. (n.d.-c). *Drama glossary*. TKI website. http://artsonline.tki.org.nz/Teaching-and-Learning/Pedagogy/Drama/Glossary

Ministry of Education. (2000). *Arts in the New Zealand curriculum*. Learning Media.

Ministry of Education. (2004). *Telling our stories: Classroom drama in years 7–10*. Learning Media.

Ministry of Education. (2006). *Playing our stories: Classroom drama in years 1–6*. Learning Media.

Ministry of Education. (2007). *The New Zealand curriculum*. Learning Media.

Ministry of Education. (2008a). *Approaches to social inquiry: Building conceptual understandings in the social sciences*. Learning Media.

Ministry of Education. (2008b). *Te Marautanga o Aotearoa*. Learning Media.

Ministry of Education. (2010). *Tu Rangatira, a Ministry of Education resource for Māori medium educational leaders*. http://www.educationalleaders.govt.nz/Leadership-development/Key-leadership-documents/Tu-rangatira-English/Introduction

Ministry of Education. (2011a). *Curriculum stories—effective pedagogy—Mantle of the Expert*. http://nzcurriculum.tki.org.nz/Curriculum-stories/Mediagallery/Effective-pedagogy/Mantle-of-the-expert

Ministry of Education. (2011b). *Attendance matters: Guidelines for implementing an effective attendance management plan*. http://ndhadeliver.natlib.govt.nz/delivery/DeliveryManagerServlet?dps_pid=IE6650538

Ministry of Education. (2015). *Te takanga o te wā—Māori history: Guidelines for years 1–8*. http://maorihistory.tki.org.nz/assets/Uploads/Te-Takanga-o-te-Wa-English.PDF

Ministry of Education. (2017). *Te whāriki: He whāriki mātauranga mō ngā mokopuna o Aotearoa—early childhood curriculum*. https://www.education.govt.nz/assets/Documents/Early-Childhood/Te-Whariki-Early-Childhood-Curriculum-ENG-Web.pdf

Ministry of Education. (2019). *Te aho ngārahu project information*. http://minedu.cwp.govt.nz/our-work/overall-strategies-and-policies/moutereo/te-aho-ngarahu/

Ministry of Education & New Zealand Teacher's Council. (2011). *Tātaiako: Cultural competencies for teachers of Māori learners*. https://educationcouncil.org.nz/required/Tataiako.pdf

Ministry of Health. (2002). *He korowai oranga: Māori health strategy*. http://www.moh.govt.nz

Morgan, N., & Saxton, J. (1987). *Teaching drama: A mind of many wonders*. Hutchinson.

Morgan, N., & Saxton, J. (2006). *Asking better questions* (2nd ed.). Pembroke.

Mutch, C. (2013). Progressive education in New Zealand: A revered past, a contested present and an uncertain future. *IJPE: International Journal of Progressive Education*, 9(2), 98–116.

Neelands, J., & Goode, T. (2000). *Structuring drama work: A handbook of available forms in theatre and drama* (2nd ed.). Cambridge University Press.

Neill, A. S. (1966). *Freedom—not license!* Hart.

O'Connor, P. (2020). Teachers hope to end 'near death' of arts in school. *Newsroom*, 21 January. https://www.newsroom.co.nz/@ideasroom/2020/01/21/994613/arts-leaders-hope-to-end-near-death-of-arts-in-school

O'Connor, P., O'Connor, B., & Welsh-Morris, M. (2006). Making the everyday extraordinary: A theatre in education project to prevent child abuse, neglect and family violence. *Research in Drama Education*, 11(2), 235–245.

O'Neill, C. (1995). *Drama worlds: A framework for process drama*. Heinemann Press.

O'Neill, C. (Ed.). (2015). *Dorothy Heathcote on education and drama: Essential writings*. Routledge.

O'Neill, C., & Lambert, A. (1992). *Drama structures*. Stanley Thornes.

O'Toole, J., & Dunn, J. (2002). *Pretending to learn: Helping children learn through drama*. Pearson Education.

Özen, Z., & Adıgüzel, Ö. (2017). Dorothy Heathcote'un yaratıcı drama yaklaşımları. *Yaratıcı Drama Dergisi*, 12(1), 1–28. https://doi.org/10.21612/yader.2017.001

Pease, B. (2002). Rethinking empowerment: A postmodern reappraisal for emancipatory practice. *British Journal of Social Work*, 32, 135–147.

Puketapu-Hetet, E. (1989). *Māori weaving*. Pitman.

Reckwitz (2002). Toward a theory of social practices: A development in culturalist theorising. *European Journal of Social Theory*, 5(2), 243–263.

Robinson, K. (2006). *Do schools kill creativity?* [TED talk]. https://www.ted.com/talks/sir_ken_robinson_do_schools_kill_creativity?utm_campaign=tedspread&utm_medium=referral&utm_source=tedcomshare

Robinson, K., & Aronica, L. (2015). *Creative schools: The grassroots revolution that's transforming education*. Penguin.

Roediger, H., & Pyc, M. (2012). Inexpensive techniques to improve education: Applying cognitive psychology to enhance educational practice. *Journal of Applied Research in Memory and Cognition*, 1, 242–248.

Sayers, R. (2011). The implications of introducing Heathcote's Mantle of the Expert approach as a community of practice and cross curricular learning tool in a primary school. *English in Education*, 45(1), 20–35.

Sayers, R. (2012). *Mantle of the Expert: The legacy of Dorothy Heathcote*. Doctoral thesis, University of Leicester.

Sendak, M. (1963). *Where the wild things are*. Harper & Row.

Sharp, T. (n.d.). Huia beak brooch: 'I just didn't think!' TKI, *Arts online—Te Hāpori o ngā toi*. http://artsonline.tki.org.nz/Teaching-and-Learning/Secondary-teaching-resources/Drama/Units-and-sequences/Huia-beak-brooch-I-just-didn-t-think!

Shaw, J. (1986). *Those who sailed with Cook* (90 mins). Visual Production Unit, Department of Education, New Zealand. Item Nos. 85/120 and 85/121, 1984.

Shuker, C. (2019). *Author interview—Saturday Morning*, Radio New Zealand National, 23 March. https://www.rnz.co.nz/national/programmes/saturday/audio/2018687901/carl-shuker-author-of-a-mistake

Shulman, L. (2005). Signature pedagogies in the professions. *Daedalus: Journal of the American Academy of Arts and Sciences* 134(3), 52–59.

Simpson, E. (1966). *The classification of educational objectives, psychomotor domain*. Research project, University of Illinois, Urbana Illinois. https://files.eric.ed.gov/fulltext/ED010368.pdf

Smedley, R. (1971). *Three looms waiting* (Part 1). BBC Omnibus documentary. https://www.youtube.com/watch?v=f5jBNIEQrZs

Smith, A. (2007). *Understanding children's development: A New Zealand perspective* (4th ed.). Bridget Williams Books.

Stoate, G. (2013). *The dialogic aspects of Mantle of the Expert pedagogy used to teach devising at NCEA level 2 in a year 12 classroom 'I don't think it's about credits—definitely not about credits'*. Master of Education (MEd) thesis, University of Waikato, Hamilton. https://hdl.handle.net/10289/7963

Swanson, C. (2016). *Positioned as expert scientists: Learning science through Mantle-of-the-Expert at years 7/8*. Doctoral thesis, University of Waikato, Hamilton. https://hdl.handle.net/10289/9974

Swanson, C. (2017). Fictional others: Expanding the possible through interactions with the fictional. *NJ*, 41(1), 14–26. https://doi.org/10.1080/14452294.2017.1329678

Tauranga, W. (2019, November 29). First encounters—A Mantle of the Expert exploration of New Zealand history. *Mantle of the Expert Aotearoa*. https://mantleoftheexpert.co.nz/first-encounters-a-mantle-of-the-expert-exploration-of-new-zealand-history/

Taylor, A. (2009). *Drama conventions*. Handout from Weaving our Stories: International Mantle of the Expert Conference, University of Waikato, Hamilton. https://mantleoftheexpert.co.nz/role-conventions-in-colour/

Taylor, T. (n.d.). *Fairy Tale problem solvers*. Planning example. https://www.mantleoftheexpert.com/resources/planning-units/context/fairy-tale-problem-solvers/

Taylor, T. (2016). *A beginner's guide to Mantle of the Expert: A transformative approach to education*. Singular Publishing.

Taylor, T. (2018). *Generating student concern for learning*. Blog post, 29 September. https://www.mantleoftheexpert.com/blog-post/generating-student-concern-for-learning/

Taylor, T. (2020). Troll hunter. *Explore more stories*. https://www.explore-more.org/stories/troll-hunter/

Taylor, T., & Edmiston, B. (n.d.). *The mountain rescue team*. https://sites.ehe.osu.edu/bedmiston/files/2011/11/Mountain-Rescue-Team.pdf

Te Rau Matatini. (2010). *Guidelines to setting up Rangatahi advisory groups for child and adolescent mental health, addiction and whanau ora services*. Te Rau Matatini, Wellington. http://teraumatatini.com/publications-and-resources/t%C4%81-t%C4%81tou-mahere-korowai-guidelines

Thomas, D. (2016). Distributed practice: A key learning technique. Blog post on Education Research Techniques website, 15 August. https://educationalresearchtechniques.com/2016/08/15/distributed-practice-a-key-learning-technique/

Tourelle, L. (1998). *Performance: A practical approach to drama*. Harcourt Education.

Webb, L. & Heathcote, D. (n.d.) *The circle of progression or teacher compass*. https://www.mantleoftheexpert.com/wp-content/uploads/2019/07/Circle-of-Progression-copy.pdf

Wiggins, G., & McTighe, J. (2005). What is backward design? In *Understanding by design*. Association for Supervision and Curriculum Development. https://educationaltechnology.net/wp-content/uploads/2016/01/backward-design.pdf (n.p.)

Wikipedia. (n.d.). *Mantle of the Expert*. https://en.wikipedia.org/wiki/Mantle_of_the_expert

Williams, M. (1922). *The velveteen rabbit*. https://digital.library.upenn.edu/women/williams/rabbit/rabbit.html

Willis, L. (2013). City of Ember—sustainable city. *Novalighting's Blog MOTE*, October. http://novalightning.blogspot.com/p/mote.html

Wood, B. (2013). What is a social inquiry? Crafting questions that lead to deeper knowledge about society and citizenship. *Set: Research Information for Teachers*, (3), 20–28.

World Economic Forum. (2020). *Schools of the future: Defining new models of education for the fourth industrial revolution*. https://www.weforum.org/reports/schools-of-the-future-defining-new-models-of-education-for-the-fourth-industrial-revolution

Index

Abbott, Luke 3, 20
ability grouping 64–65, 80
action
    drama element 220, 221
    five levels of meaning-making 252
    in positioning theory 47, 48, 49–50
active listening 86
aesthetic dimensions 13, 28, 32, 35, 38, 74, 101, 144, 167, 184, 207, 225, 228, 229, 234–36, 239, 251, 307, 318, 326–27, 332
affective domain 43, 44, 117, 237–38
agency 46
    see also power relations; repositioning; powerful positioning
    students 7, 27, 28, 31, 32–33, 46, 49, 122, 134, 147, 160–61, 200–04, 211, 309, 330, 331
    teachers 201, 341
    young children 270
"ages and stages" viewpoint 39–40
aho/interweavings (microplanning and teaching) 121–22, 154–55, 214–15
    aho 1: keeping things safe and applying limits 157–60, 204
    aho 2: building relationships and fostering social practices 160–64, 204
    aho 3: taking on multiple perspectives 164–67, 191, 195, 204, 207, 280, 300
    aho 4: questioning 167–69
    aho 5: travelling in and out of worlds and through time and space 170–74, 195–96
    aho 6: introducing dramatic tension 174–79, 191, 196 (see also tensions)
    aho 7: moving between different teaching modes 179–84
    aho 8: using drama strategies and conventions 184–99, 204–05 (see also drama conventions; drama strategies)
    aho 9: working with power: status, agency and positioning 200–04, 205 (see also powerful positioning)
    aho 10: encouraging critical thinking and reflection 204–09 (see also critical thinking; reflections)
arts
    arts-rich learning 330
    devaluation 37
Arts in the New Zealand Curriculum (Ministry of Education) 116
assessment 211–13, 258, 274, 275, 318, 330, 331, 341–42
Auckland Theatre Company 8

backstory *see* framing and backstory
Batt, Tanya, *Imagined Worlds* 268
behaviour challenges 278, 319
biculturalism 281, 335, 336, 337
blocking 260, 261
blogs 210, 212–13
Bloom's taxonomy 42–43, 44, 237–38
body language 13, 167, 168, 178, 181, 183, 194, 200, 226, 306, 310
Bolton, Gavin 159
    Dorothy Heathcote's story 16, 39
    Drama for Learning (with Dorothy Heathcote) 3, 38–39
Bowell and Heap, *Planning Process Drama* 240–41
Brock, Terry 7
brotherhoods strategy 69, 74
    brotherhoods and otherhoods tool 254–56
Bruner, Jerome, three forms of representation 44, 180, 183 224, 225, 236–37, 326
"building belief" 220

Cardy, Lynne 8
Centre for Curriculum Redesign (CCR) 327-29
character education 27, 327, 328, 329
child-structured dramatic play 16-17, 25, 34, 41, 42, 74, 100, 178, 181, 183, 184, 220-21, 261, 269, 270, 276, 332
   see also projective play; socio-dramatic play
circle of progression see teacher compass tool
citizenship 27, 329
client 30, 38, 109-12, 120, 123, 151, 170-71, 221, 286, 324
   examples of clients 109-12
   mythological elements in client's world 299-300
   pre-planning 126, 127, 133, 134-36
   rolling-role arrangement 272-73
   selecting the enterprise 344-45
   in Shark Tank example 80, 81, 84, 88-89
   in Toy Museum example 54, 57, 60, 66, 67, 68, 71, 72
co-construction 28, 32, 33, 133, 147, 155, 160, 164, 169, 200, 201, 210-11, 220, 287, 321
   see also collaborative activity
   principles of improvisation tool 259-62
cognitive domain 42-43, 117, 237-38
coherence 198, 310
collaborative activity 30, 39, 44, 58, 161-63, 177, 254, 258, 270, 293, 296, 319, 323
   see also co-construction; responsible team
   Fullan's "six Cs" 329
   teaching in collaborative settings 271-73
collective identity 30
commission 3, 14, 17, 38, 120, 123, 151, 170-71, 183-84, 195, 201, 204, 205, 221, 222, 324, 325
   completion 315
   description 26, 30
   examples of experiences commissions 109-12
   focusing learning with a narrow commission 136, 293-95
   and frame distance 240
   in Objects of Significance example 97
   pre-planning 126, 127, 134-37, 138, 141, 143, 280
   rolling-role arrangement 272-73
   selecting the enterprise 344-45
   in Shark Tank example 79-81, 83, 86, 87, 88, 90, 91, 136-37, 152, 195
   subject specialities 275
   time manipulations 314-15
   in Toy Museum example 54, 55, 63-64, 72, 73, 195
   weighing up when to use 286-89
commission model 13, 19-20, 23, 24, 25, 26, 286-89
communication 27, 329
compact 12, 185-86, 187, 194, 195, 196, 197, 217
company 18, 30, 31, 90, 109-12, 120, 270, 315, 316
   Augmented Reality Solutions (Shark Tank) 77, 78-80, 84, 86-87, 88-89, 90, 91, 132, 134, 152, 153-54
   History Mystery toys (Toy Museum) 54, 60-61, 62-63
   see also responsible team
compassion 307, 323, 324, 327, 330, 332
   see also empathy
complexity 205, 325
Connecting Curriculum, Connecting Learning research project 4-5, 29, 30-31, 319
continuum of engagement 164, 222-23
conventions 12, 38, 184, 185, 187, 193
   see also drama conventions; role conventions; social conventions
core elements 12, 29-32, 38, 120-21, 122, 124, 125, 145, 150, 155, 221, 286-89, 328
   see also drama elements; weaving metaphor
corporate practices 90, 296, 316
courage 330
COVID-19 pandemic 8, 323, 324, 331
creative writing 54, 55, 290-91

Index

creativity 27, 37, 128, 152, 167, 173, 193, 250, 252, 254, 264, 280, 324, 325, 326–27, 329

critical distance 253–54

critical thinking 27, 87, 122, 169, 204–09, 252, 254, 257–58, 329

culturally responsive and sustaining practice 37, 73, 92, 98, 107, 114, 280–84, 327, 335–39, 343

    see also biculturalism; Māori; multiculturalism

curiosity 330

curriculum

    see also drama curriculum; *New Zealand Curriculum (NZC)*

    four-dimensional model (CCR) 327–29, 339, 340

    Fullan's "six Cs" 27, 329–30, 339

decoding complex texts 75, 80, 90

deep learning 27, 28, 136, 147, 176, 251, 254, 271, 293, 329, 330

    in Objects of Significance example 93, 102–3

    in Shark Tank example 78–81, 87

    in Toy Museum example 60–63

democratisation of information 324–25

"describe then interpret" strategy 207–08

design-based learning 19

Dewey, John 208

dialogic inquiry 50, 78, 165

digital technology 14, 19, 53, 80, 85–86, 129, 134, 139, 156, 173, 194, 220, 258, 272, 274, 298, 323–24, 330, 331

dimensions of dramatic imagination 13, 91, 94, 100, 234–36, 249, 250, 332

"disturbance factors" 18

divisions of culture planning tool 226–30, 284

divisions of culture tool 226–30

Downey, Renee 7, 219

drama conventions

    books and information on use of conventions 187–88

    commission model 286, 287, 289

    examples of practice 199, 267

    examples of widely used conventions 188

    Heathcote's list of role conventions 189–92, 193–95, 196, 197–98, 224, 230–31

    labelling 188–89, 225

    microplanning and teaching 184–99, 205, 217

    in a mini mantle 265–66

    selecting 224–25

    sequencing 225–26

    to support interpretation 208

    using "on the hoof" 196–97

drama curriculum, Arts learning area 21

drama elements 13, 21, 220–22

drama for learning 17, 23, 24, 28, 91, 120, 124, 126, 183

    collaborative and social skills development 270

    descriptions 13, 16, 25, 31

    Heathcote & Bolton, *Drama for Learning* 3, 38–39

    process drama strategies and conventions 13, 32, 33

    teaching modality 32, 33–34, 216–17, 235, 265, 266, 267–68, 270, 300, 328

    use of six dimensions of dramatic imagination 235

drama games 266

Drama New Zealand 2, 3, 20–21, 343

drama strategies 14, 38, 65, 122, 143, 165, 176, 180, 217

    commission model 286, 287, 289

    examples of practice 199

    labelling 188–89

    microplanning and teaching 184–87, 193–99

    in a mini Mantle 266

    selecting 224–25

    sequencing 225–26

drama techniques 13, 21

"drama to explore people" 16–17

dramatic imagination *see* dimensions of dramatic imagination

Dramatic Inquiry 53, 269, 287, 289

    see also inquiry learning

    aligned with school values and

culture 337-38
New Zealand context 107
description 13
five levels of meaning-making 252
Mantle of the Expert relationship 23-26, 116
professional development 8, 93, 279, 338
school use and growth in interest 7, 8, 22, 92, 279, 337, 338, 342
teaching 8, 9, 97, 121, 122, 158, 162, 187, 230, 264, 276
three modalities tool 215
dramatic performance 42, 181, 182-83, 184
dramatic play
see also child-structured dramatic play; socio-dramatic play, play
drama elements 220-21
drawings 228-29
dropping to the universals tool 205, 257-58, 332

economic purpose of education 327
Edmiston, Brian 5, 23, 31-32, 49, 161, 179, 180, 302
The Mountain Rescue Team (with Tim Taylor) 268, 314
education, New Zealand
historical injustices 340-41
history of progressive education 340-41
priorities for 21st-century 334-42
Education Review Office 22
effective vs ineffective new pedagogies 330-32
elements of drama 13, 21, 220-22
embodiment of learning 25, 28, 36, 76, 90, 165, 206, 207, 237, 278, 300, 306, 320, 326
emotions 144, 152, 238, 306
emotional distance 238-40, 241, 242
emotional engagement 62, 135, 159, 216, 239, 241
emotional safety 158-60, 306-07
empathy 27, 32, 36, 37, 143, 144, 158, 223, 300, 310, 323, 332, 343
see also compassion

empowerment 45
enactive form of learning/representation 44, 180, 183, 224, 225, 236-37, 326
enactive, iconic and symbolic tool/triad 224-25, 236-38
ethical issues 3, 23, 72, 75, 87-88, 90, 91-92, 133, 136-37, 138-39, 153, 167, 207, 270, 291-92
Eurocentrism 98, 227, 282
evidence-based practices 332-34
expert positioning see powerful positioning

facilitator voice 69, 97, 235, 247-48, 249, 267, 302
fictional context 30
financial literacy 60, 72
five levels of meaning-making tool 91, 105, 106, 251-53
focus 126, 127, 129-31, 220, 249, 293-95
in Shark Tank example 75, 80, 131
Foucault, Michel 45-46
four-dimensional model of curriculum (CCR) 327-29, 339, 340
frame analysis 40-41, 47
frame distance 30, 93, 98, 106, 159, 238-42, 288, 310
framing and backstory 30, 41, 47, 73, 87, 120, 143, 151, 191, 221, 278
communication frame 219
double framing 241-42
handout on building the frame/backstory 345
mapping 149
pre-planning 126, 127, 132-34
in Shark Tank example 134, 154-55
subject specialists 274
freedom 200-01, 202
Freire, Paolo 45
Fullan, Michael
effective vs ineffective new pedagogies (with Langworthy) 330-32
"six Cs" 27, 329-31, 339

gagging 260, 261
generalist approach 324-25

generic tasks grid 139, 339, 346–47
Gilbert, Gay 7, 212
Goffman, Erving 40–41
grace element in teaching 307–08, 317
group culture 39

Hall, Michelle 7
Hanly, Tamsin, *Critical Guide to Māori and Pākehā Histories of Aotearoa* 93
Heathcote, Dorothy
    biography and documentaries 16
    Drama for Learning (with Bolton) 3, 38–39
    dramas 21
    links to New Zealand 20–21
    Mantle of the Expert development 15–20, 31
    Mantle of the Expert: My Current Understanding 6
    models within her practice 16–20
    "Paradigms regarding views of children" 1
    Three Looms Waiting 115
Heick, T. 42–43
history, New Zealand 8, 281–82, 283, 339
hook 69, 121, 123, 126, 127, 148, 150, 216–19, 228, 275, 304
    see also signs and symbols
    dramatic hook 216–17, 219
    expert hook 218–19, 275
    inquiry hook 217–18, 219, 275
    in Objects of Significance example 99–101, 217, 218
    in Shark Tank example 76–78, 153–54, 217
    in Toy Museum example 56–60, 216–17
Hulson, Maggie, *Schemes for Classroom Drama* 268

iconic form of learning/representation 44, 180, 183, 224, 225, 236–37, 326
icons 226
ideas
    as physical forces 114–15
    as viruses 115

imaginative activity
    dimensions of dramatic imagination 13, 91, 94, 100, 249, 250, 324–36, 332
    Fullan's "6 Cs" 27, 329
    imagination warm up activity 266
imagined and real worlds
    avoiding deceit 301–04
    commission model 286–89
    dialectic between the two worlds 241
    dramatic performance feeding into imagined world 182–83
    dual awareness (metaxis) 30, 34–38, 171–72, 206, 302, 328, 332
    engagement with the imagined world 3, 19, 35, 59, 96, 102, 146, 162, 163–64, 193, 222–23, 294–95
    Eurocentrism 282
    multiple perspectives 36, 37, 73, 93, 97–98, 164–67, 170–71, 172, 195, 207, 289, 296–97
    mythological elements 297–300
    names used for people, companies and entities 289–91, 292–93
    in Objects of Significance example 94–96, 98, 99–101, 102, 104
    participants with specific learning needs 276–78
    point of connection 219
    power dynamics 206–07, 209
    pre-planning 134–38
    real-world learning 331–32
    setting up the imagined world 150, 151, 220–22
    in Shark Tank example 76, 77–78, 79, 81–82, 84, 86–87, 92, 154
    signalling the imagined world 37, 61, 64, 71, 99, 171–72, 181, 184, 186, 229, 230, 249, 270, 277, 291, 302, 303, 304–05
    signing 227–28
    specialism 325
    teaching in collaborative settings 271–73
    in Toy Museum example 56–57, 62–63, 66, 70, 73–73
    travelling in and out of worlds and

through time and space 170–74
working with fictional others 316–17
improvisation 16, 17, 27, 51, 78, 150, 155, 172, 177–78, 181, 182, 192–93, 219, 235, 250, 293
    principles of improvisation tool 259–62
indices 226
inquiry learning 32–34, 124, 217–18, 267, 300, 329
    see also Dramatic Inquiry
    in Shark Tank example 80, 81
    in Toy Museum example 64

kākahu 18, 113, 115, 116–17, 118
    see also weaving metaphor
Knighton Normal School 3, 8, 107
knowledge 327, 328
    prior knowledge 333, 338
    social and cultural perspectives 36
korowai see weaving metaphor
kotahitanga 163

language 9, 32, 37, 63, 77, 80, 90, 99, 106, 160, 163, 164, 167, 169, 224, 239, 264, 277–78, 312, 332
    see also body language; three teaching voices tool
    inclusive language 77, 203, 204
    persuasive language 55, 78
Langworthy, M., effective vs ineffective new pedagogies (with Fullan) 330–32
learning
    see also deep learning; drama for learning; inquiry learning; problem-based learning
    arts-rich learning 330
    Bloom's taxonomy 42–43, 44, 237–38
    Bruner's three forms of representation 44, 180, 183 224, 225, 236–37, 326
    design-based learning 19
    meta-learning 36, 327, 328
    multi-modal learning 179–80
    project-based learning 19, 329
    social and cultural contexts 39, 40, 44, 73, 98–99, 105–06, 107, 114, 139, 280–84
    learning and development theories 39–51
lesson plans, pre-existing 268
licence 200–01
literacy learning 72, 226, 254, 256

"man in a mess" drama 16
Mantle of the Expert
    see also weaving metaphor
    and 21st-century educational priorities 322–32, 339, 340, 341–43
    in New Zealand 20–23
    core elements 12, 29–32, 38, 120–21, 122, 124, 125, 145, 150, 155, 221, 286–89, 328
    descriptions 13–14, 17, 26–29
    development 15–20
    early years and junior classrooms 269–71
    evidence of effectiveness 332–34
    New Zealand examples 109–12 (see also Objects of Significance example; Shark Tank example; Toy Museum example)
    opening modalities 215–19
    participants with specific learning needs 276–78
    preparatory activities 265–66
    reasons for name 17–18
    relation to four-dimensional model of curriculum 328–29
    relation to other pedagogical approaches 23–26, 329–32
    senior students 275–76
    starting out on using in the classroom 263–65
    subject specialist settings 273–76
    theoretical underpinnings 38–51
"mantle of the expert" as a convention 188
Mantle of the Expert Aotearoa website 22, 26, 39, 210, 213, 268, 282
Māori 216, 237, 242, 336, 338
    see also weaving metaphor
    in Objects of Significance example 93, 98–99, 100–01, 102–06, 107
    Shark Tank role 82–83
    suggested teaching themes 283–84

te ao Māori 7, 37, 73, 83, 91, 98, 114, 144, 281, 283, 284, 335, 336, 339
te reo Māori 9, 12, 101, 139, 336, 339
tikanga Māori 48, 113, 117, 124, 139, 158, 281, 284
mapping 146–48, 280
    experiential phase 151
    initiation phase 150–51
    narrative arc 150–53
    reflection/transformation phase 151–52
    in Shark Tank example 152–54
    template 147–48, 149–50
meaning-making, five levels 91, 105, 106, 251–53
meta-cognition 36, 206
meta-learning 36, 327, 328
metaphors 114–15, 144
    see also weaving metaphor
    as a distancing device 241–42
    Māori 336, 339
    Otaika School, Northland 337–38
metaxis 35
    see also imagined and real worlds
microplanning 147, 154–57, 212, 240, 273, 274–75, 331
    see also aho/interweavings (microplanning and teaching); teaching
Miller and Saxton, *Into the Story* 268
mindfulness 36
"mini mantles" 265
modes 179–80
    see also teaching – teaching modalities
multiculturalism 284, 335, 337
multi-modal learning 179–80
multiple perspectives 19, 27, 29, 105, 117, 173, 184, 204, 231, 280, 307, 324
    drama for learning 31, 32, 126, 300
    imagined and real worlds 36, 37, 73, 93, 97–98, 164–67, 170–71, 172, 195, 207, 289, 296–97
    preplanning 143–44, 145, 146
    process drama 16
    signature pedagogy 122, 157, 164–67
mythological elements 297–300

names of people, companies or entities in imagined worlds 58, 60, 61, 78, 283
    alternatives to real-world names 108, 126, 134, 135, 289–91
    avoiding light-hearted names 136, 292–93, 309
narrative arc 17, 150–53
narrative, poetic, reflective categories tool 225–26
narrator/storyteller voice 57, 93, 94, 96, 100, 106, 155, 179, 181, 234, 235, 248–49, 267, 319
"neuromyths" 334
New Zealand
    history teaching 8, 281–82, 283, 339
    priorities for 21st-century education 334–42
New Zealand Curriculum (NZC) 12, 20, 21–22, 36, 72, 83–84, 85–86, 90, 106, 109–12, 123, 149, 185
    see also drama curriculum
    and assessment 212
    framed as professional tasks 30
    Mantle of the Expert planning process 284–86
    teaching in depth 317–19
"no penalty zone" for learning 35
"now-immediate time" 170

Objects of Significance example 92, 163, 192, 202, 228, 234, 247, 265
    commission 97
    continuum of engagement 223
    deep learning 93, 102–03
    implementation and the hook 99–101, 217, 218
    learning objectives 93
    links to curriculum 106
    outcomes 105–06
    planning 92, 93–99
    tensions 97, 102–04, 176
opening modalities 215–19
Otaika Valley school, Northland 7, 23, 337–38

participants 126, 128–29, 151, 153–54, 155–56, 157
   see also co-construction; imagined and real worlds; power relations; powerful positioning; repositioning; responsible team; role taking and shifting; students
   dropping to the universals tool 257–58
   limits and constraints 157–60, 201–02, 204
   needs of participants who come and go 319–21
   questioning by participants 168–69
   questioning of participants 251–52
   recording the learning 210–11
   safety 157–60, 306–07, 310
   two-step response tool 253–54
perspectives
   see also multiple perspectives
   shared perspectives 30, 132, 143
   shifting perspectives 171, 172
persuasive language 55, 78
persuasive writing 55, 67, 68, 72
physical positions 48
physical safety 157–58
Piaget, Jean 39–40
Pieces of Dorothy (documentary, Burgess) 16
Pirini, Elicia 200, 293
planning 113, 280–300, 331
   see also microplanning; weaving metaphor
   and curriculum 284–85
   divisions of culture planning tool 284
   examples: Objectives of Significance 92, 93–99
   examples of teacher blogs 212–13
   examples: Shark Tank 75–76, 128–29, 131, 136–37, 139–40, 142, 143–44, 196, 284–85
   examples: Toy Museum 54–55, 73–74
   existing planning, use for getting started 268–69
   four stages 124–25
   stage 1: laying out the whenu—pre-planning and research (see pre-planning; research)
   stage 2: choosing the overall shape—mapping 146–54, 280
   stage 3: interweaving the aho—microplanning and teaching (see aho/interweavings (microplanning and teaching))
   stage 4: defining and appraising the work—recording and assessment 209–13 (see also assessment)
   subject specialists 274–75
play 16–17, 26, 332
   see also child-structured dramatic play
   child-structured dramatic play 16–17, 25, 34, 41, 42, 74, 100, 178, 181, 183, 184, 220–21, 261, 269, 270, 276, 332
   projective play 18, 41–42, 181–82, 183, 269
   socio-dramatic play 16, 34, 41, 170, 220–21, 261, 270, 314
Playing our Stories (Ministry of Education) 21, 268
positioning theory 46–50, 203
   see also expert positioning; physical positions; powerful positioning; repositioning; social positions
power relations
   see also agency; expert positioning; repositioning; powerful positioning
   constructs 36, 301
   within corporate structure 90, 296, 316
   critical thinking and reflections 206–07, 209
   early years and junior classrooms 271
   imagined and real worlds 35, 37
   teacher-in-role voice 250–51, 271
   teachers and learners 27, 28, 31, 32–33, 35, 45–46, 47, 49, 90, 122, 160–61, 200–04, 267, 308, 313
   teacher's eight power positions 231, 232–33
   theories 45–46
powerful positioning 17, 31, 32, 33-4, 120, 125, 177, 200, 203, 249, 267, 278, 314
   hook 218–19, 275
   teaching modality 32–34, 48–49, 50, 124, 215, 218–19, 267, 328

see also agency; expert positioning; power relations; repositioning
practice theory 50
pre-planning 125–46, 147, 196, 273, 280, 339 *see under* planning
    four handouts to help with pre-planning 344–49
problem-based learning 55, 175, 211, 323, 329
    simple, complicated and complex problems 205
process drama 2, 13, 23, 24, 26, 27, 38, 162, 170, 183, 220, 225, 241, 265, 276, 306, 311
    Bowell and Heap, *Planning Process Drama* 240–41
    description 14, 16–17, 25
    examples 21–22
    exploring process drama 267–68
    huia beak brooch example 94
    imagined and real worlds 34
    reflections 2, 16
    strategies and conventions used by in drama for learning 32, 33
    students with specific learning needs 276
professional learning and support 279, 342–43
project-based learning 19, 135, 329
projective play 18, 41–42, 181–82, 183, 269
    see also child-structured dramatic play; socio-dramatic play
psychomotor domain 43, 44
purpose of an activity 186, 187, 193, 194, 196, 197

questioning 167–69, 300, 324, 333
    five levels of meaning-making tool 251–53
    "What if …?" questions 54–55, 141–42, 174, 177

real and imagined worlds *see* imagined and real worlds
recording the learning 209–11, 212–13
reflections 31, 120, 121, 122, 125, 156, 222, 233, 264, 269, 281, 306, 324, 337, 338

events of the imagined world from back in the real world 35, 36, 38, 248
    examples of experiences 109–12
    five levels of meaning-making tool 251, 252, 257–58
    microplanning and teaching 157, 158, 160, 165, 166, 167, 171, 182, 183, 184, 195, 204–05, 206–07, 208–09, 211
    narrative, poetic, reflective categories tool 225–26
    in Objects of Significance example 101, 105
    preparatory activities 266
    process drama 2, 16
    professional learning 279
    reflection/transformation phase 151–52
    in Shark Tank example 75, 78, 81, 92, 153
    six dimensions of dramatic imagination 235
    teacher compass tool 243, 246
    teaching in role 250, 311
    in Toy Museum example 53, 68, 72, 74
registers and positions tool 230–33, 332
relationship building 39, 122, 160–64
relationship shifts 240–41
repositioning 27, 31, 32, 49, 50, 120, 202–03, 297, 300, 305–06, 321, 325–26
    see also agency; expert positioning; power relations; powerful positioning
research 145–46, 280, 295–96
responsible team 3, 18, 30, 123, 151, 162, 171, 201, 202–03, 221, 240, 270, 273, 300–01, 325
    see also commission; company; expert positioning; participants; powerful positioning; repositioning
    alternative perspectives 48–49, 296–97
    keeping the sense of one team 315–16
    pre-planning 126, 131–34
    selecting the enterprise 344–5
Robinson, Ken 326–27
role conventions 14
    enactive, iconic and symbolic tool 224–25
    Heathcote's list of 33 role

conventions 189-92, 193-95, 196, 197-98, 224, 230-31
role function in relation to frame distance 239-40
role taking and shifting 40-41, 46-47, 297, 308-09, 325-26
    de-rolling rituals 305-07
    drama element 220, 221
    dramatic role 41-42, 65, 83
    resistance to role 311-13
    Toy Museum 70
    working with fictional others 316-17
    see also "shadow role", teacher in role, responsible team, client
rolling role 13, 14, 18-19, 23, 24, 25, 26, 272-73

safety 157-60, 310
    emotional safety 158-60, 306-07
Sanctuary (drama, Department of Education) 21
"Scarf Game" ("This Is Not A ...") 266
Schliecher, Andreas 323, 324-25
school networking 342-43
science experiments 83-84, 90, 152-53, 317-18
"shadow role" 60
Shark Tank example 74-75, 178, 182, 183, 192, 195, 199, 312-13, 320
    commission 79-81, 83, 86, 88, 90, 91, 136-37, 152, 153-54, 195
    continuum of engagement 223
    implementation and the hook 76-78, 153-54, 217
    learning objectives 75, 80, 131
    links to the curriculum 83-84, 85-86, 90, 317-18
    mapping 152-54
    outcomes 88-89
    planning 75-76, 128-29, 131, 136-37, 139-40, 142, 143-44, 196, 284-85
    research 146, 295
    science experiments 83-84, 90, 152-53, 317-18
    signs and symbols 144-45
    tasks 139-40, 152-53

tensions 81-88, 142, 153, 166, 176, 196, 316-17
things that could have been done differently 90-92
Sharp, Trevor 94, 97
Shulman, Lee 50
signalling the imagined world 37, 61, 64, 71, 99, 171, 181, 184, 186, 229, 230, 249, 270, 277, 291, 302, 303, 304-05
signature pedagogies 50-51, 122, 124, 156-57, 200, 201, 214, 326
    see also aho
signs and symbols 126, 127, 144-45, 270, 332
    see also hook
    divisions of culture tool 226-30
Simpson, E. 43
skills 327, 328, 331
social constructivist theories 39-40
social conventions 14
social inquiry 19, 286
social positions 48
social practices 50, 122, 157, 160-64, 201, 203, 284
    see also collaborative activity; relationship building
social purpose of education 327
sociocultural theories 39
socio-dramatic play 16, 34, 41, 170, 220-21, 261, 270, 314
    see also child-structured dramatic play; play; projective play
sound-based work 85-87, 90
space see time and space
specialisation 324-26
stalling 260, 261
stealing 260, 261
storylines 47, 48, 49-50
storytelling 69, 72, 182
    see also narrator/storyteller voice
strategies 184
    see also drama strategies
student-led inquiry 33
students
    see also participants
    agency 7, 27, 28, 31, 32-33, 46, 49, 122,

134, 147, 160–61, 200–04, 211, 309, 330, 331
   early years and junior classrooms 269–71
   senior students 275–76
   specific learning needs 276–78
subject specialist settings 273–76
Swanson, Carrie 317
symbolic form of learning/representation 44, 180, 183, 224, 225, 236–37, 326
symbols *see* signs and symbols

tasks 126, 127, 137–39, 141, 163, 202, 280, 285, 318
   generic tasks grid 139, 339, 346–47
   Shark Tank 139–40, 152–53
   subject specialists 274–75
Tātaiako (Ministry of Education & New Zealand Teacher's Council) 114, 149
Tauranga, Whakarongo 8
Taylor, Allana 224
Taylor, Tim 3, 8, 20, 31, 198, 201–02, 228–29, 243
   A Beginner's Guide to Mantle of the Expert 38, 133, 216
   The Mountain Rescue Team (with Brian Edmiston) 268, 314
Te Whāriki (Ministry of Education) 116, 149
teacher compass tool 96, 180, 243–47, 318–19
teacher in role (TIR) strategy 186, 188, 191–92, 196, 250, 265, 267
   early years and junior classrooms 271
   overcoming uncertainties 308–11
   registers and positions tool 230–33
   role function in relation to frame distance 240
   steps for signalling 304–05
   unsignalled role 301–04
teacher-in-role voice 94, 102, 106, 155, 218, 235, 247, 249–50, 267
teaching 300–21, 331
   see also aho/interweavings (microplanning and teaching); microplanning
   agency of teachers 201, 341
   avoiding deceit 301–04
   avoiding temptation to pre-teach 313–14
   code of ethics 303
   dealing with resistance to role 311–13
   ensuring the curriculum is taught in depth 317–19
   grace element 307–08, 317
   professional learning and support 279, 342–43
   subject specialists 274–75
   teaching in a collaborative setting 273
   teaching modalities 32–34, 179–84, 215–19, 267–68, 300, 328
   three teaching voices tool 247–51
technological change 323–24, 342
   see also digital technology
Telling our Stories (Ministry of Education) 21, 268
tensions 31, 32, 35, 38, 109–12, 120, 122, 149, 280, 300, 308, 310, 325
   Haseman and O'Toole's types of tension 177
   Heathcote's list of 12 levels of tension 141, 177
   introducing dramatic tension 174–79, 196, 217
   levels of tensions in order of subtlety 348–49
   New Zealand Curriculum drama element 220, 222
   in Objects of Significance example 97, 104–05, 176
   pre-planning 126, 127, 140–42, 174–75
   productive and key tensions 142, 149, 151, 175–76, 191, 196, 205
   in Shark Tank example 81–88, 142, 153, 176, 196, 316–17
   in Toy Museum example 54, 64–68, 176
themes, New Zealand examples 283–84
Those Who Sailed with Cook (drama, Heathcote, Shaw) 21
three forms of representation 44, 180, 183, 224, 225, 236–37, 326
Three Looms Waiting (BBC documentary,

Smedley) 16
three teaching voices tool 247-51
   see also facilitator voice; narrator/storyteller voice; teacher-in-role voice
tikanga Māori 48, 113, 117, 124, 139, 158, 281, 284
time and space
   drama element 220, 221
   manipulation in the imagined world 173-74, 195-96
   using manipulations in time 314-15
time shifts 240-41, 248
TKI website (Ministry of Education) 5, 180, 187-88
TLIF (Teacher-led Innovation Fund) projects 7, 23
TLRI (Teaching and Learning Research Initiative) projects 4-5, 22-23, 337-38
Towler-Evans, Iona 5, 20, 170, 288
Toy Museum example 53, 72-73, 158, 168, 178, 195, 202
   commission 54, 55, 63-64, 72, 73, 195
   continuum of engagement 223
   deepening the learning 60-63
   exhibition opening 69-72
   implementation and the hook 56-60, 216-17
   learning objectives 54
   links to curriculum 72
   planning 54-55, 73-74
   tensions 54, 64-68, 176
   things that could have been done differently 73-74
"trading game" 166
transformation 151-52, 195
Treaty of Waitangi/Te Tiriti o Waitangi 91, 166-67, 281, 335, 336, 339, 345
"truth button" or "truth serum" 168-69
two-step response tool 253-54

University of Waikato 2, 3-4, 6, 7, 22-23

value 61-62, 63, 73
values 133, 252, 327, 337-38, 345
versatility 325-26

virtual environments 14, 79, 134, 139, 153, 154, 192
   see also digital technology
Vygotsky, Lev 40

Walshaw, Julia 3, 147, 268
weaving metaphor 18, 113-19
   aho/interweavings 121-22, 154-55 (see also aho/interweavings (microplanning and teaching))
   gathering materials 119-20
   mahi whatu/working the weave 122-23, 150
   models and patterns 123-24, 147
   ngā aho tapu/ the sacred thread 121
   ua/hems and edges 123
   whenu/core elements 120-21, 150
Weaving Our Stories conference, 2009 4, 22, 251
"What if …?" questions 54-55, 141-42, 174, 177

"Yes Let's" game 56, 266

www.ingramcontent.com/pod-product-compliance
Lightning Source LLC
Chambersburg PA
CBHW060303010526
44108CB00042B/2618